KING
OF
CONS

KING
— OF —
CONS

Exposing the Dirty Rotten Secrets of the
Washington Elite and Hollywood Celebrities

AARON TONKEN

NELSON CURRENT

A Division of Thomas Nelson, Inc.

Published in Nashville, Tennessee, by Nelson Current, a subsidiary of Thomas Nelson, Inc.

Nelson Current books may be purchased in bulk for educational, business, fundraising, or sales promotional use. For information, please e-mail SpecialMarkets@ThomasNelson.com.

Special credit due to photographer Peter Halmagyi. For more information visit www.PHphoto.us.

Library of Congress Cataloging-in-Publication Data
Tonken, Aaron.
 King of cons : exposing the dirty, rotten secrets of the Washington elite and Hollywood celebrities / Aaron Tonken.
    p. cm.
  ISBN 1-5955-5000-3
 1. Tonken, Aaron. 2. Swindlers and swindling—United States—Biography.
 I. Title.
  HV6692.T66A3 2004
  364.16'3—dc22

2004020804

Printed in the United States of America
04 05 06 07 08 QW 9 8 7 6 5 4 3 2 1

Dedicated in loving memory of

Alicia Buttons

Carol MacNeil

Michael Moskovitz

Pauline "Patti" Rieder

Lois Thomson

It has been a blessing for me to have dear friends who stepped forward immediately to help when I got into trouble and have shown great sympathy to my plight. I could never have made it without the extreme patience, compassion, love, and generosity of my good friends. I love you all . . .

Joni & Jody Berry

Steven Fox

Bradley O'Leary

Ken Roberts

George Bird

Philip Levy

I don't know if I would still be alive today if it weren't for the both of you. You have been my friends, protectors, and in many instances served as my conscience. I will be forever grateful. I promise you and all my friends that the kindnesses extended to me in times of trouble will not have been given in vain. The second chance in life that has been offered to me will be filled with the good deeds seen in a godly life.

CONTENTS

Contents

one

HAIL TO THE CHIEF

The event was wonderful. I can't thank you enough. And I'm very grateful for the boost it gave Hillary's campaign.

—BILL CLINTON,
Handwritten Personal Letter,
August 18, 2000

In a land of moral imbeciles, I knew I could be king.

That's the way I'd always figured it, anyway. Turns out I was right. Hollywood is that land, and, in order to be crowned, all you have to do is determine what its denizens desire and find a way to score it for them.

In the summer of 2000, at the age of thirty-four, I had made it to the top.

On a hot August morning, I was heading west on Sunset Boulevard, past Beverly Hills, through Bel Air and Holmby Hills, to Brentwood. It's a gorgeous drive, with the Santa Monica Mountains, cut by a seemingly endless procession of rugged, wooded canyons off to the north.

The road also passes through some of the priciest real estate on the planet. Around every bend in the road is the multi-million-dollar home of a movie star, producer, director, or businessman, each more spectacular than the one before.

I was driving my black Mercedes convertible—top down. I've never cared much about material possessions—I still lived in a cheap, one-bedroom West Hollywood apartment with no air conditioning—but I knew that in my adopted city, image was everything. If you wanted to climb the ladder of success, one of the first steps was to look the part. Which demanded a luxury automobile. So I leased the Benz.

But now here I was on the top rung. I was about to throw the greatest celebrity bash ever—bringing in the most powerful man in the world, the president of the United States, to party down with a galaxy of Hollywood's brightest stars. It was the biggest achievement of my life, though I scarcely had a moment to stop and savor it.

Simply thinking about what I was trying to pull off was enough to drive me nuts. Actually doing it—attending to the thousand and one details that go into producing a gala event, while simultaneously massaging some of the entertainment industry's most fragile egos—made me a nervous wreck. In addition to the normal strains of producing a Hollywood gala, however, there were my own financial problems. They hung over my head like a death sentence. Additionally, there was my knowledge that, while this big-ticket event might appear totally legit to an outsider, it wasn't. I tried not to think about it.

AT BRENTWOOD, I TURNED onto Mandeville Canyon Road, which winds through the wooded hills for three or four miles before reaching the entrance to the magisterial estate where the tribute would be held. Formerly owned by Hollywood leading man and matinee idol Robert Taylor, the estate now belonged to Ken Roberts, a friend who made a fortune in the radio business. Known simply as The Ranch, the incomparable spread was 112 acres. When I asked him if he'd like to host the president, Ken told me, "Well, you know, I'm not a Democrat." But then added with a smile, "Of course, I'm not a Republican, either. I'm an American. So . . . ah, why the hell not?"

As I neared the grounds, the last three-quarters of a mile were punctuated with checkpoints and lined on both sides with about a hundred unmarked law enforcement vehicles—Secret Service, FBI, state and local cops. There would be more officers on the grounds, of course, and snipers were positioned at key vantage points among the mountains ringing the white-fenced estate.

All this police presence because of my party, because President William Jefferson Clinton was coming. I was the one who had made it all happen. No one else. Me, a high-school dropout from a small northern Michigan town who, not long ago, had been living in an L.A. homeless shelter. Thinking of the accomplishment, I pulsed with excitement, pride, and apprehension all at once. My one regret was that my dad, a highly-respected physician who passed away in 1987, was not there to see that his only son had finally made something of his life.

After passing through the last security gauntlet, I was finally on the asphalt horseshoe that fronted the spectacular main residence. The monstrous stage was erected at the top of the horseshoe and was ringed with lights. It had columns on either side, rising tiers to hold Ian Fraser's seventeen-piece orchestra, a Jumbotron TV screen, and an apron that left plenty of room for speakers to address the audience, and performers to dance and sing.

I was thrilled.

On the great lawn that fans out from the residence, two thousand director's chairs had been set in place, with copies of the tribute book and a gift bag of the performers' CDs laid on them. The director's chairs were just one indication of the class and attention to detail that I brought to all of my functions. (Another was my use of personal couriers to deliver guests' tickets to them.) Each of the canvas backs was imprinted with the name of the event:

The Hollywood Gala Salute to
President William Jefferson Clinton
August 12, 2000

And everyone could take these home as souvenirs at the end of the evening. Onstage, Cher was rehearsing the song I had requested, "If I Could Turn Back Time," dressed in jeans and a T-shirt. I sat and watched her for a while, enjoying a little quiet time before I really had to get down to work. Such moments of pleasure were few and far between. Mostly, I was hurrying from place to place, trying to make sure that everything was picture perfect.

I'd hired an event planner who managed the monstrous job of seating, among many other details. Seating was always a pain for big events such as this because of the swarms of *schnorrers,* a Yiddish word for cheapskates, who wanted free seats.

But more trouble than the freeloaders were the stars themselves. These people are Excedrin City. I'd hired some hands just to keep track of them. Who was going to show up, who was a late cancellation, and how did that affect the order of performance? Was anybody in a snit over his or her dressing room, food, spot in the show, or whatever? With a lot of celebrities, you have to baby them and give in to their most outrageous demands. If you don't, you can find yourself without a star— they'll just walk out and leave you high and dry.

For instance, Natalie Cole reneged. Michael Douglas was supposed to show, and didn't, along with Goldie Hawn and Jack Lemmon. I had paid for them and listed them on the invitation, but the publicist who was supposed to arrange things let me down. I signed up Brian McKnight to perform, but the sponsors vetoed him because they felt he wasn't big enough, and the show was already overcrowded.

We really wanted Rosa Parks to come and toast the president. But when we invited her, her assistant demanded that we pay her to appear and send a Gulfstream IV private jet to bring her. This led David Rosen, national finance director for Hillary Clinton's Senate campaign, to joke that Parks had "come a long way, from the back of the bus to a G-4." We went back to Parks's assistant, told her we couldn't possibly spring for the Gulfstream, but could arrange for a first-class commercial flight for her and her assistants. "Miss Parks simply *must* have a private jet," she said. "What about Air Force One?" We were already way over budget, and President Clinton was not going to swing by and pick her up on his way. Much as we would have liked to have Rosa Parks, we had to pass.

That might seem like a lot of disappointment and confusion (I thought I'd even nailed Stevie Wonder but his assistant and I were never on the same page), and maybe it was. But it was quite common when you were preparing for a big benefit show. Despite everything, most of the entertainers I'd invited were there and ready to perform, including Cher, Patti LaBelle, Sugar Ray, Toni Braxton, Melissa Etheridge, Michael Bolton, Paul Anka, and Diana Ross. Who needed Michael Douglas anyway?

THE CLINTON GALA WAS TWO THINGS. For one, it allowed celebrities who were politically sympathetic to rub elbows with their favorite Baby Boomer. There's nothing movie stars love more than hobnobbing with political stars, and many politicians are suckers for Hollywood dazzle. It's harder to keep them apart than to bring them together. But also—probably more important to the first couple—the evening was a fundraiser for Hillary's Senate campaign. And *that* would lead to a world of troubles.

At the time of the Salute, I had been at the intersection of Hollywood Boulevard and Pennsylvania Avenue long enough to know that improprieties sometimes happen when the Left Coast meets Washington. Though I was relatively new to the political fundraising scene, I'd become increasingly aware that much of what I saw—and participated in—was questionable on many fronts. So I turned myself deaf and blind and deliberately ignored the potential consequences. If this was the way business got done, who was I to object? I was rising to the top, and no trivial, white-collar laws were going to get in my way.

As I stood greeting people on that August evening, I saw, huddled together, three men: Peter Paul, a longtime friend, business associate, and personal mentor of mine, who had financially underwritten much of the event; Hillary Clinton's national finance director, David Rosen; and Jim Levin, the top Clinton fundraiser and Chicago nightclub owner, with whom we'd planned the gala and who had finally secured the president's participation.

I overheard them talking about a guy who hadn't arrived yet. He was a Japanese national named Tendo Oto, the president and CEO of Venture Soft, a Tokyo Web animation outfit. He was in negotiations with the evening's event sponsor Stan Lee Media—the company built on profits from Lee's comic creations, such as Spiderman—to launch a joint venture that would bring the U.S. company's globally branded superhero and fantasy story franchises to the Asian marketplace. Peter Paul was then virtually running Stan Lee Media and was heavily involved in the deal. The formation of that company, SLM Japan, would be announced on August 15, just three days later.

In the meantime, I knew that Mr. Oto really wanted to be there, presumably to cement some of his American connections. But it is against the law for foreign nationals to contribute money to domestic political campaigns, and since this event was raising cash for Hillary, he should have attended for free or not at all. It hadn't happened that way. Instead, as Brian Ross later reported for *20/20*, Oto had given Paul twenty-seven thousand dollars, which was then funneled into the campaign fund.

They were now discussing what to do about this guy, whether they'd have to sneak him in or not. They'd already decided he couldn't attend the post-entertainment dinner with the Clintons, though he'd paid enough. It was too risky.

The final arrangement was surprising. As Paul, Rosen,

Levin, and the White House staff worked it out, Oto was seated directly behind the president during the show. If they were hoping for a low profile, they didn't get it. The following week, *US* and *People* both ran the same photo of Bill Clinton at the gala, with Oto clearly visible in the background.

I STOOD TAKING IT ALL IN: the service staff from Spago (L.A.'s legendary hotspot) in their crisp white shirts and black slacks, moving expertly through the crowd; the men in their Armani suits and year-round tans; the gorgeous women in their Rodeo Drive clothes and jewels, from stores like Chanel, Dior, Valentino, Cartier, and Harry Winston. Some of the celebs were wearing jewelry that I gave them.

But for most of the reception and cocktail party, I attended to last-minute details. I rushed around to the various rooms and suites that were serving as celebrity dressing rooms to make sure that the performers had everything they wanted and would be ready at their appointed times. By the end of the evening, some of the rooms—in particular, the office used by musical group Sugar Ray—would be totally trashed, with food ground into the carpets, wine spilled on the furniture, pictures knocked off the walls . . . the whole Johnny Depp treatment.

When the president's limousine pulled up, I grabbed my close associate Cynthia Gershman, a Beverly Hills philanthropist and big underwriter of the evening. We joined the elite group of greeters: Peter Paul and his wife Andrea, Stan Lee and his wife Joan, estate-owner Ken Roberts and friend

Virginia Loving, Jim Levin, and David Rosen. Photographers were also on hand to record the moment.

Out stepped Bill, Hillary, and Chelsea—warm, engaging, and cheerful, with big smiles on their faces. I had the honor to escort the first family out to their seats—arm in arm with the first lady, the president and his daughter following close behind.

The crowd gave the Clintons a standing ovation. It was a dizzy whirl of smiles and camera flashes, passing influential *Variety* columnist Army Archerd and his wife Selma, John Travolta and his wife Kelly Preston, and Whoopi Goldberg. Bill gave a big hug to Muhammad Ali and his wife Loni and stopped to chat for a moment with Brad and Jennifer. Pitt and Aniston had been married less than two weeks earlier. Bill extended his congratulations.

AT LAST, IT WAS UNDERWAY. Stan Lee, co-host of the Salute, bounded up to the podium and welcomed everyone to what he called "Woodstock West." Then, after offering Clinton a post-presidency job as a superhero in one of his comics, he sat down. The spots were dimmed, leaving the stage bathed in soft blue light, and Ian Fraser's orchestra played "Hooray for Hollywood." It was a beautiful scene.

Shirley MacLaine, looking splendid in her flowing white dress, gave the opening tribute to Clinton. Then came Patti LaBelle, followed by a documentary video showing Bill Clinton's childhood in Hope, Arkansas. And then a slew of performers.

Briefly, in order: Jimmy Smits basically calling Bill Clinton an honorary Latino; Sugar Ray; more video from Hope; comedian Red Buttons talking about his first meeting with the president (he had replaced David Spade, who made the White House nervous because they thought he might tell Monica Lewinsky jokes); four little girls reciting poems about what they'd do if they were president; Toni Braxton singing seductively; Anjelica Huston offering an Irish toast; Melissa Etheridge performing "Come to My Window."

Etheridge thanked the president for making her feel welcome in Washington and creating an atmosphere in which she was comfortable coming out as a lesbian (which she did at his inauguration). In the tribute video, you can see Bill Clinton wiping away the tears.

Then: Dylan McDermott and Alfre Woodard speaking; Michael Bolton belting out "When a Man Loves a Woman"; film of Hillary recalling her first meeting with Bill; and Whoopi saying, "What a ride it's been."

Cher came out next, in her butt-hugging jeans, turquoise, sequined top, high-heeled boots with silver fringe, and blue-streaked hair. Her stylist had obviously worked his tail off. She sang "Life after Love" and my chosen song. Muhammad Ali, still looking youthful, followed with his wife, who did all the talking.

Then: film about the birth of Chelsea, and Bill as a parent; Paul Anka doing a Clinton-specific version of "My Way" (which he wrote) and "Freedom for the World," accompanied by a Jewish cantor and a full, white-robed choir; more from Hope; and a very frail Gregory Peck pleading for more gun control.

Diana Ross came out next, in a yellow feather coat over a strapless yellow gown, covered in appliqués. She sang a medley, considered the hit of the evening. That was good for her ego, since it was her first public performance after her recent tour, which had been abruptly cancelled due to poor ticket sales.

After Ross, Hillary paid tribute to her husband on screen; there were a few words from Ted Danson and Mary Steenburgen, who dissolved into tears of gratitude; and then the show's climax.

It began with film of Roger Clinton singing "Circle of Friends" at Bill's first inauguration, which then segued neatly into Roger singing the same song live to his brother—both men noticeably older (and wiser?) than they'd been eight years earlier. The event was capped by fireworks and a thunderous standing ovation.

When the applause subsided, the first family mounted the stage, and both Bill and Hillary spoke. Then everyone rocked to the Clinton anthem, "Don't Stop Thinking about Tomorrow." As Bill, Hillary, and Chelsea exited stage right, I was there, the first to greet them. There were hugs and kisses all around.

The "private" sit-down was yet to come—a lot of noshing and schmoozing—but the big show was over. I could finally take a breath.

THE SOCIAL WHIRL CONTINUED until after two in the morning. When the presidential party finally left, I walked them to their car, along with Travolta, Preston, Patrick Swayze, and Wesley Snipes.

Just before they got into the limo, I handed the president gifts from me, Stan Lee, and Peter Paul: for him, a custom humidor and a handmade gold watch worth tens of thousands; for Hillary, a necklace that cost eight grand. The first lady disliked it and later sent it back.

Before my car arrived, I had my last fond glimpses of this gathering of the rich and famous. I watched them drive off into the night. I may have been the ultimate outsider growing up, but not any more. Now I was in, and *they* were my people.

But not for long. In less than three years I'd be busted. Instead of chronicling my stunning successes, *Variety's* Army Archerd would be writing about my criminal misdeeds; I'd be talking not to presidents and movie stars, but to the FBI and other federal agencies, handing over more than two dozen boxes of letters, e-mails, receipts, and invoices, cooperating as the government pursued a multifaceted investigation into the corruption that lay hidden behind all the glitter.

And little did my Hollywood friends suspect that, when I began talking to the feds, they would be launching prayers up to whatever gods they believed in—prayers that went like this: "Please, please don't let him mention my name . . ."

two

STAR STRUCK

*I appreciated your personal attention . . . you
are the perfect host.*

—ALMA VALENZUELA,
Office of Congressman Ed Pastor,
Personal Letter, November 19, 1991

With her stunning good looks and impeccable taste, my mom,
Anita Mirves Tonken, couldn't help but stand out in the small,
blue-collar town of Alpena, Michigan.

When it came to material possessions, her instincts were
flawless. The expression "keeping up with the Joneses" should
have been coined for her. Despite her intense dislike of the
unsophisticated town, she tried to make the best of things,
throwing the biggest, most lavish parties in town. For my bar
mitzvah, she blew right past the Joneses.

I assisted. Unlike most kids my age, I loved this stuff. I was
involved with almost every aspect of planning the affair. I
especially liked the expensive engraved invitations, how they
looked and how they felt in my hand. Though I would far
exceed my mother as a producer of glittering tributes, this was
where it all began.

I pestered my mom and dad to invite regional celebrities she'd never met, a terrible embarrassment for her. Among many others, she tried to snag the governor, the state attorney general, and our U.S. congressman, Robert Davis. For weeks, I eagerly anticipated the mailman's arrival, hoping to find an RSVP from someone of consequence.

None of them came, of course. But there were compensations from many of the no-shows, in the form of checks, savings bonds, and other gifts. I raked in thousands.

The whole idea of giving gifts was big in my family. My father, Dr. Harvey Tonken, was generous to a fault, and my mother loved nothing better than showering friends or relatives with outrageously expensive presents. For me, the youngest of three and the only son, nothing was too good. Looking back, I realize my dad spent tens of thousands on my bar mitzvah. It probably crushed him with debt.

When the big day arrived, a huge tent was erected on our lawn, which had been specially manicured for the occasion. There were flowers everywhere. Along with a giant inflatable Humpty Dumpty and fifteen-foot inflatable clown on the ground, a blimp flew overhead that said, CONGRATULATIONS AARON. Over three hundred people came. This included Alpena's "A" list, if there was such a thing, all the doctors and lawyers and prominent business people. Other friends and relations flew in from all over the U.S. and Canada, where my father had formerly practiced medicine.

The bar mitzvah was orthodox, and my mother decorated the temple beautifully with ferns. The service is the religious highlight of the ceremony, and it was completely traditional. Amazingly, my reading of the scriptures in Hebrew was flawless. I know this made my family proud of my accomplishment.

I don't know if it ever happened again.

MY PROBLEMS WITH MONEY began at an early age.

The cash I received at my bar mitzvah had been converted into U.S. savings bonds, which were locked in the dining room cabinet where my mother kept her fine china and silverware. I, of course, got hold of the key. Whenever I wanted, I would remove some bonds, take them to the local bank, and cash them in. I'd use the money to buy flowers for girls in the Miss Alpena beauty pageant. I also bought a ton of riding equipment for the horse my father had given me, like a fancy saddle and sterling silver bridle.

I got caught when the president of the bank called my parents one day to make sure they knew I was coming in repeatedly and cashing my savings bonds early, for which there was a penalty. My parents were ticked. To them, it was theft, but I didn't see it that way. I was only doing what I had to do to get what I wanted, with no thought for the consequences—a pattern of behavior that would really land me in trouble later on.

My father responded to my actions by redoubling his efforts to turn me into an ethical person. He desperately wanted me to develop a sense of responsibility, so he secretly paid a couple of local businesses to give me jobs. I bussed tables at Dave's Pizza and, after that, did cleaning work at the Alpena Music Center (where I actually spent most of my time gossiping with the owner's wife). I hated both jobs and spent weeks hassling my dad about them until he allowed me to quit. A lot of time would pass before I was able to see what he'd been trying to accomplish.

I was no better at school than at work. While my two sisters (who practically lived in the library) excelled, I could hardly keep my head above water—socially or academically. I had been diagnosed some years earlier with attention deficit hyperactivity disorder and placed on Ritalin. But ADHD would only make a tough situation worse. From a very early age, I suffered from bad facial tics and involuntary head movements. At thirteen, I was entering middle school, which is always a difficult transition. But try adding hyperactivity and twitching to the mix. I was able to fake it for a while—bringing home Bs. But eventually, my grades went into a nosedive from which they never recovered. I never did graduate high school. Years later, I tried for my GED. I had to take the test four times before I passed it. Just barely, I'm sure, since I scored below the state average in every category.

There were other conflicts as well. My dad was kind, sensitive, and devoted to my mother. He honored her in the home, never spoke words of anger to her that I heard, and always put her first. But there was tension. Raised Jewish, Harvey later converted to Christianity. This wasn't something of which my mother approved. In fact, playing off Mom's prejudices, neither did my sisters and I; we regarded all non-Jews as inferior. We looked down upon his religion and even made fun of it in his presence. To say it strained relations is beyond understatement.

All told, my dark and troubled youth would only make the lights of Hollywood glow all the brighter.

DURING MY LAST YEARS IN ALPENA, seventh and eighth grades, I really developed my lifelong addiction to celebrity. I also got involved in politics for the first time. It was not so much that I was interested in ideology, but politicians were famous and powerful, and that attracted me. In addition, I developed my budding talent for organizing, especially fundraising functions, and discovered that I had a real gift for the art of the schmooze. I became quite brazen about cold calling dignitaries I didn't know, often asking favors of them.

I really wanted to be an entertainer. But the facial tics killed that dream. The next best thing seemed to be hobnobbing with the rich and influential. I pestered my parents to invite the local luminaries to the house, so that I could meet and study them. I wanted to know what they thought, what they talked about, how they'd gotten where they were, how they moved through the world. I desperately wanted to be successful—to be one of these people—and felt certain that some day I could.

I started with Dan MacDougal, a candidate for state representative, by licking envelopes and handing out bumper stickers. *Boring.*

I wanted in on the real action. So I took it upon myself to organize a fundraiser for MacDougal.

Although I was only fourteen years old, I did it all: rented the armory, arranged the entertainment, made the banners, balloons, and posters. It was a pretty precocious thing to do, not to mention pushy. But I truly thought the candidate would thank me in the end, maybe bring me into his inner circle. Not surprisingly, I had no idea of the proper way to go about the task and knew nothing about election law. And because MacDougal had no idea what I was doing, no one from his team told me what I was getting into. I didn't realize you were required to form an official fundraising committee and identify the committee as the sponsor of the event.

As a result, I didn't achieve what I'd been trying to accomplish. In fact, MacDougal's political opponents recognized immediately that there were campaign finance irregularities and pounced all over them. Whether they cost MacDougal the election I don't know. But he did lose.

I probably should have learned from this experience to pay attention to political campaign laws. Not me. During my Hollywood heyday, I unknowingly broke many more of them.

The fact that my first foray into politics had been in a losing cause didn't make me back off—now I had a passion to make it fly, to achieve. I turned my attention to Robert Davis, the congressman who hadn't come to my bar mitzvah. He was a Republican, which didn't go down well with my father, a lifelong Democrat. But Davis was what we had, our district's incumbent. I did some local leafleting for him, plus tormented my dad, until finally he handed over some money for the campaign.

After that, my dad became a regular contributor, a major compromise for him that I never appreciated back then. My father betrayed his political principles solely to open a door for his scheming son. It worked.

Eventually we became somewhat close with Davis and his wife. I even stayed at their home in the Virginia suburbs once. For a week I had an in-depth exposure to D.C., touring the halls of Congress, working in Davis's office, being photographed with Ted Kennedy, and having dinner with then-Speaker of the House Tip O'Neill.

My Washington experience was an education. I was thrilled. By my standards, I had hit the big time. But my parents had other ideas.

AT SEVENTEEN I FOUND MYSELF on the street. I couldn't hack it in school—public or the two boarding schools my parents had tried. I couldn't really hack it at home, either—I was too difficult for my mother to handle. For the next five years, I drifted around, taking odd jobs along the way, staying with friends and relatives in Ontario, Michigan, West Virginia, Pennsylvania, and Arizona.

It was there in Scottsdale where I met Gilbert Ortega— "the King of Indian Jewelry," as he was known. I'd seen Ortega, driving around town in his white Rolls Royce. That kind of car gets your attention.

Ortega was a fourth-generation Arizonan, whose family roots went back to seventeenth-century Mexico. He'd grown up dirt poor, one of seven kids. But he had an eye for quality. As an adult, he began working in his dad's reservation trading post, on the New Mexican border. From there, he moved to Gallup and started a chain of Indian stores that eventually stretched across the Southwest, from Texas to Arizona. When he died in 2003, there were twenty-two of them. I knew I could benefit by ingratiating myself to him.

One night, at the Hyatt Regency bar—where the in crowd hung out—I walked right up to him and introduced myself as a psychologist. I knew he wouldn't talk to a wandering high-school dropout. The ruse didn't play, but he hired me anyway. It turned out to be an important break.

Despite his career in jewelry, Ortega really wanted to be a country singer. He had even made a tape of himself, performing his own songs, such as "Send Me the Pillow that You Dream On." As a result of his interest, he had befriended quite a few country stars. So when he planned a grand opening celebration for his newest store—in the fancy Scottsdale Galleria mall—Gilbert wanted some of them to attend. I arranged that. It was my first experience with bringing celebrities to an event, and I liked it.

Gilbert wanted Waylon Jennings and his wife Jessie Colter to attend the opening, along with Tanya Tucker and Mae Boren Axton, the mother of Hoyt Axton and coauthor of the song "Heartbreak Hotel." He knew them all. But I was the one who went out, sold them on the idea, and convinced them to juggle their schedules and make an appearance. I had the talent.

It wasn't just my sweet talk that made it happen, though. Gilbert was only willing to offer these people airfare and accommodations in return for their time, thinking, with his monstrous ego, they were coming just for him. I knew that wouldn't cut it and pushed Gilbert to throw in some nice gifts. He hated the idea but came up with a few things, not enough in my opinion. So I took some jewelry from his stores and gave it to them, telling them it came from Gilbert. That did the trick. They all showed.

Luckily, when Gilbert found out my little secret, he didn't mind, because he was happy with the results. It was good for business to have the stars there, and doubly good to have them serve as walking advertisements for his products.

For my part, I didn't think of what I did as theft. I was merely trying to please Gilbert, by doing what he should have done to get what he wanted, and I succeeded. Unknowingly, however, I was setting a pattern of behavior that would eventually lead me into a world of hurt.

But I wasn't satisfied with just having country stars there. I wanted people from politics too. So I started cold calling, a skill I'd honed a few years before.

You see, when I was touring Washington with the Davis's, I lifted Jackie Onassis's number from an acquaintance in Washington. I'd been obsessed with the former first lady since my childhood. So, at the age of fifteen, I called up Jackie O. She was surprised but very gracious. She asked how old I was, undoubtedly perplexed as to how I got her number. But I did most of the talking. It was a rare pleasure and my first taste of celebrity schmoozing.

Cold calling someone famous didn't seem like a big a deal to me. In fact, it was easy. I imagine that surprises most people. Few would even do it, and those who could get through would probably be tongue-tied. Not me. I felt completely at ease talking with celebrities. Moreover, I had a gift for putting them at ease. And, I found, once you have someone feeling comfortable, you can ask almost anything of them.

For the Ortega event, I phoned Rose Mofford, who had become governor of the state after Evan Mecham was impeached. She knew Gilbert and agreed to attend. I also cold called the Arizona attorney general, Grant Woods, and he came. So did Congressman Ed Pastor. The Galleria bash was my first experience mixing the worlds of entertainment and politics. It would not be the last.

Gilbert was pleased with the result. "Given the chance, Aaron can do many things," he wrote of me. "I recommend him without any reservations."

Woods also wrote a letter of recommendation for me: "I am confident that Aaron will put forth the ultimate effort. . . ."

So did Governor Mofford: "It is a privilege to recommend Aaron Tonken. He is a highly motivated and ambitious individual. . . . His public relations skills are excellent. . . . Please give this hard-working young man the opportunity to produce great results for you."

All in all, I'd done something pretty big. But my dreams were bigger still, and to realize them I needed a more expansive stage. If I wanted to associate with the stars, I had to go where the stars were, and that was a long way from Alpena.

three

PRISONER AT ZSA ZSA'S

When I left Arizona, I had stars in my eyes and almost nothing in my pockets. Just seven hundred fifty bucks, total. I hit Los Angeles in my motorized eyesore—a beat-up Buick station wagon with the laminated vinyl siding peeling off. It had brought me a long way, and I only had a little further to go.

My destination was the home of CiCi Huston, whom I had met through a friend back in Arizona. Known more formally as Celeste, she was one of legendary filmmaker John Huston's many ex-wives and the ex-stepmother of actress Anjelica Huston.

Desperate to gain entrance into the Hollywood scene, I coaxed CiCi into letting me stay at her place and work as her assistant. I did mainly menial chores for her prized horses, feeding them and mucking out the stalls. I had to put the manure very carefully into a number of plastic bags then set them out at the street for removal. The garbage man got paid extra for taking CiCi's crap. I didn't.

She was a habitual gossip and backstabber, who never missed an opportunity to belittle or attack me. I could hardly avoid her daily personal assaults; she made fun of my appearance, even my car (which she wouldn't even allow me to park in her driveway). But I figured I could endure the abuse if she introduced me to stars. I had to push her to do it, but she did come through—sort of. I didn't know it at the time, but CiCi had largely alienated herself from the community.

My initial star contacts were sporadic. Bo Derek stopped by one day. The Schwarzeneggers were neighbors, but Arnold never visited. Maria Shriver did make it over on occasion, so her kids could pet CiCi's horses. And there was the time John Forsythe drove by in his beautiful black Porsche and blew a kiss to CiCi. Not the biggest names in the biz, true, but for me a star was a star. I eventually did meet Arnold, even if it only was for a few minutes at Patrick's Roadhouse, out on the Pacific Coast Highway.

The real breakthrough came when I convinced CiCi to introduce me to her former friend Zsa Zsa Gabor. Now you must understand that Zsa Zsa was to me the epitome of Hollywood glamour. She was exotic, classy. Who cares if she slapped a cop once or twice . . . or wasn't in any memorable movie . . . or, for that matter, had no discernable talent? She was a star, and I *just had* to be in her orbit.

"No," CiCi said when I first suggested it. "I don't see her any more and don't want to be involved with her. I don't even know what I'd say to her. We have nothing to talk about." It wasn't going to be easy, but my pestering eventually wore her down, and she caved.

"Hello Daaahling! Sveethaht!" I overheard Zsa Zsa say when CiCi called. "Vat you vant?"

The pair chitchatted for a while, talking about their mutual interest in horses, with CiCi frequently putting her hand over the receiver and making fun of Zsa Zsa's accent. A Hollywood friendship to be sure. In the end, they made a date.

"S—," CiCi said after she'd hung up. "Now I've gotta go to lunch with her because of you."

"You didn't even *mention* me," I whined.

She laughed. "Well," she said, "when we go to lunch, I'll tell her all about you. Don't worry."

They had their lunch, and CiCi came through for me, although it wouldn't be long before I would wish she hadn't. CiCi had gotten me an appointment to interview for a job as the actress's "assistant." I had no idea what was in store.

I WAS VERY EXCITED the morning I drove over to Bel Air Road. It was an exclusive street in an exclusive section of the city; along with Zsa Zsa and her sister Eva (in different houses), President and Mrs. Reagan lived there, as did Elizabeth Taylor. It was also quite hilly. I was sure that at any moment the ancient Buick, which was clanking ominously, was going to die on me. But it didn't. Just my luck.

The house had an intercom that Zsa Zsa herself answered.

"Come in, daahling," she said as the wrought iron gates

opened for me. I went up the drive and parked way off to the side, so she wouldn't see the condition of my car.

The estate itself—1001 Bel Air Road—was fabulous, a yellow two-story house with a pool, a rose garden, and an incredible view of Beverly Hills and Los Angeles. But I didn't smell roses when I exited my car. I'd stepped in dog crap; there were piles of it all over her cracked driveway.

From the door, I was led to an office by a Polish maid to await Zsa Zsa's entrance. And what an entrance it was. Overweight and about seventy-five at the time, she still thought she could get away with wearing a nearly see-through negligée. It almost worked, what with her excellent facelifts, silver blonde hair, milky white skin, and really nice jewelry.

She didn't shake my hand and barely even looked at me. We talked for maybe five minutes, though I could barely understand her because of her thick Hungarian accent. She asked me some personal questions, and I gave her some made-up answers. Then she said I was hired. I had no idea I was the fourth "assistant" she had taken on that month alone.

THUS I WENT TO WORK FOR the Princess, as she liked to be called. I guess this was because of her marriage to Prince Frederic von Anhalt, who was supposedly from some line of Prussian nobility, though I later learned that he mostly traded on his heritage by selling royal titles to commoners and wannabes. What a piece of work.

Zsa Zsa treated him like a gardener, not a husband, and they had separate bedrooms. That could have been because von Anhalt seemed more like a queen than a prince to me. He never tried anything with me, though. Maybe he felt making a pass at a Jewish guy was beneath him. The specialty of von Anhalt's German Shepard, Schatzi, was "killing vucking Jews," he told me. Von Anhalt thought that was a real hoot.

The job went badly from the start. While taking heaps of verbal abuse, I rushed around answering the phone, fetching drinks from the kitchen, and fending off bill collectors. There was a deluge of letters from department stores, clothing stores, credit companies, and others, all demanding immediate payment. There were lawsuits pending for past due bills. There was one correspondence from a very famous name in designer clothes, whose store was located on Rodeo Drive, telling her that she had to stop "buying" his dresses, wearing them once, then returning them. It was clear he was through cutting her slack. If she persisted in this behavior, she would be permanently barred from his store, he said, before warning her to "keep her fat Hungarian ass out."

I was stunned. Rich people didn't live this way. They paid their bills because they could. Bill collectors on the doorstep all the time, that was something that happened to poor folks. If having money didn't free you from those hassles, then what was it for?

Even opening the "friendly" mail could be a painful experience. There were always invitations to this or that ritzy private party, though Zsa Zsa didn't go out much. I remember opening one, while she was there with me, that asked her to attend a big birthday bash for Stanley Black, a prominent Beverly Hills developer. When she saw what it was, she said, "Those vucking Jews, always showing off their money. I won't go."

Zsa Zsa's shocking words barely had time to register with me. I was just too busy trying to hang onto my job. Still star-struck, I would endure anything in my effort to hang on. In the end, however, I couldn't. It was clear that I didn't have the right skills for the assistant position—her "secretary," as she called me—and I lasted only about a week. But she didn't fire me; I simply got demoted. That didn't bother me, since I'd been out of my element, anyway. And in truth, I was grateful to remain employed.

From assistant and office worker, I went to cleaning house, raking leaves, making deliveries of her new line of special pink cream that was supposed to eliminate facial lines, and serving as her personal driver. I was in charge of cleaning the cement courtyard where they let their lhasa apso and Schatzi, the Jew-killing shepherd, out to take a dump.

I remember the first time I cleaned Zsa Zsa's bathroom. She had a shelf with, literally, dozens of prescription medications on it. Lithium, Percocet, sleeping pills, all kinds of stuff. I'd been raised in a doctor's family, but I had never before seen such a collection of drugs. I asked a friend what they were. "Mood levelers," he said.

It wasn't working.

The general housecleaning was a Herculean effort. There was a lot of old furniture—not nice antique old, but crummy old—and even that hadn't been kept up. The carpets were ancient and stained, the bedding was filthy. There were holes in the walls and fleas everywhere. What parts of the house I was allowed to see looked like Dresden, after Hitler. Schatzi must have felt right at home. Still, I did my best to spruce it up and got no credit for my efforts.

And little money, for that matter. It was Zsa Zsa's strategy, I would learn, to take live-in help on at the beginning of the month, then find an excuse to fire them at the end, when the first paycheck was due. She didn't quite play me that way—despite the way she yelled at me, pushed me around, and even slapped my face from time to time. Maybe she liked me.

As her newly-appointed driver, it was one of my duties to take Zsa Zsa to her Simi Valley ranch in her beautiful, four-door, dark blue two-hundred-thousand dollar Bentley. The Princess controlled the money; the Prince was relegated to driving a crappy Buick station wagon just a few years newer than my crappy Buick station wagon. We took the trip about an hour's drive north of Bel Air a couple of times a week.

One Sunday afternoon, Zsa Zsa threw a party out at the ranch. Since she didn't actually own the place—just rented space for her horses—all she could use was a room that adjoined the horse stalls. She set up a card table inside the barn for the food. There were flies everywhere. It was really gross, but funny too, all these people trying to eat amid hundreds of buzzing flies and the stink of the stables.

In preparation, Zsa Zsa had her Polish maids whip up a special pot of her famous Hungarian goulash for the affair. That dish was her marital secret, she said. It was how she'd snagged her husbands, all seven or eight of them. They fell for her goulash. Sure enough, at the party, people came and ate it and complimented her on it.

I got a good laugh out of that, because I knew what went into the famed dish: cut-up hot dogs and sauerkraut, basically. The cheapest possible ingredients—that was it. I got nauseous just having to smell it on the ride out. I couldn't bring myself to eat one bite. Yet here were all these guests fawning over Zsa Zsa Gabor's goulash.

Typical Hollywood. If you had any star power at all, people would tell you whatever you wanted to hear.

DESPITE THE DIFFICULTY working for Zsa Zsa, living with CiCi was proving even worse. She had a new boyfriend, and so I needed new digs. I tried an old, decrepit hotel—all I had money for—but couldn't hack it. So I did the one thing I shouldn't have: asked Zsa Zsa for a favor.

"All right, daahling. You can move into the guest house. But you are sooo verry handsome, ve vill have to break you in verry slowly. The Prince will be sooo jealous of you."

She said I could work for her full time, in return for which I could live for free and draw a small salary. Yeah right. Despite all my misgivings about Zsa Zsa and the Prince, I was thrilled. Not only was I getting out of my cesspool of a hotel, I was going to live in Bel Air! With Elizabeth Taylor and the Reagans as neighbors! Nothing else mattered.

I gathered up my few belongings and headed over to Zsa Zsa's that night. When I pushed the button at the gate, the Prince came on over the intercom.

"Vat are you doing here?" he asked me.

I told him I was moving into the guest house.

"No vay," he said. He muttered something in his thick German accent that sounded nasty, then added, "Go avay," and cut me off. Zsa Zsa hadn't told him anything about our little arrangement. But then, after a screaming match between Zsa Zsa and the Prince, she let me in.

"Come back over, daahling."

The cottage that was to be my new home was a disgrace. I got so many flea bites the first few days I was there, I had to go to the emergency room and get a shot. That was a trial in and of itself, because of course the first thing the hospital wanted to know was how they were going to be paid. I had no cash, checks, credit cards, or health insurance. I gave them a line about how I didn't have my insurance card with me and would send them my policy number later. What other option did I have?

Living at Zsa Zsa's full time, I could see firsthand the turnover in personnel. She went through assistants, cooks, maids, and Mexican yard workers faster than her famed goulash went through the digestive tracts of her unsuspecting husbands. The poor Polish girls were my best friends there. I would be shut out of the house, starving, and they would pass me fruit and chicken through the bars that were over the kitchen window, like I was a monkey in a zoo. But nearly every month, I'd have to make friends with a new set of girls.

AS IF THE DRAMA IN THE HOUSE wasn't bad enough, there was the ongoing tragicomedy with Zsa Zsa's sister Eva. You probably remember Eva from the popular television show *Green Acres.* She was the talented Gabor sister. Eva lived a couple of blocks away in a nice, clean, immaculately maintained home. She was very elegant and slender, very attractive for her age, and still respected in the Hollywood community.

Eva used to say, "Oh, you should've come to vork for me instead." But that was just the kind of luck I was having in Hollywood. I hook up with a Gabor sister, and it's the wrong one.

What's worse, I had some perverse sense of loyalty to Zsa Zsa. "Thanks, but I'm happy over there," I lied to Eva.

On the surface, the Gabors got along with each other pretty well, but Zsa Zsa was extremely jealous of her more successful sister. She would constantly ask me if I thought she was more beautiful than Eva, and, of course, I would always have to tell her yes, even though she was a good five sizes larger.

One hot summer day, I was driving the Bentley back from the ranch when Zsa Zsa suddenly went on a tirade, spouting off horrible, nasty things about Eva—she was no good, she stole movie parts from her, whatever. I could decipher about half the rant because it was delivered in Zsa Zsa's thick Hungarian babble. After she had vented her unintelligible vitriol, she turned to me and said, "Right?"

Right? Right about what? I had no clue. Of course, a wiser man than I would have agreed with the old cow regardless. But for some reason—maybe it was the heat, or maybe I'd hit my threshold of Zsa Zsa's bitching—I didn't. Zsa Zsa screamed at me to pull over and get out. She left me there on the side of the road halfway between Simi Valley and Bel Air. I had to take a cab home.

She also sent me, one time, on an errand to Eva's to deliver a jar of Zsa Zsa's special pink anti-aging cream, her famous "beauty secret." Zsa Zsa tried to sell the stuff to whoever would pony up a few bucks. There were cases of it in storage. No one was buying, and no wonder. I tried it on myself once, thinking: *Hey, Zsa Zsa looks young for her age, what could it hurt?* A lot, actually. I had an immediate allergic reaction. It literally burned my skin, and guess what—I had to go to the hospital again.

In any case, I dropped off the jar of cream to Eva and returned home. When I buzzed Zsa Zsa to let me in the gate, she yelled over the intercom: "Vell, did you get a check?"

A *check?* I had forgotten. I'd been told to be sure and pick up the money for the cream, but I'd gotten to talking with Eva, and that just slipped my mind. We're talking about something like fifteen bucks here. Between sisters, no less.

"No," I said, suddenly fearful. "I'm sorry, I forgot it."

"Then go and get it," Zsa Zsa insisted, and wouldn't let me in until I did.

So, like a good little slave, or "white nigger" as Zsa Zsa would often call me, I trudged back to Eva's, asked her to write a check for fifteen dollars, and took it back. I was utterly humiliated.

I WAS MAKING NO MONEY and getting so little to eat that I became frantic to find another job, even applied at McDonald's. Finally, after much pounding of pavement, I landed a gig at Macy's department store. Real work at last. I was pumped.

When I told Zsa Zsa the good news, though, she was

furious. I couldn't go my first day, she insisted, because I had to drive her out to the ranch instead, an engagement that had not been scheduled. The new job was only part time, I reminded her, and I could still take her to the ranch after I got off. No go. She was not going to have me slaving for someone else.

I stuck to my guns this time. I went back to the guest cottage, dressed in nice clean clothes, what little I had, and set off for work. I got as far as my car. There the old station wagon sat, one of its tires as flat as a pancake. Of course I couldn't prove it, but I knew that Zsa Zsa had ordered one of her yard workers to puncture the tire. I just knew it.

By the time I got the tire changed—I had to call up a friend to help me out—I was hours late for work. I went anyway and told my supervisor the truth (though who could have believed me: Zsa Zsa Gabor slit your tires?). *Sorry,* my boss said. *You can't be late your first day. You're fired. Company policy.*

I trudged back to Zsa Zsa's.

"Now you can take me to the ranch," she said smugly.

Slave that I was, I did too. But I think that was the moment I realized I had to get away from this woman, before she drove me stark raving mad. I had no money, no job, no skills, no alternate place to live, nothing. But I had reached a new low of desperation. And I knew I had to escape from Zsa Zsa's concentration camp—with the dogs and the fleas and the scraps of food through prison bars—and the key to my deliverance came in the form of a trip to Europe. The Prince and the Princess would be gone for two weeks, and when they returned, I told myself, I'd be gone for good.

I KNEW IF I WAS GOING TO BREAK FREE, I needed quick and easy money. Zsa Zsa had never really paid me, and clearly had no intention of ever doing so. I was trying to think of a way to work my unfortunate circumstances to my advantage. So when inspiration finally struck, when I finally realized my horrible living conditions could actually be my salvation, I snapped into action.

I called up the *Globe,* a supermarket tabloid, and offered them the real story on Zsa Zsa Gabor's house. They bit. A reporter named John I. Jones was assigned to me and took me to lunch at the Four Seasons Hotel in Beverly Hills. I spoke into a tape recorder as he asked me questions, and he laughed himself silly at my stories. John was a real nice guy, even loaned me fifty bucks out of his own pocket for food and gas.

That night, after the interview, I gave John a tour of the Gabor house, where he snapped pictures of the place. He was, like I had been, appalled. I provided him with a photo of Zsa Zsa (one that made her look even more bloated than usual) that he could use for the cover.

Sure, it was a terrible thing to do. I still felt a loyalty to Zsa Zsa, and this was absolute betrayal. But, at the same time, I figured she had it coming. The woman had broken me in spirit, leveled me financially, emotionally, and every other way she could. So we plowed ahead.

The *Globe* had agreed to pay me five thousand dollars for my exclusive story of being imprisoned at Zsa Zsa Gabor's. It was plenty to start me on my new path. But what I didn't realize at first was I wouldn't be paid until two weeks after the story hit the newsstands. Big problem. My boss and the Prince would be home well before I received any cash. I needed some traveling money, and fast.

Then I was hit with another brilliant, if devious, idea. I remembered the many times Zsa Zsa had been trying to get home in her Bentley, only to get stuck behind one of the many buses that gave tours of Beverly Hills and Bel Air. *See the homes of the stars!* That kind of thing.

Whenever she was recognized, the tour leader would honk his horn and point at Zsa Zsa, whereupon the passengers would click away with their cameras. Sometimes they would even wait outside of the gates for her to pull out. Zsa Zsa hated this. She would cuss a blue streak in English and Hungarian every time we encountered one of those buses.

So I figured if these tourists wanted to see the homes of the stars, I'd give them a very, very intimate look. I'd take them inside the gates, inside the house, let them see what a dump it was, everything. I called up one of the tour companies, and we cut a nice deal. I even called a rent-a-cop company and hired an armed guard to stand inside the door, just to make the whole thing seem special. I also diverted a little money to the Polish maids, to ensure they'd go along with the program and because, like me, they needed the extra cash.

We ran people through, in groups of fifteen or twenty, for around half an hour each. It was a sight: star-stuck tourists wandering through the dilapidated mansion, expressions of awe mixed with pity, stepping over dog turds and swatting fleas. They got their money's worth.

I remember one couple in particular, a husband and wife from Wisconsin, all decked out in their extra-large-sized polyester outfits, with raised eyebrows, looking around the

"Moulin Rouge"—that's how Zsa Zsa referred to her rec room—which was done up in red and featured a pool table, dance floor, strobe lights, and bar. It was as moth-eaten and unkempt as the rest of the house.

"Somehow," the wife sighed and said, "I never dreamed Zsa Zsa Gabor could live like this." *Priceless.*

I wound up making about thirty-three hundred off the tours, which went on for six or seven days. But in the end, I was found out. Someone had apparently tipped off Eva, who investigated my little money-raising scheme and reported it to her sister. The Polish girls, friends as always, alerted me to what had happened, and I knew it was time to scram. Fortunately I had the money to make a new start.

So when Zsa Zsa phoned me from her plane back to the States, I was ready.

"Daahling," she said, all sweetness and light, "the Prince and I are on our vay home. And ve have a vonderful surprise for you."

And then, faintly but distinctly in the background, I heard von Anhalt say, "Yeah, an administrative opening at Auschwitz."

"Really?" I said. "Well, vuck you," and I hung up.

UPON LEAVING THE NIGHTMARISH WORLD of Zsa Zsa's, I was relieved—believe it or not—to settle into a homeless shelter called the Chabad House. I had first found out about the place while watching TV one day while the Prince and Princess were away. Flipping through channels, I had come across a most peculiar sight, Jewish rabbis in black, long-tailed suits dancing around. It was the funniest thing. They were having a fundraiser for the Chabad organization and were dancing in front of the tote board that showed how much money had been pledged. Jon Voight—a nice man who later became my friend—was the celebrity helping attract donors, and he was there, dancing too.

The organization offered different programs for drug addicts, street people, what-have-you, and ran a homeless shelter named Chabad House. I remember thinking at the time, *God help me that I should wind up in a place like that.* So that's where I went.

The shelter was run by members of Chabad Lubavitch, a Hasidic missionary movement that provides services to Jews in many countries around the world. Their stated philosophy is this: "No Jew should ever be lost to the Jewish people, no Jew must ever be lonely." After the terrors at Zsa Zsa's, that sounded really comforting to me.

There were a lot of rules, though. You had to eat kosher, for example, if you wanted to take advantage of the one meal a day they offered. There were weekly chores to be done. You had to go to worship services every morning, and you had to wear *teffilin.* These are leather straps that are wound around the right arm and hand in a prescribed fashion with one strap placed on the head. Both straps include a small square box containing four Bible verses inscribed on pieces of parchment.

Chabad House took anyone, regardless of race or religion, but everyone was expected to participate in these observances of the Jewish faith.

Therapy sessions were mandatory, as well. I welcomed

that. The entire time I'd been in California, there had really been no one I could tell my troubles to. I'd been accumulating my emotional scars in isolation, so it was great to have people who would listen to me and whom I could rely upon for understanding.

All things considered, it was the most wholesome environment, by far, that I'd been in since I arrived on the West Coast. What a start it had been. From CiCi Huston's to Zsa Zsa Gabor's to a homeless shelter. I was really going places. I figured I was about as low as one could get and had no place to go but up, and I would soon meet the man who could take me there.

four

PETER PAUL
AND MERRY

P_eter Paul was forty-two_ when I met him in early 1993. He was average height, average build, had dark thinning hair, and sported a close-cropped beard. He dressed smartly, usually in a blazer, collared white shirt, dress slacks, and dress shoes. For as long as I've known him, I've thought he was older than his age.

I took to Peter immediately. He was everything I aspired to be: brilliant, sophisticated, a little mysterious, incredibly articulate, a great storyteller, someone who moved easily through both the business and entertainment worlds. During my formative days, he would be my mentor.

He had agreed to meet me at the Palm restaurant, on Santa Monica Boulevard. John I. Jones, the _Globe_ reporter, had introduced me to a guy named Jack, a young fellow about my age, who in turn told me about Peter and, knowing my desires to network with Hollywood's best and brightest, suggested I meet with him. Peter, he told me, had connections.

I touted myself all through lunch—a skill I perfected while looking for jobs in my stint at Zsa Zsa's—and Peter seemed duly impressed. He invited me back to his office. Peter worked out of the Bank of America building, at the corner of Beverly Drive and Wilshire Boulevard: exactly where I longed to be, in the heart of Beverly Hills, just one street removed from Rodeo Drive.

His space was several floors up, with windows wrapping around two walls, gorgeous views of the city. Even more impressive to me was his collection of autographed photographs on display. Peter was pictured with astronaut Buzz Aldrin, Muhammad Ali, Tony Curtis, Helen Hayes, Charlton Heston, and every president since Nixon. The photos took up a whole wall. I knew then and there that this was the guy I had come to Hollywood destined to meet, the one who could provide me with a passport into the world of the rich and famous.

Of course I didn't realize at the time that he had serious problems with many of these people. Peter had a Rolodex full of burnt bridges. But he still had a Rolodex, one of the best in town, and that was enough for me.

Peter had come to Los Angeles via Miami with an impressive list of credentials. An attorney who specialized in international law, he'd been president of the World Trade Center. He'd once represented Salvador Dali in an art book publishing deal and had worked with architect I. M. Pei. For a while, he managed Buzz Aldrin, during promotion for a book on the twenty-fifth anniversary of the moon walk.

Initially, that was the only side of Peter I knew. I had no idea he was a convicted felon who'd been disbarred in Florida after a 1979 conviction for attempting to defraud the Cuban government. I also wasn't aware that he'd been busted for possession of cocaine and had done prison time. And I wouldn't find out until two years later.

But truth be told, I don't think knowing that would have changed much. He had what I wanted, and I was ready to do whatever I needed to get it. Besides, with the Cuban deal, he thought he had the blessing of the U.S. government. And the drugs, he maintains to this day, belonged to someone else. Maybe. I hate drugs, and know nothing about them. But even if he were lying about both the drugs and the Castro scam, I'm not sure it would have made any difference to me.

The important thing was Peter had relocated to L.A. to reinvent himself, as so many others have done, myself included, and he was obviously enjoying success in his new life.

I begged Peter for a job, even though I had a lousy track record, no useful skills, and no idea what I wanted to do. All I knew was I had a Trump-sized entrepreneurial spirit—I just needed a firm hand to guide me. And so after much pleading and self-promoting, Peter was willing to take a chance.

My duties were not really defined. Peter simply said, "I'm interested in seeing what you can do. Show me."

PETER'S PRIMARY FOCUS at that moment was managing the career of romance novel coverboy Fabio. You remember: the guy with the accent as thick as his pecs and a full head of long blonde hair women would die for. Fabio had done all right as a model, but Peter had much grander ideas for him. He believed Fabio could be recast as a romantic icon, a champion of women, especially—no joke—on the issue of the lack of respect for women in the romance publishing industry.

Initially, no one knew there was a real person behind those sexy cover photos. Peter changed all that. He brought Fabio off the cover and gave him a promotable identity. He even secured Fabio a book deal as a romance novel author, even though he seemed barely literate to me. Since Fabio was in such demand as a model, Peter threatened to enjoin publishers from using his image on their covers unless they put his name on the cover as co-writer. It all worked. Fabio was reborn—no longer just a hunk, but a hunk with heart.

I was always cordial to Fabio when he came around, but he seemed to dislike me from the start. I think he resented the attention I was getting from Peter as his new protégé. Fabio didn't want Peter to focus on anything but Fabio. Nevertheless, he was my first assignment.

Peter wanted to have a big Hollywood "coming out" party for his boy. The venue: someplace hip. The guests: celebs. My kind of assignment.

Peter introduced me to Mark Fleischman who, for almost five years back in the eighties, had run the famous Studio 54 in New York, after its original founders went to jail. From there Mark moved on to Hollywood, where he opened Tatou. Designer Peter Nygard and TV personality Robin Leach, among others, were his partners in the new restaurant and nightclub, which quickly became a trendy gathering place for the stars.

My job was to get together with Mark, take Peter's Rolodex, and make the party happen. Sounded tough.

Especially when the party was in "honor" (if you can even call it that) of a talentless lunkhead like Fabio who had absolutely no status in the entertainment industry. But it really wasn't.

In Hollywood, there are some stars who'll show up for anything. They come out of the woodwork. As the saying goes out there: *A lot of people will attend the opening of an envelope.* With few exceptions, celebrities love to be wined and dined—it makes them feel special on somebody else's nickel. Plus, they can rub elbows with other celebrities. I quickly discovered that one of the best ways to get a star to your party was to casually tell him or her which other stars were going to be there. Thus I could get Celebrity A by dropping Celebrity B's name, then turn around and get Celebrity B by mentioning Celebrity A, and they all would show up. I played the ego rackets and won big time.

Of course, it helped that we were partying at Mark Fleischman's Tatou. Tatou was trendy and already had a cast of regulars. This was not entirely an accident. Mark would often comp celebrities the first time they came to eat, because they in turn both attracted more business and sometimes became repeat customers themselves. Nikki Haskell (who peddled a line of vitamins called Star Caps and billed herself as the "Diet Queen to the Stars") was one who capitalized on this. She claimed to be a part owner of the club. I don't know if that was true or not, but she did bring in second-rate celebs, who got free meals out of it, just as she did.

I picked up on this technique early on and talked Mark into giving me my own house account. I'd cold call show business people and invite them to Tatou, to have dinner either with me alone or with some other big name that I used to entice them. I did this for years, and Mark always went along with the scheme because of the illustrious guests I brought through the doors.

This was my first taste of the good life. Still living at Chabad, with its one square meal a day, I was half-starved yet suddenly eating in one of the best restaurants in town. And putting it on a tab. Only in America. Or rather, *only in Hollywood.*

I lined up some of the regulars, such as Victoria McMahon, the newly ex-wife of Ed, and Carol Connors, the singer/songwriter who co-wrote the "Theme from Rocky," sang lead on "To Know Him Is To Love Him" for her high school classmate, Phil Spector, and was once Elvis Presley's girlfriend. By the time I met Carol, she was snidely referred to as the town schnorrer. Her schnorring would continue throughout my career.

Once Peter firmed things with Mark on the financial arrangements, date, and time, I dug into the Rolodex. I knew every name in there. These were the folks I had come to California to meet, and now I had the unmatched pleasure of talking to them on the phone, inviting them to this party I was putting together. I loved every minute of it. Even if it was for the benefit of a cheesy ingrate like Fabio.

I secured Red Buttons and his wife Alicia, Lorna and Milton Berle, Cesar Romero, Loretta Swit, Anne Jeffreys, Roxanne and Jack Carter, and Florence and Sid Caesar. Sure they were no longer on Hollywood's A-list, but they were legends and would become regulars at my events. Young Hollywood would, not surprisingly, look down on these old stars, completely oblivious to the fact that they would be just like them one day, if they were lucky enough to last. But I never did. I appreciated real talent. For me, getting someone like Red Buttons—who has won all three of the highest acting honors: Academy Award, Golden Globe, and Emmy—was a privilege. Whenever some young celebrity would say to me something like, *Red Buttons, oh, isn't he dead yet?* I would reply, *Would you please take out your Oscar and show it to me?* That'd always shut 'em up.

I also snagged Michele Phillips, Kris and Bruce Jenner, Lois and Buzz Aldrin, and even Dr. Ruth Westheimer. I talked the famous producer Freddie Fields, who came with his fourth wife Corinna, into serving as co-host for the evening, along with out-of-towner Sally Jesse Raphael, whom I had cold called.

The party was, if I do say so myself, a huge hit. Photographers were everywhere, squeezing off shots of the arriving celebrities. Sally Jesse and Freddie Fields stood out front with their spouses, alongside Fabio, greeting people as they rolled up. When Dr. Ruth arrived, Fabio, in a rare moment of inspiration, swept her up in his arms and carried her inside. The photographers went nuts, snapping away. That turned out to be the shot of the night. It was published in *People* and all over the world.

Everyone was happy. Mark Fleischman got a lot of publicity for Tatou. Fabio got a lot of publicity for himself. Peter moved Fabio's career along. The stars got free food and drinks and laughs. And I'd organized my first celebrity event in Hollywood—a stunning success. And all it really took was a Rolodex, a few cold calls, and my one verifiable talent: schmoozing.

ONE OF THE WAYS in which I sought to ingratiate myself to the Hollywood community and make valuable, practical connections was to hang out around the pool at the Four Seasons Hotel, where many celebrities stayed while doing publicity interviews. It was a technique I had adopted while still living with Zsa Zsa. I'd put on my best clothes, walk around like a paying guest, and mingle.

It was there that I met Stuart Goldberg. Stuart was handsome and, right off the bat, very nice to me, offering welcome relief from the contentious Hollywood behavior I was slowly getting used to. A very successful criminal attorney from Chicago, Stuart had given up his practice and moved to Hollywood to try to make it as a screenwriter. Already in his forties, Stuart still hadn't had much luck.

But he was well connected and able to introduce me to important and influential people. Like Chen Sam, for instance—a publicist for Elizabeth Taylor and a close friend of hers as well. When I found out that Stuart knew her, the wheels started turning in my head immediately. Maybe I could work through Chen Sam to organize my first charity event.

"Let's put something together for the Elizabeth Taylor AIDS Foundation," I said to Stuart. That was Taylor's big charity, one that she'd founded in 1991, after losing her friend Rock Hudson to the disease.

"Come on," I said. "This will be a great opportunity to meet some more people in the business."

I had some underwriters in mind, but Stuart was a bit wary. He hadn't yet seen me in action and didn't want to put his relationship with Chen Sam at risk. An even bigger hurdle for him, no doubt, was the fact that I was talking about putting on a major charity event while I was still a major charity case. But with a commitment from the underwriters to fly to Los Angeles, he was game.

The meeting would be held at Elizabeth Taylor's Bel Air home, not far from Zsa Zsa's in space, but a world away in class. I was overwhelmingly excited and twitching as usual. Here I was, homeless and living in a shelter, and I'd managed to pull off this unlikely meeting. The amazing thing was, it hadn't really been that hard. I was figuring out the game as I went, and I was a quick study. All that was required was to bring together two groups of people—the wealthy and the famous—who didn't know one another but had interests in common. I only wished that my mother and father could have been there to see it.

Elizabeth Taylor was still the star of stars, even if she didn't do movies any more. Getting a private audience with her was quite a feat. Oddly, although I was thrilled and my tics were working overtime, I wasn't nervous. This was my niche. I was completely comfortable around the stars. I expected success.

Once inside, I sat on a plush white couch, and the first thing that happened was that Elizabeth's husband (now—surprise, surprise—ex-husband) came traipsing through. She had met construction worker Larry Fortensky, who was almost twenty years younger than she was, at the Betty Ford Clinic, then married him. He was working on a project out back involving the pool and clomped by in his muddy work boots.

Chen Sam brought us soft drinks while we waited. Like I said, I wasn't nervous about meeting Elizabeth Taylor—in fact, the whole thing seemed kind of surreal—but I was nervous about something else. My friend from the *Globe*,

John I. Jones, had been pleading for my assistance ever since he heard I was going to her house. He wanted me to look in the refrigerator and report back to him what kind of medications I could find. There would be a lot of money in it for me, he said. I'd told him no from the start. But still, it was on my mind the whole time. The money could bring me a car and an apartment of my own. Very tempting.

When the star came in, she transformed the room.

Often when you meet a star in person, you're surprised at just how different they are from their screen images. They look old and haggard. Not Elizabeth Taylor. Though she was in her early sixties, she was still beautiful. Her hair was nicely done, and she was dressed in casual slacks and an oversized sweater that was pulled down to thigh-level. Her weight was under control. She had very little makeup on, which seemed to accentuate her natural beauty.

Chen Sam introduced us all. Elizabeth shook our hands, thanked us for coming, and sat down next to me. She was very gracious and soft-spoken, educating us about her passionate support of AIDS research.

I gave my best spiel, proposing a grand charity concert with lots of stars performing. She seemed to be going for it. She told us she thought she could get Janet Jackson and some other big names. After I'd said my piece, she took my hand, looked right into my eyes, and thanked me. I felt privileged to be there. I realized it was an honor to be with this woman, not because she was a star, but because she was a humanitarian.

While the conversation continued, I excused myself to go to the bathroom. On the way back, I took a little detour, through the kitchen dining area where I saw, on a shelf, a couple of Oscars. I had never seen one before in real life. I couldn't help myself. I had to hold one. It was thrilling.

At the same moment, I looked for the fridge. I had a fleeting thought that I might actually peep inside and come up with some juicy tidbits for the *Globe*. I let it pass. I'd been down that road before and didn't want that type of behavior to define my Hollywood career.

I was especially pleased that I resisted when Elizabeth later confronted me about the earlier story I sold the *Globe* and about the tours of Zsa Zsa's house. I was mortified. I'd sort of been hoping no one had noticed, but apparently Chen Sam had spilled the beans. My reputation preceded me.

"You shouldn't do those kinds of things," she told me. "Especially in this town, it's just *soo* small. But"—she smiled mischievously—"because it was Zsa Zsa, you should be all right." I was relieved and embarrassed at the same time.

The event never came off, but I was not overly discouraged. I'd proven I could bring famous and influential people together for a common purpose. Translating that into an actual charity event was just a matter of time.

ABOUT THAT SAME TIME, Stuart also introduced me to a wealthy family from New Mexico named the Maloofs. The Maloof family, under the leadership of the matriarch, Coleen, presided over an enormous financial empire that built its initial fortune through the distribution of beer and liquor within the state. From there, they diversified into banks, hotels, and casinos throughout the Southwest. They loved also sports franchises. They once owned the Houston Rockets, nearly acquired the San Antonio Spurs, and went on to purchase the Sacramento Kings. In 1996, the Maloofs were ranked as the richest family in New Mexico, with a collective net worth of four hundred fifty million dollars. My kind of people.

With Coleen overseeing all the family enterprises, the various businesses were run day-to-day by her five children, sons Joe, Gavin, Phil, and George, and daughter Adrienne. I would eventually meet all members of the family, at different times, at the Four Seasons, where they would stay as they shuttled back and forth between Albuquerque and L.A. They were new to the scene but wanted to make useful connections as they expanded their operations into California.

The Maloofs were not sophisticated, but they were honest, hard-working, decent people. I quickly became friends with them all. Especially Coleen, who, since I almost always got along famously with older women, took to me immediately.

Right away, the gears started turning, and I began to try to think of some kind of event I could put together *with* them, or what I might be able to do *for* them. Here was a source of real money; together, we could surely achieve great things. I began by introducing the Maloofs to Peter Paul, then worked out a lunch meet with Barbara and Nancy Davis (mother and daughter in one of Hollywood's wealthiest families). The date ended with generous donations from the Maloofs to the Davises' favorite charities. But the masterstroke was yet to come.

Adrienne Maloof was getting married in the late summer of 1993. The wedding would be back in Albuquerque, which seemed to me like the dark side of the moon by then. So I

suggested they hire me to arrange for some top-level entertainers to fly down and perform.

It was kind of a bluff, since I couldn't really guarantee any
performers until I tried. But I knew a fair number of celebrities at that point.

"Who do you want?" I asked.

Well, they said, Charlton Heston would be nice. His presence would add a great deal of dignity to the event. And how
about, for musical entertainment, the rock group Kiss? They
were one of the brothers' favorites.

"No problem," I said, all the while thinking the whole
notion of pulling in major acts like that to Albuquerque, for a
stranger's wedding, for free, no less, was simply preposterous.

I did know Charlton Heston, though, and his wife Lydia.
I'd cold called them once, schmoozed them, and invited them
to dinner at Tatou. They'd accepted.

The Hestons were gracious, lovely people, both strong in
character—that was obvious. They never acted like prima
donnas, as most stars did, expecting others to obey their every
whim. On the contrary. The Hestons were always kind to me,
grateful and appreciative of my efforts. They never held out
their hands for gifts or favors, which made them a rarity
among celebs, as I was soon to learn. And I treasured every
minute I spent with them.

As I got to know the Hestons, I visited their home, where
I learned that Lydia was a highly-skilled photographer. She
had accompanied her husband to many locations around the
world, where he was acting in films, and taken scads of
pictures. Many were framed and mounted in the house.
Stunning stuff.

I suggested she have a public retrospective, where she could display her work and sell it if she wanted to. We could make a party out of it. It'd be at Tatou, which was ideal because there was a small art gallery attached to the restaurant. Lydia, though flattered, was shy and hesitant about my offer at first, but after talking it over with her husband, she gave her consent. I cleared it all with Mark Fleischman, and we were on.

While in the process of putting this together, of course, the Maloof wedding came up. I loved the Hestons dearly for themselves, not merely their prestige, and I was reluctant to impose on them. But thinking of the doors that the Maloofs could open for me, I asked Lydia if she thought her husband might be willing to attend the ceremony, not as payback for the exhibition, but as a favor.

No one was more surprised than I when Charlton said yes. Better than that, he agreed to read scripture at the ceremony.

I was walking on air. Moses was going to Albuquerque, to read the Bible at my friend's wedding. *Damn, I'm good,* I thought. I called the Maloofs, who were as thrilled as I was, though not completely aware of the magnitude of my accomplishment. Charlton was doing all this just for the travel expenses. Unheard of in Hollywood.

Kiss was another matter. I personally didn't know anyone in the group, but I did know someone who did: Fabio. Oh well, a connection's a connection.

Since we weren't on the best of terms, though, I had Peter Paul speak to him for me. Next thing I knew, we had a dinner date at the Four Seasons: the Maloofs, me, Peter, Stuart Goldberg, Gene Simmons and Paul Stanley of Kiss, Stanley's wife Pam, and Gene's partner, the actress Shannon Tweed.

Things moved quickly from there. Simmons and Stanley apparently liked the Maloofs and, amazingly, agreed to sing at the wedding, again just for expenses. They even promised to transport their personal soundstage to New Mexico for the gig. To be honest, I have no idea why the band agreed, except for the possibility that Gene Simmons, known to be as sharp in business as he is on stage, thought the Maloofs were a good connection to have.

When the big day arrived, I was sick and couldn't make the trip to Albuquerque. But the Hestons went as scheduled, as did Gene Simmons and Paul Stanley, along with Milton Berle's wife Lorna (who had talked her way into a free trip). Those were my celebrities. I couldn't have been more proud.

Even without my presence, everything went as planned. The Maloofs were ecstatic. And I'd shown yet again, as I had with the Fabio party, that I had the skills necessary to pull off an event involving the rich and the glamorous. It was a strange ordeal: Charlton Heston and Kiss performing at a wedding for strangers in the middle of New Mexico, arranged by a nearly penniless kid with no name, no clout. Oh yeah, and Casey Kasem came too.

The absurdity of the situation was not lost on Gene Simmons. According to some friends, as the aging rocker was preparing to go on stage, he turned in their direction and muttered, so that everyone could hear, "What the f— am I doing here?!"

LYDIA HESTON'S PHOTO RETROSPECTIVE at Tatou, on September 15, 1994, was wildly successful. It was attended, and written up the next day in Variety, by top columnist Army Archerd. Celebrities by the score were there, mostly those of the Hestons' generation: Milton Berle, Ernest Borgnine, Tony Curtis, Gregory Peck, and many others. The one person, though, that I really wanted was Chuck Heston's old friend Jimmy Stewart.

I'd begged Stewart to come, but it wasn't meant to be. He was, in many ways, the anti-celebrity. He cared nothing for schmoozing, for the food, drinks, elbow-rubbing. He'd allow us to put his name on the invitations as a co-host, and that was it. Nothing would persuade him to show.

So, feeling like I needed someone of equal stature to replace Jimmy, I pursued Ronald Reagan. I had found in Peter Paul's trusty Rolodex the phone number of Reagan's penthouse office at Fox Plaza in Century City. I cold called and got through to John Hall, a staffer at the office and a great guy. John would bend over backward to help people, so long as it didn't come anywhere near compromising his boss—he was very protective about that. And he never wanted anything in return. From time to time, I would offer him gifts in appreciation of favors he did me. He always refused them.

He did, however, accept an invitation to join me for dinner at Tatou, where he brought along Fred Ryan, Reagan's chief of staff. They enjoyed the evening tremendously and sent a very nice thank-you note on the president's stationery that I still keep and treasure. That was the beginning of a friendship with John that endured for many years. In the future, when I wanted to impress clients by arranging a quick visit with Ronald Reagan, John would almost always oblige me.

During the course of the dinner, I casually asked if the president might be able to make it to the Lydia Heston show at the Tatou Galerie. John said he'd check but was doubtful because Reagan was due to speak that same evening at a California State Republican Party fundraising dinner. I just knew that was a no.

Later, John got back to me and said the president would agree to have his name associated with the event, but showing up would be difficult. Still, Charlton Heston was not only one of his oldest friends but a longtime political supporter. And so, after much juggling, John and I pulled it off.

Former President Ronald Reagan and first lady Nancy would attend the cocktail reception preceding the dinner honoring Mrs. Heston and then make his way to the fundraiser. He could stay for about an hour.

I was ecstatic. I immediately got to work redesigning the engraved invitations so they would include his and Nancy's names as co-hosts. I got on the phone, and the rest was a breeze. With Reagan coming, everyone wanted a ticket.

The only thing to worry about then was the exhibit itself. I was terribly afraid that many of the guests would be schnorrers, just there for the free food and drink. I was concerned the night could be a bust, and a real embarrassment for Lydia Heston, if nobody bought any of her work.

So I raided Peter Paul's checkbook and handed out money to some friends, instructing them to buy Lydia's photos. Probably not necessary, but she did sell out.

Nancy and Ronald Reagan's appearance at the cocktail party was the highlight, of course. I'll never forget their arrival at Tatou. The president was preceded by his Secret Service entourage, stern, strong individuals in suits that stationed themselves around the room, their tiny microphones plugged into their ears. Just like the movies. The former president and first lady were elegant and gracious and put up with my endless introductions to people they didn't know, having their picture taken with stranger after stranger. Everyone wanted that for a souvenir.

The night was a blast, but a financial bath for me. Mark Fleischman and I had underwritten the cost of the cocktail reception and subsequent dinner. I felt like it was worth spending money in order to expand my list of connections. Whatever it took. This attitude would get me into trouble later on. Boy, would it.

CONSIDERING MY SUCCESS with the Adrienne Maloof wedding, I definitely wanted to maintain my relationship with the family.

I hadn't made a great deal of money off of my efforts on Adrienne's behalf—in truth, it wasn't that much to begin with, and then I had to split it with Peter Paul—but that didn't bother me. I felt the best of times were yet to come. Since the Maloofs were so pleased with what I'd already done with them, I persuaded them to participate in another event I was putting together.

Ivana Trump was hosting a party in October at her sixty-sixth-floor penthouse apartment atop the Trump Tower in New York City. It was in celebration of the publication of her book, *Free To Love.* Peter had parlayed that into a joint affair with Fabio, who had a new romance novel coming out. It was an informal charity fundraiser as well, so there would be lots of good, free publicity.

Another resounding success. The Maloofs wound up donating fifteen thousand dollars to the Muscular Dystrophy Association. Shamefully, I diverted that money into Peter Paul's account, in order to cover expenses we had run up on some other event. It was wrong, and I knew it. But I was desperate. It was the first time I did such a thing, and, unfortunately, it would not be the last.

five

HOOKING UP

If there's a star in the heavens, Aaron Tonken
will have the contact.

—RONALD K. DOLLINGER,
Executive Director,
Friends of Sheba Medical Center,
Letter, June 15, 1994

Late in 1992, while hanging around the Four Seasons pool,
Stuart Goldberg told me about a new couple in town. They
were from Chicago and were living at the hotel until they
found a permanent place in the area. Their names: Joseph and
Kay Kimberly Siegel.

Joe was a commodities trader and former president of
Siegel Trading, one of the largest firms on the Chicago
Mercantile Exchange. He'd been busted for conspiracy, tax
fraud, and rigged trading, for stuff he'd done back in the mid-
seventies. He was fined and put on probation.

Kay, much younger, was Australian, the granddaughter of a
Welsh coalminer. She was very attractive, and would have been
even without the numerous facelifts, courtesy of the famous
plastic surgeon, Dr. Steven Hoeflin of UCLA. Kay was very
big on anti-aging strategies. A few years later, she would found
the Siegel Life Project at the UCLA Center on Aging.

What a pair they were, with their garish jewelry that screamed *nouveau riche*. Diamonds. Gold. All the flashy stuff. A gold chain around Joe's neck. A painfully obvious toupee perched atop his head. They would often show up dressed in matching Versace outfits, and Kay, instead of starting with "Hello," would say, "Versace, head to toe Versace!" and pose like a fashion dummy.

When Joe and Kay met, they were both married. Kay left her husband, who subsequently jumped out a window to his death. Later, according to Hollywood gossip, Kay and Joe's wife had a knock-down, drag-out fight on the floor of the Exchange. Kay won, and Joe divorced his wife. The two married in a full, traditional Jewish ceremony, after Kay convinced Joe's father she was actually Jewish, which she wasn't.

When I met the Siegels, though, I knew none of this. To me, they were simply another charming, wealthy couple who wanted to work their way into the glamorous Hollywood social scene.

So I befriended them, and the three of us started hanging out.

They would invite me to dinner, sometimes three nights a week, and only to the finest five-star restaurants: the original Chasen's in Beverly Hills, Jimmy's Restaurant in Century City, and the Bistro Gardens. As strange as it may seem, the Siegels would swing by the Chabad House, take me out to eat at some pricey nightspot bristling with celebrities, then drop me back at the homeless shelter.

Of course, I knew why. Kay wanted to meet stars, and I had the connections.

They lived in Century Woods, a very glitzy neighborhood, with Wallis Annenberg, the daughter of Walter Annenberg—

former ambassador and billionaire who founded *TV Guide* and *Seventeen* and owned newspapers and radio and television stations—on one side and Patricia McQueeny, Harrison Ford's manager, on the other.

The house itself was a fabulous, marble-floored, two-story palace that Kay loved to show off. It was decorated almost entirely in silver with huge silver S's holding the curtains back, and even silver toilet seats. Whenever guests were over, Kay would absolutely have to give them the tour which consisted of her bedroom, cast in a ghastly peach color (*Poor Joe*, I would always think whenever I saw it); her extravagant jewelry collection, displayed as if in a museum; and, laid out on the bed and draped over every piece of furniture, her cherished fur coats. Now, as you probably know, Los Angeles is semi-tropical, and there's not much call for fur coats at any time of the year, but Kay had a slew of them from Chicago, and Joe had a matching full-length mink, as well.

One day, Kay hosted lunch at her home. She invited Patricia McQueeny. I brought the actress Rita Moreno and her husband. There were a few other friends and neighbors there, as well. At one point, Patricia made the mistake of complimenting Kay on her china. That was all it took. Suddenly, Kay, who was sitting at the head of the table, popped right up, brushed the food off her plate, and turned it over, saying, "Versace." She then turned over all the silverware and did the same thing, naming the brand and how much she paid. I could have died. To Kay, everything was about the price tag.

Still, I tried to stay in their good graces, believing their wealth and power couldn't hurt my lowly situation. In fact, I thought it could help quite a bit. I introduced them around as best as I could and, in the summer of 1993, helped the Siegels throw a big garden party at their home by bringing out my usual galaxy of stars.

I also told them I was looking to make some new contacts among charitable wealthy people, since I was thinking about getting into the business of producing charity fundraisers.

"Well, I have someone for you," Joe said. "You should meet the Gershmans."

Oh, how little did I know then where that one simple sentence was going to lead me. And what a profound effect following that advice would have on my life for most of the next decade.

I'd never heard of them, but naturally I asked Joe to tell me more, even though I could see Kay scowling in the background.

"Cynthia and Harold Gershman," he said. "They're very wealthy."

"What does he do?" I asked.

"He's in the lease-back business."

I had no clue what that was.

"He owns land and buildings all over the country," Joe said. "Then he leases them back to major department stores, things like that."

"How wealthy would you say he is?"

"I don't know," Joe said. "If I had to guess, I'd say a hundred and fifty million. Or more. And they have a charitable foundation. They give away a lot of money."

My interest was piqued. "How can I meet them?"

At that point, Kay exploded. "That Cynthia," she said, "I can't stand her! She's an awful person!" And on and on like that, a real tirade.

I could see this was a bit of a delicate situation. I didn't want to alienate the Siegels; they'd been friends who had shown a lot of kindness toward me. But it sounded like the Gershmans would be good contacts to have. A charitable foundation would be a great thing for me to be allied with. It would turn out to be the most fateful connection of my Hollywood career.

I MET THE GERSHMANS through Carol Connors, the Oscar-nominated composer and world-class schnorrer who co-wrote the lyrics to the "Theme from Rocky." I knew her mostly from the restaurant, Tatou, where she was a hanger-on, a frumpy middle-aged woman trying to hold on to her looks—with facelifts, nose jobs, red hair dye, too much makeup, and overly loud clothes—and, like Rocky in the first film, fighting a losing battle. The meet was scheduled for the night of Lydia Heston's exhibition party.

Problem was, the Siegels were also coming, and although Kay and Cynthia were former friends—Kay had romanced Cynthia like crazy when she first came on the scene, giving her a Judith Lieber handbag and trying to work her way into the Gershmans' circle—those bridges had been burned, and Kay now hated Cynthia's guts. She couldn't find enough bad things to say about her. A tried and true Hollywood relation-ship, for sure. It was funny in a way, because they were both social-climbers with tons of money and little taste. Starf—ers, as the type is known around town.

I tried my best to keep things quiet, seating the two couples on opposite sides of the room, facing away from one another, and seating the Siegels with stars such as Shirley Jones from *The Partridge Family*. But that evening marked the end of my relationship with Joe and Kay Kimberly Siegel. She couldn't tolerate my budding relationship with the Gershmans.

And that should have been that, with no real harm done. However, in Hollywood, nothing outside of the movies has a simple ending. Feuds can go on for years, turning people inside out with bad feelings. What happened in my case was that, after the party for Lydia Heston, Kay Siegel was bent on revenge.

She did some research into Peter Paul's past, and when she found out about his previous felony convictions, she wrote up the story, printed it out, attached an old newspaper clipping about him, and faxed it to people on the VIP contact list I'd generously given to her at her summer party.

She also began spreading rumors about me. She cold called Barbara Davis, the well-known Hollywood socialite, whom I knew only slightly and whom she had never met, and said that I was going around claiming to be on the board of directors of her charity—something I never did. She also told people that I had a criminal past, if that's what you call a minor arrest as a teen.

She didn't completely succeed in ruining my credibility, of course, but her efforts did have something of the desired effect. One day, Barbara Davis called me out of the blue, at my office in the Bank of America building. I was pleased to take the call, thinking she wanted to thank me for the hundreds of thousands of dollars in cash and in-kind contributions thus far that I'd raised for both her diabetes charity and her daughter Nancy's charity.

Fat chance.

Instead, she turned loose on me, cussing me out good, ticking off details from Kay's smear job. I tried to set the record straight, with no success. That was the way in the community: rumors were easy to start, hard to stop. Damage was often done before you even knew what hit.

Peter Paul wasn't surprised a bit. In fact, he'd tried to warn me. When I had introduced him to the Siegels, he saw right through them and tried to explain to me how there were two levels to Hollywood society: the lowbrow types, who have somehow managed to acquire a lot of money but not much class to go with it, and the upper-crust people, who tend to be richer, have more breeding, and are more exclusive about whom they associate with. He told me to watch out for those who acquired money without the necessary class. I didn't listen and got burned.

Finding out about Peter's past criminal record, in addition to the further stresses of Kay's betrayal, was a cold, hard lesson in the tactics of the wealthy, and my relationship with Peter was never the same. We would gradually part ways.

Meanwhile, I was getting hardened and mistrustful—in other words, becoming a regular Hollywood mover. I was learning that you had to be careful on whom you turned your back in this town. You never knew when you would find a knife planted deep in the middle of it.

I HAD BEEN STRUGGLING to ingratiate myself to the rich and powerful, and the Gershmans, it seemed, were the mother lode.

Hal Gershman looked exactly like Colonel Sanders, right down to the white suit. The big difference though: the Colonel's hair was real. Hal wore a blatantly cheap toupée. You could see the tape showing. Seriously. What is it with these guys? To top it off, he was the only bald man I ever knew who, with a rug on his head, still had dandruff. And though he might have been worth a hundred fifty mil (by Joe Siegel's estimation), he didn't spend any of his fortune on clothes. His entire wardrobe was seventies vintage, cheesy polyester, covered in little rips and stains.

A far cry from the lovely and graceful, though vexatious, Kay, Cynthia was often described as "gnome-like," which is, I suppose, a euphemistic way of saying "short and fat." Like a troglodyte emerging from a cave, Cynthia would merely greet you with a grunt, not a hello. In the art of conversation, she was a minimalist. Her clothes were tacky and shapeless at best, no matter how expensive they might be. She sported fake eyelashes that went in every direction but the right one. And her head was crowned with a cheap, blonde hairpiece that never seemed to be adjusted correctly and looked like the Leaning Tower of Pisa.

The first time I visited their Beverly Hills home, I thought, *Geez, it's worse than their clothes.* Right out of the French bordello school of home decor. There was a sunken living room all done in white vinyl, a hideous maroon sofa right in the middle of it, chintzy ornaments scattered around, and a cheap piano no one could play. An African room sported skulls, bones, spears. Another room filled with jade and ivory.

All Cynthia ever wanted in life was to be a movie star. I would eventually pay producers and movie companies to give her roles, paying as much as a hundred thousand dollars for as little as two speaking lines. She'd mumble through her lines, which would later end up on the cutting room floor. She never made it to the big screen—not once.

Instead of fame, though, she got money. She'd married into a ton of it. Cynthia had met Harold while sitting on a stool in some Hollywood bar. His wife, Julia, had terminal cancer at the time. Looked like a golden opportunity. Cynthia would come by and hang out at the pool with Hal, while Julia was dying inside the house. As soon as Julia passed away, Cynthia moved in, and they later married.

Hal Gershman was an exceedingly nasty man, with a snide, dirty little laugh and enormous ego. He was abusive to his wife—often calling her a "f—ing c—" in front of other people—and estranged from his children. He cheated on Cynthia over and over and particularly liked young Asian-American girls. Once, when he broke up with one of his little tarts, he let the car he'd given her sit out in front of his house—a constant reminder to his wife—until he got a new lover. One night a week was designated as "date night," during which Hal did whatever he wanted and encouraged Cynthia to do the same.

"If you don't like it," Hal would tell Cynthia, "move out." She hadn't had sex with him for several years now and used to say openly that was the one area in which "he isn't selfish. He loves to f—. Just not me any more."

But as much as he loved young women, Hal's first and most enduring love was money. That was what he really cared about. And he was, despite his wealth, the cheapest codger you'd ever meet. When he needed his Rolls Royce repainted, he took it to Earl Scheib.

As bad as he was, though, the man did in fact control a charitable foundation—probably for the tax breaks—and I knew this could mean big bucks for my own events and maybe a modest living for me. So I stuck it out, in spite of the constant insults and abuse (hey, at least I wasn't the only one), and, believe me, earned every penny I got from him.

Hal and Cynthia—then Cynthia alone after Hal died—were the people I dealt with most closely during my charity fundraising career in Hollywood. They (or she) helped underwrite many of the most glittering events I put on, including the Hollywood Gala Salute to President William Jefferson Clinton in 2000.

Virtually as soon as I met them, late in 1993, I enlisted their support, convincing them to serve as co-hosts at the Ivana Trump/Fabio book party and to contribute fifteen thousand dollars from their foundation to muscular dystrophy.

Diet Queen Nikki Haskell later described to me Ivana Trump's reaction to my newfound friends, quoting her and imitating her accent: "Vat der vuck are these horrid people, the Gershmans, co-hosting wit me? They are so common, and him looking like Kernel Sanderss!"

FUNNY STORY: STEPHANIE POWERS, former co-star of the hit TV show, *Hart to Hart,* was looking for new backers for her charity, William Holden Wildlife Foundation (WHWF), which she had founded in order to continue the work begun by the actor William Holden in Kenya. Holden had fallen in love with African animals, and he set up the Mount Kenya

Game Ranch, which was dedicated to the cause of wildlife conservation.

She invited me to her house on Hutton Drive in Beverly Hills to talk about it.

I, in turn, told her that I represented Cynthia and Hal Gershman. They loved animals, I told her (true enough, I guess—they did love their pet poodle, T.J.), and would like to become involved with her foundation. I played them up as wonderful, philanthropic people. The reality, of course, was that they didn't care about her charity in particular; they only wanted more new stars to invite to their get-togethers that I was trying so desperately to arrange.

I put Stephanie on the line with Cynthia. They talked. Cynthia agreed to send over some money for the WHWF, but, as she always did when I brought her new people, she practically forced Powers to agree to attend one of her parties in return.

Reluctantly, Stephanie agreed to attend an upcoming Gershman party. They were potential large benefactors. What choice did she have?

I was pleased, since I'd delivered yet another star, based entirely on a cold call. In my enthusiasm, however, I failed to realize something. The Gershmans threw two parties a year at their home, and two more at Jimmy's, or some other trendy restaurant. By chance, the next one, the one I had steered Stephanie Powers to, was at their place. Which meant there was a problem—a pretty big one—that I should have anticipated.

When Stephanie arrived and was shown into the Gershman home, she was immediately confronted by their vast, grotesque array of stuffed animals. All African! I mean, they had heads on the walls, zebra skins on the floor, a whole room dedicated to Africa, in which they displayed their huge (probably at least partly illegal) ivory collection.

Poor Stephanie nearly puked. Hal just laughed. Cynthia had no idea what the problem was.

Needless to say, the three did not become fast friends. Stephanie wouldn't dare step foot in their house again. The Gershmans had that effect on people.

I MET THE ELLISES through an attractive young businesswoman named Mitzi Price. She would later become my landlady. I had met Mitzi at Tatou and liked her immediately. She was a ticket broker, among other things, and wanted a table for ten for a fundraiser benefiting Elizabeth Taylor's charity, American Foundation for AIDS Research (AMFAR), for which I was selling passes. This event was the hottest ticket in town—held at the Playboy Mansion, with *Cirque du Soleil* slated to perform, and an exclusive pre-event cocktail party at the Bel Air Hotel where you could actually meet Elizabeth, as well as Charles Bronson and many other celebrities. Mitzi just had to get some tickets, so I obliged.

About a month later, Mitzi called to thank me and told me the tickets had been for a nice couple who had just moved to L.A. from Chicago. Their names were William H. and Diana Roque Ellis. They were well-to-do—Bill was the owner of the Farley Candy Company, the country's largest private label candy manufacturer and second largest producer of bag candy—and they were very interested in gaining entry to the town's upper crust. They were also generous contributors to charities.

I had figured out by then I could make a nice living bringing wealthy business people and entertainment industry celebrities together. Though I had no credibility, and no résumé to speak of, I could still make things happen simply by talking a good game. In the smoke-and-mirrors world of Hollywood, that was all that really counted anyway.

One of the surest ways of hooking up stars with wealthy businesspeople was to get the latter to donate large sums of money to a celeb's favorite charity. That was the shortcut to the top. If you helped big stars with their pet organizations and brought them big money, most of the time you could make direct contact, bypassing agents, managers, publicists, and all the other layers of protection that stars surround themselves with—the people you never wanted to deal with anyway, since they would never help out unless there was something in it for them.

But fundraising was a cutthroat game. In any given week, you could usually find several big black-tie bashes going on around town. Competition for the stars' time and the donors' money was fierce. I got very good at it, very fast, for two reasons: First, I had the gift of schmooze—I could talk a Bedouin into buying a sandbox. And second, I realized early on that stars are for sale. Or, as I used to put it, *you could buy them with a watch.* And I would.

Needless to say, the candy couple was right up my alley— new to town, eager to crack elite social circles, big on giving to charities. That they were worth three hundred million or so was all I really needed to know. Mitzi was correct. There was every reason to believe that we would have a mutually profitable relationship.

Accompanied by Peter Paul, I met Diana Ellis at the Sports Club L.A. on Sepulveda Boulevard in Westwood. She was a sweet woman, svelte, with long brown hair, swarthy skin, and the exotic beauty suggested by her ancestry, which was half Armenian, half Scotch/Irish. I liked her from the start.

She had hired publicists to work for her, and other Hollywood operator types. She'd even brought in a psychic. They all failed. None of them was getting her the kinds of intros she wanted.

Could I do it? "Yes," I said. "I can do it, and I'll do it well."

I told her that, for openers, I could hook her up with the Davis family, one of the premier families in town and one of the world's richest, as well as Ronald Reagan. These were big names to drop and, since nobody in town did this kind of thing for free, I asked her for ten thousand a month to start and held my breath.

Diana didn't bat an eye. She probably had to keep herself from drooling over the names I mentioned so casually. She was so hot to start climbing the social ladder she wrote me a check for the whole ten grand on the spot and invited me to her home to meet her husband . . . although she asked me not to mention our little deal.

I shared half the money with Peter. Despite the fact that I'd done all the work, he still had the Rolodex.

The next day, I drove out to the Ellises' place. They lived in Bel Air, not far from Zsa Zsa's, on St. Cloud Road. The house, a completely remodeled older home worth eight million, was across from Johnny Carson's ex-wife Joanna and was formerly owned by Tony Curtis and Sonny and Cher, among others, including pop star Prince. It was spectacular. I entered through big wrought-iron gates set in a wall surrounded by shrubs and flowers. The grounds were beautifully landscaped with gardens and koi ponds. I knew it must cost a fortune to maintain a place like that, and I saw a number of employees working on the upkeep.

I parked in a courtyard. A houseman answered the bell and showed me in. Inside was just as impressive. The house was probably twenty-five thousand square feet, with guest wings, winding staircases, an enormous kitchen, a full commercial-sized gym, and so on, all furnished and decorated by Diana, who had impeccable taste, a nice change of pace from my usual clientele. Many of her paintings—she was a portrait and figurative artist—hung on the walls. There was plenty of indoor staff in evidence, as well.

The houseman left me in the foyer as Bill Ellis came in. A self-made multimillionaire originally from Appalachia, he was about six feet tall, with gray hair and glasses, old enough to be Diana's grandfather.

I gave the Ellises what was quickly becoming the Aaron Tonken tour of Hollywood. With the help of John Hall, I got them a meeting with Ronald Reagan, who was gracious, as always, offering them jellybeans from the jar on his desk, chatting with them, allowing them to take pictures, granting them a subsequent tour of his Bel Air home, at my request, and giving them a set of presidential cufflinks with his signature on the back. This was a gift that the former president reserved for special friends. He did it because I asked.

I also arranged a meeting between them and the Davises.

Marvin Davis had made an enormous fortune in the oil business and later got involved in such ventures as buying and selling Twentieth Century Fox and the Beverly Hills Hotel. He is one of the real movers and shakers in Hollywood, always listed in the Forbes list of wealthiest people in the world, with a net worth currently set at four billion dollars or more.

Daughter Nancy, I knew, was active in the fight against multiple sclerosis, even suffering from the disease herself. I had helped her enormously with her annual event, the Race To Erase MS, brought celebrities to her fundraisers, got people to donate valuable items to her charity auction, and raised money—lots of it—for her, never asking for anything in return except the satisfaction of helping fight this disease.

So I set up a lunch with the Davises and Ellises, which led to Diana Ellis handing over fifty-thousand dollars for the Race To Erase and the same sum to Barbara Davis, her mother, for her Carousel of Hope Ball, which benefited the Children's Diabetes Foundation. That was the beginning of the Ellis/Davis association. Bill and Diana would continue to contribute the same amount each year, right up until their divorce. In addition, Bill pledged a ton of "in-kind" contributions: Farley candy for gift bags, auction items, etc.

It was an important moment for me. Lots of charities have to scrape and beg for that kind of money, or pray that they raise it during their one yearly fundraiser. I'd delivered a hundred grand in one afternoon, over lunch, just like that, and arranged a meet between two powerhouse couples. I felt like a peddler of influence.

I was, to say the least, very pleased with myself. I was getting ahead while becoming connected in Hollywood society, which, make no mistake, was my primary goal. Yet, at the same time, I was helping raise money for people who really needed it. Doing well for myself by doing good for others. That was the way I looked at it, in the beginning.

Over the course of the next several months, I continued to provide Diana Ellis with entrées into the social circles she so desired to move in, and she continued to pay me under the table. It was a nice arrangement, and I made some decent money. We held parties at her house, to which I invited celebrities I knew: Stephanie Powers, Fabio, Kay and Morey Amsterdam (whom Bill loved), Martin Landau, and Jean and Casey Kasem. I also introduced them to Dr. Steven Hoeflin, the renowned plastic surgeon I met through Kay Siegel, a local hero in the collagen-infused town of L.A.

I also, much to my own surprise, was able to hook the Ellises up with Frank Sinatra. I cold called Barbara, Frank's fourth wife, who sponsored the nonprofit Barbara Sinatra Children's Center, and told her I had some potential donors for her. So she invited my clients to her annual charity event in Palm Springs. Bill gave her a check for ten thousand dollars, plus some extra for Diet Queen Nikki Haskell, who was riding along on the Ellises' dime. Schnorrer that she is, Nikki had bugged and bugged me about it, until I agreed to push Diana to include her.

Even more exciting than the event, though, Barbara invited the Ellises back to her home after the gala, and they got to have their pictures taken with her and Frank. It was a once-in-a-lifetime experience, a rare opportunity to spend a little time with one of the century's biggest singing stars. It turned out to be one of Frank's last public appearances.

"BASICALLY," I TOLD DIANA, "what I want to do is bring a special, special event to your home. Not just featuring local personalities, but world-renowned people too. It would be unique and really elevate your standing in the community."

I was pitching her on a very ambitious project that came to me in a moment of blazing inspiration: we should stage a benefit for Israel's Sheba Medical Center, a huge complex that was the Middle East's largest hospital at the time, featuring many patient care options that were available nowhere else in the region. The center was heavily supported by American citizens through the Friends of Sheba charity, and I'd made the acquaintance of Ron Dollinger, the foundation's executive director. Had even gotten his go-ahead on the project.

The event, I told her, would attract not only top-drawer Hollywood stars but international political figures as well. Always a big deal. It'd be incredible, a real feather in her cap, I said.

She was piqued, I could tell.

"I've done a lot for you and your husband," I went on, "but this will be by far the biggest thing yet. And it's going to take some money to pull it off. I need to be compensated, more than usual."

I took a deep breath and asked for eighty-five thousand dollars. I was desperate for the cash. I'd moved into an apartment in West Hollywood and needed to pay rent and buy some new furniture. In addition, with the help of Peter Paul, I was leasing a blue BMW convertible. If I was going to be a mover and shaker in Hollywood, I had to move and shake in style.

With Diana's support, we approached Bill.

I was nervous. First, I there was the amount I was asking

for—eighty-five thousand dollars just for my fee; there would be additional event expenses—to produce something that was, after all, a charity event. I knew it was justified. I was working very hard and getting extraordinary results now, and deserved to be paid like a professional. Paying me would be worth it, considering how much my efforts would bring in for the Center—at the required pledge of twenty-five thousand dollars per couple, it was going to be a great deal—and how much resulting prestige would then come Bill and Diana's way. But that didn't allay another concern of mine. I doubted Bill would fully understand what I was talking about, raising money that would be sent to Israel for a Jewish hospital. Neither he nor Diana was Jewish. In fact, I wouldn't have been surprised if he was looking for the horns on my head. What I was asking might not have been unique, but it sure was unusual.

My fears were for nothing; in the end Bill trusted me. I gave him the same spiel I gave Diana, told him this event would be the crown jewel, solidifying their social status, and he sat down and wrote me a whopping-big check.

And with that, my career in the field of charity fundraisers began in earnest.

The Friends of Sheba benefit was a huge success. Dennis Ross, the U.S. ambassador to Israel, attended, as did the two major guests of honor: Mrs. Jehan Sadat, widow of the slain Egyptian president and Nobel Peace Prize winner, and Mrs. Leah Rabin, wife of the Israeli prime minister Yitzhak Rabin, who would himself be assassinated a year and a half later. They were there to be the recipients of the humanitarian awards. Kirk Douglas was on hand to present the awards. Natalie Cole sang.

I even arranged for foundation director Ron Dollinger to introduce Bill Ellis to Haim Saban, one of *Forbes's* four hundred wealthiest men in America, a giant in the entertainment industry, and a major donor to the Democratic Party (he got a front row seat at the Clinton Salute). The two would eventually work out a business partnership, between Farley Candy and Saban Entertainment, which owned the rights to the kids' TV show *Mighty Morphin Power Rangers*, among other things.

What a night. It was the first time I had ever organized an event of such extravagance.

It was also a learning experience for me, a very disillusioning learning experience. While setting up the entertainment for the show, I discovered Natalie Cole would only perform at the benefit for a price. Twenty-five thousand dollars to be exact, in addition to whatever special perks are written into her standard contract. Charity or not, Natalie did not come cheap.

But I would also discover that this was the rule, not the exception, as far as celebrities were concerned. With few deviations, no one would sing, dance, play music, or tell jokes without pay. And we're talking substantial sums of money here, tens of thousands of dollars or more, that are going to artists' fees, off the top. These come directly out of an event's proceeds, and thus represent cash that could go to the charity, but doesn't.

That's not the worst of it. Even if they weren't performing, stars sometimes demand yet more thousands of dollars worth of expensive gifts, simply in order to entice them to grace a fundraiser with their presence. Again, this represents money the charity doesn't get. You wouldn't believe how much is siphoned off. I call it *taking from the needy to feed the greedy.* All perfectly legal, of course—assuming these celebrities report such gifts on their tax returns.

ONE OTHER INTERESTING FOOTNOTE to the Friends of Sheba affair:

Jack Gilardi was a self-styled Hollywood "superagent" who worked out of International Creative Management (ICM). He was sort of ridiculous. A short, stocky Italian guy in his fifties, who liked to make out how tough and important he was. He was Charlton Heston's longtime agent and had previously handled Nancy Sinatra and Annette Funicello, to whom he was married for fifteen years. When I met him, he was far past his prime, but he did score me two last-minute additions to the guest list: O.J. Simpson and his girlfriend.

The date of the Sheba event: June 11, 1994.

The following day, Nicole Brown Simpson and Ronald Goldman were murdered.

six

STONE COLD

Paul said how pleased he was that Carolco had finally decided to cast Sharon Stone as Catherine Tramell [female lead in Basic Instinct*].*

"She is Catherine Tramell," Paul said.

Since Catherine Tramell was an ice-pick wielding, manipulative, omnisexual, sociopathic killer, I asked Paul what exactly he meant by that.

"Sharon is evil," he said.

"You mean as Catherine Tramell."

"No, as Sharon."

—JOE ESZTERHAS,
Hollywood Animal

Do you think I'm as pretty as my sister?" Kelly asked me the first day I met her. She was a sweet, cute girl with shoulder-length, dirty blonde hair. Kind of average. Definitely not the gorgeous sort Stuart usually went out with. Still, she was nice, and we hit it off immediately.

But I was stunned by her question. "Do you think I'm as pretty as my sister?" I couldn't believe she had put me on the spot like that. What it said to me, what I knew from that moment onward, was that she lived and suffered in the shadow of her larger-than-life sister.

"Sure," I stammered. "Of course you are." I paused, then added, "And you're sweet inside." Best I could do.

But it was a downright lie.

You see, I very much wanted to get involved with Planet Hope, Kelly's very own charity, whose focus was homeless kids. My friend Stuart Goldberg, who was dating Kelly at the time, knew I would be interested—since it looked as though I might have a future as an event organizer—and set up the lunch. But I also lied because it was her sister I wanted to meet. Her sister was the charity's co-founder. Her sister was one of Hollywood's most glamorous stars. Her sister was Sharon Stone.

And she had the nerve to ask me, "Do you think I'm as pretty as my sister?"

RAISED IN PENNSYLVANIA in a blue-collar family, Sharon was the one who had made it out to L.A. first, parlaying her great looks and brains (she reportedly has an IQ of 154) into two highly successful careers, initially as a model, then as a movie star. Kelly followed along the road to Hollywood, as did older brother Michael. I think Kelly had delusions of herself as a star, like her sister (whom she sometimes called "Queenie"), but her looks, which she had obviously inherited from her father, just weren't going to cut it.

So in 1991 Kelly founded Planet Hope and ever since has worked full-time on its development. By the time I met her, she was still struggling to get it off the ground. I knew I could help and was eager to cement the relationship with the Stone family, so I convinced the Gershmans to throw a party at their place.

"They want to do it as a celebrity brunch at their house," I told Kelly, much to her surprise and excitement. "I'll bring a bunch of stars; they'll kick in the money for expenses, plus contribute to Planet Hope. The only stipulation they made is that Sharon would have to be involved."

I knew the Gershmans would never go out of their way for Kelly Stone, who was less than nobody in their eyes. But Sharon was a different matter. To have the sexy superstar come to their house would be a real social coup. And the fact of the matter was, I hadn't discouraged them from making that a condition. I wanted Sharon there too. I believed that making her acquaintance would be a real shot in the arm for my career. Turned out to be more like a shot in the head.

Kelly assured me if we could put the Planet Hope fundraiser together, Sharon would show. With the Gershmans' backyard as our site and Sharon Stone listed on the invitation as co-host, I would invite a bunch of stars to come, even put some of their names on the invitation list. All for free, of course.

Since this was in the early phase of my career, I still wasn't making any money from my promotional efforts. I was doing it, hopefully, to enhance my presence in the Hollywood community and strengthen my connections. That was enough. I believed that the payoff would come later, when I was well established. But I had no master plan for that. I was making it up as I went along.

So Kelly and I were now a team. She even offered for me to move into her offices on the Paramount lot. Jackpot. As a part of Sharon's package deal with Paramount, they had provided her with a small, two-office bungalow on the studio lot, for her and her assistant. Since Sharon never used the offices, she gave them to her sister for the headquarters of Planet Hope.

It was perfect timing. By the beginning of 1994, I had already fallen out with some key people in my life, such as Peter Paul, the Maloofs, and the Siegels. That was just the way of Hollywood. Relationships were ever shifting and changing, as people competed for ever-higher positions in society. You always had to be careful what you told your best friend today, because he or she might be your enemy tomorrow.

SO THERE I WAS DRIVING MY BMW through the Paramount gates right up to Sharon Stone's office. I thought I really had it made, imagining myself as a big-shot producer arriving for the morning shoot. It was all I could think about, and, in Hollywood, the *only* thing to think about.

There, you were either involved in the entertainment industry or you were a leper. Likewise, even though I'd been raised in a family where a firm education, blue-collar work, and the simple life were appreciated, where service to others was valued, and even though my dad was a hard-working, honored, much-loved physician, I was beginning to think the only thing that mattered in the world was "the biz." That was the spell Hollywood spun. Making something of yourself as a doctor, small businessman, farmer, police officer, whatever, it didn't mean a thing to those in the land of make-believe. Saving lives wasn't anything compared to producing a major motion picture.

That was the prevailing mindset. I slowly stopped

respecting people's achievements in any field other than entertainment. I was interested only in meeting, befriending, and
working with celebrities, producers, high-profile industry
executives, and the mega-rich. That was it.

Kelly and I worked well together—I gave Kelly all my
most powerful links, including my entire mailing list, which
featured addresses, home and office phone numbers, and fax
numbers of a large group of stars and wealthy potential
donors and represented a major upgrade for Planet Hope's
resources. But we decided to keep our first event simple.

We knew we wanted to honor Bill Mack, a famous sculptor
from Minnesota, and give him the opportunity to meet people
who might buy his work. Bill was a client and friend of Chris
Harris's, Kelly's publicist, and had done a famous bronze nude
that was modeled after Sharon Stone, although she tried to
deny this, for some strange reason. Bill donated a lot of his art
to charity, a generous man through and through.

But the chief attraction, of course, would be Sharon. Once
we had her, many more celebs would follow, and then we had
a good chance of attracting the wealthy (our target donors) to
mingle with the movie stars.

But would Queenie show? That was the sixty-four-thou-
sand dollar question. Kelly said, *Yes, of course.* She was a
cofounder of the charity, after all. I was more skeptical. Sharon
had a reputation around Hollywood. Voluminous articles had
been written on the topic. She was self-centered, would do
anything to get what she wanted, used people and discarded
them, and so on.

Two things I can say about Sharon Stone: (1) I never slept
with her, and (2) more important, for my and Kelly's purposes,

I never saw her lift a finger to help Planet Hope. It was a pain in both cheeks to get her to commit to making even the briefest of appearances, and then you still had to worry until the last minute about whether she was really going to show.

Furthermore, Kelly was terrified to ask her for favors. Her own sister. It took forever for Kelly to finally get up the courage to call Sharon and nail down a commitment. When she did, she had to beg. She even enlisted the support of her older brother, Michael, who had been hanging around, trying to break into the business.

They were often a pathetic pair, the outcast siblings of Sharon. It was humiliating to see Kelly pleading with her famous sister once she finally got through to her. Often, Kelly would even have to deal with Sharon's publicist first, trying to line up support before speaking directly to Sharon, and beg for a meager hour or two of Sharon's time. And then there was Michael. He was always hitting me up for money because he couldn't hack it in L.A., threatening to blow my relationship with Kelly if I didn't "loan" him what he needed to support his lazy existence. All I wanted was for Planet Hope to succeed, and I had to deal with this eye-crossing bunch.

Stardom, and the pursuit of it, changes people. You've heard it said, I'm sure, a million times, but it's absolutely true. It turns people into monsters and families into feuds. Even if you were blood-related, if you didn't bow down at the throne of celebrity and kiss tail, you could be cut off. And that's what worried me.

A no-show from the divine Ms. Stone would be a bust for Aaron Tonken and a dire situation for Planet Hope.

I TOOK KELLY ALONG with Chris Harris over to the Gershman estate so they could envision the setup. It looked nice enough from the outside. You passed through wrought iron gates up the short drive to a spacious, one-story, white brick Mediterranean-style house, with several brown-shingled mansard roofs spaced along the facade. In the open garage, you could see the matching convertible Corniche Rolls Royces Hal had bought, along with a Cadillac, a station wagon, and an ancient bright-yellow limo.

The problem was the inside. And the backyard. And the Gershmans themselves.

They'd told me a hundred times how they'd had to remodel the whole interior recently because of a fire that had broken out one night while they were at dinner with Danny Thomas and his wife. Probably should have left it as is. The place was a designer's nightmare, a tacky relic from another age. Years later, after Hal died, a movie company would ask if they could use the house as a location for a few scenes in the movie *The Rat Pack.* It would serve as the setting for Dean Martin's home in the sixties. The producers said they wouldn't have to change a thing. (And they did use it, but instead of paying Cynthia, they gave her a few lines in the movie, which naturally were cut from the final print.)

The kitchen was filthy, littered with food wrappers and packets of half-eaten cookies, dog food for their little red poodle T.J. spread everywhere, the refrigerator stuffed with smelly leftovers Cynthia had bagged home from restaurants. In the family room was a huge skylight, about five feet by five feet, made of colored plastic. The room looked like a set from *The Poseidon Adventure* where the ship had turned upside down. At any minute, I expected Shelly Winters, Gene Hackman, Red Buttons, and Ernest Borgnine to come crashing through.

Outside, things weren't much better. The garden furniture was all rusted and weeds were growing everywhere. We had to get creative.

First, we decided the party would be held out back, where the swimming pool was. There would be a long table set up by the garage, for check-in, then guests would be led around the side to the backyard, never gaining entry to the house. This was not uncommon when rich people hosted an event. Often they didn't want strangers traipsing through their home; they didn't want to worry about theft and breakage. And that's how we put it to the Gershmans, rather than that we were too embarrassed for anyone to peek inside.

There would still need to be a great deal of sprucing up. Weeds had to be cut. There were things that needed to be moved or hidden, like the rusty furniture and these tacky, white faux-Greek statues.

"I just want it to look like people with money live here," Chris told me while suggesting improvements, "and not that they do all their shopping at Wal-Mart."

Kelly's one major contribution to the organizing of the event, and it was a big one, was to persuade a number of fine restaurants to provide food for the occasion. This is no small task. It involves persistence and a lot of hard work—you have to convince restaurant owners that the publicity is going to make it worth their while—and Kelly brought it off quite well. Stations would then be set up below the pool on the tennis court, with all of the fabulous food laid out there.

So we had a place and an underwriter. I use "underwriter" loosely because nothing ever came for free with Hal. He might underwrite some expenses, at my direction, through the foundation, but he always wanted to get it back from me in equal amounts, in the form of "gifts" like luxury cruises and trips to Europe.

We also had the food and one star attraction. But that wasn't enough. We expected to fill a lot of tables with people who paid a great deal of money—not so much for the philanthropy but the chance to rub elbows with stars. We needed more elbows. That's where I came in.

Out came the trusty Rolodex, and my trusty dialing fingers—some say the fastest in the business—and I started calling celebrities. Some I knew, some I didn't.

"Hello," I would say, "Kelly and Sharon Stone would like to cordially invite you to join them for an afternoon brunch for the benefit of their charity, Planet Hope."

That was the initial spiel. Then, as I got commitments from celebs, I could drop their names too, would even put them on the formal invitations. First one I tried was Tom Arnold, cold called, and he accepted. I called Jackie Collins. She also accepted. And not only did she accept, she refused to be comped. She paid for her ticket herself, the only celebrity who did.

I guess my early scores went to my head, so I decided to try Tom Cruise. No luck there. Bruce Willis turned me down too. And there were some stars I wasn't allowed to call because Sharon disliked them for one reason or another.

But for the most part, I was remarkably successful. The final version of the invitation looked like this:

Planet Hope along with Stephen Baldwin, Jacqueline Bissett, Jackie Collins, Cathy Lee Crosby, Johnny Depp, Charlene Tilton, Melanie Griffith, Robert Guillaume, George Hamilton, Penny Marshall, and John Ritter cordially invite you to join us personally for AFTERNOON BRUNCH in honor of Internationally Renowned Sculptor Bill Mack hosted by Cynthia and Hal Gershman at their Trousdale Estate 412 Robert Lane, Beverly Hills, California 1:00 P.M. Sunday afternoon, June 26th, 1994. To celebrate the unveiling of Mr. Mack's rendering of his newest sculpture dedicated to the promise of *Planet Hope*.

CYNTHIA AND HAL GERSHMAN welcomed guests by singing, "Catch an Arriving Star." I was mortified, afraid our stars and donors would turn away right then and never look back. Fortunately for us all, they persevered.

And what a lineup it was. There was Faye Dunaway, Leonardo DiCaprio, Dean Cain, Anthony Michael Hall, some of the *Beverly Hills 90210* crowd, Diane Ladd, Ed Begley Jr., Lorna Luft, Jerry Vale, Terry Moore, and Sidney Poitier. My regulars were also there, of course: Red Buttons, Lorna and Milton Berle, Michelle Phillips. We even welcomed Steve Ford (the actor, and President Ford's son), John Hall (from President Reagan's office), Steve Wasserman, Gloria Allred, and Selma and Army Archerd (who wrote up the event for *Variety*). And, of course there were the schnorrers, Nikki Haskell and Carol Connors. Chris Harris told me Carol had such an inflated opinion of herself that she once demanded, and got, a refrigerator before she would grace a certain charity event with her presence.

But the best news was that our feature attraction, Sharon Stone, actually showed up, something of a surprise to me. Sharon had, as usual, been making all kinds of excuses, citing the stalking incidents and death threats she'd received after the release of *Basic Instinct.* It was no joke, apparently. Kelly had seen some bruises on her sister. But Sharon had bodyguards now, and I had brought in almost a hundred thousand bucks for the charity, with much of that money contributed specifically for the right to spend an hour or two with Hollywood's biggest sex goddess. So her arrival was a blessed relief to everyone. She came in a red sundress and was the center of attention, especially that of the Gershmans.

Cynthia was dying to have a picture taken with her, and so finally Hal marched up to Chris Harris and said in his low voice, "G—damn it, I want Sharon Stone over here *right now,* for a photo with us."

Chris crossed the lawn and relayed the message, "The lady of the house would like you to go over there . . ."

"No," Sharon said. "I'm staying here."

Cynthia took the initiative to approach Sharon and introduce herself. Sharon left. She and DiCaprio made their way to the pool, sat on the edge, took off their shoes, and dunked their feet in the cool water. Anyplace else, it might have been an entirely normal, natural thing to do on a sweltering summer day, such as it was. But not in Beverly Hills.

It wasn't a casual maneuver at all, but entirely calculated. The unveiling of the Bill Mack sculpture was about to take place, and Queenie's response was essentially, *Hmmm, how can I upstage that? Let's see what I can do to attract some press attention.* Sharon made sure she was noticed by splashing the water with her feet and displaying her cleavage to maximum effect.

Chris kept saying to her, "Okay, would you get out of the pool now?" He, at least, felt some responsibility to Bill Mack, as well as to the people who were there to meet her. She ignored him.

So when Michelle Phillips saw photographers rush over and snap pictures of the wading starlet, she took her shoes off and hopped in as well. Pure Hollywood. Everything was always about publicity, how to get it and keep getting it.

Finally, in utter frustration, Chris asked Judy Ellis of *Life* to pretend she wanted to interview Sharon for the magazine, fighting fire with fire. One sure way to get her out of the pool and stop her from further detracting from the ceremony: offer her more publicity. Pure genius.

Of course, when Sharon finally did recognize Bill Mack, the honored guest, by commenting on one of his statues, it was still all about the angle and only when the press was all ears. In his *Variety* column, Army Archerd mentioned the fundraiser was to honor "Bill Mack, who created a sculpture of a reclining, nude Sharon Stone," who had told Archerd she hadn't posed for it. "It was someone younger and prettier," she said.

Clever move on her part. First, Sharon upstages the guest of honor, a brilliant sculptor who's also a kind and decent man who had donated tens of thousands of dollars worth of his work to charity (whereas she, whose primary claim to fame is having flashed her crotch on the big screen for a fleeting instant in her one hit movie, is donating an hour of her time). Next, she gets the press to focus primarily on her at the event. And finally, she gets even more publicity by playing humble— *oh, that couldn't possibly be me, she's too pretty*—all the while craftily drawing attention to her own good looks.

Oh well, at least Cynthia eventually got the picture she wanted. It was of Sharon Stone in her red sundress with her feet in the Gershmans' pool. She treasured it. To the last days I spent with Cynthia, she kept that photo taped to the wall over her desk in the kitchen. It matched her taste perfectly.

MY RELATIONSHIP WITH KELLY and Stone Canyon entertainment was not long-lasting. I had come up with what I thought was a brilliant idea, using my connections in Arizona to create a big charity event in Scottsdale. Taking Planet Hope on the road.

A new alliance with Allison Goldwater, granddaughter of Barry Goldwater, the former senator and presidential candidate, proved promising, as she worked like a dog, raising money, selling tickets, lining up local sponsorships.

I rustled up the talent, nabbing old acquaintances Tanya Tucker and Rita Coolidge, both of whom agreed to perform for free, as well as Leslie Nielsen, Marlee Matlin, Peter Fonda, Reggie Jackson, Sugar Ray Leonard, Milton Berle, Red Buttons, Gary Busey, and several other stars who agreed to attend just for expenses. Naturally, I used the same line I'd used for the Gershmans' event: "Sharon and Kelly Stone would like for you to attend a benefit with them," blah, blah, blah, and everything was going along fine, except that Sharon was the same old on-again, off-again harpy, and in the end failed to show.

Despite the fact we were getting great coverage from the tabloids and entertainment television, Sharon's absence confused donors and upset the other stars. Kelly was really hurt and surprised. I was just pissed. That's when I made my fatal mistake and took out my frustrations on Kelly's mom, telling her face-to-face what a horrible child she had in Sharon.

Kelly found out about the incident, and that was that.

Personally, I felt like I got out none too soon. Kelly continued to organize fundraisers, now with a nice list of honorary board members to put on her stationery, thanks to me, and on December 4, 1995, she produced the inaugural Planet Hope Ball. It was black-tie, with President Bill Clinton acting as honorary chairman, and was held in the Crystal Ballroom of the Beverly Hills Hotel. Ultra-classy, or at least it was supposed to be. Except for the fact that Sharon Stone was coming.

Chris Harris would later tell me what happened that evening.

The occasion was designed to honor Lee Iacocca, whose daughter was good friends with Kelly, and who had supported the charity both with cash and with access to his personal mailing list. Bill Mack had been working for six months with Sharon, creating a *bas relief* sculpture of her. It was worth about forty thousand. In recognition of Lee's efforts on behalf of the charity, Bill was going to present the donated sculpture to him at the ball.

Bill had also made two crystal plates that would be

awarded that evening, one to Iacocca and the other to Sharon Stone for the help she'd given Planet Hope. What a joke.

When Sharon arrived at the cocktail hour, she immediately went over to Chris and said, "So what's happening? What are we doing?"

Chris responded, "You're going up on stage to receive a couple of awards, one from Bill Mack and one from this little nine-year-old homeless girl named Lupi Tapia that we found—"

Sharon immediately interrupted, "I am not going to do that!"

Jan Moran was there too. She was the international fragrance expert and author of the book *Fabulous Fragrances*. Her company had co-sponsored the ball and in return was supposed to get a plug. Sharon was to accept free gifts from them on the stage.

"I'm not going up on stage," Sharon said flatly, when reminded of her role.

Chris was incensed and shouted at her, "You know what you are, Sharon? You are a bitch from hell! You have a whip in one hand, a surprise in the other, and living with you would be like be living with Norma Desmond."

Sharon, true to form, attacked Chris with her cell phone, smashing him on the wrist. She called security and told them he was out of control and should be locked out of the room. Chris announced to the press that Sharon was refusing to participate in the event. The whole thing was a fiasco.

Later that evening, when Chris Harris was due to receive the Angel award, for all the free promotional and public relations work he'd donated to Planet Hope, Sharon wouldn't let him go up on stage to accept it. Instead, she forced Kelly to put it in a dirty brown paper bag and carry it over to him.

"Take it back," Chris said upon delivery. "And shove it up Sharon's *ass!*"

seven

UNCLE MILTIE
GOES COUNTRY

Shortly after I met the Gershmans in September of '93, they in turn introduced me to Milton Berle and Lorna, his fourth (and final) wife. In no time at all I was thick as thieves with the Berles. In fact, by November, I was organizing a second wedding anniversary celebration for them at the Hotel Nikko, where I persuaded many of my celebs to hold their parties. (After Chabad, I struck a deal with the Nikko: I lived there rent free if I helped on the PR front by keeping celebs around—make it seem like a hip joint.)

It was a gala affair, with virtually every old comic and Jewish entertainer in town attending. Tova and Ernest Borgnine came, as well as Rosemarie and Robert Stack, Ann Jeffreys, Cyd Charisse, Renee Taylor and Joe Bologna, Connie Stevens, Norm Crosby, and Martin Landau. Tony Martin and Jerry Vale sang. Laughs were furnished by Milton's old pals, like Jack Carter, Jan Murray, Red Buttons,

Don Rickles, and Sid Caesar. Two hours of fabulous entertainment, which if you had to pay the performers' going rates would have cost hundreds of thousands. Luckily, they weren't charging their going rates; they did it for free because it was Milton.

The biggest joke that night, however, was the running commentary on the state of marriage in Hollywood.

At 2:00 A.M. I got a call from Peter Paul, who I'd invited to the party and was staying at the Nikko that evening. He told me he needed me in his room right away but wouldn't say why. Now, the last thing in the world I wanted to do at that hour was hang out with Peter, who was obviously drunk. But he insisted. So, I threw on some clothes and went.

Peter was there with Susie Fields, a gorgeous blonde who was divorced from the music and movie producer, Ted Fields, of the Marshall Fields family. They had gotten loaded together and decided on the spur of the moment to get married. At two o'clock in the morning. *Nuts.* Others were there, including actor Martin Landau. Everyone was wasted. Martin was smoking pot.

I told Peter he was out of his mind.

"No, we just discovered we're in love," he said. "We have to do it now! And I want you to be my best man!"

"You can't get married in a hotel room at two in the morning, just like that," I said.

"Oh, yes you can," Peter said. "The minister's on her way."

And she was. Peter and Susie had called 1-800-WEMARRYU, which will provide a minister anytime, anywhere.

The minister showed up half an hour later and performed the ceremony. I was best man, just like Peter wanted. A couple of months later, presumably after they'd sobered up, Peter and Susie had the marriage annulled.

Ah, Hollywood romance.

OVER THE NEXT YEAR, I spent a lot of time with the Berles, trying to ingratiate myself to them by inviting them to my galas, making him the guest of honor at many, and showering them with attention and favors. I worked hard to help Milton's wife Lorna and her daughter Susan Moll (married to Richard Moll of *Night Court*) launch *Milton,* a magazine for cigar smokers, but the advertisers just weren't biting. Lorna eventually had to sell. She was able to sell it at a profit, however, because the ad accounts she did have—ones I got for her—carried a lot of cachet, including Cartier Jewelers and Alfred Dunhill of London. Not that I ever saw a penny of it.

But then, I struck gold. At a Planet Hope event in late 1994, I had the brilliant idea of seating Milton and Lorna with Steve Wasserman and his wife Jessica Klein, who I had met and become friends with through Stuart Goldberg. Steve and Jessica were one of the hottest young writing duos in town, the talent behind the mega-hit TV series *Beverly Hills 90210.*

All four of them got along famously. They joked and laughed and carried on. Milton gave Steve a cigar and showed him how you were supposed to smoke it. Pretty soon, Steve and Jessica were asking Milton if they could write a part for him on their show. Were they kidding? Did they have to ask? Milton Berle had practically *invented* television. He was not going to turn down an opportunity to return to his old love.

Besides, although Milton Berle was a living legend in show business, his star had long since faded—he was eighty-six years old, after all—and while you could still get him out for parties and Friar's Club roasts, he just didn't work much any more. He didn't get too many offers.

So with both parties eager to proceed, they wrote him in. Milton played a formerly-famous sitcom actor who'd been stricken with Alzheimer's Disease. He was a huge hit. So good, in fact, he was nominated for an Emmy as "Outstanding Guest Actor in a Dramatic Series."

Berle had won Emmys before, including one in 1978 for lifetime achievement. To win another in the twilight of his career would have been "the icing on the cake," as Lorna put it. But as with the Oscars, capturing an Emmy is not a simple thing. You have to get out there and promote yourself and your work.

Lorna started pushing me to come up with something that would generate publicity for Milton. This was not the first time. She was always asking me to do things for her husband, saying stuff like "you know how much he loves you," or "he would really love to have you be the one who does this," and I would always oblige. Though it was BS, of course, I bought it—not because I didn't know a line when I heard one, but because I had such a driving need to prove my worth.

So under intense pressure from Lorna Berle, I came up with an idea for a spectacular event that would showcase Milton and, hopefully, provide the kind of media exposure that would cause voting members from the Academy of Television Arts and Sciences to take notice and vote for him.

My plan was to take Milton on the road—to Nashville, Tennessee!

WHY I THOUGHT OF NASHVILLE for Uncle Miltie, I'm not sure. Partly it was the simple fact that I loved country music and had already met some of its legends, like Tanya Tucker, Waylon Jennings, and Mae Boren Axton (co-writer of "Heartbreak Hotel," Hoyt Axton's mother, and one of the most prominent women on the country scene). Probably, it also had something to do with the fact that Nashville was the entertainment center for middle America. A Hollywood star visiting there would certainly make a bigger splash than if he simply did something in his own hometown, where there was always competition.

I also had my own agenda. I wanted to expand my contacts in that segment of the industry. I'd been approached by a friend of a friend who lived in Nashville to do something for his charity. That gave me the notion to organize a huge fundraiser in the form of a concert featuring performances by big-name country stars. I thought this would be easier to achieve than something involving pop singers, because C&W artists generally tended to be more grounded and—for lack of a better word—normal than the hardened music executives on the East and West Coasts.

To make it happen, I needed to meet more of those stars, as well as affluent people in the country music world who might be persuaded to help underwrite such an event. So I put this idea together in my head with the Milton Berle publicity tour, and the Tennessee trip was born.

I called my man in Nashville. No problem with regard to the fundraiser idea. He could arrange a meeting for me with agents, producers, managers, executives, the kind of folks who might go for it.

Then I explained to him about Milton Berle. Could he help

me there as well? The two different events would cross-pollinate each other, I said. If I had a sit-down dinner for Berle with a group of country stars, then some of them might later agree to perform at the fundraiser. Perhaps he could arrange something with . . . I had no idea whom to try, and he came up with the name "Tammy Wynette." That was fine. Though I'd become acquainted with her ex-husband, George Jones, back in Arizona, I'd never met her.

Naturally, I said, I would cover the cost of the food and so on. That was typical of my approach, promising to put up the cash for something that would be of no financial benefit to me, while not having a clue how many dollars we were talking about.

I asked him for one other thing, as well. Could he get Milton some radio or TV time?

A few days later, I got a call back. Yes, Tammy Wynette would love to host a sit-down dinner for Milton Berle and sixty-five or so other guests at her home. She would take care of inviting some of her old friends, country music stars, to join us. In addition, I got Milton lined up for a spot on *The Ralph Emery Show* (who is something like the Johnny Carson of the South) and on another radio talk show.

So we were in business.

I organized everything, including first-class airfare and luxury accommodations for Lorna and Milton Berle. Which would've been fine, if that was where it ended. In Hollywood, it rarely ended with the star, since every one of them had peripheral people who simply had to be included. In Milton's case, this meant Hans, his personal assistant. Then Lorna pressured me to bring Leslie, her daughter from a previous marriage, and Leslie's husband. I finally agreed.

I invited and paid for a few others I was hoping to impress and get in my corner for other events—including Norby Walters and his wife Irene (whom he called "Tootsie"). I believed that Norby was a well-connected guy who could deliver artists to perform for free and that he would be useful when we were planning the big concert with the Nashville VIPs. Bad decision. He was connected, all right, but not to the kind of people you'd want to meet. Looking back, I'd have to say that if there was one guy I never should have been mixed up with, it was Walters. And that's picking through a very sordid lot.

NORBY WAS A FAST-TALKING, unattractive man with a big nose and a mouth to match. He drove a Bentley and loved to brag to me about how often he cheated on Tootsie.

Norby, typically, would scream rather than talk, half the time in Yiddish, whether you were Jewish or not. He was insulting and obnoxious. A friend of mine used to say that "whenever Norby Walters exits a room, he leaves a trail of anti-Semites behind him."

I got involved with him because of a guy named Lloyd Bloom (who was someone a mutual friend had introduced me to earlier). Bloom had told me he was Norby's partner at one time, before screwing me on some deal or other. I recalled that conversation when looking through Peter Paul's Rolodex and spotting Walters's name. I cold called him, we talked for quite a long while, and we wound up doing some things together.

A few months afterward, in late August 1993, Lloyd Bloom was shot to death in his Malibu home. There was no murder weapon present, no signs of struggle or forced entry or robbery. The killer was never found.

I didn't know Norby Walters's background until later. He'd been born Norby Meyer and raised in the Brooklyn neighborhood controlled by Murder, Inc. He had a lot of ties to organized crime. After running a restaurant for a while, he became a hotshot music and then sports agent.

In the late eighties, he and Lloyd Bloom were busted for racketeering. Authorities alleged that they secretly signed dozens of college athletes to contracts before their college eligibility with the NCAA had expired. Michael Franzese, a former Colombo crime family captain who fixed professional games and organized gambling for pro athletes, testified at the trial. Franzese, who had been born again and turned state's evidence, said that he allowed them to use his name to threaten athletes who either didn't want to sign or who wanted out of their illegal contracts. There were also allegations of fixing. "Our goal was to get as many players as we could sign and get them to influence the outcome of a game," Franzese said.

Norby (along with Bloom) was convicted in 1989 and sentenced to five years in prison. But in 1990, the conviction was overturned on appeal because of jury instruction error and the failure to sever the two cases. Two years later, with the case reopened, Walters pled guilty to two counts of mail fraud (of the schools his athletes attended). That, too, was overturned, in 1993, a couple of months prior to Bloom's death. "It was all tossed," Norby Walters says today.

Like Peter Paul, and so many others with a criminal past, Norby had come to Hollywood to reinvent himself, and that's what he was in the process of doing when I invited him and his wife to go to Nashville with us. I don't think he ever intended to help me get talent for the big concert I was planning; he was just using me for a free ride and the chance to make some new contacts of his own.

UPON ARRIVING AT THE NASHVILLE AIRPORT, we were met by a special group of greeters. They, as well as the limo drivers, all had Southern accents, and Milton didn't stop making fun of them the whole time we were there.

"Where are we?" he would say. "Land of the s—kickers?" Over and over. Lorna would hush him up, seeming halfway embarrassed.

Then, when we got to the hotel suite and I opened the curtains, we found that we were looking across at a hospital with a huge cross on its side.

"What the f— is that?" Milton said.

That's how Milton was. He didn't have respect for religion in general and Christian Southerners in particular, and he didn't mind showing it. The whole time we were in Nashville, where there's a church on every street corner, he would make derogatory remarks like, "Aren't there any f—ing Jews in this place?"

Over the next two days, as I listened to this stream of abusive talk, I couldn't help but think: *No wonder middle Americans hold Hollywood in such contempt. How could they not, when we have such contempt for their values?* But no one ever saw this ugly side of Hollywood's most beloved performers. And so when we were in McDonald's the next morning, adults and children alike flocked around the aging legend in awe. Milton loved the attention.

Milton appeared on *The Ralph Emery Show* first, and it was great. Though he was an old man, and moved frustratingly slowly most of the time, when he got on stage he was transformed. He lost about thirty years. He was in his element. He spoke and sang and told jokes with great energy, in a voice grown young and strong again.

There was press attending Milton's appearances, and I had hired a video monitoring service that captured entertainment-related news. It was hitting the wires. "Milton's Country Tour," they called it, or "Uncle Miltie Goes Country." Eventually, he showed up on *Entertainment Tonight* and other national shows, all hyping Milton as a major contender for the Emmy.

For lunch, Mama Mae (as she liked to be called by those closest to her) had asked if I would bring my entourage to her home in Hendersonville, about twenty miles out of town. There would be seventy-five to a hundred people there, including executives from the board of directors of the Grand Ole Opry. The mayor would give a speech in Milton's honor. I couldn't say no to Mama Mae. So I told her we'd be there.

We trudged off to Hendersonville in the ninety-degree heat, with Milton dressed as always in his hat and full-length, brown trench coat. Milton looked tired from all the traveling and schmoozing. *This had better be short and sweet,* I decided.

The lunch was served outside in the direct sunlight. We were all frying, not used to the muggy Tennessee summers. Lorna and Milton ate fast, while Norby shot bull with some music industry execs. The mayor welcomed Milton on behalf of the people of Hendersonville.

As we were preparing to leave, I was approached by several of the Grand Ole Opry's producers and pressed to get Berle to appear live on the stage, in front of several thousand, or at least tape something for the show, with its TV audience in the millions.

I took them over to meet Milton, so that he could tell some jokes and they could get to know him a little before making their formal request that he do the Opry. Milton clowned around with the producers for a while, then said, "Yes, I'm really looking forward to the Opry, so I can meet Little Jimmy C—sucker. Ooops . . . I mean Dickens."

Jimmy Dickens was an old-time, beloved Opry performer, and Milton had meant this as a joke. Wrong guys. It was the kind of thing that might go over at the Friar's Club, but we were a long way from there. No one laughed. Needless to say, the invitation to have Milton appear on stage at the Opry was never offered.

WE HUSTLED BACK TO NASHVILLE, where Milton rested up. That was what I wanted to do as well, but no such luck. Lorna had to take me shopping.

I'd made the mistake, back in L.A., of telling her about a famous designer of Western attire named Emmanuel. He had outfitted stars such as Marty Stuart and had a shop in Nashville. Mae Axton told me about him. She loved him.

That was all Lorna needed to hear. Coincidentally, there was a charity event coming up later in the year with a Western theme, and she got it into her head that she simply must have an Emmanuel design to wear to it. That'd be unique in Hollywood, she thought. It'd make her stand out. So she forced me to go to his store to pick something up.

When we got there, she looked and looked, all the time hinting about what she most loved. I knew what she was doing: rich as she was, she still wanted me to pay for it. That would win me favor with her and Milton, but I hesitated. The place was very, very expensive, and I'd already spent most of what I had on the trip. I could not afford the added expense. Foolishly, however, I succumbed to her unspoken pressure and offered to purchase a gift for her.

Big mistake. She selected a rhinestone-studded jacket, hand-made, with an intricate design. In addition, they hand-fitted it for her and added a few individualized details. It cost a fortune, sending me even deeper into my personal financial black hole.

That evening, the seven of us piled into one stretch limo (paid for by yours truly, of course) and went to the dinner hosted by Tammy Wynette and her husband George Richey. Lorna had been pleading with me ahead of time to speak to Milton. She wanted me to tell him that if he got up after the dinner and did a routine, he shouldn't use any of his foul-language material.

I promised her I'd pass that along, but actually I was kind of interested to see what he would come up with off the cuff. Plus, he was one of those comedians who, once he's on stage, either gets carried away with himself or stops giving a hoot. Once that happens, it doesn't matter what he's agreed to. If he starts getting foul-mouthed, there's no stopping him.

Tammy lived in a very nice house, though it would be considered modest by Beverly Hills standards. She and her husband were out front to greet us, along with a camera crew from NBC. Tammy was a delight, a very classy woman. I was thrilled to meet her, and they seemed equally thrilled to meet Milton Berle. Happiness all around.

Lorna kept whispering to me how impressed she was that I had pulled this off, and all I could think was, *Yeah, anything for old Uncle Miltie.* Because, in reality, it was a pretty bad business decision to be throwing my money at this thing. I mean, it wasn't like I was doing it to promote some hot younger star like Jim Carrey; an oldie like Milton wasn't likely to give me much of a return on my investment.

What kept me upbeat about it was that I held on to the illusion that I would cut a deal for my big charity concert because of the connections I made here. Then I would get all my money back and even profit some. Stupid, stupid. I was still dripping wet behind the ears.

Tammy gave us a mini-tour of the house. Milton was very cordial, as he could be when he turned on the charm. The house was filled with prominent country singers and comedians. Paul Overstreet was there, and so was Charlie Pride, one of the only black country stars and the first one inducted into the Country Music Hall of Fame. I was particularly excited to meet Crystal Gayle. She was so beautiful to me, inside and out. I remember playing her records over and over when I was a kid back in Alpena, and I had pressured Mae Boren Axton hard to make sure Crystal came. Which she did. Mama Mae was great.

Dinner was beautifully set up in a sunken area of the living room. Everyone got a table favor: an 8x10 autographed photo and a boxed set of videos of Milton's work. The latter I had to order from one of his nephews in Florida. As always with Milton, nothing came for free.

Then Milton got up to give a little speech and tell a few jokes. Lorna looked at me and asked me with her eyes, *Did you speak to him?* I ignored her, but when Milton's patter began to get a little nasty, she convinced Norby Walters to handle the matter. Norby got up, walked slowly over to Milton, and started talking to him.

Now, this is something you never want to do to any comedian, much less Milton Berle, when he's *on.* You're interrupting his act and risk his turning his full wrath on you. To make things worse, Milton was a little hard of hearing, so Norby felt compelled to speak very loudly. He was practically yelling at Milton not to let his jokes get too dirty. And all in Yiddish!

Milton finally turned to him and yelled back: "WRONG ROOM!!" Meaning almost everyone in the room was puzzling over what this bizarre man was shouting in some foreign language. Lorna and I, though, were laughing hysterically.

Norby sat down. Then Milton launched into one of the forbidden jokes.

"Here is my beautiful wife, Lorna," he said, waiting until she stood up. "My lovely wife, Lorna. You know, we were married not too long ago, and on our wedding night I asked her to bring home something black and sexy. So she did." Pause. *"Charlie Pride!"*

Lorna was embarrassed, but everyone laughed uproariously. Even Charlie. Milton had done what he does best: win a crowd over. He was a hit.

After dinner, Milton sat for about forty-five minutes and autographed all of the video box sets. These were stars themselves, who were lining up to get his signature.

It was a heartwarming sight, all going along perfectly until Lorna, afraid that her husband might be getting tired, asked if he was ready to go. And just like that, he turned on her, humiliating her with the nastiest words, right in front of everyone. You see, that was also Milton. He could go from charming and pleasant to absolutely vicious in the blink of an eye. I'd seen it many times before.

Even so, Milton finished his autographing session, and lots of pictures were taken. It was great publicity. The story made all three network news shows in Los Angeles.

The next day, I and the business portion of my entourage—including Norby—went to the meeting with the music business people. I don't think Norby impressed them much, with his New York jive chat and haphazard Yiddish thrown in. But it looked as though they were interested. We talked about plans and schedules and ideas for the production. The talent managers were willing to commit their clients, and that was the biggest hurdle.

Problem was, Norby was too lazy to see it through, and I don't think anyone else was prepared for the amount of work it would take. That dumped everything into my lap, and I just hadn't learned the ropes well enough in 1995. A few years later, I would have brought it off, and brought it off big. But at that point I lacked the experience, as well as the necessary aggressiveness, to succeed through sheer force of will.

Thus I was leaving Nashville empty-handed. For a two-day trip I was out over fifty grand with nothing to show for it. Well, actually Lorna Berle did thank me. But Milton, never.

He didn't win the Emmy, either.

THOUGH I'D FALLEN INTO the stressed-out state that would often be the norm for the rest of my Hollywood career, I was feeling upbeat enough, with all my successes, to celebrate. In September, I was turning thirty, and as usual I was thinking big. I guess I'd grown accustomed to all the lavishness I was surrounded by in Hollywood, where it wasn't unusual for someone to spend forty grand on a birthday bash for their kids. *If they could do it,* I figured, *why couldn't I?*

Besides, I was still foolishly thinking that money spent on entertaining movie stars was simply a business expense and that cash laid out now would flow back to me at some point in the misty future. I hadn't yet tumbled to the fact that, for the most part, the only thing accomplished by showering stars with gifts was whetting their appetite for more gifts.

I certainly wasn't thinking about that in the summer of 1995. All I knew was that I had decided to throw myself the thirtieth birthday party to end all birthday parties. Not only did I want to surround myself with the stars who had become my "friends," I wanted to fly in members of my family too, so I could impress them with how high I had risen. I couldn't consider myself a true success until my family knew about it.

Finding a place to have the party was no problem. I was still living for free at the Hotel Nikko, and they still needed PR. So we made the arrangements.

The next thing to do was order the invitations. For this, I knew just who I wanted. I was very taken with a stationer that Nancy Davis had used for the invitations to her son's bar mitzvah, a hilarious story in itself.

You see, I was still working with Nancy, volunteering my

time, resources, and many corporate connections to help the Race To Erase MS, despite the ugly things her mother kept saying to her and others in the community about me. I also got her some celebrities for the bar mitzvah. I convinced David Copperfield to make a short video congratulating her son, and I got noted photographer Howard Bingham to persuade his old friend Muhammad Ali to attend.

When Muhammad rolled up and realized that he was at a Jewish temple, though, he refused to get out of the limo. He just waited in the car until the religious section of the ceremony was over, then was driven to the Davis's house for the big party, where he signed autographs for the kids. A bizarre sight to say the least, because here was Muhammad Ali at a bar mitzvah, signing, of all things, Muslim religious pamphlets.

Anyway, I'd been impressed with the bar mitzvah invitations. They were kind of garish, very extravagant, and I loved them. So when I went to the same company to get mine, I knew I didn't want a simple card. I wanted something special, and the company came through with a spectacular one.

They were delivered to my invited guests in a large 8x12 box. Inside was a postpaid RSVP card with gold script. The invitation was on the box itself. It had black borders and was etched in gold. A gold star of Hollywood was prominent at the very top, along with a gold Oscar. On one side was a plastic palm tree with a wire that had stars hanging from it. There was also a plastic representation of a movie director sitting in a chair, a camera, and one of those clackers they use to signal the start of a scene. The text read:

You Are Cordially Invited to a 30th Birthday Celebration
Starring Aaron Tonken
Friday, October 13, 1995-6:30 P.M.
Cocktails Dinner Dancing
Imperial Ballroom, Hotel Nikko, Beverly Hills
Cocktail Attire

The invitation's crowning touch was a little button underneath "Cocktail Attire" that said "Push," and, when pressed, played, "There's No Business Like Show Business," sung by Ethel Merman. Many friends have saved those invitations to this day. They cost thirty-five bucks. Each. I ordered a hundred and fifty of them.

Though I was spending money I didn't really have, I was determined not to skimp on anything. I hired a fourteen-piece orchestra, for example.

And stars, of course. In order to impress my family, I needed a room full of stars. So I invited all my regulars, along with everyone else I could think of.

Norby Walters offered to bring some stars I didn't know. The catch was he wouldn't do it for free, even after I'd paid for his trip to Nashville and everything. Norby didn't do favors for friends. He charged me fifteen hundred. Per star. Then he showed up with several *alta cockers*—our Yiddish expression for "old timers." People like Edie Adams, whom at that point I'd never even heard of.

My own family was represented by my aunt, uncle, cousins, and sister Heidi. I flew them out and put them all up, of course. I wanted my mother there, but she refused to come. Maybe she didn't want to admit to herself I had finally achieved something in life. In a way, Anita's no-show was no surprise, considering that my grandmother had recently died. Not that she was delayed for mourning. Mom didn't even attend her own mother's funeral. I think she was just trying to forget that some of us even existed.

The party was another smashing success. I greeted everyone at the door, flanked by two of the most gorgeous models in town. The orchestra was seated on a special stage I'd had built for them, under the word *Hollywood,* spelled out in lights. There was a huge dance floor. At every table, I left the party favors: a life-sized chocolate Oscar and a CD with songs by some of the artists who performed.

There were more than 125 people in all, including: my family members, my pal Stuart Goldberg and his mother Rhea, Alicia and Red Buttons, Mae Boren Axton, Paul Overstreet, Lorna and Milton Berle, Michelle Phillips, Roxanne and Jack Carter, Joni and Norm Crosby, Gretchen Becker and Martin Landau, Florence and Sid Caesar, Lydia and Charlton Heston, Steve Wasserman, Jessica Klein, Kelly Stone, Tootsie and Norby Walters, most of the cast of *The Young and the Restless,* Gary Coleman, Kato Kaelin, Edie Adams and her husband, Marilyn and Monty Hall, Cynthia and Hal Gershman, my assistant Chad Mouton, and a long list of others. The only ones who didn't make it, whom I really wanted, were Steve Lawrence and Eydie Gorme, my favorite performers in the world.

Among all the gifts I received, two in particular stand out. First, Mae Axton gave me an inscribed book of poetry, *From the Window of My Heart (Poems To Live By),* that was written by her and illustrated by her son Hoyt Axton. I still have it today.

Second, Paul Overstreet had come, bringing his whole

beautiful family at his own expense. As his gift to me, he sang several of his award-winning country songs. I was both flattered and touched.

The festivities went on until midnight.

It should have been the crowning moment of my young life, but wasn't. As glorious as it was, the guest of honor couldn't really enjoy his own birthday bash. I just had too many dark clouds hanging over my head.

First, there was the expense. The affair cost me forty thousand dollars, which I covered with a private loan. More than most Americans made in a year, and I'd blown it on a party.

And then there was the Tommy Lasorda benefit, which would be the first charity event for which I was the sole producer. It was going to be held on October 15, only two days after my birthday gala. I was a nervous, twitching wreck over it. It was a horror.

But it was *huge*.

eight

DODGER BLUES

I personally can attest to the fact that Aaron is a very sincere and caring individual whose extraordinary ability to raise charitable funds has been overshadowed by the very people he counted on to perpetuate the fundraising [i.e., celebrities].

—STEVEN FOX, *Founder and Former Director of the Tommy Lasorda Jr. Memorial Foundation*

What I needed was a major hit. Something people would talk about.

I'd taken a couple of shots at breaking into movie production and failed. But at the same time, I was steadily honing my craft as a fundraiser and professional schmoozer, and that seemed more likely to be where my future lay. To move ahead, I needed something that would raise my profile in the community, that would dramatically expand my network of star connections, that would put me in touch with more sources of future funding, and, last but not least, that would get me out of debt.

Sure, I'd helped raise over a hundred thousand dollars for Planet Hope. But I wanted to do a mega-bash, something that would raise millions. And I wanted to do it solely on my own, where I was in control from start to finish. I was ready, or at least I thought I was.

I went through the trusty Rolodex and decided to make a cold call to Tommy Lasorda, an icon in the Los Angeles area. I called his home and spoke with his wife Jo. I told her that I produced fundraising events and asked if she and Tommy would be interested in doing one for their favorite charity. At the time, I didn't even realize that the Lasordas had founded their own charity a couple of years earlier. It was the Tommy Lasorda Jr. Memorial Foundation, in honor of their late son.

Tommy Jr. was homosexual and had died at the age of thirty-three. As I would later find out, while Jo Lasorda was very close to her son, Tommy Sr. had had a very difficult time accepting Junior's sexual orientation. This made for an awkward situation when the young man succumbed to AIDS. Tommy Sr.'s way of handling it was always to say his son passed away from pneumonia, and leave it at that. Thus the foundation created in Tommy Jr.'s name was in no way AIDS-related. Its mission was simply to help kids in need.

I didn't know about any of this at first and wouldn't have cared if I did. The only important thing was that the Lasordas were a perfect fit. I needed to put on something big, and the foundation needed a sizeable infusion of cash.

We met for dinner at Tatou. Jo and Tommy Lasorda, Steven Fox, the executive director of the foundation, and me. Steve was a Jewish guy around fifty, over six feet tall, with a muscular build and brown hair. I found, as I came to know him, that he was a very thoughtful person, honest, inquisitive, quiet, and gentle, yet strong at the same time. He was tough when he had to be, but mostly kind and generous, and he liked to laugh a lot. He was a longtime friend of the Lasordas, very loyal to them, and would become an important influence in my life as well.

I ordered five different desserts, winding up with a plate of assorted chocolates in front of me. "Like chocolate, do you?" Steve joked. Then we got down to business. I pitched them hard, telling them that I wanted to organize and produce a huge gala that would raise some serious money for the foundation. I described a star-studded night to them. Not that I knew that many top stars personally, but I was confident that Tommy's name would be sufficient to draw them in. I was right.

The real hurdle was, as I discovered later, that the Lasordas had already been burned, at one of the earliest fundraisers held for their new charity. The event was a roast held in Las Vegas, featuring Tommy's old friend Frank Sinatra and a lot of other stars, for the joint benefit of the foundation and Barbara (Frank's last wife) Sinatra's Children's Center. When Frank, who was in declining health at the time, got up on stage and began repeating the same jokes more than once, several people came and ushered him from the room. He never returned to his seat for dinner.

This enraged his wife, who stormed into the accounting room, then demanded, and made off with, the evening's proceeds. The Lasordas got nothing. After that, Frank would never even return his friend Tommy's phone calls.

Thus, the Lasordas must have been at least a little wary going in. But still they were impressed with my pitch and wanted to move forward. I received the go-ahead to start planning an event to raise money for the construction of a sports center in Yorba Linda—to be named after Tommy Jr.—that would be a place where local kids could go after school, instead of hanging out in the streets. If I could bring in a million or two, that would be an enormous benefit to the foundation.

In addition, Steve Fox offered me space in the offices of his company, Lasorda Leasing, on Alondra Boulevard down in Paramount, southeast of the city. I could move in immediately—a godsend. I hadn't had a real business address since I left Stone Canyon.

Every day I was commuting the eighty-minute round trip from the Hotel Nikko to Paramount, where I worked like a dog on this project, from early in the morning until eight or nine at night on weekdays. Steve would also let me in on weekends, so I could put in another ten hours on Saturdays and Sundays. I also legally registered the first business that was truly my own: Aaron Tonken and Associates. I was very proud.

Yet despite all this hard work and continuing success, I was still sinking lower and lower into debt. I never managed my business well, could never get ahead. Problem was, I never took the time to learn how to run things in a professional manner and go through the proper channels, as Steve and others continually counseled me to do. Steve was a great resource, a highly successful businessman with decades of experience, and I should have gone to him with questions, for guidance. At a bare minimum, I should have hired a real accountant to keep watch over my cash flow. But I didn't do any of these things. I felt like I could do everything myself.

I hadn't changed a bit from my years as a spoiled child recklessly lavishing gifts on others, stealing from my own funds just to do so.

Only now, the stakes had been raised.

It was a shame. Because I was now well on my way to producing events that would raise millions for charities and, later, political candidates. Everything I did was the best. Yet, I was never appropriately compensated for my efforts. In fact, the more successful I became, the further I fell into debt. I had an obsessive, admittedly irresponsible desire to make people happy, even at my own extravagant expense.

But in the end, the privileged benefited the most. I was out my money, yes, but the real tragedy was that my stupidity led to many worthy causes getting hurt along the way.

SINCE THE LASORDA EVENT was such a major undertaking, I needed help. So I brought Chad Mouton and another assistant, Steve Gottlieb, along with me from Stone Canyon. I put them on salary, even though I had very little income, paid Chad extra to drive to work in Paramount, and overpaid Steve. Overpaying was always my downfall. But that wasn't the worst of it. I also felt I really had to add someone to the team with experience in the entertainment industry, someone who had produced events and could deliver stars. And so I made the mistake of turning to Norby Walters.

Steve Fox tried to talk me out of it. He was convinced that Walters was a slimeball who could do me no good. Though he hadn't met the guy, he knew Norby's reputation from the stories that were still appearing on tabloid TV like *Hard Copy*. He also knew that Norby had recently been involved in some questionable ventures with a business associate named Michael Bass.

Bass was a legendary ex-con who'd fled the country after being involved in a series of events so bizarre no novelist could have made them up. Among other things, Bass had: tried to steal a boxer out from under Don King; been accused of ripping off hundreds of thousands of dollars from a charity fundraiser for beloved AIDS poster child Ryan White; duped half of Hollywood with a phony Tribute to Boris Yeltsin party on Oscar night; and allegedly been assaulted by actor Corey Haim with a BB gun. In 1993, authorities began looking into several Bass events that involved missing monies, including one featuring Milton Berle that left Milton furious. Predictably, Bass then disappeared, only to surface in Russia of all places, where he was last seen selling pricey tickets for a gala tribute to Diana Ross at Moscow's Golden Palace casino. Diana never showed.

This was the kind of company Norby kept. He'd even been involved in the Berle fiasco that led to Bass skipping town. You'd think I would have been bright enough to realize I shouldn't bring someone like Norby into fundraising events with me. Nope. I was blind to his faults, and I begged Steve Fox at least to meet him. Reluctantly, Steve agreed.

Afterward, his advice was exactly the same: *Stay away from this guy.* Of course, I hired him anyway. And Steve, bless him, stuck with me. I don't know why. As Norby began teaching me the dirty tricks of the trade, Steve was always there as a positive role model. He even advanced me the start-up money for the Lasorda event, out of his own pocket.

The day that Norby walked into the office, he announced that he could deliver a slew of stars to our gala, for free. Well, *free* in the sense that the stars wouldn't charge us to appear (not always the case, as I would find out). No, the stars were free, it was *Norby* who wasn't.

This was one of Norby's scams: he would talk celebrities

into attending fundraisers, then charge the charities an exorbitant fee for his services. The charities, who usually didn't know how to approach stars on their own, or have much success at it, would go along, thinking they had no choice. So the money they had to pay Walters came right off the top, diminishing the amount that actually went to their cause. It was disgraceful. Shamefully, though, I would do it too, just like Norby taught me, at times when I was desperate for money. If you had the connections, it was a sure way to raise some quick cash.

What made Norby's actions doubly wrong was that he specialized in B- and C-list celebs. In other words, these were primarily people out of the spotlight who were delighted to receive any kind of publicity. They would have come to any function, anytime, anywhere. All you had to do was know where to find them, and then ask. But many charities didn't know that, and those were the ones Norby targeted.

Norby wanted to be involved in everything, right off the bat. He set himself up as my mentor, even though I had a much better one right across the desk from me in Steve Fox. But Norby convinced me he knew the ins and outs of this business better than anyone, that he could really help me get ahead. What was really happening though was that he was tapping into my substantial list of contacts and using them for his benefit. Or charging me a hundred dollars for every three numbers he gave me out of his own Rolodex. I was laying golden eggs for him, not the other way around.

I don't know how much he profited in the long run. Most were turned off by his obnoxious, fast-talking, Yiddish-spouting, in-your-face, New York ways. I had to keep him away from a lot of my clients.

Norby did teach me some things, however. He showed me the proper way to write letters asking for money, and how to do presale solicitations. Regrettably, much of his curriculum had to do with how to lie to my clients and cut corners. For example, I discovered that when I registered my business, I should also have applied for a commercial fundraising license. I didn't know you were required to have one to do what I was doing. But Norby waved it off as unimportant.

"Fuhgeddaboudit," he said in his accent. "They'll never know. Just make sure you cover you're ass. As long as the charities are happy, you'll be fine." Yeah, I wish.

BASICALLY, THE PROCEDURE for organizing each of my charity or political fundraisers was more or less the same, and a step-by-step examination of what I did with the Lasorda benefit will show how it all works.

The first thing to determine was what kind of event it was going to be. It could be held in the afternoon, evening, or night. It could range from a casual brunch to a cocktail party to a full-tilt, black-tie ball. There could be featured speakers, panels, awards, auctions, and a whole host of other ceremonies. Food could be hors d'oeuvres or a multi-course, sit-down dinner. There might or might not be entertainment. All this had to be nailed down at the start.

With the Lasorda benefit, there was no doubt. We would have a star-spangled mega-bash, at night, with dinner, guests of honor, auctions, performers, everything. This was very ambitious for my first time out, but the more elaborate you got, the more money you were likely to bring in. It was that simple, and my goal was to hit the seven-figure mark. Anything less would be a major disappointment.

The next thing you need, if you want the event to take off, is an honoree. It doesn't matter what you are honoring him or her for; it's all BS anyway, just an excuse for a party. What *is* important is that your honoree be the most prominent person you can get. The bigger the guest of honor, the bigger the names of those who will come out to see and be seen. Stars attract other stars. It also helps if you tap someone who has never been honored before, what I called a "virgin honoree."

I already had Tommy himself. He was probably as beloved a sports figure as had ever been associated with Los Angeles. Everybody knew Tommy. But we didn't want his own charity honoring him. We needed someone else and, after considering a number of possibilities, we settled on Billy Crystal. Why? Like I said, it's all BS.

When I presented the idea to Jo Lasorda, she was skeptical. She'd always had trouble getting Billy to commit to anything in the past, she told me. He was hard to get. *No problem,* I replied. I was absurdly confident, considering that I'd never tackled anything of this magnitude before. *Leave that to me,* I told Jo. *I know what to do.*

I sat down with Norby and Steve, and we composed a letter. It reminisced about Tommy Lasorda's longtime friendship with Billy Crystal, talked about his son and the charity founded in his name, and asked Billy to be the guest of honor at a foundation fundraiser during which tribute would be paid to him for . . . well, for being Billy Crystal. It was reasonably heartfelt, I thought, although the words were ours and not

Tommy's. We passed it along to Tommy for his approval, and he signed it. Then it was hand-delivered to Billy's office at Castle Rock Entertainment.

Billy said yes. And fast!

A major coup. We'd landed Billy Crystal, a big Hollywood star whose name could go out over everything. We had the person, now we needed the place.

My goal was to find the hotel that would rip off the charity the least. While these places would provide the kind of space required for a gala—their giant ballrooms—they charged for everything else, such as food, drinks, valet parking, and table service. They charged a lot, and made huge profits.

Seems immoral or almost criminal, doesn't it? To have these huge, glittery, expensive events in order supposedly to raise money for charity. "It's just the cost of doing business," some will say. But consider that the total bill for an event such as I was organizing can easily run four hundred thou. Remember that in addition to providing food and drink, you also have to pay to fly your performers and honorees in, and sometimes to fly their families with them, and then you have to pay for everyone's accommodations and transportation expenses. After all, celebrities won't make a trip to the mailbox without travel expenses. And with the caliber of people we're talking about, it has to be first class all the way.

Now, it does sometimes happen that a genuine philanthropist will underwrite the full cost of putting on a show, thereby allowing all money taken in to go to the charity. But that's rare. Very rare. Usually, underwriting by individual and corporate sponsors will be partial, and the rest must be made up out of receipts. Most commonly, expenses total between 40 and 70 percent of the take. The charity gets only what's left over.

Wouldn't it be so much better if charitable people would simply give the money directly to their chosen cause? you ask. Of course it would. But the cruel reality is that it often takes a party to get folks to give. They're willing to part with lots of money only if in return they get to participate in all the glamorous proceedings, and to be publicly noted for having taken part. Writing a check and putting it in the mail isn't fun, isn't exciting; hanging out with movie stars is. Let's be frank, most contributors aren't doing it simply out of the kindness of their hearts.

Because I wanted to save wherever I could, I planned to make the rounds in Beverly Hills, checking out the different hotels' facilities, meeting with caterers, inspecting menus and venues, getting prices. Then I would sit down and compare the different packages and see which one made the most sense for what I wanted to do. This was exactly the right way to go about it. Problem was, it never happened.

What happened instead was that my partner Norby Walters said, *Oh no, just leave all the arrangements to me.* He promptly set up a meeting with the people in charge of ballroom events at the Beverly Hills Hotel, and that, as you may know, is one of the most expensive places in town.

They offered the Crystal Ballroom, which was gorgeous, I had to admit. In addition, the hotel itself recently had been purchased by the Sultan of Brunei and was just reopening. The Lasorda benefit could be the inaugural event. The resultant publicity would be terrific, everyone assured me.

Norby Walters, the experienced one who was supposedly guiding me in this process, pushed for the Beverly Hills Hotel.

I don't know if the hotel was paying him or what, but he really lobbied for it, insisting that if I wanted to get the best people out, then I should go with the best hotel.

Of course, no one bothered to tell me that this hotel in particular would not offer a free room to any performer or special guest, nor gave the slightest discount. Not on anything. Nor did I know that selecting the Beverly Hills Hotel was going to cost me a number of paying guests. I later heard of Jewish couples who wouldn't even enter the building because they believed the new owner was anti-Semitic.

I picked it anyway.

After the decision was made, we went over the menu. Once again, I was trying to save money. I ordered the least expensive of everything, including the "rubber chicken" that all of the hotels are famous for serving at these affairs. The food was basic: salad, main entrée, dessert. I was thinking that would be it. Silly me.

We had to have an open bar, Norby said. So that all those stars coming out for the extended cocktail hour and silent auction would have someplace to drink. On top of that, he insisted that we have two bottles of wine—one red, one white—at each table. This, of course, would send our expenses skyrocketing, since the hotel wanted thirty-five dollars a bottle to serve their cheapest house brand.

I was a non-drinker from a family of non-drinkers. Plus this was a charity event. In my naïveté, I didn't see why people had to have alcohol. Norby looked at me like I was nuts. "You can't expect your guests to pay thousands of dollars and then not have free wine at the tables," he said.

As it turned out, I was later able to get someone to donate

the wine, many thousands of dollars' worth. But the hotel still demanded sixteen dollars a bottle to uncork and serve it. Sixteen bucks? That was a ripoff, and I knew it. I told them I'd go around to each table and do the job myself. But in the end I gave in. I had no choice.

The final price they quoted me for catering was $110 per person. With six hundred fifty coming, that added up to the tidy sum of $71,500. *Ouch.*

Then there was the problem of the bar to deal with. Norby insisted on an open bar; I thought guests should pay.

"You don't understand," Norby said. "It's an investment. You get these people drunk, and then they will bid wildly on the auction items."

I didn't want that. This was a charity affair. People should buy these things out of generosity, I thought, not because they were intoxicated and didn't realize what they were doing. What he was suggesting seemed almost like a sacrilege to me. Once more, I was showing what a novice I was. We finally compromised on a partial open bar. Up went the price again.

By the time I walked out of the Beverly Hills Hotel, I felt battered. But at least the deal was done. Everything involving the hotel was arranged. Now we had to line up a dinner chairman.

The dinner chairman is the person who agrees to send out letters on his stationery, asking others to lend their good names to the dinner committee, attend the event, and buy tickets. Later, the chair's name goes at the top of the committee list on the general invitation.

If you want to have a really successful fundraiser, it's very important that your committee list, which is printed down the left side of the invitation, have the best names on it. When the names are impressive, they encourage others to participate; they suggest that this is the *in* thing to do that night. The most desirable names are those who usually don't do functions, who hold high positions in the entertainment industry, or who are A-list stars.

Unfortunately, I gave Norby the job of finding a dinner chair, and he got me a meeting with Donald T. Sterling. For a fee, of course. Sterling was a big-time real estate developer, rumored to be one of the wealthiest men in the state of California, and owner of the NBA's perpetual losers, the L.A. Clippers. He was crass and arrogant—he actually put his net worth on all his stationery, which said something like "one billion dollars in assets." He also held himself out to be this major philanthropist when in reality, by reputation, he was cheaper than Hal Gershman. Just try getting a dime out of him. Donald T. Sterling turned out to be not much of a catch—a local laughingstock would be more like it—but that didn't stop us from forging ahead.

With Billy Crystal and our dinner chair in the fold, the presale solicitations could be sent. These are simply letters on event stationery that ask the recipient to make a financial contribution, donate an item for the live or silent auction, or purchase a sponsorship. Sometimes they can be used to tap into the recipient's mailing list as well.

The initial presale letter would be from the guy at the top, in this case Tommy Lasorda. Norby taught me how to write a template for this (for another fee), then I just had to get Tommy to sign it. Should have been a simple matter. It was his own charity, after all, a memorial to his only son. But

Tommy seemed oddly disinterested in the whole thing. If it was difficult to get his signature, it was impossible to get him to work on bringing in money. I learned early on that I couldn't count on either Tommy or Jo to pick up the phone and become involved personally in any of the fundraising, nor to assist us in any significant way. It would be Steve, Norby, and me, and our assistants, who would make it happen.

As my career progressed, I would find that this was generally the case, more often than not, that a charity's namesake will barely lift a finger to help with a benefit.

Thus, I had to push and push on poor Steve Fox until Tommy finally signed, and the letters could go out. Though it had been difficult, I was very optimistic that we'd get good results. I had quite a mailing list at this time, to which I was able to add names from Steve's and the Lasordas'.

But Norby taught me that you didn't stop with the initial letter. You did a follow-up a couple of weeks later, this time with the signature of a different supporter of the charity. Norby drew this one up for me (for yet another fee), and I got Larry King to sign it.

Larry was one of the big names I'd managed to enlist. I'd also snagged Rob Reiner to emcee, Alan King to do the opening monologue, and Tony Bennett to sing. This was going to be big. The ballroom could seat six hundred fifty, and I was going to put six hundred fifty bodies in there.

Meanwhile, the fancy auction items were starting to come in. Collecting these probably seems like fun, and it can be, but it brings on its own share of headaches. As donations begin to arrive, you have to hire an event planner to catalogue them and later to coordinate the auctions themselves. You also have to lease space to store the stuff until the big night, and some of the items can be sizeable. I actually wrote to Roger Penske of Penske Racing, asking him to contribute a Mercedes. I lobbied him hard for that, and eventually he did give us one. It didn't arrive in time for this benefit, but I used it in my second Lasorda event.

Anyway, the point is—and this is just one small example—that there were always dozens of expenses that might seem minor at first, but that could quickly mount up. And they were mounting, all right, along with the list of special favors people were asking. It was worse for someone like me, because I was green and for the most part didn't know what I was doing. At the same time, I was desperate that this, my first big production, be a success. I didn't want the foundation to get a penny less than they could, so I paid out of pocket for things I shouldn't have.

The pressure was intense. Steve was fronting money, but I still had to borrow more and more, or put off people who wanted to be paid. I had bill collectors on my butt the whole time, and for long afterward.

THERE WERE PROBLEMS, OF COURSE. Norby Walters was being a royal pain in so many ways. He was in charge of lining up additional stars to attend, which he did. For his usual fee. The trouble was that he was bringing me B- and C-list people who would have come anyway, on the weight of Tommy Lasorda and Billy Crystal's names. But I was thinking that with stars more is always better. I didn't care who he got, or how he did it, as long as the ballroom was filled with famous faces.

In addition, Norby insisted that I put him in charge of the seating for the event. He twisted my arm, saying it would be a disaster if he didn't do it. For all I knew he was right; I'd never tried to seat such a large number of guests before. So I gave him the job. For a fee, do you think? Guess.

This turned into a disaster the night of the event, when we discovered that Norby had been giving away free tickets to members of his family and had seated them at some of the most prestigious tables. So when Mike Piazza and Eric Karros showed up, they found themselves seated in the "North 40," as we called the area farthest from the stage.

Tommy was enraged. He went up to Steve Fox and said, "What in the hell is going on? My players are not going to sit against the wall."

Steve took this to Norby, who said, "Well, sorry, there are just no more seats."

"Then move your family," Steve said, "and put the Dodgers in the good seats."

When Norby refused to do it, Steve threatened to have security come and throw his entire family out the door. That got it done.

Also, on the entertainment front, we were having the normal difficulties. Tony Bennett, whose career was enjoying a resurgence, had agreed to come and sing his three songs for "free," which merely meant he wasn't going to charge his normal artist's fee for the performance itself. I still had to pay to fly him in and put him up, and to provide meals and ground transportation. Ditto for Danny Bennett, Tony's son and manager. And his quartet. First class all the way, of course.

Tony would only stay at the Peninsula Hotel, which was one of the costliest in Beverly Hills.

In addition, Danny had told Steve that his father liked to arrive in a city a couple of days before he was scheduled to perform, so that he could rest up and prepare. At the expense of the foundation, Fox reluctantly okayed the extra two days' lodging. Though the Peninsula had kindly offered us discounts for the out-of-town celebrities I booked with them, you can see how easily unexpected expenditures mounted up once an event was underway.

On top of that, when the Bennetts arrived at the hotel, Danny called Steve to say that actually what Tony had always really wanted to do was stay in the presidential suite. He was in the process of moving his father. The presidential suite cost over two thousand a night.

Steve hit the roof. "No way," he said. "The foundation is not going to pay for that. If Tony wants to stay in the suite, we'll pay what we originally agreed on, and he'll have to pay the difference himself."

After that, it really got ugly. Danny threatened that his father would pull out if he didn't get to stay where he wanted. Steve replied that if Tony Bennett reneged on his commitment, the Lasorda Foundation would ruin him in the press. Danny made some derogatory remarks about Steve; Steve told him to watch his step.

After Danny insulted him one last time, Steve said, "Okay, stay right there. I'm on my way over."

"And what are you going to do when you get here?" Danny asked.

"I'm going to write your instructions on your forehead, so

you will know," Steve said.

"F— you!" Danny said, and hung up.

Fox did go right over there too, but he couldn't locate Danny Bennett. No answer at his room. Steve never did find him. But he did get through to Tony, and when he told him what had transpired, Tony said not to worry. His room was fine. He wouldn't move into the suite, and he would perform as scheduled.

So, in the end, it all worked out. But that's a good example of one of the endless minor headaches an event producer has to endure when he works with stars and, even more so, the people around them. Every time. And, relatively speaking, this one wasn't so bad. As you'll see, matters can get much, much worse.

THE BENEFIT ITSELF WAS A DELIGHT, a beautiful night. The stars rolled up in their limos, stepped out under the overhang, and made their way up the red carpet into the Beverly Hills Hotel, as it if it were the Academy Awards. Stanchions were set up on either side, and behind them there were dozens of reporters and paparazzi, getting pictures, mini-interviews, and video footage from the celebrities as they arrived.

To get to the Crystal Ballroom, you passed through the lobby with its potted palms and pineapple-shaped, buttery leather kiosk seats and headed left down a long hall to a winding, descending, carpeted staircase. A tapered chandelier hung from the ceiling deep into the stairwell, and wall sconces held antique glass vases.

On the lower level, there was first a lobby where the silent auction was set up on several long tables. The bar was there as well. The walls were peach colored, and in the center was a huge chandelier with a hundred lights shaped like roses. Then there was the ballroom itself, also done in peach, with another rose chandelier. There was a full stage with a velvet curtain at one end, a small balcony with wrought iron railing at the other, big arched windows to the left, reflected in equally large arched mirrors to the right. It was lavish, to say the least.

Army Archerd reported the evening in his *Variety* column, specifically mentioning the full-size Steuben crystal baseball bat we awarded Billy Crystal "for his homeruns in the charity ballpark." Alan King started the show with Rob Reiner emceeing. Jay Leno surprised everyone by appearing to introduce Tony Bennett. Archerd failed to mention, however, that after Tony Bennett's standing ovation, the audience wouldn't shut up while he tried to sing. They were so loud he could hardly hear himself. In an attempt to quiet them down, Tony tried to perform his second song without the microphone. That didn't work either, so he quit right in the middle. I was supposed to get three songs; I got one and a half.

This wasn't untypical of Beverly Hills socialite crowds. They were often rude and disrespectful to performers. Steve Fox said later that it was partly due to the fact that Norby Walters—who was greeting everyone with his incredible BS line: "Never too big to say *hello!*"—was going around doling out wine, getting everyone as intoxicated as possible. They were partying so hard by the time Tony appeared that they barely knew where they were.

IT SEEMED LIKE, DURING THESE YEARS, there were a number of celebs who couldn't help but make things difficult for me, one of whom was Rodney Dangerfield.

Rodney was living at the Beverly Hilton Hotel at the time and was known for wandering around the lobby half-stoned, with his fly open and his shirt hanging out of it. I was friendly with him for a while, but couldn't handle his wild behavior—the man was constantly high, asking for dope. Mean and vicious, too.

One time, Cynthia, Hal Gershman, and I had bought a table to a black-tie event, and Cynthia, as usual, bugged the hell out of me to get a celebrity to sit with them. I was going crazy with other projects at the time, so I did a hack job of it. I got Rodney. He came with his date—a gorgeous, very much younger, blonde Mormon girl—dressed like a slob, smelling of booze.

Among the honorees was the president of France—there was some kind of commemorative tribute going on—and at one point Gregory Peck stood up and toasted him. Peck talked about World War II and what good friends of America the French were.

Then, in that loud voice of his, Rodney said to his group, "The only thing the French did was tell the Nazis where the Jews were hiding!" Everyone at the table was mortified except Hal Gershman, who laughed his head off. Cynthia, as usual, didn't get it.

A few moments later Peck, tall and distinguished in his tuxedo, proposed a toast. As everyone lifted their wine glasses, he said, "Vive la France!"

At that, Rodney jumped to his feet, raised his fist with fingers clenched and his thumb jabbing toward his crotch, and shouted, "Vive la France THIS!" The crowd closest to us fell silent. Security came to our table, asking Rodney to leave. He did. But on his way out, he asked me for a joint.

That was Rodney Dangerfield. So it was no surprise to me when he showed up at the Lasorda benefit, which was cocktail dress, in a jogging sweatsuit, unshaven, smelling like he hadn't bathed in a week, and seemingly loaded.

Steve spotted him at the check-in table, walked over, and said, "May I help you?"

"Do you know who I am?" Rodney contentiously asked. "I was invited to this event by Norby Walters." It was true. Norby had, of course, comped his pal.

"Yeah," Steve said, "I know who you are. Do you know who I am?"

That took Rodney by surprise. "No, who?"

"I'm the guy who is going to keep you out of here."

God, I loved Steve.

"Why?"

Steve sighed. "Because you stink and you're not properly dressed. Go home and take a shower, shave, and put on the right clothes."

Rodney did. And when he came back, Steve let him in.

No wonder Mr. Dangerfield gets no respect.

THE FINAL ACCOUNTING was a nightmare. The gross receipts went to the foundation that Jo Lasorda controlled, and then the expense money was paid back out to Steve Fox, who had generously fronted the cash for the event. Poor Steve was continually inundated with bills that he hadn't counted on, or that were much higher than expected. When all was said and done, we had taken in about $650,000—much too low, due mostly to the free tickets all the schnorrers had demanded and that I (and Norby) had foolishly given out. We had $400,000 in expenses—too high, due to the mistakes I made and the overages I was coerced into. Thus, we were able to clear only about $250,000. Now let met tell you, most charities would have been satisfied, even thrilled with, a quarter million. But I had set my goals much higher and was personally disappointed. Worse for me, the Lasordas were extremely upset.

One day, Steve told me Tommy was coming into the office to give me a "talking to" about my handling of expenses. *Just let him do it,* Steve said. *Just sit there and take it.*

Tommy immediately got almost nose-to-nose with me and screamed into my face, with spit spewing out of his mouth, like I was an umpire who'd just made a bad call. I barely heard the words, I was so stunned. I'd worked my fingers to the bone for the foundation, with virtually no help from the Lasordas.

Of course, I was as shocked as anyone that a mere 40 percent of the money we raised actually went to the foundation, although this was certainly not uncommon with charity galas.

As I was quickly coming to see, there was no avoiding this ugly truth about the business: people use these things for their own purposes. Vendors make exorbitant profits supplying the various goods and services needed; entertainers (even if they waive their performing fees) get comped for airfare and hotel rooms; and freeloaders (who are too cheap to even buy the basic ticket) come to mingle with the stars and sponge up food, drink, and goodie bags at the charities' expense.

Worse, sometimes people outright steal, as happened with the auction. After the event, we noticed some smaller items missing. Steve Fox called the people we'd hired to conduct the affair, and, after not returning his calls for two weeks, they finally admitted they took the items. *I guess you can always sue us,* they told him.

DESPITE ALL THE UNPLEASANTNESS, the Lasordas allowed me to produce another fundraiser for the foundation—Fight Night. I set it up to happen at the Ritz Carlton Hotel in Phoenix. I liked doing things in Arizona because it was familiar territory and it allowed me to touch base with old friends like Attorney General Grant Woods.

The idea behind the Fight Night fundraiser was that we would honor a real boxer and invite celebrities to pretend to spar with him. For the Phoenix event, I scheduled Sugar Ray Leonard and Tony Danza. Leonard agreed to appear for free. Danza committed, although he had to remain in L.A. for most of the day to film an episode of his sitcom. He said he would come if we would charter a jet to fly him down there for the evening, and then return. Which we did: a twin-engine King Air plane that cost the charity forty-eight hundred dollars for the fuel to fly to California and back.

But then, Danza didn't show at the airport, which we found out about at the very last minute (when these thing always happen). Steve Fox called and told Danza in no uncertain words what he thought of him.

"Well, I never really committed," Tony told him.

"Oh yeah?" Steve said. "Then why are you apologizing to

Tommy? I never would have sent a plane for you if that were the case, you lying piece of s—. The least you can do is make good on the money the foundation put out to fly you down here."

Tommy was reaching for the phone at this point, and Steve handed it back to him, saying disgustedly, "Some friends you got."

That was that. Danza didn't show, and the plane returned home. He never did reimburse the foundation, either. The expense had to come out of the benefit's proceeds.

Despite such fiascos, approximately a hundred twenty-five thousand dollars was raised for the foundation that night. The Lasordas, however, were still burning over the first event, and I didn't produce anything for them again.

But I did keep working—I was really beginning to fly.

nine

My Girls

I'm not particularly a fan of horse racing, and I don't gamble, but I was always dreaming up new ways to make money and develop new promotional ventures, and one day, as a budding entrepreneur, I recalled a trip I'd taken long ago.

Shortly after I had moved out of my parents' home in the mid-eighties I went to live with and work for a friend of the family, Jim Thomson. My parents couldn't handle me, and so his family took me in for a while. Jim ran a balloon business entitled Dynamic Displays, which sells giant inflatables for a wide range of events, including city Thanksgiving parades, the Olympics, and Super Bowls. I worked in sales, organized parades, and trained and supervised the many on-site volunteers who were needed to maneuver the giant inflatables (some of them sixty feet tall) down the street.

It was then, while soliciting business by phone, that I'd hooked up with a woman who ran a parade and festival in

Florence, Kentucky, who invited me to come down for the Jim Beam Stakes, a race that was just beginning a rise to national stature under its new owner, Jerry Carroll.

I went, had tons of fun, and got to meet a number of prominent people: Lee Greenwood, Wynonna Judd, former president Gerald Ford and his son Steven, both of whom I would be associated with later in California, and even Dr. Henry Heimlich, who developed the Heimlich Maneuver. It was a real thrill for me and an early taste of celebrity hobnobbing.

Naturally, I also tried to sell Jerry Carroll, the new owner, some of our inflatables. At the time, I didn't make the sell. But in 1996, now many miles, many years, and many achievements beyond the balloon business, I called Jerry out of the blue and tried to sell him on something entirely different.

"Jerry," I said, "I work with a lot of Hollywood stars, and I can bring a group of them to Kentucky for the Jim Beam Stakes. It'll be great publicity for the race. Some of them could perform, and others will just be there to be seen. I can get them to do it if you simply pay their expenses. And my fee, which is ten thousand dollars."

It was an incredible deal for him. His sponsors would love it, and it would greatly raise the profile of the race. He said yes.

So I brought Milton Berle, Red Buttons, Sid Caesar, Jasmine Guy, Harry Hamlin, and several others. Neil Sedaka sang. Everyone was happy. The stars had a ball; I made my ten grand. It worked out so well that Jerry Carroll invited me to do it all again next year. He promised me much more money and eventually a long-term contract.

With those promises in hand the following year, I, like an amateur gambler, raised the stakes too quickly, bringing in more stars, making the event more spectacular, and subsequently crapped out. The whole thing turned into a fiasco, even though it began with such promise.

We had a great cast of characters: John Forsythe, Linda Evans, Jerry Van Dyke, Barbara Eden, Molly Ringwald, Dean Cain, Catherine Oxenberg, Blair Underwood, Paula Abdul, and Wayne Newton, who, like always, was a big hit.

But things turned sour the first day. A horse broke its leg during the last race. They had to euthanize it, right out there on the track. It was horrible and proved to be an omen of ill fate for the weekend's festivities.

Later that night, Jerry Carroll hosted a private restaurant cocktail party and dinner for the stars and showed up drunk. He stepped up right in Wayne Newton's face and insulted him. I was mortified. Wayne had flown in from Vegas at his own expense, come to his party, and asked for not a dime. Wayne should have just decked him on the spot, but of course is too much of a gentleman for that.

Later still, poor Catherine Oxenberg was in her hotel room, when Carroll showed up outside the door and began beating on it, yelling, "Let me in, let me in!" She had no idea what he wanted with her, but thought the worst. She was terrified. The next day, when she told me the story, I had to apologize profusely to her for Carroll's inexplicable behavior.

All of this, of course, was prelude to the fight over money. I'd already determined I wasn't going to speak to Jerry Carroll ever again after the way he'd treated my guests. But he still owed me—a lot. And when it came time to pay up, he simply refused.

Needless to say, this was an absolute disaster for me. Already in desperate financial straits, I had put out a lot of money for the stars' expenses and made cash payments to others—especially Dean Cain, who never did anything for free but always wanted cash upfront, and Barbara Eden, whom I'd given ten grand because Carroll had a thing for her and wanted her there (I guess he dreamed of Jeannie more than most). I'd been promised reimbursement for this, and now I wasn't going to get it. I should have sued but ate my losses instead. I couldn't afford a lawyer and didn't want the endless hassle of legal proceedings. Like a shark, if I didn't keep moving I was going to die.

THE WORST OF THE JIM BEAM STAKES fallout involved Paula Abdul. I really wanted to get in with her, so within a few weeks of meeting her, I was gifting her with Cartier jewelry and lavish items from Alfred Dunhill, spending tens of thousands on her. I thought I was improving my client list by courting her like this. In reality, as I was to eventually find out, I was giving her way too much in relation to her market value—this was years after the huge success of her debut album and years before her reemergence as the kind-hearted foil to Simon Cowell on *American Idol.* Oh, if only they knew.

Paula, as it turned out, was a chronic whiner. She would grouse and kvetch about every little thing. Once I tried to help Paula out by getting her a new publicist—she later dropped her and told me she was getting calls almost every day, with her complaining about how awful her life was.

Anyway, I was seeing a lot of Paula at the time of the Jim Beam Stakes. I asked her if she'd do me a favor by going there.

Not to sing, just to show up. She said no. I offered to pay her a hundred thousand to do it. She said yes. People later told me that was about ninety-five grand more than her going rate, but I was, unfortunately, getting used to throwing around large sums of money that I didn't actually have. Though it was completely irresponsible, I figured I'd probably be able to pay her out of the long-term money Jerry Carroll was going to give me. God, what a fool I was.

When I got stiffed by Carroll, I had to tell Paula I couldn't pay her the hundred thou immediately. I offered to set up a payment schedule, and she told me what I could do with myself. She sued me for the whole amount.

I woke up from a nap one day to Leeza Gibbons on the TV, telling all about the lawsuit. Two years before, Leeza herself accepted thousands of dollars in jewelry and other gifts from me, for her, her husband, and her children, for hosting a charity cocktail reception at her home. I'll get into that in a minute.

Paula appeared on the broadcast to say I had "messed with the wrong girl" and she intended to collect every penny owed her. Sweet and wronged, but tough as can be. Of course, there was no mention of all the things I'd done for her: the travel expenses, the jewelry. No one even contacted me for my side of the story. The report only said they had "tried" to reach me—like I was that hard to find: Leeza knew me personally and had all my phone numbers.

There *was* a silver lining to all the nastiness with Abdul, though.

Paula hired Philip Levy as her lawyer in her suit against me, which ended with my consenting to an entry of judgment against me and in favor of Paula. I never was able to pay her any of the money, but I did get to meet Phil, who later became my own lawyer and, more important, a close friend, a relationship I am so blessed with and have enjoyed to the present day.

Phil also represented Paula in her later divorce, after which he was forced to bring an action against her for non-payment of her bill, totaling about thirty-five thousand dollars. When asked in court why she wouldn't pay, Paula declared:

"You just don't understand. I'm down to my last million!"

PAULA ABDUL WAS BY NO MEANS the first diva I had the displeasure of dealing with. In fact, one year earlier I had come face-to-face with true Hollywood royalty (and a royal pain in both cheeks) in the form of Melanie Griffith.

It started in 1995 when I met Melanie's famous mother, Tippi Hedren, the beautiful, petite blonde who starred in Alfred Hitchcock's 1963 movie *The Birds.* Hedren chaired the ROAR Foundation, which maintained the Shambala Preserve, a place on the edge of the Mojave Desert that provided a sanctuary for endangered animals. These were mostly big cats, lions, tigers, cheetahs, etc., that hadn't come from the wild. They'd been born in captivity and become orphaned or been cast-off by their owners.

I got involved with Tippi because I liked her and I loved animals, but also because I thought I'd be able to produce a lot of really successful events if I had a famous actress like Melanie Griffith to help out.

Wrong again.

Melanie, like so many children of Hollywood stars, turned

out to be a spoiled brat who hated the idea of lifting a finger to help anyone, much less her mother, whom, as far as I could tell, she berated every chance she got. Tippi was often reduced to tears as she told me how much her daughter hurt her.

But I plunged ahead, organizing a fabulous three-tier event for December 16, 1995, to be called Humane for Hollywood. Leeza Gibbons, who had her own very popular TV talk show at the time, offered her house for the cocktail reception. The party would then move to the Thunder Roadhouse, which was on Sunset Boulevard in the heart of the Strip, for dinner. And the evening would end with a nightcap at Alfred Dunhill of London, in Beverly Hills.

Melanie Griffith and her future husband, actor Antonio Banderas, were to be among the featured star attractions and co-hosts. Tippi was supposed to line them up, which she did, sort of. That is, Melanie grudgingly agreed, after I paid her with thousands of dollars' worth of Alfred Dunhill luggage for her and Antonio. It was one of my first experiences with providing gifts to a star to help a charity function along. It would certainly not be my last.

So the happy couple were coming. But just a few days before the event, Melanie wrote her mother a hateful, vitriolic letter, which Tippi read to me. Melanie said, to put it politely, that she didn't want to be involved in petty affairs like this, and accused Tippi of using her, and all kinds of other terrible things. Put succinctly, she said, why didn't her mother just get the hell out of there, move back to Los Angeles, and forget about the damn animals.

Then she refused to help us with publicity. A professional publicist friend of Tippi's had offered to donate her time and expertise in this area, but Melanie wouldn't cooperate. Melanie personally called the publicist and said, "I don't care that you are doing this event for free. I will do no publicity to help you out, no matter what. *None!*"

This turned out to be a serious problem, since Leeza Gibbons had offered to devote an entire show to ROAR and the fundraiser. They were going to put a phone number up on the screen, so that people could call donations in. The producer told me they never did that sort of thing.

I tried to work through the publicist to get Melanie Griffith to change her mind.

"Tell her this," I said, "I know you told us *no press*. But this is a once-in-a-lifetime opportunity. It's Leeza Gibbons for an hour. It'll be great for your mom's charity."

The publicist tried. But this was Melanie's response: "I thought I told you no f—ing way. No f—ing *publicity!* I am not doing *anything!*" And she hung up on the publicist.

Despite Melanie's lack of cooperation, the event was proving hugely popular. Leeza had specified that there should be a limit of two hundred guests at her home, but the requests kept pouring in. I didn't want to turn anyone away since each ticket bought meant a donation to the charity. Finally, there were four hundred people coming. Leeza wasn't happy, but I calmed her down by giving watches to her and her husband, and other expensive gifts to her kids.

A whole host of stars came to the cocktail reception at Leeza's: Loni Anderson, Dennis Hopper, Patrick Swayze, and many others, including Melanie and Antonio, who were late, naturally. I didn't know until the last second if they were actually going to show at all.

Cynthia Gershman was there too, of course. Always ready with a tactful remark, Cynthia, upon meeting Tippi Hedren, said to the glamorous star of *The Birds* as well as *Marnie,* not "Hi" or "How are you," but, "When can I meet Melanie Griffith and get my picture taken with her?"

The house that Leeza Gibbons lived in was a beautiful Mediterranean home that used to be owned by Joan Crawford. It had been completely redone and modernized, of course, but one of my friends who was there joked that he'd gone through the closets, looking for the coat hangers Crawford hit her kids with.

When it came time to adjourn to the Thunder Roadhouse, I found myself riding in a limo alone with Melanie Griffith and Antonio Banderas. It was a freezing cold night for Southern California, and Melanie, who was wearing a full fur coat to an animal rights charity event, complained the whole way.

"I always have to f—ing rescue her and her f—ing charity," she said about her mother.

Banderas was quiet but friendly; he seemed like a nice guy. I wondered why he was with Melanie. Maybe it was what she could do with those collagen-pumped lips—some of the biggest I'd ever seen. Made her look like a freak.

Of course, it could be those lips hadn't been altered at all, but were merely the result of years of pouting as a Hollywood brat.

I MADE INITIAL CONTACT with most celebrities through friends of friends or my patented cold call. But it took money to get to Natalie Cole. Twenty-two hundred dollars to be exact.

That was my winning bid to lunch with her, the result of a silent auction held at Nancy Davis's annual Race To Erase MS charity fundraiser. I had been wanting to meet Natalie for some time. And I admired her music, as well as her father's. I thought we'd get along. Besides, it was for a worthy cause.

We met at the Grill on the Alley, just off of Rodeo Drive, considered to be one of the places to see and be seen in Beverly Hills. It was where many film industry executives met with actors and their agents for power lunches. It was also one of the restaurants with which I had a relationship—which meant in return for bringing celebrities there, I got preferred seating and a house account that I naturally couldn't afford.

Nancy invited herself to the lunch, along with her friend Lynne, a type I became very familiar with in Hollywood, what I called "The Best Friend." These were primary sycophants, people who didn't seem to have much identity of their own, but who gained status simply by being known (and often announcing themselves) as the best friend of someone rich and famous. They would follow their idols around, agree with everything they said, and kiss tail at every opportunity. This seemed to work equally well for both parties.

But I could tell that Lynne was here for reasons beyond filling her "best friend" role. Nancy had brought her along in a desperate attempt to keep some distance between Natalie and me. She was, in essence, protecting her turf.

Nancy didn't want me becoming too chummy with "her" celebrity. Those who host, sponsor, or produce events are always in competition with others trying to do the same. Forget the charity part: fundraising is a cutthroat business. Once you get a celeb on your side, you want to keep them there.

And in Natalie Cole's case, matters were further complicated by the Davises' relationship with her. Natalie liked to hang with the fabulously wealthy as much as they liked having her around. To show her appreciation, not only did Natalie help raise money for the Race, she also performed at many of the Davises' private functions for free. This made her, even more, one of "their" stars, and it made me just another competitor. God forbid she and I hit it off, and Natalie appear at one of my own charity events.

The plan worked, too. Though the lunch was pleasant enough, it seemed carefully orchestrated. Every time I began to have any kind of meaningful dialogue with Natalie Cole, Lynne would butt in with stupid questions, pretending an interest in subjects she couldn't have cared less about. This effectively prevented me from connecting with Natalie. I paid the bill, and that was that for two years.

In 1996, however, lunch with Natalie went up for auction once more at the Race To Erase MS. Again, I spent over a thousand dollars and won.

Once again, I chose the Grill, and once again, Nancy showed up with her pal Lynne in tow. This time, though, I was better prepared. I brought along a new friend and benefactor of my own, Raymond Caldiero, who at the time was the senior vice-president of Northwest Airlines and had previously been a senior vice-president and assistant to Bill Marriott of Marriott Corp.

As Ray kept Lynne and Nancy occupied, with Nancy pushing him hard to donate free first-class air travel with Northwest for her next fundraiser, I focused completely on Natalie, and this time we really connected. She was sweet and kind and genuine. I was glad to finally meet a kindred Christian soul in this town, since I was struggling with my own faith— something I'll explore in later. I thought she would be a good influence on me. I didn't really know about her past at that point. It wasn't until I read *People* magazine's cover story, several years later, when they were discussing her just-published autobiography that I learned about her years of drug and alcohol addiction, and prostitution.

After lunch, I said to everyone at the table that I was presently representing Alfred Dunhill of London in some promotional activities and suggested that we all go over to the store on Rodeo Drive.

"I'll try to use my influence to get them to give you a few things," I told Natalie.

They took the bait. No one hesitated for a second. What I really meant was that, since Natalie Cole was a well-known singer, the people at Alfred Dunhill would probably give her some stuff so they and I could use that in our promotions. Places such as Dunhill liked to be able to say to their clients something along the lines of, "Natalie Cole was just in. Would you like to see what she bought?" Many publicists in town worked this way, hooking up celebrities with stores to promote their products.

So off we went.

Let the shopping spree begin.

I spent about eighteen grand that day. Dunhill gave me a nice discount, but the goods didn't come free. To me, it was part of the cost of doing business. I believed I was currying favor with a celebrity, hoping that would lead to her doing things for me in the future.

And it worked. By the time we were finally done, Natalie had given me her home phone number.

THE KEY TO A WOMAN'S HEART, I found early on, was jewelry. And it was the best way I knew to win and hold onto relationships with female celebs.

The way I was able to provide such extravagant gifts was by establishing relationships with prestigious stores such as Dunhill, Seidler's of Boston, and Cartier. As a part of my charity fundraising efforts, I would go through upscale magazines and tear out advertisements by luxury companies selling cars, boats, motorcycles, vacations, jewelry, and so on. I would then send them one of my standard presale letters on event stationery, signed by a big star, with a further list of dozens of celebrities who had agreed to be on the committee, or to participate in some other way.

The company would then be invited, by our big star personally, to take part in our live and silent auctions. Included was a form for the vendor to fill out, specifying what he wanted to donate to the live or silent auctions, or both. It usually worked. In some cases, it was a one-shot deal, but in others I would use them over and over. I secured goods to auction, the charities got money, and the stores got publicity. I would also arrange for celebrities to attend things like new store openings or special shows, with the expectation that I would get money, gift items, or other favors in return.

It was an arrangement beneficial to all parties, except me. The problem was, these places were often willing to sell me very expensive items for my personal use, at a discount. They knew I was giving the stuff to famous personalities, and to have a star wearing their jewelry was a walking advertisement for them. Very good for their business, not so good for my finances. I had house accounts with these luxury vendors. Big mistake. My desire to please my friends and clients, by doling out pricey jewelry, just drove me deeper into debt. We're talking hundreds of thousands of dollars' worth, to Natalie Cole alone.

I had worked particularly hard to get Brooke Shields to two events sponsored by Cartier, showering her with jewelry, paying for a beautifully-tailored tuxedo from Alfred Dunhill for Andre Agassi to wear in their upcoming marriage ceremony, as well as a pair of watches. Brooke took it and took off without so much as a thank-you note.

After lavishing all this jewelry and gifts on Shields, Abdul, Cole, and all the rest of the women I was courting, I ran up quite a bill. Never thinking, *How am I going to pay it?* Just charging away like there would never be a reckoning. It was like I was on crack. The spending was an addiction, just like any other, and I couldn't break the habit because the alternative was far more horrifying to me: losing my relationships with the stars. Money was their lifeblood.

My tab came to nearly one million dollars with Cartier alone. I had nothing like that kind of money. Steve Fox ended up covering half of it for me. The rest, I just ignored. Cartier never came after me. I don't know why. Probably because they decided it wouldn't be worth all the negative publicity of a lawsuit to try to squeeze something out of me that they knew I didn't have. It would make them look bad to have gotten in so deep with me, no matter what. Maybe they even figured my promotional efforts had been worth a few hundred grand.

I lucked out with Cartier. I would not be so lucky with others.

SOMETIME IN MID-1996, Jill Eisenstadt, a great lady who worked for the public relations firm Loving & Weintraub and would later become Arnold Schwarzenegger's publicist, approached me with a job. A very upscale European clothing/ department store called Etro was scheduled to open its first American branch on Madison Avenue in New York, on October 25. And since I was often working with high-fashion stores, and had one of the best Rolodexes in town, they wanted me to pull in a few Hollywood personalities for the grand opening.

They promised to pay me and guaranteed that Etro would provide giveaways for the celebs, in the form of a twenty-five-hundred-dollar gift certificate for clothes each, and another for their spouses or companions.

It sounded like a good deal all around. Even though I knew that there were many competing events in that time slot— including the glitzy Carousel of Hope Ball in L.A.—and that, therefore, many of the top names would already be committed, I took it on.

As was often the case, and just as often to my regret, we agreed to everything on a handshake basis. I was fairly new at this game and seldom thought to get a firm contract in writing. Besides, Hollywood is a business based on handshakes, and I was just following its example.

Jill faxed me a list of fifty suggested stars the company wanted, just twelve days before the event. Not much notice. But I did the best I could and in the end lined up Dean Cain, Neil Sedaka and his wife, Lorna and Milton Berle, and a group of hot, young TV stars. They committed not only to the opening but to the after-party as well.

I arranged first-class airline tickets for them, along with ground limo transportation and accommodations at the St. Regis Hotel, one of the most expensive and elegant in New York City. On her end, Jill had sent out press releases, set up in-store promotions, and so on. All based on the assurance of personal appearances by my celebrities.

Then, almost at the point where I was walking out the door to go to the airport, Jill called.

"I'm sorry," she said. "I didn't get authorization to pay the expenses of the stars. Not the travel or the hotel bill. And . . . the store isn't going to give them any gifts, either." Nor, it seemed, was I going to get paid.

"Huh?" was all I could get out.

"I don't know what happened," she said. "Either they reneged on their promise, or it was all a big misunderstanding."

I was stunned. I'd already charged the airfare and was responsible for the accommodations. Not to mention the fact that the stars were attending, in large part, in order to receive all the free clothing. I never would have done this if the store wasn't backing it, I said. What should I do now?

"I guess you'll just have to cancel the stars," Jill replied.

Are you kidding? I can't do that. We're already on our way, I thought, then told her I'd get right back to her.

As a test, I called the celeb I was closest to, Milton Berle. I got Lorna on the phone and said, "How would you feel about canceling and not going to New York?"

"*What!?*" she said.

"There's been a . . . . mixup."

"Look," she said, "Milton is sitting on the edge of the bed putting on his pants right now. If you cancel, we will never go to or support anything of yours again."

"Okay," I said. "See you at the airport. Don't worry, I'll take care of everything."

I phoned Jill back and said, "We're coming. We'll have to figure all this out ourselves."

What "figuring it out" actually meant was that, as usual, I would foot the bill for the entire trip, including travel expenses and the stars' shopping sprees at Etro. Neither Jill nor Etro nor Loving & Weintraub came through with one single cent. It strained my relationship with Jill for a while, but eventually I decided she had been used as well and that the blame lay with her employer and the store. She tried to make it up to me in other ways, but it crushed me financially.

In the meantime, though, I had to come up with the money. The only way I could do it was to get a crooked business associate of mine to charge everything on his credit cards, then pay him back plus 25 percent interest with a loan I got from Steve Fox.

I got totally hosed on the Etro event. When all was said and done, I spent eighty thousand on the trip, not including the interest on the loan. I should have just cancelled and accepted the consequences. But I didn't. I still had the mindset that it was critically important to keep the stars happy, no matter what. I didn't want any damage to my reputation. I was mortally afraid I would lose what I had.

Up today, down tomorrow—that was the way of life in Hollywood. It was why wealthy stars always took handouts, because they never knew when the gravy train was going to run out of track. And I was much the same. I did whatever I had to do to stay on the rails, which, of course, eventually led to a monumental train wreck.

IT WAS QUICKLY BECOMING APPARENT to me that in the world of celebrity fundraising, the only real charity cases were spoiled stars and their associates. The events were called benefits, of course, but the ones that benefited the most were the rich and famous, who use these affairs, not to help the needy, but for their own self-aggrandizement. Some can be bought to show their faces; others attend simply to get their pictures in the papers; still others will take any freebie they're offered. But corporate sponsors are also making out, accumulating the goodwill value of being associated with a noble cause. Manufacturers and retailers profit, as well. They know that donating one item can result in the future sale of many similar items.

Then there's the media, which benefits in more ways than one. Obviously, stars generate stories they can put into print or on TV. But that's not where it ends. There are as many ways to exploit a charity as there are people to think them up. For instance, consider my involvement with the magazine, *Vanity Fair.*

Vanity Fair is an upscale magazine for upwardly mobile people who, they hope, will buy the upscale products they advertise in their pages. Their viability as a publication depends upon their success at getting and holding the kind of clients who will be repeat advertisers, and thereby pay the freight. They'll do anything to keep these folks happy. Understandably, the more prestigious the client, the more they're willing to do. Which is where people like me come in.

I got hooked up with *Vanity Fair* because of a mega-event called Friends Helping Friends that I was just in the beginning stages of organizing and producing. As one of my first steps, I sent out many letters seeking support for the Friends gala. One of them ended up on the desk of Jean Karlson, who at the time was director of creative services for the magazine.

Jean called me, and I took a meeting with her. She was impressed with me and especially with my vision for the event. It looked like a good fit. I needed sponsors; she was looking for something young and hip to associate some of her clients/advertisers with. So *Vanity Fair* became one of the sponsors of the Friends night. Jean did a great deal for us, bringing in Calvin Klein and Halston and other big names.

But it all came for a price. Corporate sponsorship was rarely a straight "just let us help you because it is charity" kind of thing. Jean requested a free full-page ad in the event journal, a thank you by name from the stage, multiple free tables, and all kinds of other extras, as we shall see. And she had me pay her, personally, a 10 percent cash commission on the value of all donations she steered my way. Anything for a worthy cause, right?

In addition, sometimes the sponsor will ask you for favors unconnected to the event they're sponsoring. That's what happened with *Vanity Fair* in this instance. Jean Karlson called me up and told me she'd been contacted by John Martens, the general manager of Neiman Marcus in Beverly Hills. They were throwing a dinner party in West Hollywood for the famous fashion designer, Emmanuel Ungaro, and Jean asked me if I could deliver some celebrities. At no cost to the store, of course.

I couldn't very well turn them down. *Vanity Fair* was doing a lot to help with my other event. So I said okay.

I asked Penelope Ann Miller, Julia Louis Dreyfuss, Jane Seymour, and others, including my constant companion, Natalie Cole. A little schmoozing, a lot of jewelry, and I had my celebs.

I PERSONALLY ACCOMPANIED NATALIE to the Ungaro dinner and was pleased to find that everything looked great. There were cocktails upstairs and one long table beautifully set out downstairs. I greeted my stars as they showed up. They all came. I wanted the evening to be perfect because I wanted to solidify my new relationship with *Vanity Fair*. I expected that it would lead to bigger and better things.

Natalie was clearly stressed. All she had talked about on the ride in was her boyfriend Francesco and their problems. The night before we had been at a performance of Engelbert Humperdinck in Las Vegas (I had paid for all of her and her fiancé's travel expenses) and things turned really sour. Natalie and Francesco were always fighting about money—which Francesco had none of—and when he went through Natalie's purse without permission, things exploded. She reprimanded him, and he pitched a fit and threw the purse across the room, all right in front of everyone. It was humiliating, but par for the course for Natalie and Francesco.

I had told her, *You should break up with him unless you*

like being mistreated. You are beautiful inside and out and have so much to give. You deserve someone who will properly love you back.

She agreed, and promised that she would do something about it. Which of course she didn't. Which led to further embarrassment for all involved, including me.

That night, at the Ungaro dinner, Francesco arrived at the cocktail reception, unexpected and unwelcome. He marched in like he owned the place, confronted Natalie, and led her downstairs where the two started to fight.

To avoid the melee, I veered into the dining room and got another big surprise. Looking at the seating chart, I discovered that Natalie was seated alone near Ungaro while I was relegated to the *schlepper* section way off at the far end. I was Natalie's "date" for the evening and should have been seated right next to her. Also, I was the one who arranged the stars, who twisted their arms when they didn't want to show, who put up his own money to secure their attendance. And now I was getting the shaft? I was pissed.

I found John Martens, from Neiman Marcus, and he didn't even know who I was.

So I introduced myself, told him I was the one who had brought Julia Louis Dreyfuss, Penelope Ann Miller, Jane Seymour, and Natalie Cole to his dinner, and explained the problem with the seating.

Coolly, he told me I wasn't important enough to be seated next to Mr. Ungaro. My mouth dropped open.

"Look," I said, "it'll be very awkward for Miss Cole to be there without me. It will make her feel uncomfortable, especially since I invited her to attend with me."

He wouldn't budge. "If you don't like it," he informed me, "you can go."

That was when I lost it. I was already becoming known around town for my emotional outbursts, and John Martens was about to find out why. I let him have one right in the face, nose-to-nose with him.

"Go f— yourself!" I shouted. Then added, "Suck my f—ing d—!" I left him standing there, stunned, and went over to the bathrooms and told Natalie and Francesco we were leaving.

They were still going at it. Before I could tell them what happened, Francesco lit into me, heaping insults on me while his girlfriend, predictably, refused to come to my defense. *Gee,* I thought to myself, *maybe if I give her another hundred thousand in jewelry it'll help.* Pretty soon, we were all screaming and carrying on. It got so bad the restaurant manager had to tell us to take it outside.

Francesco shoved Natalie into his car. I got into mine and drove home. I was sure our little scene was going to make the tabloids, but luckily it never did. I was also worried that the incident might screw up my relationship with *Vanity Fair,* but when I called Jean Karlson to tell her what had happened, she said not to worry. She didn't like John Martens very much, he was a big snob, and besides, we had a more significant event to keep working on.

My reward for my long-term relationship with *Vanity Fair,* which continued through the aforementioned Friends Helping Friends event, the Family Celebration event in 2001, and later included my convincing Natalie Cole to perform inexpensively for a group of their top advertisers, as well as getting Wayne Newton to open his entire estate to them, was a hatchet job article on me that they ran in August of 2003, fraught with inaccuracies

ANOTHER WOMAN I MET at this time was Joan Collins. I asked for it. I wanted to meet her. Joan represented the very essence of Hollywood glamour to me and many others, and I believed she would be an excellent addition to my Rolodex.

"Aaron," a colleague of mine that worked with Collins told me as we set about to arrange a meeting with her, "as your friend I have to tell you, she's really greedy. Everything with Joan is always *more, bigger, better,* you know what I mean? Even though she has more money than she knows what to do with, she still doesn't like to pay for anything. I'd be careful with her if I were you."

I should have listened.

I, of course, had that supreme confidence that I could take control of any situation. Things worked out for me, I thought, one way or another. Besides, I hoped she might actually be a little like her sister, Jackie, a really decent person who never allowed me to comp her for anything.

When she wasn't at her home in Europe, Joan Collins lived in the Sierra Towers on Doheny Road, right where Beverly Hills and West Hollywood meet. It's an ultra-ritzy, high-rise condominium complex, with apartments in the half-to-three million dollar range. A lot of celebrities, like Diahann Carroll and Sidney Poitier, live there.

I told her I'd like her to be one of the stars that came to my events. I told her she'd get gifts, expensive jewelry. She said okay, and we shook hands on it. As a token of good faith, I asked her to call Jane Seymour, to get her to come out for the Ungaro dinner, which Jane did. Then we embarked on one of the costliest journeys of my life.

As I've said, I had a relationship with Cartier, whereby they would discount jewelry to me, and I would gift stars with it. They were also supposed to support my charity events. In 1997, Cartier was celebrating its one-hundred-fiftieth anniversary, with all sorts of events planned, capped off with a glittery, black-tie gala at the Metropolitan Museum of Art on Fifth Avenue in New York. Cartier wanted it to be the party of the year. So they gave me a call. They wanted celebrities. To protect my discount arrangement with them, and my house charge account, I agreed to round up the usual suspects for free.

I also decided to bring out Joan Collins. If there was anyone who truly belonged at a celebration of one hundred fifty years of Cartier jewelry, it was the queen of *Dynasty*. Joan Collins, now in my coterie of stars, agreed. But first there was the matter of our little quid pro quo. I offered to take her to Cartier, prior to the celebration, and buy her a watch. How little did I know, this woman was in a league all her own.

When we got to the Beverly Hills Cartier, as agreed, I let her pick out a watch, a super expensive one, of course. And that should have been the end of it. But it wasn't. "Oh, by the way," she explained in her most charming, persuasive tone, "I have a bit of a predicament. You see, my daughter is getting married, and I *so* want to give her a really nice wedding present. Can you help me out?"

Joan knew a mark when she saw one. I had the big red

bulls-eye right in the middle of my back. I said, "Sure, go ahead and get something for her."

She picked another watch, absurdly expensive. Then she said she really wanted to get something for her future son-in-law, as well. What could I do for her there?

At this point, my colleague took me aside and said, "Aaron, you agreed to give her a watch. You don't have to give her anything more. . . . It's too much, too soon. It's not how things are done in this business. Her family is her concern, not yours."

He was talking to a wall. Joan Collins was going to get whatever she wanted. It was a business expense for me, and money well spent, I thought. The son-in-law got his watch as well, and now we were ready to tally up the bill. After the discount, it came to seventy thousand dollars. That's right, seventy grand for three watches, discounted.

Joan left feeling very pleased with herself, I suspect. She'd scored a fine piece of jewelry for herself, plus taken care of her wedding present expenses, all at no cost to her. Who wouldn't be happy? And still it wasn't over. I promised to take her to Etro the next time we were in New York, merely a month or so later.

Both she and I were in the city on separate business, and we went to the high-priced fashion store. I had helped—to say the least—with their opening six months earlier and had an account with them. *Fine*, she said. When we arrived at Etro, I told her to pick out some gifts for herself.

What followed was an orgy of spending the likes of which none of us had ever seen. Not me. Not my colleague. Not even the staff at Etro, one of whom made a point of telling me how stunned she was. But it was Joan Collins doing the buying (with me paying), and that was great for them.

Etro features high-end, mostly European clothing, jewelry, and housewares, and it's eight stories tall. Joan simply started at the top and worked her way to the bottom, floor by floor, saying *I'll take this* and *I'll take that*. She took everything from clothes to luggage, right on down to plant holders and custom garbage cans. Yep, *custom garbage cans.*

It was like watching a swarm of locusts. Plenty of the items she picked were things she already had, of course. But that was Joan, and he knew it. The stuff was free, there was a sucker standing there waiting to pay the bill, and so she was going to help herself. Simply because she could.

"Aaron, can you afford to do this?" asked my colleague. "Are you taking care of yourself here? You have to learn how to say no. You don't understand these people. I do. I was raised in this business. They will take advantage of you, then turn on you. I don't think you should be doing what you're doing."

And once again, I didn't listen.

For her pièce de résistance, Joan got together with the store management and told them she wanted everything shipped to various locations. She didn't have to carry anything. She walked out of the store without a bag.

When all was said and done, I wound up charging a hundred forty grand to my Etro account. One afternoon, one shopping spree. Together with her Cartier haul, Joan had picked up over two-hundred-thousand's worth of luxury goods without having to fork over a dime. Not a bad haul.

But I got it back on my end, right? When she went to all those celebrity bashes with me? No, sir.

At the Cartier celebration at the Museum of Modern Art the following night, Joan didn't show. In fact, she never appeared at a single one of my events. And still I tried to ply her with gifts to come out.

She always blew me off. Once she even called David Niven Jr., who was chairing a charity event I was organizing, to complain that she hadn't gotten some gift I'd promised her and that therefore I wasn't a man of my word. This after all the hundreds of thousands in gifts she'd received from me. Unbelievable nerve.

Joan Collins was probably one of the greediest, most irresponsible person I ever met in Hollywood, and that is saying a lot.

"HOW ABOUT FOR TEN THOUSAND?" I asked Natalie, knowing full well it was my own money on the line and nobody else's. Ralph Destino, the chairman emeritus of Cartier, had asked me on the spot to persuade Natalie Cole to perform at their big celebration, and now I had to persuade her. She gave me a look, and so I started going up. I didn't stop until I got to seventy-five.

At that point Natalie said, "Cash?"

"Yes," I said. What an idiot.

Seventy-five grand for one song, just one of many cash payments I made to her (and numerous other stars) over the years. The payments meant a great deal to her—money in hand without having to deal with agents or publicists, and their fees, and without having to put forth much effort. In this instance, Natalie got such applause for "Paper Moon" she did an encore, "Route 66." Maybe for two songs she thought I got my money's worth. I don't know what she did with all the cash. I can only hope that she properly reported it as income.

But why did I do it, when I was burned again and again by contentious stars with little sense of shame and no sense of loyalty? Why did, as Steve Fox would continually put it to me, I continue to throw good money after bad? *You can't buy these people's friendship,* he would say. *They will take and take until you can't give any more, and then they will drop you.*

Why? It's easy, really: I'd made it. I was living the life that had been my dream since I was a small child. I'd accomplished grandiose things, with the odds stacked heavily against me. I was very proud of what I'd achieved. In a few short years, starting from zero, I had made myself a person to reckon with in Hollywood. I was hobnobbing with the elite in that town. Some of the most important people in the biz were coming to me, and me alone, for favors only I could deliver. For a man who refused to do drugs, tossing around money, buying the affections of celebrities was one hell of a high.

All the while, though, I was living hand-to-mouth. I never turned a profit from these spectacularly expensive events. Quite the contrary, I fell deeper and deeper into debt.

But I still felt like I was getting somewhere. Natalie Cole and I were growing closer. In part, because she was one of my few friends who was a practicing Christian. We prayed together and sometimes went to church together. I liked going to Natalie's church, which was all African-American and located in the Crenshaw area, a poorer part of Los Angeles. Not only was I enjoying the religious experience, I was being immersed in another culture, a very different one from the phony Hollywood society I frequented the rest of the week.

Natalie once gave me a devotional that I treasure to this day. Inside, she enclosed a handwritten note that said:

Dear Aaron,

Here is the devotional pamphlet I told you about. Read it *faithfully*. Ask for *wisdom* and *spiritual maturity*. Pray for guidance.

God hears and He is faithful.

> With Love,
> Natalie

This kind of feminine attention was something I craved but rarely received. Part of it, I'm sure, goes back to the coldness of the women in my own family.

There was always conflict in my home, growing up, and much of it seemed to revolve around my relationship with my mother and sisters. When I first moved out as a young man, I went to live with the Thomsons, longtime friends of the family who owned the inflatables business. While I was there, Jim helped me understand my family better; he knew us all very well and helped me think through some of the problems. I was surrounded by passionate, highly opinionated, strong-willed women. Everyone wanted to be top dog. My sisters were high achievers—they excelled at school. Yet I, who was a terrible student, got the favored treatment. It was a situation that was bound to lead to conflict.

Jim remembered one time when I'd taken a light globe off a lamppost and stood in the middle of the road in front of my house, screaming for my mother until she appeared. When she did, I dropped the globe right in front of her. It shattered into a million pieces. I told him that I always craved attention, yet at the same time I wanted to be disciplined. Or, at least, have someone *care enough* to discipline me. Instead, I was largely ignored.

My father gave me a beautiful quarter horse, which I named Sadat Straw. I loved him, rode all the time. We kept the horse on a farm where my dad rented space. Also stocked with ducks, chickens, geese, and other critters, I would be driven almost every day to the farm after school by our maid. It was partly to play with the animals, but also to keep me away from home for a little longer. My two sisters hated to be anywhere near me. Eventually, dad built them separate bedrooms above the garage, and that was their sanctuary. The rooms were officially off limits to me, which was undoubtedly for the best. Not that it didn't hurt in the long run.

I never did develop a healthy relationship with either of my sisters and am still totally estranged from Melissa, the elder of the two.

Heidi and I were on-again, off-again as adults, with our high point coming at the Clinton Salute, to which I invited her. I helped her out financially after I became successful in California while she was in medical school. I really wanted my sisters to love me and tried hard with Heidi. I flew her to L.A., put her up in the Beverly Hills Hotel, wined and dined her, took her to parties, and gave her lavish treatment. All for naught. Our relationship ruptured after I got in trouble with the law. In my time of gravest need, when families are supposed to come together, I got nothing.

My mom and I pretty much split ways after my father died

in 1987, not that we were close then. I'd always loved my mom. But she was very self-involved, and I required extra effort. No doubt about it: I was difficult. But rather than try to understand me, she sent me to boarding school. Rather than show me the love I needed, she had me leave home because I was a pain. I don't put all the blame on her, but I can't deny she bears some of it.

Without that feminine affection in my life as a child, when I was older I went pursuing it by other, more costly means.

ONE OF THE REASONS I had come to Los Angeles in the first place was because I wanted to experience for myself a swinging lifestyle that could be more easily acted out in the anonymity of a big city. Well, as they say, be careful what you wish for.

I was incredibly naïve when I arrived in California. I'd only had two sexual experiences at that point, neither of them great. And during my early days in the City of Angels, I didn't have much of a chance to make sexual contacts. I had no money and was earning very little. CiCi Huston kept me on a tight leash, I was a virtual prisoner at Zsa Zsa's, and later I lived at the Chabad homeless shelter. None of these places was exactly conducive to bringing home a date. In addition, I had few friends at first, and I was very focused on making my way upward in the entertainment community. I didn't have a lot of free time.

As my situation improved, though, so did my opportunities.

This meant I had to confront the central conflict of my life, between my sexual appetites and my religious faith.

My father, you see, though raised Jewish, converted to Christianity and practiced it for the rest of his life, to the chagrin of my mother and her family, who were all observing Jews. He was extremely devout: church on Sunday, Bible class, scripture-reading, and full reliance on God for daily guidance. Though he undoubtedly wanted to share his belief in Jesus with his children, he was not allowed to. He hid that, as though it were an awful, dirty secret. Still, I noticed.

The Thomsons were also devout Christians. While staying with them, I began to seriously study the Bible. By the time I was in my early twenties, I too had converted.

They had been taking me to the church Jim was pastoring, the evangelical Baptist congregation in Amherstburg, a small town on the Detroit River south of Windsor. It had been largely populated by African Americans who fled to Canada before Emancipation. There, surrounded by a community made up of the descendants of slaves, I was baptized. Perhaps it was fitting, since the Jews had themselves been so often enslaved.

I had finally converted for real, fulfilling, as I saw it, my Judaism. This meant that I accepted Jesus Christ and expressed my desire to live according to biblical teachings. It would still be many years before those powerful words of Christ would really take hold in my heart and turn my life around. But it did, at least, prick my conscience when it came to matters in the bedroom.

I knew that sex outside of marriage was a sin, but I had undeniable urges. I struggled with myself, trying to decide what to do. Compounding the problem, because of my schedule and career-focused lifestyle, I was hardly in the running for a long-term relationship. I couldn't put in the time for more serious, emotional involvement. Besides, I was over-weight, with a facial tic and very low self-esteem. It didn't seem likely that any normal person would want me anyway. In the end, I "resolved" the dilemma by doing the worst possible thing. *I paid for sex.* And my actions would lead me spiraling downward into a hell of sex addiction.

For many years, this was my life: I worked like a dog, ate, slept, and had lots and lots of sex. That was it, nothing else. Since the work I did was unbelievably stressful, I had to have some form of release. I didn't smoke, drink, or take drugs, thank God. But I did become addicted to food, and to sex.

MY RELATIONSHIP WITH NATALIE deepened through 1997. We would go on dates with other couples and on trips together. We were never romantic, but sometimes, we'd lie in bed together and watch TV and snack after her performances, sharing some of our most intimate thoughts and feelings. I looked up to her for the person she was inside, not because of her fame. One day, when we were riding in a limo together in New York, she said, "You know, you are so wonderful. You are almost perfect." It's what every guy longs to hear—*almost.*

Francesco certainly wasn't perfect, but that didn't matter much to Natalie. One day, Francesco mentioned that he thought about opening a small café on Little Santa Monica Boulevard in Beverly Hills. Natalie wasn't about to stake him, so I volunteered to lend the money to get started—a hundred thousand dollars. I made out like it was no big deal, just something I'd do because I loved Natalie so much as a friend. Of course, I had to borrow it, and putting together that kind of purse sometimes takes a while. Not that Natalie proved too understanding. After two weeks, Natalie jumped on my back: "Are you going to give Francesco the money or not?" I felt so pressured that I just did it. I borrowed seventy-five thousand and handed it over. I asked for nothing in return and took Natalie at her word when she told me Francesco was good for it. The restaurant opened and closed within a couple of months. I was screwed. The money was gone, and I had no way of paying it back. Neither Natalie nor Francesco ever suggested that they might make good on the loan, not even "someday." They didn't even thank me.

Still, the gifts kept flowing, as I learned slow and hard. I bought a Land Rover as a surprise gift for Natalie's son Robbie, a thank you for something or other she had done for me. When I delivered it, she told me bluntly she really would rather have had the cash. So I sold it and gave her the money, about forty thousand dollars.

I threw her a lavish birthday party at L'Orangerie, with a guest list of a hundred or so. It cost me thirty grand, but I really didn't mind because it made Natalie happy. Afterward, she told me I treated her better than any of her husbands ever did, and said how much she loved me. I guess we had what you would call a symbiotic relationship.

As the year wound down, I approached her with an idea that had been percolating in my head for a while. I knew how much she admired her father, Nat "King" Cole, and believed he deserved to have something set up in his name, something substantial, something that would keep his memory alive for the ages.

I pitched to her the idea of endowing a center at UCLA, where kids who were interested in the arts could get financial assistance. I thought that would be the perfect way to remember her dad. Of course, it would take a lot of money to get it going—I figured at least a million—but I thought I could get Cynthia Gershman to commit that much over several years. We would then hold fundraisers to keep the project going. It was very ambitious, but that had never stopped me before.

I told her I envisioned holding several big musical events a year to create awareness and generate funding. If she could get other prominent entertainers, maybe friends like Whitney Houston or Tina Turner, to join up with her, I was certain we could get millions from companies and private donors. This was what I was good at.

Although hesitant at first, Natalie slowly warmed to the idea and agreed to let me approach the dean of the School of Arts and Architecture at UCLA. I talked with him several times, going back and forth with the idea. They were definitely interested, not to mention excited to meet Natalie Cole, and eventually we set up an appointment for December 9.

I was psyched! This was a different kind of project altogether, one that could have meaning for years and years to come. I thought of all the kids who could be helped with their education, with our efforts and in her father's name.

The meeting lasted about two hours, and it went great. UCLA was definitely jazzed. Natalie was too, but she continued to be concerned about our ability to carry through with it.

It was a major league dream. We were talking about constructing a building and funding scholarships on an ongoing basis. I reassured Natalie as best I could and scheduled a second meeting. We were continuing to move forward.

And then it all came crashing down. The project, the relationship, everything.

We were having brunch one afternoon at the Bel Air Hotel, just the two of us, when Francesco stormed in and made a terrible scene. It was like the Ungaro incident all over again, and once more she took it, the screaming, the yelling. This time it was all about me. For whatever twisted reason, Francesco had decided he didn't want me in Natalie's life any more. He gave her an ultimatum, right there: she was to stop seeing me, as a friend or associate or anything.

It was bad. I knew that, but I clung to the desperate belief that Natalie wouldn't give in to Francesco's demands this time, that she would hang on to the best friend she'd ever had and dump this verbally abusive SOB.

It was a foolish hope. Natalie needed Francesco, whatever it was that he did for her, more than she needed me.

After all of the great times and the intimacies and the hundreds of thousands of dollars in cash and gifts, she didn't even have the courage to call me. Instead, just after Christmas, she sent me a fax. An excerpt:

[Y]ou know the dynamics of this past year have been sometimes overwhelming. I needed to make a decision—right or wrong. And to choose between friends and someone you love—well it's not easy. But I want you to know how much I have appreciated our times together. . . . In my heart, I am praying that, somehow, there will be a way we can again be even better friends—all of us.

Right now, I am working very hard on my relationship with Francesco, both of us are working through some very difficult issues, as you well know, and I don't want to jeopardize that in any way.

In other words, Natalie was sorry, but I was out of the picture. It broke my heart.

ten

WITH FRIENDS
LIKE THESE . . .

David Schwimmer *agreed to* meet me at his home in the Hollywood hills, just north of Sunset Boulevard.

A friend of mine, also in the business, also a young, successful actor with his own television series, had agreed to set up the original meet, an absolute thrill for me as *Friends* was quickly becoming the hottest show on TV. From the moment I discovered the connection, the gears started turning, and I was envisioning an elaborate charity event involving the entire cast, my most prestigious fundraiser yet. I was pretty good at generating concepts now, and I quickly came up with a catchy title, Friends Helping Friends.

I would have preferred to take a meeting at one of the trendy restaurants frequented by people in the industry. That way, if I ran into important people I knew, I could impress David with the quality of my contacts. In addition, people who were strangers to me might see us together and, because I was having lunch with a famous TV star, want to approach me and get to know who I was.

At that point, I hadn't yet learned that in Hollywood it's often better to keep a low profile, to not broadcast what you're doing. The town is full of ruthless individuals—your competitors for celebrities' attention—who will attach themselves to you when they see you working with the rich and famous, and then try to steal them from you.

I showed up at David Schwimmer's home at the appointed hour, got buzzed in, and David escorted me out to his backyard, where we sat by the pool and talked. He had some ideas himself, but basically didn't know how these things worked, so I laid out the whole event for him. I said we would definitely need the entire cast of *Friends,* and that we would honor them in some way. I knew Matthew Perry's agent and was sure I could get him, but David would have to help me with the rest.

He said he'd talk to the cast, find out what they would and wouldn't be willing to do. One thing he was sure of was that they would have charities of their own they'd like to raise money for.

How about him? I asked. What charity would he particularly like to benefit? The Lookingglass Theatre Company, he said. I had no clue what that was. He explained that it was a nonprofit theater group in Chicago that had given him his professional start. He wanted to reciprocate by helping them out, and he wanted them to get the majority of the money. Who cares about starving kids in Africa? These were starving actors!

Uh oh, I thought to myself. *I don't think this is going to get a very good reception in L.A.* I didn't know anyone who would support something like this when there were much more worthy causes. "David," I said, "I think it will be difficult to build this event around a small, Chicago-based theater group. We'll need to have a big local charity involved in order to assure ourselves of a strong ticket base."

Well, those were the people *he* wanted to back, he insisted. He'd have to see what the other actors came up with.

In truth, my relative inexperience was blinding me to the reality of the situation. I potentially had the cast of *Friends* on the line. That in itself was the draw. People would come out to meet them no matter what organization was benefiting.

SHORTLY AFTER OUR MEETING, David called and told me that the rest of the cast was in. Of them, only Courteney Cox had specified a charity she wanted to benefit, the Archer School for Girls. Another small organization, I thought, but at least it was local. I still held to my mistaken notion that we needed one more, a big-time outfit, and I went out and got the John Wayne Cancer Institute on board.

Had I bothered to consult Charity Navigator, a nonpartisan, nonprofit agency that evaluates thousands of different causes, I would have found that both the Archer School and the JWCI get very low ratings (i.e., less money taken in goes to charitable recipients, more is spent on expenses). And a lot of people thought Lookingglass was a joke. *Who the hell are they?* I'd get asked. *David Schwimmer's charity of choice*, I'd say, and that would shut them up.

David and I also discussed disbursement of proceeds and decided that each charity would get an equal one-third share.

Little did I realize how that was going to come back to haunt me.

So we had our agreement in place. Everything was a go for a huge gala with the whole cast of *Friends*. I couldn't have been happier with what I'd pulled off. The big brass ring was sitting there, waiting for me to grab it. Nothing was going to stand in my way.

The first thing I did was contact Cynthia and Hal Gershman. I knew they would provide financial help because they never passed up the chance to rub elbows with the stars and make it look like their foundation was doing some good. Of course, their contribution only came to twenty-five grand, peanuts compared to the eventual expense.

In return, there were the standard favors to be done. Whenever word got out that a new, spectacular event was being organized, it was like hanging a sign out your window that said: *Let the rip-offs begin.*

The Gershmans demanded to be on stage, where they would be publicly recognized (and ridiculed, under people's breaths) for underwriting the whole dinner, which they didn't do. I also had to give them a full-page ad in the tribute journal (a five-thousand-dollar value), with photographs, and seat celebrities at their table. Plus I had to "gift" Hal with his usual payment, in this instance a luxury trip to Europe for four that cost about as much as he had "donated"—thereby making him guilty once again of *self-dealing*, which he had done with me on numerous occasions. This time, the tickets came from the charity's silent auction.

And starting with this event, there was another special Gershman condition. They wanted national press coverage for the things they were doing. No budging on that. Cynthia felt she had gone as far as she could with self-promotion; now she wanted someone to get her noticed by the media. A professional publicist, in other words, who would help her attain a higher profile and therefore, theoretically, advance her acting career. Cue laugh track.

Norby Walters jumped in with both feet, too. My "friend" and business associate convinced me that I needed him to make sure plenty of stars would be in attendance. Idiot that I was, I believed him. Almost anyone else could have told me that the *Friends* would bring out the stars *en masse.* But I was too insecure to trust that. I had to be absolutely certain that there would be *some* celebs at the tables, even if they were B-list or worse. Norby wanted to bring ten stars, who would come for free, but demanded, surprise of surprises, twenty-five thousand to make it happen. I eventually agreed to fifteen. What a deal.

I'D ARRANGED WITH THE BEVERLY HILTON HOTEL to hold the main event in their ballroom, along with the welcoming cocktail party and a concurrent silent auction. But I wanted something extra, something that would make my gala stand out as different from all the others going on, something that would make this truly an affair to remember.

What I came up with was a second, pre-event cocktail reception, for gold and platinum donors only, to be held at the home of Engelbert Humperdinck. I chose Engelbert because I loved his music and thought it would be great to honor him. I knew his star had faded, that he was considered something of a joke in the industry. But I hadn't forgotten him, and if I could do something to help restart his career, I wanted to. Maybe putting him with the kinds of people who would come out for the young, hip cast of *Friends* could do it.

Besides that, there was the mystique of Engelbert's house itself. It was a landmark Hollywood estate, a spectacular place, all pink, right on the south side of Sunset Boulevard, and had been previously owned by Rudy Valee. It had also once belonged to the fifties sexpot actress Jayne Mansfield. There was a heart-shaped pool out back, where Jayne had once been photographed frolicking in the nude.

There was one more consideration. When I sent out my invitations to potential contributors all over North America, being able to offer the VIP option was a big advantage. I knew there were a lot of people who would pay, and pay well, for the opportunity to do some socializing at a star's home.

I approached Scott Dorsey, Engelbert's son and manager, with the idea, and he loved it. Of course the incredible publicity value and the honor and pleasure of doing charity work weren't enough. Dorsey demanded a payment of twenty-five thousand in cash, and gifts on top of all that. That'd get us the use of Humperdinck's home and a couple of songs at the main event. We would do the VIP party outside, around the pool (mainly because the interior, surprisingly, was rather shabby). I agreed.

For a co-host with Engelbert, I landed Ann-Margret. Another major accomplishment. Ann-Margret rarely went out any more and was known for never doing this sort of thing.

Next, I developed an honoree dinner committee to put down the left side of the invitation. It was totally A-list. I had sent out the committee solicitation letter, over David

Schwimmer's signature, and it worked like magic. Warren Littlefield, then-president of NBC Entertainment, the man who had forged it into the top-ranked network, had agreed to be dinner chair. Below his name there were forty-five others—stars, network TV and film studio executives, and other high-profile industry types—including Jason Alexander, George Clooney, Janice and Billy Crystal, Jay Leno, Garry Marshall, Arnold Palmer, Gwyneth Paltrow, Don Rickles, Brooke Shields, and Marsha and Robin Williams.

At the same time, I was working on a special guest of honor. If honoring *Friends* was going to bring in the younger set, then we needed someone to attract the older crowd. I wanted Bob Hope. No easy task. I had to negotiate for a long time with Linda Hope, his daughter, because Bob was ninety-four years old and nearly deaf and blind. But I persisted, and in the end got the commitment. That was one of his last public appearances, and another real coup for me.

For my master of ceremonies, I needed an experienced comedian and called on Marc Gurvitz for assistance. Marc was a great, ethical guy who worked at Brillstein-Grey Entertainment, managing such celebrities as Dana Carvey, David Spade, and Chris Farley. He would help out in providing stars for my events but never asked me for a thing in return. Whenever I offered him money or gifts, he would tell me he preferred that I make a donation to Hollygrove, his favorite charity, instead. I think I've made it clear how unusual that is.

I knew that Marc also represented Jon Lovitz, and that's who I wanted for my emcee. Marc asked him. No response. So I offered Lovitz a ten-thousand-dollar watch and, I guess, that was the ticket. He committed.

In addition to a big-name emcee, I wanted to be able to say on my invitation: *with Special Performances by . . .* So I started calling talent.

I thought three was about the right number for performers, along with Engelbert, and I wanted diversity. My first call was to Marty Stuart's manager, whom I had met in Nashville and gotten along with. No problem. Marty would come and do two songs for no compensation, just expense money. A great start.

Tony Bennett was next. I really wanted him, but I didn't want to deal with his manager/son again. Thus I approached him through his publicist. After a lot of back-and-forth, we struck a deal. Tony would perform for free, but I had to pay the usual expenses: airfare and hotel (the Peninsula, of course) for him and his quartet. As an additional condition for getting Bennett, I also had to kick in free tickets and an all-expense-paid trip for his publicist. Oh well.

With two down, one to go, I was running out of time. The invitations had to go into the mail, and I wanted all the performers' names on it. I turned to the one person I thought was a true friend, Natalie Cole. Okay, she said, she'd do it. For twenty-five thousand, in cash, for two songs. Plus another forty-five thousand or so in Cartier jewelry. I was disappointed that she didn't cut me some slack, do me a favor, as a friend, just this once. Or at least for the charities, who would be, essentially, paying for the expense out of their proceeds. But she didn't relent, and I gave in. She knew I was in a tight spot.

That completed my performers list. The invitation now could be printed and sent out. It was gorgeous. Many pages long, with a page for each honoree featuring a bio and photo, and a spread on Engelbert's house and its history. Okay, I'd spent more than I'd hoped to, both on Natalie and the invitation itself, which along with the tribute books would end up costing me sixty thousand dollars. But what the heck. I knew that we'd have no trouble filling all our tables. We were going to pack the place, which meant a huge crowd, since the ballroom at the Beverly Hilton could accommodate a thousand people. And that meant big bucks in return.

Concurrent with producing the invitation, I had to come up with the auction solicitation letter, and it was a beauty. I got Jay Leno to sign it, and it went out to hundreds of potential donors. I suspected this was going to pique corporate America's interest, and I was right.

With these companies, I lent a personal hand. I had crisscrossed the country in the past couple of years, as I forged new contacts in the private sector. Now I cashed them in. There was my friend Ray Caldiero, the senior vice-president of Northwest Airlines, who came through with donations of airline tickets. Ray had, in turn, introduced me to the CEOs of Bausch & Lomb, Reebok, and Northrop Grumman. I worked them all, as well as BMW, Seidler's of Boston, Cartier, and many, many more. I'd gotten very good at closing the deal.

I was relentless in ferreting out donations, never taking *no* for an answer. In the end, a lot of what we got for the live and silent auctions was due to personal corporate contacts and cold calls I made. I was especially aggressive with the TV sponsors of the *Friends* show itself, telling them that this was a way to give a little back to the people who had provided them with such massive exposure, and they did come through.

My assistant, Chad Mouton, had also developed a computerized database, filled with thousands of names of individuals and companies to solicit, and we did a massive mailing from that.

AS BEST I COULD, I TRIED to involve the *Friends* cast, but getting them to assist was like pulling teeth. I asked David to put me together with the rest of the cast, so I could make my pitch. I went down on a Saturday while they were taking a break from a meeting with the series' producers, showed the six young stars the layout of the invitation and auction solicitation letter, and asked them for names of well-to-do people they thought might want to contribute.

The two Matts, LeBlanc and Perry, seemed distant and disinterested. The girls were much more cooperative, particularly Courteney and Jennifer. They would be the only ones who ever even provided lists. From the rest, I got nothing.

However, the contributions were pouring in. Nearly everyone we contacted wanted to be a part. The final tribute journal lists the following as the main sponsors of the evening: BMW of North America, British Airways, Mitchell Fox of *Vanity Fair*, Halston, and Calvin Klein. In the end, my mailings and cold calls brought in about $1.4 million, retail value, in donations of luxury items for the auctions, not counting those packages on which it was impossible to put a value.

We had everything from two new BMWs, a car and a motorcycle, to a non-speaking, walk-on role on an episode of *Friends*, to a set of fishing rods with an all-expense paid fishing trip to Alaska to go along with it. A few other examples, taken directly from the live auction list, were:

***PRIVATE SCREENING AND RECEPTION FOR 50—Private screening for fifty of your closest friends of a newly released film at the Charles Aidikoff Screening Room on Cañon Drive in Beverly Hills, California. And, to make it even more special, there will be a cocktail reception for you and your guests hosted by Hymie's Fishmarket. Make your plans for any mutually agreeable Sunday . . . between now and January 31st. Donated by Charles and Gregg Aidikoff, this is at least a $5,000 package . . .

***DIAMOND COLLAR AND EARRING SUITE by Seidler's Jewelers of Boston— Gentlemen . . . your ladies will love it! A Diamond Collar and Earring Suite . . . 18 karat yellow gold and pavé diamond three section collar with 42 Russian cut diamonds weighting a total of 2.10 carats of superior color and clarity. Matching earrings are done style with a pavé diamond center with 24 Russian cut diamonds weighing a total of 1.04 carats of superior color and clarity. Valued at $18,000 . . .

***19 DAYS DOWN UNDER—The two of you will fly to Sydney, Australia, on Air New Zealand, Business Class, and then spend six days & five nights at the fabulous Conrad Jupiter Hotel on Australia's Gold Coast. Then it's back to Sydney to board your Seabourne Cruise for an unbelievable thirteen-day cruise to Auckland, New Zealand, in your private suite. The value on this nineteen-day dream vacation is over . . . $35,000

***"HOW TO HOST A MURDER" with your FRIEND, DAVID SCHWIMMER—You and your guest will spend the evening at the home of David Schwimmer playing Decypher's "How to Host a Murder" . . . you'll have dinner too . . . and you never know what other celebrity might drop in to play with you. If you'd like to spend the evening with David, here's your chance! Priceless . . .

***LUNCH WITH YOUR "FRIENDS"?—This evening is all about friends. You can join the Cast of Friends . . . for lunch . . . at David Schwimmer's home . . . and your Chef will be the one and only Wolfgang Puck . . . serving up a fabulous array of his specialties from Spago. This is definitely a one-of-a-kind luncheon . . . for you and three of your friends . . . this is something that money can't buy . . . but it will tonight . . . Minimum bid $10,000

Sadly, the last two live auction items—which may have been the two most enticing on the entire program, and undoubtedly the most unique—never happened. Just before the auction, David Schwimmer told me some of the other cast members of *Friends* weren't comfortable with the Spago-catered lunch, and I was forced to cancel it.

The murder mystery night at David's fared even worse. The package brought a high bid of twelve thousand dollars. A father had bought it for his nine-year-old daughter, who had flown in from Arizona for the fundraiser.

David came up to me right there on stage and said it didn't

sell for enough, that he was worth more, and that he didn't want to honor it. It was a terrible scene. I was doubly embarrassed because I had worked out a deal with the game company based on David's word, and, as a result, they had given me a lot of money and products for the event.

There went who knows how much in proceeds, out of the charities' pockets. But those were the kind of developments you had to learn to live with in the land of broken promises.

"I WILL GO ON RECORD SAYING I did deliver cash to a number of celebrities on Friends Helping Friends. I don't know [how much] was in those envelopes. I didn't ask." So said Adam Buttons, son of Alicia and Red, in an interview with *Vanity Fair*. I had hired Adam, as a favor, to be an assistant and courier, using him, during the run-up to the event, to dole out cash to celebrity after celebrity. Apparently, the word was out on me, on my loose purse, and everyone had their hand extended. Adam eventually quit, in part because he said he didn't like the idea of being a "bagman" for these transfers. Nevertheless, the money kept rolling out.

Now, let me say that there is nothing illegal about paying a movie star to attend a function, or to perform at one. Unethical, perhaps, but not illegal. But it is a sort of fraud—even if not by a strict legal definition—when neither donors who give their money, nor the charities who receive it, are aware that a portion of event expenses is going into the pockets of some very wealthy people who are *supposedly* donating their time and talent.

But other activities were decidedly more questionable. For example:

Several stars from my events—whom I unfortunately can't name because of ongoing FBI and IRS investigations—had me prepare for them tax letters for the full amount of what their normal fee would be. Let's say a singer usually charged a hundred thousand for a forty-five-minute performance. I would verify in writing that this person had in fact donated his or her time to the charity, and that the donation had a street value of a hundred grand. This was almost always an inflated number. In the first place, they often placed an overly optimistic value on their services, much higher than they could get in the real world. And in the second, they weren't giving a full performance, just doing a song or two. But for tax purposes, they'd deduct the whole amount, whatever I specified, as a charitable contribution.

This is bad enough. It's clearly immoral, and of questionable legality, but perhaps still a wicket they could wriggle out of. Here's something worse: Some of the stars would then have me make the under-the-table payments in cash, jewelry, travel, or other luxury items, in an amount equal to or exceeding their performance fee. Yet they would still ask for and receive a tax letter thanking them for their "free" performance, and this letter would go to their accountants, presumably to be filed for a full tax benefit.

Still, onward we went. As the donations and sponsorships started piling up, so did the requests for special favors. One of the reasons a gala like this can result in such a small net profit for the charities is because of these freebies. For example, Delta Airlines would donate four or six free tickets, and in return demand a free table for ten. Or a jeweler would donate a ten-thousand-dollar watch and want six dinner tickets. Plus, because it was an auction, you never knew what something was going to sell for.

Put a bunch of rich people in a room, lubricate them with alcohol, and anything can happen. I once saw a guy pay twenty-five thousand for a dog. But other bidders may get off on the cheap. So at the end of the day, you might have given a corporation tickets worth, say fifteen thousand, but taken in only five thousand for the donation that those tickets were swapped for. Not a good trade-off.

And then, of course, there were the chronic schnorrers. They would pester me for free tickets until I was tearing my hair out and would finally give in. Often the worst schnorrers would promise a future favor in return. Uh huh. Just try to collect on that one.

Seating was always a nightmare that I wouldn't wish on anyone; it seemed to bring out the worst in people. People who felt they'd been shortchanged by their table location would do anything—scream at you on the phone, throw a temper tantrum, beg, literally cry like a baby, whatever—in order to get you to make a change. Sometimes you'd fill their request just to shut them up.

Publicists were the worst. They would promise that some star or other would attend, then threaten to cancel after the fact if I did not meet their demands. Either I came up with some free tickets or their client wouldn't show. Some of them would even demand freebies when their clients *weren't* coming, just for having *tried* to get them.

Some donors would want free ads in the tribute journal,

publicity for them, in return for donations (again, something I was selling for five thousand bucks). Some would want a journal ad *and* free tickets. At the Friends Helping Friends event, some demanded both of those *plus* a couple of passes to the VIP cocktail party at Engelbert's (spots free to those paying fifteen or twenty-five thousand per table).

Donors for the gift bags might also expect to be compensated with tickets. Now, we're not talking about some cheesy little brown bags with a couple of party favors inside. No, my gift bags were really amazing. At the Friends event, every patron got *two* of them, each the size of a piece of luggage, filled with sunglasses, books, full-size bottles of Calvin Klein's newest fragrance, Halston perfumes, jewelry, CDs of the night's performers, the finest chocolates, canisters full of fancy candy, games, and on and on.

We set out two thousand of those bags and still came up short. Two weren't good enough for some of our esteemed guests, I guess. They had to steal other people's as well.

ANOTHER COMPLICATION AROSE because of *Vanity Fair.*

The only thing the magazine really did for our event was bring in two of its advertisers, Halston and Calvin Klein. In return, though, they demanded to be listed as a primary sponsor, a free table for ten, and a full-page ad. It was a lot, but that wasn't all.

Jean Karlson called me and said Halston had decided that one of the conditions of its sponsorship was to be that the three female *Friends* stars had to wear Halston cocktail dresses that night. I've never known whether the demand actually came from the company, or if the magazine originated it in order to butter up its advertiser. It doesn't really matter. It was another unreasonable demand that thankfully the girls agreed to.

And again that should have been the end of it, but *no*. *Vanity Fair* figured, I suppose, that since I'd delivered on that demand, they'd push me for more. They called and told me that Halston was going to pull out if I didn't get some additional stars to wear their clothes, as well.

What the f—? I said. I thought Karlson was kidding. She wasn't.

So I had to contact a publicist, who had some clients that were coming, and get her to persuade them to wear Halston, or I was going to lose a top sponsor. Remember this is after agreements have already been made—bargaining for more after the fact and threatening to pull out if the demands are not met is, in my mind, nothing less than greedy bloodsucking. The publicist delivered Tiffany Amber Thiessen, but it cost me some cash and precious free tickets. She was unable to get Alicia Silverstone but wanted more free tickets just for trying! When they see you treading water, the sharks start circling.

And *that* should have been the end of it, right? Guess again. The next call was about the other major sponsor *Vanity Fair* was delivering: Calvin Klein. Now, that company supposedly was threatening to yank its support too, unless the male cast of *Friends* wore Calvin Klein. But when I got an agreement from them to do so, the ante was upped yet again; now the entire waitstaff was to dress in CK as well, both at the main event *and* at the Engelbert reception. Ye gads! Couldn't these people think of a few more ways to exploit a charity fundraiser?

Still, I couldn't afford to lose Calvin Klein. They were on the invitation, helping to underwrite, donating gift bag items, etc., etc. It was important to try to appease them, so I went to the hotel waitstaff and the caterer for the VIP reception.

I was in the middle of negotiations with them when the phone rang. It was Jean Karlson. *Again.* Oh yeah, she said, it was important to Calvin Klein that the waiters be good-looking, young men who would properly show off the clothes.

I hit the roof.

Most of the waitstaff at the hotel were Mexican Americans, middle-aged or older, a good number of them overweight. Hardly any were the "model types" the company was looking for. Round and round we went. Finally, we compromised. I would use a specialized agency to supply the help for the VIP reception, and they would wear Calvin Klein. The hotel staff would be dressed by Calvin Klein as well, but it would be the regular waiters.

Vanity Fair, indeed.

THE EVENING OF THE EVENT, just before the VIP reception at Engelbert Humperdinck's, I got a call from Alan Marguiles, who manages both Engelbert and Ann-Margret. Ann-Margret wasn't coming, he informed me. She didn't feel like it. Note that he didn't even have the decency to lie and say she didn't feel *well*; nope, she just didn't feel *like it.* As if it were no big deal. This was the co-host of the reception, listed on the invitation, whom some people would be coming specifically to meet. She lived only a couple of miles away. And she was reneging on her agreement because she didn't *feel like* honoring it.

I was boiling but had to keep it bottled up. There was nothing I could do. I still had a spectacular night to oversee.

The grounds at the reception were beautifully appointed, the weather was nice, and, best of all, the people the VIPs had come to see (Ann-Margret excepted) were uniformly gracious and cooperative. Though it had been costly to stage, I felt it would bring in additional donor money, and it did.

Everyone gathered around the heart-shaped pool, having cocktails and chatting, taking advantage of photo ops. Warren Littlefield and Engelbert Humperdinck were only too happy to have their pictures taken with my sponsors, but mostly people wanted to be photographed with the cast of *Friends.* So I arranged all of them into a group and then, one by one brought my special guests down for the photos: the chairman of BMW North America; Steve Florio, the head of the Condé Nast publishing empire, who with Mitchell Fox and Jean Karlson had flown in to represent *Vanity Fair;* and many others, including, of course, the ever-present Gershmans.

Cynthia and Hal nagged and nagged me, saying, "When are we getting *our* picture taken?" over and over, until I finally dragged them to the head of the informal line of people waiting. Hal squeezed into the shot at one end, with his tacky white suit and bad toupée dangling, while Cynthia tripped and fell into Engelbert Humperdinck's lap. She wouldn't get up, even though the wind had whipped her dress up to her waist. While everyone laughed nervously, she insisted that the picture be taken that way. Engelbert was a good and gracious sport and went along with it. God only knows what the cast of *Friends* were thinking.

As the reception wound down, I was informed, a little late, that Engelbert had a bit of a sore throat and wouldn't be able to sing at the main event. Since I still had Natalie and Tony and Marty, it really wasn't much of a problem. The real crises were waiting for me at the Beverly Hilton, as I found out when we all made the short trip over to the hotel.

The first thing that happened was that the cast of *Friends* didn't go to the VIP room, along with the other attending celebrities. They and their escorts were taken to a private room, where they "rested up" for the main event. This was a crass avoidance of one of their primary jobs. You want your honorees to mingle with the high rollers, because that's one of the things the big donors are there for—if you schmooze them they'll be more inclined to part with even more money for the charities.

That all left me, the producer, in a familiar bind. I didn't want to harangue the cast about it and risk having them walk out altogether. But in order to avoid that, I had to cover for them, to make some lame excuse to the people who were asking me where they were, and who had paid good money to meet them. Egg on my face no matter what. It just went with the territory.

Unfortunately, that was my minor dilemma. The big disaster hit me right in the face when I went to check out how the silent auction was doing.

Because of the magnitude of the fundraiser, I had hired an event manager—yes, there are such things—to take over some of the work, namely: receiving, cataloguing, and safely storing the auction items; transporting auction items to the ballrooms just prior to the event; setting them up, along with eye-catching displays; making up bidsheets, attaching them to clipboards, and putting these out next to the appropriate silent auction item; stuffing gift bags; setting out gift bags and tribute journals for every guest; gathering bidsheets after the silent auction and tallying them up; collecting money from the winners; and sending those lucky people home with their proper prizes. These are small tasks but absolutely critical to the success of any fundraiser.

It was imperative that all those things run smoothly, and the event manager was paid a pretty penny to make sure they did. Nonetheless, it was quite a heavy workload, and I realized that. So I kept in close contact her, checking on how she was doing, offering additional help if she needed it. *No,* I was assured each time, no problems. Everything was going great.

Well, except for one teensy little detail.

To my horror, I discovered my hire had utterly failed to carry out one of the most important assigned tasks: half of my auction items didn't have a bidsheet beside them, including the two BMWs! No one could bid on them. People probably thought the car was there for decoration.

Insane with rage, I went looking for my manager. She was nowhere to be found. Days later, when I finally caught up with her, she laughed it off as a minor screw-up. But the damage was incalculable. What it meant was that at the end of the night, I was going to have a roomful of leftover auction items, simply because they'd received no bids. This was devastating for the charities, and a real headache for me, as I would then have to figure out how to properly dispose of all this stuff.

There was nothing I could do. It was too late to re-set the silent auction. It was only supposed to be an hour long to begin with, and it was winding down. Besides, there were obviously no extra bidsheets to put out. I just had to bite my tongue and carry on with the live auction. It was during this, while the auctioneer was working, that David came up to me at the side of the stage and told me about the cancelled items. Lord, what else could go wrong?

Of course, from the point of view of the guests, I'm sure it looked like a huge success. It was a glamorous night, with a host of stars attending: Tom Selleck, Jason Alexander, and many, many more. The entertainment was great. Jon Lovitz was very funny, and the three singers were at their best. The crowd loved it all.

Then the cast accepted their FRIENDShip awards from Warren Littlefield, each of the members receiving a sterling silver plate by Christofle, given for "Creative Achievement—Ensemble Comedy." As the program put it, "The round tray was chosen for its clean simple lines, echoing the idea of a global community of people helping people. Christofle has been the silversmith of choice for generations of royal families, countless estates, embassies, ocean liners, and luxury hotels, and joins hands with the American Foundation for the Performing Arts in celebrating the selfless efforts of some of Hollywood's royalty."

Anyone who knew the truth would have laughed. Selflessness was nowhere in sight.

Then came the highlight of the evening for me, when the cast of *Friends* and everyone else paid tribute to Bob Hope. As Mr. Hope got up and waved, the orchestra played "Thanks for the Memories." The crowd went wild and gave the legendary comedian a standing ovation for over two minutes.

Following that, the cast went backstage, where Bob Hope joined them, and many pictures were taken. And then . . . they left! The event wasn't over yet, and my guests of honor had split. Later, Stephanie Powers told Cynthia that they went next door, where they had drinks at Trader Vic's. Once again I was angry, not to mention embarrassed, since several people came up and asked me, "Where are the *Friends?*" and I had no answer.

The day after it was over, I began to get calls. Guests called to thank me and tell me how spectacular the night had been. Other charities were on the phone, wanting to know if I could do something similar for them. Jean Karlson told me what a great job I'd done and how impressed *Vanity Fair* was, and how we'd do more things together in the future.

It should have been my moment to bask in the glow, but I couldn't because I was looking at the numbers. Despite the hundreds of tickets we'd sold, and all the fancy auction items, our gross was only around a half million, with about a hundred twenty-five thousand net to split among the three charities. Not good. In fact, in order to even make it to the plus side of the ledger, I had to forego my salary and pay some additional event expenses out of my own pocket by borrowing money. I took responsibility for the shortfall, and it cost me dearly.

Some of it was my fault, true. I'd spent way too much to bring stars to the event and hadn't budgeted the rest of the expenses well at all.

On the other hand, the biggest snafu of the night—the one that cut the bottom line the most—was the unsold silent auction items. I was left with nearly a quarter million dollars' worth of goods and services: jewelry, luxury trips and cruises, and the like, plus the BMW sedan and motorcycle. That was a pain, because I was going to have to arrange for some kind of second auction to get rid of the stuff. But at least it would mean much more money for the three charities down the road.

I figured I could get a hundred seventy-five to two hundred thousand for the leftovers in a special auction and split the proceeds out so that each charity would walk away with a minimum of a hundred grand. Not great, but not bad, either. I even made a quick call to the Lookingglass Theater and learned that their previous best fundraiser had brought in twenty-eight thousand. They would undoubtedly be ecstatic to get nearly four times that from a bunch of people on the other side of the country who had never heard of them. Or so I thought.

WHEN I EXPLAINED THE SITUATION to David, he was furious. Understandably enough—the amount raised was much less than he'd hoped for.

As a result, things got nasty—bullying correspondence from his attorneys, meetings with mine, the whole *megillah*. Because of the fallout, in fact, Schwimmer has filed a lawsuit against me. In the end, Lookingglass did get their money; though I can't say the same for the Archer School for Girls or the John Wayne Cancer Institute. The charities got screwed, and I had no choice in the matter. I was just happy never to hear from David's lawyers again.

I still had to deal with my own guilt. I borrowed some

money to give to the John Wayne Cancer Institute and, over the next few years, raised more for them from other events of mine and with a substantial private donation I persuaded Cynthia Gershman to make. I pretty much made it all up to them, although the sour feeling I left them with right after Friends Helping Friends never completely went away. I never was able to make good with the Archer School, though I told their executive committee what happened face-to-face. One of them burst into tears when I broke the news. I have rarely felt as bad and embarrassed as I did that day.

That, finally, was the bitter end of Friends Helping Friends. As things worked out, *Friends F—ing Friends* would have been more like it.

eleven

IN THE MONEY

A *couple of months after* the Friends Helping Friends gala, there came an event of far-reaching importance to my life and career, and it wasn't even one that I produced: the death of Hal Gershman.

Around November of '97, Hal went into the hospital with chronic congestive heart problems. Doctors tried putting in a stint, but it didn't work. He slowly got weaker and sicker. It was obvious he was dying.

No one sent flowers. No get-well cards. Few visited. He'd amassed so much material wealth, which he could have used to do so much good for so many people, but he'd chosen not to. This was his tragic reward. Even his estranged children continued to keep their distance.

One evening, when he was so near the end, as I was escorting Cynthia out of her husband's hospital room, Hal woke up, called me over, and said, "Cynthia is a good woman, please take care of her. I want you to take care of her."

I told him I would.

The following day, Hal Gershman died.

Cynthia called me from the hospital to tell me. "I don't know why, but I just can't cry," Cynthia would say to me then, and to everyone else for the next several months.

That night Cynthia went home, and she and Hal's son Ron cut checks for fifty grand apiece to tide them over until the will was read.

The funeral was short and simple. I attended with Cynthia. Ron and his wife Kathy came, but not Hal's daughter Gloria or any of his grandchildren. I kept my distance from Ron. As far as I knew he was broke. But he was still burned at me for a trip to London I gave him that didn't go as he hoped—the two British Airways first-class tickets were waitlist and the luxury hotel was sub par, in his mind. Some gratitude.

Immediately after the burial, Cynthia was ready to party. Since Hal and Cynthia were Jewish, it would be expected after his death that his wife would *sit Shiva,* the Hebrew term for mourning the deceased. She could hardly pretend to mourn the passing of her husband, who'd really been that in name only. On the contrary, it was a huge load off of her. What she wanted most was to go out to dinner. Or, as some of her friends put it, Cynthia was *"sitting Shiva* at Spago!"

Naturally, she made me go with her. From that day onward, I never heard her speak of Hal again.

EVERYONE WAS NERVOUS over the reading of Hal Gershman's will. Toward the end of his life, even though he had apologized to Cynthia for treating her badly as a husband, he was still his old self. I knew that he had been meeting with his attorney, intending to cut just about everyone down.

"They don't need to drive Ferraris and Rolls Royces," he said of Ron and Cynthia. "They should all work for their own money."

Of course, his idea of cutting Cynthia back was to reduce her monthly allowance to fifteen thousand dollars, a sum that would make most other Americans quite happy. But not here in La La Land. Cynthia had a lifestyle to keep up, and she didn't feel able to do it on a meager fifteen grand a month. Likewise, Ron had a lot of expenses, with an ex-wife, kids, and other family and legal obligations.

So everyone was kind of holding their breath, as Ron met with the estate attorneys and other lawyers, not knowing what Hal had managed to do before he died. We waited for about a month before it was all finally settled, and then we learned that he hadn't made any substantive changes.

There were a lot of gray areas, but what it primarily boiled down to was this: Cynthia, Gloria, and some of the grandkids would get monthly payments of eighty thousand, while Ron would get more by virtue of being administrator. Cynthia got the condo in Palm Springs, a dump valued at a hundred thirty-five thousand. Ron and Cynthia each got a Rolls. The main house in Beverly Hills was left in the estate, which owned it, but Cynthia had a lifetime right to live there, all expenses paid for: taxes, upkeep, and whatever.

Now, you'd think that eighty grand a month, mortgage-free,

would be sufficient income for anyone, even in Beverly Hills. But not these people. Both Ron and Cynthia complained bitterly that it just wasn't enough.

To deal with the assets remaining in the estate, a board of three trustees was created, consisting of Ron, Cynthia, and City National Bank. Boy, did that ever change Ron and Cynthia's relationship. Before, Ron hated Cynthia's guts; now that he might need her in voting situations, she was his best pal. Ron and Kathy even took Cynthia out to dinner once a month. I think the unspoken agreement they reached was that neither would look too closely at what the other was doing. They just needed to stay close, in case Gloria would cause trouble for them.

All of this was kind of beside the point, as far as I was concerned. To me, the most significant thing was that Cynthia had been left in sole control of the Gershman Family Foundation. This meant that I would have a substantial amount of input into what she did with its millions of dollars.

Honestly, these financial matters were furthest from my mind at the time of Hal's death. I was instead concerned about Cynthia who, as dense and embarrassing as she could be, was still someone that I pitied and, in some way, loved. Moreover, I'd promised Hal on his deathbed that I would take care of her; that meant something to me.

Slowly but surely, though, it dawned on me how totally my situation had changed. *Power, prestige, access,* those were the buzzwords in Hollywood. And one of the best ways to bring those things into your life was either to have money, lots of money, or to be able to get it. Now—as Cynthia Gershman's closest friend and confidant, one of her only true friends—I was in that position.

Of course, in order to tap into it, I soon realized, I would have to make some major lifestyle concessions. I think I knew what I was in for as soon as she invited me to Spago to, essentially, celebrate her husband's demise. Clearly, I was the one she wanted around her in the days to come. If I was to become her advisor, I was going to have to build my life around her, to be with her, be available to her 24/7, give up my personal life, stop traveling to New York, and abandon my plans to expand my business into the East Coast. It was a difficult decision, considering that I had little idea what I was getting myself into. Professional babysitter and escort is what it felt like.

I gave it a lot of thought, and I decided to take the plunge.

Everything had changed. My life had entered a new phase and would be completely transformed. From now until my eventual downfall, I would be Cynthia Gershman's friend, advisor, agent, confidant, go-fer, financial consultant, social planner, political fixer, and last but hardly least, constant companion. She expected me to call her first thing in the morning and last thing at night, and a couple of times in-between on those rare days when I didn't see her. Cynthia and I never had sex (thank God, she was in her seventies), nor did we set up house together, but in every other way we were, in effect, getting married.

THROUGHOUT THIS PERIOD I was working with a guy I'll call Wayne McFeely. I met him late 1995, at the time of the Lasorda and Tippi Hedren events. Wayne was in the real estate business, but at the time we met, his life was in the toilet, due to his cocaine habit and the bad real estate market. He drove around in an old Jeep and had a beautiful home in the Hollywood Hills that he was selling, after having stripped it of furniture to make money. He was one step away from bankruptcy and reduced to turning tricks to feed his addictions and pay his other bills.

I was badly in debt, as usual, and getting deeper, desperate for money myself. I thought Wayne was the kind of person who could help me. Stupid me. Turned out the help was the other way around. I took him in as my confidant and, eventually, business associate and got him back on his feet.

In return, Wayne taught me the joys of loan sharking and money laundering.

For nearly four years, I ran a lot of my financial transactions through Wayne. He was the one with the key to it all: an American Express card on which we could run up as big a bill as we wanted, something I didn't have. So when I needed to buy something, and didn't have the cash, I'd charge it to Wayne's card. We ran that card from regular to gold and on up to platinum and the black card.

The problem was, of course, that I would then have to come up with the money to pay it off at the end of the month and, in addition, to pay Wayne the 25 percent he would tack on for providing me with this "service." I borrowed and borrowed some more, first from Steve Fox, then from a succession of other friends, then from one event to pay for another. He opened bank accounts left and right under his name and shuffled money around.

And that contributed to my ultimate downfall. I had no

feel for the flow of money. I was terrible at bookkeeping and never hired a proper accountant or a sane financial advisor. Instead, I surrounded myself with people like Wayne McFeely, thinking he was on my side, but he was just a guy who knew a good-hearted chump when he saw one.

When people saw me coming, hands were extended. Palms up, of course.

I ran up bills, bigger and bigger ones, then borrowed the funds to pay them, or had Wayne shift money through his many accounts for me. This was critical, because I always made sure that the charities got their fair share. That was my mission, and in order to get the money to them, sometimes I had to dodge my creditors. It was a very shaky house of cards. Somehow, though, I kept building it, higher and higher, for the better part of a decade, without it falling down. But collapse it would, eventually. It had to.

Meanwhile, Wayne made out like a bandit. From the less-than-zero he started with when I met him, he was able to completely resurrect his former real estate business, where he bought old tear-down houses, worked on them, and resold them for a huge profit. He was also able to support his hooker-and-cocaine habit on my money.

The worst, however, was yet to come.

It was only late in our relationship that I would discover the true extent to which he used me. He would present me with the credit card statements each month, showing me how they had been paid off in full, with the money I gave him. But that wasn't the whole story. Unbeknownst to me, he was charging back items to American Express, either by claiming that they were unauthorized expenditures or that his card had been lost or stolen. That was my relationship with Wayne, a nightmare for sure.

Eventually, I fired him, and got him entirely out of my life, shortly before A Family Celebration in September of 1999. But not before taking up with someone just as bad, someone to whom Wayne had introduced me.

His name was Blake Lindquist. He was the kind of guy who could only flourish in a place like Hollywood, and he too would handle much of my finances. He was around six feet tall but very fat, over three hundred pounds, always sweating profusely. The skin of his face was a ghastly orange from all the makeup he wore. He had some of his own special scams, such as the slip-and-fall lawsuit, of which he was a master. But his real love was gay porn. No joke. He was a videomaker who would cruise the Internet, or wander the streets of West Hollywood, searching out photogenic men. When he found a likely prospect, he'd approach the guy and offer him a job acting, telling him it was a commercial gig, for alcohol or underwear or whatever. Then, after Blake got the guy back to his office, he'd make the real pitch: *Hey son, how'd you like to be in an "adult" video, starring YOU!* As hard as it is to believe, the line worked. Everyone was looking for their "big break." Sometimes it didn't matter where it came from.

Blake's idol was Larry Flynt. He wanted to be the gay equivalent and had pictures of Flynt all over his office. His nickname: "Chubs, the porno producer." He loved it, would always laugh when he said it.

What was definitely not funny, though, were the fake receipts he wrote up for video services provided to my many charity events. These were either completely phony or represented severely inflated overcharging for footage that he actually produced—really bad and unprofessional stuff. *(You paid for this junk?* people would say to me.) I disgracefully went along with it because he was also "helping" me with my cash flow problems by freeing up some extra money to pay off greedy stars and their handlers, something I was too ashamed to do out of legitimate expenses. He'd split the take with me (minus the skim, which I didn't know about), then charge me five grand as the cost of the transaction.

Every time I thought of going to the authorities about Blake, he would threaten to take me down with him, destroy my reputation. It was a technique Wayne also used to keep me loyal and quiet. Cause them any trouble, they'd say, and they'd out me to the stars as a scam-artist. Career killer, right there.

ONE OF MY DREAMS had always been to become a TV or movie producer, and it was inevitable that, at some point in my career, I would try to branch into this illustrious area.

I had previously met Suzanne Somers and her husband/manager Alan Hamel when I tried to get Suzanne and Natalie Cole involved in a Home Shopping Network deal together, which didn't work out. But I stayed in touch with them and, after Hal died, brought Cynthia Gershman to Suzanne's gorgeous mountaintop Palm Springs home for lunch.

I had contracted to recruit someone to perform at the Associates for Breast and Prostate Cancer Studies annual gala, and I had targeted Suzanne. I figured Alan, who was eyeing the production of charity functions on his own, would see some future potential in an association with Cynthia. In return for my introducing Alan to Cynthia, I thought, Suzanne would possibly agree to do the ABCs event for me.

Nobody in town wanted to do the ABCs event. It had a reputation for being a collection of rude, gauche, and low-class people who were disrespectful to performers. I begged Alan to let Suzanne do it. Not her whole Las Vegas show, just a couple of tunes.

"Of course," Alan said. "We'd love to help you and your charity."

But not, as it turned out, before I offered him first-class tickets on British Airways, jewelry, and a lot of other stuff—the value of which came to three times what Suzanne Somers was paid for her entire Vegas routine.

When I was late getting their gifts to them, Alan sent me a vicious letter on Thighmaster stationery:

Suzanne and I have waited long enough! I want you to know that if we don't get our airline tickets and jewelry within five business days I am going to take out a full page ad in the *Hollywood Reporter* to tell the entertainment community about you.

I'd grown so used to this kind of bloodsucking behavior that it barely registered with me any more. I got their stuff to them, continued to cultivate Alan and Suzanne, sending her flowers and gifts in thanks for her performance, and before long I was mixed up with Alan in yet another deal. This time, he went right for my big weakness, my desire to make movies. He had a great opportunity for me. Or so he said.

Alan introduced me to his son, Stephen, whom he said was good friends with Keanu Reeves (true), and for whom Keanu would do anything (not). Stephen was a writer, photographer, and wannabe filmmaker who was struggling to make it, and, rather than helping the boy out himself, Alan put him with me. He could get Keanu Reeves to commit to a movie, I was told, and Stephen had the right one just waiting.

Sounded good to me, and as usual I jumped all the way in before knowing how deep the water was.

Alan and I spent hours on the phone and in meetings with him educating me about the ins and outs of the movie business, telling me what a great opportunity this was, how it would make me money and at the same time legitimize me as a producer with a Keanu Reeves movie on my résumé. Of course, what he really wanted were my resources.

The first step was to establish a company, which we called Midas Films, LLC. I financed the startup and paid thousands to have someone (provided by Alan) draw up our business plan and more thousands to the lawyers necessary to handle the legal details. I was listed as co-chairman of the firm, along with Stephen.

Stephen was our source of properties. He had several scripts and treatments awaiting development. One was *Hunger*, a remake of the 1966 Norwegian film about a starving writer, transplanted to Washington D.C. Another was *The Dumbheads*, a road comedy about a mother and daughter that was also envisioned as a spin-off TV series. Suzanne Somers was going to star in it (naturally), and Jenny McCarthy (who still had some heat on her at the time) had been persuaded to lend her name to it.

The only thing these projects lacked was the financing, which is, of course, for better or worse, the most integral part. As time passed, I began to realize that part of Alan's plan was to hook Cynthia Gershman into underwriting them—he kept asking me how much she was going to invest. Luckily, I never allowed her to get sucked in, and meanwhile, he didn't drop a dime into the pot.

The project we were really concentrating on, though, was our biggie, a period piece called *King Midas.* Everything was set, Alan and Stephen told me. The film was budgeted at sixteen million dollars. The cast was committed, supposedly: Keanu Reeves, Anne Parillaud, Joaquin Phoenix, Vittorio Gassman, Olivia Fougeirol, and Denis Lavant. Vittorio Storaro would be director of photography, Milena Canonero was designing the costumes, and Dean Tavoularis was going to be production designer. Principal photography would begin in the autumn of 1998 at Cinecittà Studios in Rome.

Impressive, right? I thought so too. So I scurried around, trying to line up financing. I talked to a lot of potential investors. The funny thing was, the first question they invariably asked me had nothing to do with the project: *Is Keanu Reeves gay?* That was what they wanted to know.

"I don't know, you'll have to ask him," was the only answer I could think of.

I took the idea to Mike Medavoy, the co-founder of Orion Pictures, whom I had met at one of my fundraisers. Mike was a legend in the business; getting him involved would have been great. But he told us the script needed a lot of work, that it would cost around a quarter of a million to get it shaped up. We didn't have it.

I tried my good friend Brad O'Leary, a wealthy businessman whom I would honor in my 1999 charity event, A Family Celebration. Even though Brad had already lent me nearly a million dollars, I asked him to consider becoming an investor. But when he kindly met with Stephen and me, Stephen was so rude and arrogant toward him—a trait he definitely inherited from his father—that I wouldn't have wanted Brad to suffer through the project anyway.

Then, after chasing another goose with a bogus financier, I was questioning everything. I had been taking the Hamels' word that all these different people were committed to *King Midas,* but I had nothing down on paper except for the plan. I asked repeatedly for something in writing. I got nothing. Just more reassurances. *You worry too much, everything's fine.* I was not reassured.

Then one day I ran into Erwin Stoff, whose firm represented Keanu Reeves. I was meeting with the manager who represented Jennifer Aniston and worked together with Stoff. I told him about my project with Stephen Hamel, and Stoff blew up.

He warned me that Stephen was always trying to exploit Keanu, that he had sold pictures and stories to tabloids about his friend, promised things he couldn't deliver, and so on. There was no way Reeves was going to do this picture, he told me flat out. No way. It was ludicrous. The whole budget would barely be enough to cover the actor's asking price.

That was it for me. I pulled out. There were a lot of outstanding bills remaining that I got stuck with. I got sued, but I paid them eventually, and that was the end of my career as a movie producer. What a waste of time and money.

And Keanu Reeves? Never met him. And I still don't know if he's gay.

AS I RECOUNT MY ADVENTURES from the latter half of the nineties, I realize I could be giving the impression that everything I touched was a disaster. This was not the case. In fact, I did many events that were unqualified successes, that raised a great deal of money and sent the charities home exuberant. Of course, that doesn't mean there wasn't plenty of bad *behavior.* This is Hollywood we're talking about, after all.

Take the following: I was ready to do another high-profile event, and I approached David Niven Jr.—son of the famous movie star—about doing something for the charity he was heading at that time, Recording Artists, Actors, and Athletes against Drunk Driving (RADD). I had two people recommend me to David: my true friend, publicist Jeffrey Lane, and my so-called friend, Barry Krost, who managed Liza Minelli and Taylor Dane, and co-managed Matthew Perry and Angela Bassett. That got me an invitation to David's home in Beverly Hills.

David and I hit it off immediately. He's extremely witty and charming. I told him I wanted to put on a great fundraising event for RADD, and he said, *let's do it.* He turned out not only to be a really nice guy, but a great person to work with. Unlike many of the stars' children in this town, he was not riding on his dad's coattails; he was very much his own man. Thoroughly professional, good at handling difficulties as they arose. David guided me and watched over everything as preparations for the event proceeded. Refreshingly, he had no secondary agenda; all he wanted was a smashing success for RADD. He was the primary reason that things went as smoothly as they did.

For a corporate honoree, David made a great pick: Suzanne and David Saperstein. Saperstein, originally from Texas, had made a fortune in the business. He'd recently relocated to California, where he was building an incredible forty-five-thousand-square-foot mega-mansion in Beverly Hills.

I got David Niven to set up a luncheon for me with Suzanne, a very elegant and beautiful lady with a great sense of humor. When I explained to her what we were planning to do, she was pleased that her husband would be honored and was enthusiastic about joining in. The Sapersteins ended up making substantial contributions to the charity. In addition, they allowed me to use their precious list of well-to-do friends and business associates, thereby expanding my base of people to whom I could go, both to solicit donations and to sell tickets.

Now we needed a celebrity honoree. I decided to turn again to Barry Krost. Barry was a short, fat, bearded, unattractive, gay Englishman, complete with heavy British accent, who dressed in unflattering clothes that made him look even fatter. He was one of those guys who's done a variety of things over the years, agent, manager, producer, whatever, making a living but never hitting it big. You meet a lot of them in the industry. He'd produced about ten films, all of them bombs. I'd crossed paths with Barry many times during my Hollywood career—including at the *Friends* event, where he coerced a twenty-five-thousand-dollar sponsorship out of me for twenty-five hundred dollars by threatening to pull Matthew Perry—and had gotten to know him pretty well.

I told Barry I needed someone good for this big event. How about Liza Minelli? Could he get her?

"Sure," he said and laughed.

I asked him why he was laughing.

"Because she's nothing but trouble," he replied. "And totally unreliable."

I probably should have listened to David Niven and gone with one of the other celebs he suggested, especially after Barry's warning, but of course I'd made my stubborn mind up. I wanted Liza, and I pushed David until he gave in.

So Barry agreed to get her, for a cash payment of ten grand. I paid it, but didn't tell David. He would have had a fit. He was an honorable man who believed in the quaint notion that charity work should not be done for personal profit and would never have approved any of these payments.

But we got Ms. Minelli, and I came up with an original name for the event: Entertaining Liza!

For celebrity co-hosts, I went back to Barry Krost, the alleged co-manager of Matthew Perry and Angela Bassett. Could he get the two of them for the reception? Sure, he said, for five thousand. Okay, okay. This actually didn't make a lot of sense, on two counts.

First of all, I already was friendly with Angela Bassett. She'd come to the Cartier gala and others, and I'd lavished tens of thousands in gifts on her and her husband. I would probably have been able to deliver her on my own. But then, I always had to consider the possibility that if I bypassed a star's manager, he or she might pull the plug on the deal at the last minute, leaving me holding the bag. As I knew him, Barry was one of those who would do it without hesitation or conscience.

Second, although I didn't know it at the time, the truth was that Barry had little to do with either Angela or Matthew, even though he claimed to be their co-manager. The other co-manager, Doug Chapin, was the guy who really handled them. So he had to be brought in as well, which meant that once again I had to pay, in the form of some expensive jewelry for Doug.

While I was at it, I hit Barry up for one more thing. Could he get Taylor Dane, whom he also handled, to perform at the main event? Sure. For another five thousand, plus a promised twenty-five thousand to Dane herself for singing (which she never got, but only because I didn't have it, not because I put my foot down).

Then Barry double-crossed me again. After he was into me for twenty grand, and the fundraiser was already planned out, he came to me and demanded that his own charity, the AIDS-related Project Inform, share in the proceeds from Entertaining Liza! Plus, I also had to add Angela Basset's charity, the Virginia Avenue Project, to get her to co-host. Otherwise, he was going to pull Matthew, Angela, and Liza herself. That put me right over a barrel. I had no choice but to go to David and explain the situation. He sure wasn't happy about it, but he saw the dilemma and agreed to let these two new charities into the mix, as long as the lion's share still went to RADD, per our original agreement.

Another crisis narrowly averted, which was good, because I was pouring lots of money into this thing. Liza Minelli was incessant with her demands, which kept escalating. First she had to bring several assistants with her, at my expense. Then it had to be a particular airline, and a particular hotel. Then her accommodation could only be the best suite in the hotel. On and on.

As if that weren't enough, Barry called and said Liza wanted to add yet another event to the whole affair, a night-before private dinner, a welcome-to-L.A. party just for her. David Niven told me not to do it, that it wasn't worth it, and we agreed we were not going to take any money away from the charities to fund it, as Barry Krost wanted to do. I was stuck again.

"I don't know what to do," I told Barry. "I can't afford to pay for it myself."

"Then," Barry said in that proper British accent of his, "you will just have to figure it out for the lady."

What with the pressure from Liza's staff, and from Barry, there seemed to be no choice. I said I would arrange it and pay for it and scheduled a wonderful five-course meal for the upstairs room at the new Chasen's in Beverly Hills. I never told David I was footing the bill—which came to around ten thousand dollars—out of my own pocket. I was too embarrassed.

Liza's assistants had supplied a list of people she wanted me to invite, mostly stars, and I delivered on that. By the time the big night rolled around, we had a guest list of a hundred. It was wall-to-wall celebrities like you wouldn't believe: Dionne Warwick, Dyan Cannon, Raquel Welch, Jon Voight, Martin Landau, legendary manager Bernie Brillstein and his wife Carrie (who was doing publicity for the main event), Red Buttons, Patricia Kennedy and Lee Iacocca, Milton Berle, Sid Caesar, Rod Steiger, Michael Feinstein, George Hamilton, on and on. Publicist Jeffrey Lane was there, and he had persuaded Burt Reynolds to host the event.

It was amazing, the show of support for Liza Minelli, how many people wanted to come out and be with her. It was a glorious evening. There was only one teensy problem.

No Liza.

I knew she was staying at the Peninsula Hotel, in the luxury suite provided by RADD, only five blocks away. Where in the hell was she?

I tracked down Susan Dubow, her publicist—who should have been watching over her client, not hanging out here—and found her deep in conversation with Barry Krost, who might also have taken some responsibility as Liza's manager.

Susan cut to the chase. Liza wasn't coming, she told me. She wasn't feeling well. I was beside myself. I'd set this whole thing up and paid for it with my own money, all because Liza wanted it. It was all for her. The room was full of people who wanted to see her. And now she wasn't feeling well enough to come to her own welcome party?

Here was the real story: We had arranged for a limo to transport Liza to Chasen's and for George Hamilton to be her escort. A half-hour into the evening, Susan got a call from George. He was with Liza, he said, and she was falling-down drunk in her hotel room. She couldn't walk, much less put on her happy face and come to dinner. It'd do more damage, in his opinion, to try to force her to go, than to let her stay where she was. Disgraceful.

Everyone knew about Liza's drinking problem. She was in a program. Alcoholics Anonymous, I think. She wasn't supposed to go near booze at all. Yet the night before, as I later learned, recording artist Michael Feinstein had her come to a party at his house and had let her drink all she wanted. And now, tonight, someone was supposed to have stayed with her, making sure she was reasonably sober when Hamilton arrived. No one did. Susan and Barry were shrugging their shoulders, saying there was nothing they could do. They had dropped the ball completely.

The evening was now an official fiasco. I filled Burt Reynolds in on the situation; then Burt did his best, getting up in front of those hundred people and apologizing with considerable grace, all things considered. He playfully put his arm around my neck as if he was going to strangle me. I have a picture of it, and though I can laugh about it now, it wasn't funny at the time. After making the fateful announcement, Burt got out of there. A number of other people left as well. Some stayed and had their dinner.

I was devastated enough at the collapse of this star-studded dinner party, but more terrified at what was to come. What if Liza didn't show for the main event? We had eight hundred fifty people coming to the Beverly Hilton Hotel, specifically to pay tribute to this famous entertainer. I couldn't let the charities down, or David Niven, who had worked so long and hard for this. The guest of honor had to *be there!*

I went over to Bernie Brillstein, for whom I had so much respect, almost in tears. Bernie shook his head. "What do you f—ing expect?" he said. He'd seen it all in his time. Still, he and his wife Carrie gave me a lot of support and encouragement. Tomorrow was going to be fine, she assured me. Which was more than Susan or Barry did. They had long since sneaked out of the restaurant and would be unreachable until the main event.

By the next day, I realized we were on the verge of a real disaster. We had to find someone strong and ballsy enough to take charge, go to Liza's hotel room that night, and escort her to the Beverly Hilton, regardless. We decided on Joe Pesci. Perfect. Someone asked him if he'd do it, and he said he would. I crossed my fingers.

By the time the VIP cocktail reception was over, I was praying that Joe and Liza were on their way. Naturally, Liza hadn't shown at the brunch we'd planned for the morning after the Welcome-to-L.A. fiasco. I expected that and would have been more surprised if she *had* attended, like she was supposed to. What was much more infuriating was that neither Angela Bassett nor Matthew Perry had showed up at the pre-VIP cocktail party they were co-hosting. Barry had some lame, last-minute excuses for them, all BS, of course. This was after the two stars' co-managers, Doug Chapin and Barry, had both been given cash or jewelry or both just to deliver them.

It was a further embarrassment for me, but I felt really terrible for David Niven, who wasn't expecting this kind of behavior and didn't understand it. These two were listed as co-hosts on the invitation, so where were they?

Worse still was that we had added Project Inform and Virginia Avenue Project as charity beneficiaries of the event, diluting the take for RADD, specifically because Barry Krost had demanded that we do it in return for his delivering Liza and Angela and Matthew. Yet none of them was there. And it was *my* "friend" Barry who had once again stiffed us. It was inexcusable. I could barely look a decent man like David in the eye, especially since I was the one who had worked so hard to sell him on Liza in the first place.

As you might suspect, I was a nervous wreck as we headed over to the Hilton. I asked Bernie Brillstein, "Do you think she'll show?" and he replied, "Don't hold your breath," and laughed.

We waited and waited—coming up with alternative plans, enlisting other performers, in case Liza didn't show—and just when we were about to give up on our guest of honor, she arrived. Joe Pesci had come through. Not that he was happy about it. When he walked passed he rolled his eyes at me as if to say, "What the f— did you get me into?" I don't know how he managed it—she was pretty smashed again—but he did. Maybe he just treated her like that guy in the trunk in Goodfellas.

Nevertheless, it was a spectacle. Liza looked terrible, like the walking dead—pale, overweight, wearing too much makeup. Her speech was slurred, her eyes unfocused, and she smiled at people without the slightest idea of who they were. Pesci gamely escorted the wasted Liza through the press line and into the ballroom, with the band playing "Cabaret," and she got a standing ovation that she most decidedly did not deserve.

Just remember who this whole thing was a benefit for: Recording Artists against Drunk Driving. And Liza Minelli shows up loaded! Incredible.

After we actually got Liza there, though, the night went pretty well. We gave out free tickets for members of the charity boards, and we raised a ton of money. Everybody went away very pleased. David Niven was totally gracious in accepting everything that had happened. That was all I'd really wanted. It more than made up for the personal financial bath I took and the dreadful behavior of Liza Minelli, Matthew Perry, and Angela Bassett, and/or their managers.

And that should have been the end of it. But, as was so often the case, there was a postscript.

Early the following morning, I was in my office, going over some other business, when the phone rang. It was the manager of the Peninsula Hotel, and he had a problem.

Liza was out of control, he said. She'd tried to charge two fur coats to the charities' account, had cleared the mini-bar out of liquor, and was demanding more at eight in the morning. She'd also left cigarette burn marks on the sofa and was acting badly toward the staff. Oh, and her dog crapped on the bed.

"We would like you to get her out of here as soon as possible," he said.

The difficulty was that all of her assistants had already flown back to New York, and so the only person left to call was me. But it was really Barry Krost's problem, not mine. I tried for hours to get him on the phone. When I finally reached him and told him what was up, he went over there, got her packed and down to the airport.

I settled the bill with the Peninsula myself. David had put up with enough already. He didn't need to be involved in the final act of her little drama. And I certainly never needed to become involved with Liza Minelli again.

CONSIDERING THE KINDS OF THINGS I've been detailing, it's easy to think everyone involved in the entertainment industry is either a boor or a rip-off artist, or both. Fortunately, that's not the case. There are some terrific people in the business, and during this period of my life I had the great privilege of getting close to one of them: Wayne Newton, as well as his wonderful family, his gorgeous wife Kathleen, their daughter Erin, and his sister-in-law (and publicist) Tricia McCone.

Of course, it didn't hurt that I was already a big fan of Wayne's. I've probably been to see his show fifteen times or more. Wayne would come out, descend down a long white spiral staircase, and walk across the stage as women screamed "I love you" and threw flowers and notes at him. It was always packed, every single booth and chair filled. At some point, he would come into the audience and hug some of the screaming women, which of course would make them scream even more.

He would also personalize his performances, talking to the crowd between numbers. He would often, whenever I was in the audience, dedicate his performance of "Danke Schöen" to me. It's one of my favorite songs. It was always an honor.

I'd met Wayne at the 1997 Jim Beam Stakes, after a lot of calls to his office, and I'd become friendly with him and his family right away. He came to handful of my functions, always paying his own way. But it wasn't until a couple of years later that I got invited to his Las Vegas estate, Shenandoah, for the first time. I was in the midst of planning A Family Celebration and had to go to Vegas to make arrangements for a kickoff party we intended to hold there at the MGM. I also wanted to see Wayne, to bring my constant companion, Cynthia Gershman, to meet him, and to talk with him about a charity he was thinking of starting, called First Americans (although that never did work out).

So the Newtons asked us out to dinner at their estate. Cynthia nearly wet her pants with excitement. We arrived in

Vegas in 110-degree heat and checked into the MGM, where Wayne was performing. His sister-in-law Tricia had booked a suite for Cynthia and me. We'd go out to Shenandoah that evening for dinner, and then back into the city to catch Wayne's show, where a reserved booth was waiting for us. This was the kind of first-class treatment Wayne and his family gave to his friends and guests. And that wasn't even the half of it.

When the hotel management took Cynthia and me up to our suite, on one of the private floors, and opened the door, our jaws dropped. It was something you couldn't imagine, that you might see only in the movies. The suite was at least five-thousand square feet, the size of a very large home, and two floors, with an elevator and a winding staircase between them. It had two master bedrooms and a full gym, sauna, pool, multiple big screen televisions, kitchen, on and on it went. It took us fifteen minutes to tour the whole thing.

I had never been in a hotel suite this nice and, rich as she was, neither had Cynthia. There was an incredible basket of fruit, cookies, and other goodies on the table, along with a note from the Newtons welcoming us. We were astounded. I called Tricia immediately to thank her and her family. It was such a kind gesture and showed both what they thought of me and how gracious they were to their visitors.

Shenandoah was even more spectacular—it reminded me a lot of Graceland. I remembered other stars who were Wayne's friends telling me how much they loved being invited to stay out there when they wanted some privacy, to get away from it all for a while. Now, as we headed up the long, tree-lined drive, I could see why.

In addition to the main house, there were several guest-houses. There were fenced areas, with beautiful Arabian horses inside, along with barns and stalls and other outbuildings, one of which housed Wayne's antique car collection that featured several vintage Rolls Royces. And there were animals everywhere. In addition to the horses, there were many dogs and a special habitat he'd built for his penguins.

Kathleen and her sister Tricia greeted us and took us out back for drinks and to wait for Wayne. There were more animals out there, a pond, ducks, even a wallaby hopping around. It was amazing.

Wayne arrived, and we went in and had an excellent dinner with the whole family, which included Kathleen, Erin, Tricia, and also Tricia's mother. Kathleen was delightful, not only beautiful but very intelligent, an attorney who helped Wayne with his business. Wayne obviously doted on Erin, a pretty, dark-haired girl who was in college. I had to do most of the talking, of course, because, as I've said before, Cynthia had trouble conversing.

After dinner, Wayne personally drove us back into the city in one of his Rollses. We were having a great time, talking and laughing. I got to call Lee Iacocca, whose upcoming seventy-fifth birthday party I was invited to, on the car phone. A real blast.

We gathered backstage in Wayne's dressing room, which was huge, while he was preparing himself for the show. There was a lot of food set out, and desserts, which I helped myself to, of course. Then we all adjourned to the theater, where we watched the show from the best table in the house. It was a truly magical evening.

I was able to visit the Newton family at Shenandoah several more times, and each one was special. Of all the relationships I made with the stars, Wayne Newton's was one of my most treasured.

AFTER HAL DIED, CYNTHIA GERSHMAN decided it was time to get serious and resume her acting career. (I know that *resume* may not be quite the right word, but that's the way she looked at it; she felt she'd given up her own dream to be with Hal, who had only held her back.) I tried my best. I paid one agent twenty-five hundred a month to find her work, ran through several publicists who all dropped her fast, spent tens of thousands in cash, jewelry, dinners, etc. in order to land her two-line speaking parts that were invariably excised from the final cut. You could probably make a pretty good comedy short if you spliced together all of her scenes that ended on the cutting room floor.

Of course, I didn't want to help her with any of this—it was a real embarrassment, and no one wanted to handle Cynthia, not even if I paid them as much as their top clients did. But Cynthia was determined and told me if I didn't help her get parts, she would pull all of the support from the events I was producing.

I now had the expertise and financial wherewithal to help other people set up charitable organizations of their own and did so for Jean-Claude van Damme, creating the Take Action Foundation, which was supposed to raise money to help disadvantaged, inner-city children. When Cynthia heard I was working with the, at that time, hot action star, she demanded to meet him and subsequently landed a role in his new action pic.

"Sure," van Damme said, "I have just the part for you." We met at Spago to discuss details. Van Damme told Cynthia that she reminded him of his mother and that he wanted to make her dreams come true. Sure enough, the next day his office called and offered to make her dreams come true for $100K. A hundred-thousand-dollar role for Cynthia. Not her salary, of course. Her payment. Or rather my payment.

Naturally, Cynthia didn't want to feel like she was paying exorbitant sums out of her own pocket for these parts, so I helped her with that, foolishly putting myself at risk by manipulating foundation funds. This is how it worked:

Back before Friends Helping Friends, I had incorporated my own nonprofit, the American Foundation for the Performing Arts (AFPA), and was preparing to apply for 501(c3) status. I thought that some day, when my career was more secure, I could turn my attention to providing help to people who wanted to succeed in this industry, as I had (theoretically). The foundation's mission, as I wrote it out, was *to provide support for students, performers, creative talents, showcase venues, workshops, theater groups, and others whose needs are apparent and ongoing.* As always with me, my vision was grand.

Initially, I set AFPA up as a pass-through foundation, to help me reorganize the way I handled money. Previously, I had approached charities, mostly one at a time, and asked if I could produce a fundraiser for them. Now, I had sufficient power to be able to organize the event first, then find several charities who wanted to benefit from it. Money from donors to the event would go into AFPA, from which I would immediately disburse it according to the percentages I'd worked out with the different beneficiaries beforehand. Everyone would get their fair share.

The foundation was not supposed to be for my use, or for any programs that I administered; this structure was supposed to financially protect me and the charities I worked with. As it worked out, though, AFPA was also ideally suited to be a vehicle for other things, darker things that I had never anticipated.

I made the mistake of putting it at the service of Cynthia Gershman. What she would do was write a check from the Gershman Foundation and make it out to AFPA. I would provide her with some kind of bogus receipt for her tax purposes, showing that the money had gone to charity. Then I would withdraw the cash and hand it off to the likes of Jean-Claude van Damme and his associates, and all the others whose only concern was how many pounds of flesh they could carve off a poor, deluded old woman.

What I failed to consider was how I was going to answer questions about my nonprofit. Did I think that no one would ever want to look at my books? Probably not consciously. When you had as many balls in the air as I did, such thoughts don't even enter your mind.

So most of the hundred grand was paid out, and Cynthia had her hot movie deal with the great Jean-Claude van Damme. And *hot* was the word for it, all right. Van Damme's epic was being filmed in the California desert in the dead of summer, with the daytime temperature rising to over 110 degrees.

I would have to pick up Cynthia around 4:30 in the morning, and drive her two and half hours to the set. Then we would sit outside in the desert and wait, with dust and sand blowing in our faces. We were so isolated I couldn't even use my cell phone to conduct any sort of business.

Cynthia had no motor home or special dressing room, of course. They just stuck her in with all the derelict extras. I swear they must have searched out every homeless person in Southern California, picked them up, and bussed them all out there to stand around in the background of their shots.

To make matters worse, Cynthia insisted on bringing her poodle T.J. along. Every hour, I would have to go fetch him water, which was a kind of relief from his incessant barking.

We sat for two days in the hundred-plus-degree heat, never seeing Jean-Claude once, or doing much of anything. Finally, on the third day, Cynthia had her big moment. In the scene, she was one of the passengers getting off a bus, and she said, "Excuse me," or something lame like that. End of the hundred-thousand-dollar part.

It made no sense to me. Here was this megamillionairess in her seventies, who had more of everything than she could possibly use, and could do almost anything with her life that she wanted. Yet she willingly chose to subject herself to this kind of abuse, complaining about it the whole time, then did it all over again the next time anyone offered.

Cynthia was furious about the experience, but would never let on to her friends. The final humiliation came when she took a group of them to a screening of the movie, and she wasn't in it. She'd been cut once again.

Yet Cynthia's demands kept escalating. She was feeding

larger amounts of money from the Gershman Foundation into AFPA.

Because I desperately needed funds to meet my obligations to my own charities, I would divert some of the cash back to her for her personal use with the rest going to my own charities, so I could continue to meet my obligations. It was always of the utmost importance to me that the charities not suffer because of the exorbitant payments I had to make to stars and the people around them. I couldn't allow those to eat into an event's legitimate proceeds.

Luckily, the Gershman Foundation was a bottomless well. Cynthia was in charge of disbursing about two and a half million a year, and she did it with gusto. She wrote checks like there was no tomorrow. It was instant access to a lot of money, so easy to do, and we both got carried away, ignoring the eventual consequences of our actions (in my case) or not having a clue what they might be (in hers). It was a situation—me in constant debt, she desperate for something she could never have—that almost begged for abuse. And as the noose that held us together tightened, the chances we took got bigger and bigger, and the day of reckoning got ever closer.

Desperate to enlist someone to take Cynthia on as a client and actually get her some decent gigs, I finally found a guy named Mark Basile, a celebrity trainer and struggling actor/screenwriter whose main claim to fame was that he was good friends with Mark Wahlberg. But he did have some connections with some smaller movie studios, and he initially got Cynthia hooked up with a couple of companies, Emmett/Furla Films and Lions Gate, which made the kinds of films that might consider someone like her.

That began a string of "parts" for Cynthia. I would pay the producers, along with a hefty commission to Basile, and she would get to believe her career was finally taking off. We're not talking chicken feed here, either. She might fork over seventy-five thou for two or three lines, and once even paid a quarter of a million for not much more. Pretty soon the word was out, all over town: *easy mark, right over there.* Now two-bit production companies were showing up right and left, offering movie roles, screwing Cynthia out of her money. Ultimately, well over a million bucks would go from the foundation to outfits that were definitely non-charitable.

As of this writing, Cynthia has not been charged with any crime related to these shenanigans, though she has been named as a defendant in a civil suit brought by the State of California against me, Cynthia, and others, for alleged misuse of charitable funds. Ironically, many times, as she wrote out these checks, I heard her say, "I hope I don't get into trouble."

The first person to catch on was Ron, Cynthia's stepson. He was upset, not so much about the financial shenanigans themselves, but because he was worried his sister Gloria would find out and make trouble. He didn't want anything to jeopardize the free ride he was getting as a trustee of Hal's estate.

On the other hand, he wanted to keep his stepmother happy, in case he ever needed her vote on something. So he was willing to turn a blind eye to what we were doing, provided she agreed to a reorganization put together by the foundation lawyer.

This was the new deal: the Gershman Foundation funds to be dispersed each year would be divided, with Cynthia getting a third and Ron managing the other two-thirds. That made

Cynthia furious—no longer would she have two and a half million to play with, now it was "only" approximately eight hundred grand. But she realized she had no choice and accepted the arrangement. As for what Ron and Gloria did with their portions, I have no idea; Cynthia was my focus.

The eight hundred thousand wasn't enough, of course. Cynthia came to me and said we could never build a decent career on a mere eight hundred thousand dollars. However, she added, it was going to be okay. The reason she'd gone along with Ron's plan was she'd figured out another way to get the money. Maybe even more than before. It was so easy, she said.

Although of course I didn't realize it at the time, what I was hearing was the beginning of the end. And, boy, do I wish I hadn't listened.

NINETY-NINE WAS A VERY GOOD YEAR for me from the point of view of the charities. The Liza affair was an excellent benefit despite her antics. In February, I produced an eightieth birthday party for Red Buttons that raised a hundred ten thousand dollars for the Friar's Charitable Foundation, and there were a couple of others, as well. After the Friends and Lasorda disasters, I had regrouped, concentrated my efforts on delivering the goods, and built my reputation back up through a string of successes. People were happy with my work. Professionally I was growing, although personally I was drowning in debt and becoming ever more desperate for "solutions" to my financial problems.

The big one of the year, though, was A Family Celebration:

One Giant Leap for Humanity, on September 26. Once again, I would deliver for the charities involved, and once again I would have to face the distractions, shakedowns, and bizarre behavior I'd become so accustomed to.

I had to pay Norby Walters twenty-five grand for making the connections to our evening's celebrity honorees—Gladys Knight and the cast of the hit TV show *The Practice.* I once asked Norby, "Aren't you afraid of getting caught, charging charities to deliver stars and then getting those stars to come for free and pocketing the money?" He just laughed. "My humanity has been rubbed away," was his answer.

Dealing with *The Practice* folks I was forced to coordinate things through Neely Swanson, the director of business affairs at David E. Kelley Productions, which produced the show. I needed her, since there were eight different actors to accommodate, and she knew it. So she hit me up for seventy-five hundred dollars. It was a payment, straight out of charity proceeds, and I shouldn't have had to make it, since all she was doing was her job. But I wanted everything to go smoothly, so I paid.

I ended up, at Neely's insistence, having to offer extravagant trips to Club Med to all of the cast. Michael Badalucco went with a companion; so did Kelli Williams and a guest. Unbelievably, a couple of years later, a friend and personal assistant of Dylan McDermott's demanded the same trip. "If you want to keep Dylan happy, you'll do this," he warned. I'd become pretty friendly with Dylan, so I did it.

Each of the cast members also got a five-thousand-dollar watch that they then had to pose wearing, to pay back the company that had provided them; as usual, commercial interests were lining up to exploit a charity function. And on top of everything else, Neely demanded separate limos to bring each member of the cast to the event and take them home. She wouldn't budge on it. Which meant the charities were out another four hundred fifty per limo.

But at least now I had my celebrity honorees. After that, the others easily fell into place. It was a kid-centered event, and they would get their awards from the Child Welfare League of America, as follows: to Shuki Levy, president of Saban Entertainment, the Spirit of Giving Award; to Brad O'Leary, president of PM Consulting, the Humanitarian Award; to David S. Liederman, former executive director of the Child Welfare League of America, the Protecting America's Children Award; to Shannon Reed, manager of entertainment sales for British Airways, the Human Spirit Award; and to Daphna Edwards Ziman, the Uniting Children of the World Award.

I was especially glad to see Brad O'Leary being honored. I'd met him several years earlier and, when he told me his daughter had MS, I introduced him to Nancy Davis, who was also afflicted with the disease. Nancy then had her personal doctor take the girl on as a patient, and he was able to help her. As a result, Brad became a very generous supporter of Nancy's Race To Erase MS and a close friend of mine.

Brad was a highly successful businessman and author and a truly decent person who helped me out financially and tried his best to keep me on the right track. He introduced me to his bookkeeper and his lawyer and urged me to use both of them to get my business affairs straightened out. But I was too headstrong. As with Steve Fox, I couldn't recognize good advice for what it was.

Also, for Brad, it didn't stop with being honored and receiving an award. He worked his butt off for the benefit, bringing in donors and raising money like you wouldn't believe, and never asking for a thing in return. Diahann Carroll—one of our co-hosts, along with Dan Aykroyd and Howie Mandel—was the same way. She is an amazing woman, a gorgeous and gracious lady. She worked very, very hard, expecting nothing in return. She was responsible for bringing in Joanna and Sidney Poitier as our dinner chairs. Appropriately, she presented Brad's award to him.

The beneficiaries of the fundraiser were to be the Child Welfare League of America and We Care about Kids, the former a large, out-of-town charity and the latter a small, local one. I brought in the Associates for Breast and Prostate Cancer Studies, part of the John Wayne Cancer Institute, in an attempt to get them the money they'd lost at the Friends event, and, to ensure we had enough of a draw, Children Uniting Nations.

To properly publicize and promote the big September event, we decided to host a kickoff event in June. It went well, despite the prima donna antics of Dionne Warwick. Where Gladys Knight had not asked for a thing, Dionne demanded that I fly her whole family out for it, eighteen people in all, and put them up. Quite a family. This was after I'd already forked over thirty-five thousand for her to help me line up performers for the main event. That's how much she charged me, even though Gladys was supposedly one of her oldest and dearest friends, and you might think Dionne would do *something* on her own dime. Nope.

Once in Vegas, she continued spending, ordering up facials, massages, movies, whatever she wanted, and charging it all to her room (which meant us). When the hotel tried to bill us ten thousand dollars for her extravagances, Sandra Furton Gabriel—one of my few inspired hires, a tough, no-nonsense woman and brilliant former producer on *Late Night with David Letterman,* whom I brought on board as stage show producer—put her foot down and refused to pay it. *This is for charity,* she told them, *get Dionne to pay her own bills.* They had a big fight, but Sandra was tough (and right) as always, and she stood her ground. I wish I had had her backbone, because Dionne then came fuming to me, and I, always trying to make people happy regardless, borrowed some money and paid the tab.

As a footnote to all this, I wound up having the last laugh. I hooked Dionne up with Barry Krost, who became her new manager. They deserved each other.

As September approached, I was getting really excited. We'd landed Ed Hall of the *Tonight Show* to be our announcer, and the lineup he'd be announcing was just fantastic: Stevie Wonder, Luther Vandross, Dionne Warwick, Patti LaBelle, and Chaka Khan. When you get so many big names, though, you're in for the usual ridiculous requests.

Vandross, for example, wanted to stay at the most expensive hotel in Beverly Hills, the Peninsula, instead of the Century Plaza where we had a deal, and I accommodated that. But then he demanded that we pay for his makeup, to the tune of fifteen hundred, plus all expenses associated with flying in his makeup artist. Total bill around five grand, for two songs. Sandra Gabriel, bless her, wouldn't hear of it. *Forget it,* she told him, *we are simply not going to do that.* Which got Luther so miffed that he refused to do his songs. This was Gladys

Knight's lifelong friend, the guy who was going to present her with the Harmony Award, threatening to renege on his commitment to her because he had to do his own makeup. Some harmony. But that was what he did, presented the award but didn't sing a note.

The day of the event, Chaka Khan had her turn. She also wanted fifteen hundred for her makeup, or she wouldn't perform. In cash, up front. I didn't have that kind of money on me, of course, so I had to go to Blake Lindquist to get it at 100 percent interest. Too bad I didn't have Sandra Gabriel with me.

She *was* there, though, for Chaka Khan's next outrage. Chaka had this horrible dress that she wanted to wear for her performance—it literally made her look about a hundred fifty pounds heavier than she was—and she wanted me to pay for it. Fifty-five hundred dollars. Naturally, I said okay and handed the bill to Sandra, who handed it right back. "NO WAY," she said. "This is a *charity* event!" I was so lucky to have her.

In the end, no cranky stars were going to spoil this night. The silent auction went beautifully, and there was an audience of about 925 for the show. It was studded with notables: Marla Trump, Patricia Kennedy and Lee Iacocca, the Reverend Robert Schuller, Ike Turner, and Little Richard. Haim Saban came to pay tribute to Shuki Levy, the pal with whom he'd created *Mighty Morphin Power Rangers*. Even Barbara and Marvin Davis attended and, to my amazement, actually paid for their table (Barbara was like a Nikki Haskell with money). I'm sure it was because the Davises had such a close relationship with Joanna and Sidney Poitier.

The performers were great, especially Stevie Wonder, who brought down the house. We had so many that we ran out of

Proud to be an American:
Lee Greenwood and me.

Meeting the Gipper:
Peter Paul and me in
Ronald Reagan's office.

Caught between two
heavyweights.

Celebrating his ninety-third
birthday at the Beverly
Hills Hotel: Uncle Miltie
flanked by Patti LaBelle
and wife Lorna.

Anything for charity: Peter Fonda, Tanya Tucker, and Gary Busey. Even though it was her own event, Sharon Stone never showed.

Hal (Col. Sanders?) and Cynthia Gershman, Yvonne Paterson Tushner, and me.

Kelly Stone, Sharon Stone, Cynthia and Hal Gershman, and renowned artist Bill Mack.

Sharon Stone making a splash, distracting press from the Bill Mack exhibition.

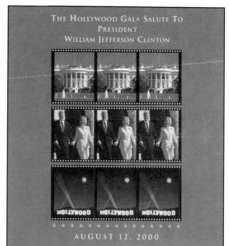

Cover of the Hollywood
Salute tribute book.

President Clinton and me.

Pennsylvania Ave. meets
Sunset Blvd. Brad Pitt
thrilled with Bill at
Hollywood Salute.

photo by: Peter Halmagyi

Dianna Ross giving her laryngologist something to worry about.

Clinton works the audience at Salute.

The first lady and me exchanging hugs at Salute.

Sharing success with one of my mentors: Peter Paul and wife Andrea.

Visiting the White House.

From a homeless shelter
to the Oval Office!

Another trip to the Oval Office:
Loreen Arbus, President Clinton,
Norman Chandler Fox, and me.

White House regular Denise Rich
and Candy Queen Diana Ellis.

Standing in front of Air Force One: Peter Paul, me and Clinton, California Governor Gray Davis standing in back.

photo by: Peter Halmagyi

The first lady and me talking shop at Senate campaign fundraiser.

Cynthia, ever-present dog Pepper, Hillary, and the man who brought them all together.

Al Gore's heart aflutter
with the promise of money.

Congressman Dick
Gephardt and the man
who brought
him Roseanne.

Where are my ribs?
Roseanne and me.

Elizabeth Taylor regales Clinton, David E. Kelley, and Michelle Pfeiffer at Family Celebration 2001.

Backstage with *NSYNC, Britney, and the president.

Larry King and me.

Honoring President Ford with the Special *Giving* Award. The former president got his money before Betty.

time and had to cut some of them out. Like Kyle Eastwood, Clint's son, who's a jazz musician, and Steven Seagal, the actor and reincarnated Tibetan monk, who brought his guitar and wanted to sing.

I was happy. The audience was happy. Best of all, the charities raised a lot of money, and they were happy. Of course, once again I didn't get compensated for all my work; in fact, I just fell further into debt. But I wasn't going to let that bother me when I could pull off spectacular events like this one.

No doubt about it, despite all my personal problems, I was riding high at the end of 1999. Under the circumstances, it was probably inevitable that I would take a trip to the intersection of Sunset Boulevard and Pennsylvania Avenue.

As the whole country prepared to enter a new century, I was about to plunge headfirst into the wild, wonderful world of politics.

twelve

THAT'S RICH

My *"break-up" with Natalie Cole* was less than permanent. A few months later, I saw her again, and our relationship would continue *on-again, off-again* until our final parting in early 2002. So it was in mid-1998 that we were in New York, having lunch at Harry Cipriani's, when a woman named Michele Laurent Rella approached our table. Natalie, as it turned out, knew her slightly.

"Hi," she said shaking Natalie's hand, "Remember me? I am Denise Rich's best friend."

Michele, I would learn, was the kind of person I described earlier, the "best friend"—someone who follows around another person who is rich and famous and nearly loses their own identity in the process. This was our first meeting, but I would be around Michele quite a bit over the next few years, and I introduced her to a lot of people. Every time, she would respond in exactly the same way. Instead of saying, "Hello, my name is Michele Rella," she would say, "Hello, I'm Denise Rich's best friend."

Honing in on Natalie, she mentioned that Denise was having a cocktail party that night at her apartment, just half a block away on Fifth Avenue. Rella invited us both. I guess she figured that if I was with Natalie Cole, I must be someone.

I asked Natalie about Denise Rich after Rella had gone. I'd never heard of her, nor of her ex-husband, fugitive financier Marc Rich.

"Oh, she's just some New York socialite. A B-list songwriter, too," Natalie said. "But she's very wealthy."

My wheels started whirring. I was always looking to meet potential donors or underwriters for my events. They might even have charities of their own that I could produce fundraisers for. I didn't want to pass up the opportunity to make a fresh contact. So off we went to 725 Fifth Avenue.

DENISE LIVED IN THE PENTHOUSE. Now, I had met a lot of monied people during my Hollywood career. A whole lot. I'd been in homes all over Beverly Hills, Holmby Hills, Brentwood, and Bel Air. But I have to say, I had never seen anything like this before.

Technically, it might be an *apartment*, but to call it that is more than a little misleading. What Denise Rich really owned was a *house*. It just happened to be located on top of a very expensive building, on a very expensive street, in one of the most expensive cities in the world.

The place was at least fifteen thousand square feet, in my

estimation, and had three levels. Inside was every amenity you could think of, including an exercise gym, guest quarters, and a state-of-the-art recording studio. And that's not counting the beautiful roof garden, with its panoramic view of the city.

Each room was impeccably furnished, with antiques everywhere, and what looked like valuable art hanging on the walls. Knowing nothing about art, I had no idea what I was really looking at. But after I became friendly with Denise, I had a picture taken of President Clinton and me in her apartment, with one of her pieces in the background. A friend of mine who saw it said that the painting was worth a fortune.

When we arrived, a butler in a tuxedo greeted us, and then someone else took our coats. There was a large number of waitstaff and other servants attending, including one who circulated with a silver tray offering the finest caviar and other hors d'oeuvres.

Though I didn't know it at the time, I would later discover that this wasn't just because she was hosting a cocktail party. This was how she lived. There was *always* a substantial staff on hand, and *always* fine caviar served when you came to her house, day or night. I knew people in California who had servants, of course. But not like this. This was *serious* staff.

Natalie introduced me to Denise, and I was taken with her right away. Besides the fact that she had some of the nicest jewelry I'd ever seen, she was good-looking, friendly, warm, and welcoming, and not at all pretentious.

Denise was busy with her sixty other guests, of course, but Michele Rella, the "best friend" who had invited us, took us under her wing. She gave us the grand house tour, then I spent most of the evening talking with her.

I told her I produced charity events in Los Angeles and elsewhere, and described some of the things I'd done. I also told her about Cynthia Gershman, who had a private charitable foundation and would help underwrite just about anything I was involved in. Natalie chipped in to say I had produced some great events.

Intrigued, Michele told me about the G&P Foundation for Cancer Research, a charity that Denise had founded in memory of her daughter, Gabrielle, who had died in 1996 of leukemia at twenty-seven. The "G&P" was for Gabrielle and Philip Aouad, Gabrielle's husband.

I was very interested in what I could do with this. Michele was enthused as well, and she called Denise over to discuss the possibilities. Denise cried often when she spoke about her daughter; you could see the great love she had for Gabrielle and how much she missed her. In the end, we decided that we'd reconvene the next day.

With son-in-law Philip and several others on hand, Denise showed a video of her daughter, who was beautiful and well-spoken and seemed very special. It was obvious that this was a terrible tragedy for all of them. And I could see that Denise wanted to do good. I encouraged her to let me organize and produce an inaugural gala. I believed we could raise a great deal of money to help endow the relatively new foundation.

I suggested Cynthia Gershman as a potential underwriter. I knew she'd be in hog heaven if she had a chance to move in a social circle like this one (although how long the relationship would last was another question). I was right. Cynthia threw in a hundred thousand, and I threw myself into organizing the event.

That's Rich

Then I got a phone call that would usher me straight into the realm of politics, and change my life forever.

DENISE TOLD ME SHE WAS inviting a few select couples to a special luncheon at her home that would be attended by Vice-President Al Gore and President and Mrs. Clinton. It would be for a maximum of a hundred people, limited to those who had given a hundred thousand or more to the charity.

Because of her contribution, Cynthia qualified, and I could come with her. I knew Cynthia would be thrilled, but I also thought this might be an opportunity for me to repair some of the damage with her stepson, so I asked if we could bring Ron Gershman and his wife Kathy. It was very presumptuous, but Denise okayed it.

This was such an incredibly prestigious invitation. The president of the United States! I was ecstatic. The only thing that seemed out of place was that Denise kept emphasizing that this was a very *private* party and stressed that I should not discuss it with anyone. I took that to mean that maybe she didn't want a lot of publicity or something.

The truth of the matter is that this luncheon was more than a reward for charitable contributors. It was also a Democratic National Committee fundraiser—a fact to which I was not privy until about a week before the luncheon. After we were packed and ready to go, Denise called to let me know the rest of the story. Now, unless we contributed fifty grand each to the DNC, we were going to be uninvited.

I really went off on her. "*What?*" I yelled. "Are you f—ing kidding?"

"I'm sorry," she said.

Now knowing Denise, I doubt she intended to mislead us. Regardless of how it happened, my butt was officially in a sling. I couldn't go to Ron and Cynthia Gershman and tell them this. If I did, it could be all over for me with them—and all those foundation dollars.

I thought it over and came up with a plan. It wasn't a very good one, and I never discussed it with anyone, but I figured it might be good enough to get us there. I called Denise back and begged her to let us all come for fifty grand, total. *Agreed.* The DNC, as a special favor, would let the four of us ride on that one donation. Without telling the Gershmans, I wrote the check and FedEx'd it just prior to the luncheon.

I'd never be able to cover the check, of course, so as soon as lunch was over I stopped payment.

WHEN WE ARRIVED AT THE BUILDING on Fifth Avenue, I couldn't believe the security. Secret Service everywhere. I'd never seen anything like it. We weren't allowed to go in the main entrance, but instead had to use a side entrance and pass through several checkpoints, metal detectors, and so on.

The Gershmans' eyes bugged when they saw Denise Rich's apartment. Ron was really envious, I could tell. Sure, they were wealthy, but not like this.

We were on the lower floor for a short time, talking to various people because the Clintons hadn't arrived yet. Then-

DNC Chairman Steve Grossman came over and said how pleased he was to meet us, especially me (whose name was on the check). It was obvious from the charm he was turning on that he thought the party had just recruited a new big donor. He was in for a surprise when he discovered I'd stopped payment.

Soon we went up on to the roof garden, where the luncheon was being held. It was beautiful, and very warm. I chatted with Patti LaBelle, met Denise's other daughters, and hung out with Natalie a little bit. When we went to our tables, I was separated from the Gershmans and seated next to Nancy Moonves, then-wife of CBS Television President Leslie Moonves. It was a great table because everyone knew and respected Nancy and Les Moonves. When people came over to say hello, the prestige kind of rubbed off on me.

The presidential party finally arrived and, after spending a few private minutes with Denise, came up to the party.

Vice President Al Gore was first to come by our table and was very friendly. Then came the president and first lady. I introduced myself. They were also both warm and friendly. I told them how glad I was to meet them and made a little small talk, then they mostly conversed with Nancy Moonves as I listened.

The highlight of the day was probably when Patti LaBelle and Natalie Cole serenaded Bill Clinton with an impromptu, *a capella* version of "Somewhere over the Rainbow." He hugged and kissed them both.

After we ate, I got a chance to spend another minute with President Clinton. I thanked him for the economic prosperity he'd brought to this country. Then Steve Grossman came and took me over to meet Hillary Clinton more formally. She was a warm woman who seemed very sincere, and focused intently on whomever she was meeting and talking to. She looked me straight in the eyes, which I loved more than anything. She made me feel like I was the only other person in the room.

This was my introduction to big-time politics, and I was hooked.

I also got a taste of the national media limelight. At a cocktail party later that evening, CNN interviewed me. I said that although I was a Republican and hadn't voted for Clinton, I was a supporter because I thought he was leading the country in the right economic direction. The interview went around the world, and I quickly realized how much publicity power was tied into these events; attending one could land you on national TV in an instant.

Of course, I wasn't much of a star with the DNC when the check went sour in their hands. They called a few times about it, but gave up. Maybe dogging a single donor for a bad check made them look desperate for cash.

MEANWHILE, PLANS FOR THE October 12 G&P charity fundraiser were coming along fairly nicely. It was highly disorganized and way over budget, but we had a great cast of characters lined up. For talent, Stevie Wonder and Natalie Cole, and many others; for honorees, Les Moonves and Milton Berle—who decided to throw a monkey wrench in things.

Part of the G&P event was paying tribute to Uncle Miltie on his ninetieth birthday, which actually fell in July of 1998. His wife Lorna told me that she and Milton wanted me to throw him a party then. Maybe Denise Rich would pay for it, they reasoned, if we also announced it as a kickoff for the October event. Remember that this would be on top of the seventy-five thousand he was getting to show up at the New York gala and be honored. Enough was never enough with Lorna and Milton.

Denise refused to foot the bill, understandably.

I should have, too. Even though I'd realized by now that Milton was never going to attract many celebrities or bring in much money, I was always afraid of losing a celebrity contact. I caved in and laid on a lavish party for him and two hundred and fifty guests in the upstairs ballroom at the Beverly Hills Hotel. There was a four thousand dollar cake in the shape of a TV with "Mr. Television" on the screen. For gifts, Seidler's of Boston came up with some stunners: a Chaumet platinum watch for Milton, along with diamond cigar-shaped cufflinks and studs, and for Lorna, a diamond and gold bracelet.

It was a star-studded night, even by my standards. Steve Allen and Monty Hall emceed. Bob Hope, ninety-five and very frail, made a cameo appearance. Tony Bennett and Jerry Vale sang. Red Buttons said, "What a turnout to see Milton for the last time!" The audience, to name just a very few, included Kirk Douglas, Frank Sinatra Jr., Angie Dickinson, Sidney Sheldon, Jacqueline Bissett, Eddie Fisher, Burt Reynolds, Connie Stevens, Carl Bernstein (of Woodward &), and Senator John McCain. Denise even flew in for it, since I had gone ahead and billed it as the kickoff to the main event. She was dressed beautifully as always, with stunning jewelry.

The party cost a fortune—an appropriate prelude to the October bash itself.

Spending on the main event was way out of control, largely due to Denise's inability to say no. She was well-intentioned, but still a novice, and didn't know what to do in an affair like this. Any little problem that came up, she would pay to try to make it go away. So, while the official take for the G&P Foundation was close to three million dollars, I'm sure there was little left over after the bills were paid. I'm equally sure that Denise made up the difference out of pocket. Unlike many others—for whom these events were their crowning social achievements and the money raised was secondary— Denise didn't want or need the self-promotion. She was serious about benefiting the charity.

Denise's novice status led to another disaster on the night of the gala. Actually, *disaster* isn't a strong enough word.

When I arrived at the Sheraton New York Hotel and Towers with Cynthia, Natalie, and some other out-of-towners, I found utter bedlam. Mobs of people trying to get in. Lines that didn't end. Something was wrong. It turned out to be an event producer's worst nightmare.

Denise had hired a local event planner to do much of the detail work, including seating, and the planner had dropped the ball. Seating is always a headache, because everyone wants the best table in the house. You accommodate as best you can, but what you want to avoid at all costs is the seating chart to be non-existent. That's what we had here.

The poor people posted at the entrance were supposed to take admittance tickets and hand out table tickets in return. They didn't have any. On top of that, President Clinton was coming, so there were additional layers of security and checkpoints. It was unseasonably hot, to boot. The cream of New

York society was here, and they were getting very cranky. We waited two hours to go through a procedure that should have taken ten minutes.

Once we got inside, I found that things were no better. Everyone had been funneled into the cocktail area, which was hot and overflowing with bodies. Thinking that maybe our names were on the tables, I went to the ballroom to check. But I couldn't get in. The ballroom doors were locked! No wonder conditions were so bad.

Oy. There was nothing to do but wait it out, which we did. Finally the doors were unlocked, and then I swear it was like the Jews fleeing Egypt in *The Ten Commandments,* except in the other direction. People fanned out, not having a clue where to go, but not wanting to get stiffed.

One couple I hardly knew grabbed me and said, "Aaron, we paid twenty-five thousand dollars for our table. *Where is it!?*"

What could I say? "I didn't do the seating. You'll have to figure it out for yourself."

I couldn't help anyone else, because I had to get Cynthia, Natalie, Ron, and Kathy settled. Cynthia had pledged a hundred grand, and already delivered seventy-five, so she was entitled to a very good table. But the only ones that were marked were a half-dozen or so up at the front, the best ones, reserved for the biggest VIPs. Those looked like they'd been tagged just a few minutes earlier. For the rest of us, it was open seating now.

I decided to brazen it out, went right into the VIP area, and snatched a table that was marked for a famous designer artist. I pulled it out of the reserved section and put Cynthia dead center, right up front. A security guard then came up to argue with me, but Natalie Cole stepped in between us and got right in his face, saying *this is my table.* He knew who she was, that she was one of the night's headliners, and backed off.

Cynthia and Natalie were set, but I still had to deal with Ron and Kathy. I went back a few rows and evicted a couple that was already seated, telling them that I was the producer and this was one of my tables. They were pissed, but gave it up. Truly, I didn't care how they felt. I'd gotten my party squared away.

Then Geraldo Rivera got up on stage, took the microphone, and addressed the crowd. He said he had the seating chart and was going to get everyone in their proper place. *Forget about it.* The din was so great, hardly anyone could hear him, and even if they did, they couldn't be bothered. They were too busy elbowing and fighting. Water glasses were spilling all over the place, and many tables were soaked.

Furious, I went looking for Denise Rich. When I passed the VIP area, I saw Dan Rather talking with Les Moonves, who did not look happy. He recognized me and asked me, very politely, to please do him a favor and get a chair for Katie Couric, who didn't have one. I grabbed one from somewhere and gave it to Katie, who thanked me, sat down, and didn't get up.

Milton Berle was furious. He'd arrived to find Bill Cosby's family and friends at his table, and he told them in no uncertain terms to get up or else he was leaving. He was on his way out—our night's honoree—when some staff member intervened and rudely displaced the Cosby people.

I found Denise backstage, intending to cuss her out. But there she was, practically in tears on Donald Trump's shoulder, hiding from the crowd. She looked like she couldn't handle any more grief. So I walked away and said nothing.

After such a catastrophe, I had every reason to fear that the show would also flop. Luckily, it didn't. People got settled at a table, some table, any table, and the rest went very well.

President Clinton spoke. Placido Domingo performed; so did Patti LaBelle and Natalie Cole. Stevie Wonder sang "Happy Birthday" to Milton Berle. Bill Cosby presented Milton with his award, while Dan Rather did the honors for Les Moonves. Celine Dion did a presentation. The crowd was filled with familiar faces. In addition to Geraldo and Katie and the Donald, Ivana Trump was there, Goldie Hawn, Star Jones, Joe Torre, Diahann Carroll, on and on. Denise even had her picture taken with the Duchess of York!

Denise looked great. I always thought she had excellent taste, but Joan Collins was a bit more catty. She used to say that whatever Denise spent, it wasn't on fabric content, meaning the outfits were too low on the top and too high on the bottom. At this event, she was wearing a purple-and-silver Escada gown into which she barely fit. When Joan saw it, she commented that Denise looked like "an expensive bejeweled sausage."

DESPITE THE ROCKY START, Denise and I became friends and stayed that way for several years. I got her a new stage-show producer and helped her out when I could. She in turn sent me startup money when I needed it for some of my fundraisers.

Denise opened doors. Hanging out with her meant spending time with her circle—except perhaps the most important couple in that circle, the Clintons. Denise was very protective of them. As far as I could tell, they had a very solid relationship. She never discussed it much and, apart from starting me off by inviting me to the luncheon, never helped me get in with them.

I would do that all on my own.

thirteen

CLINTONMANIA

*My kindness flows from . . . a deep appreciation
for all you have done this year for Democrats,
including me.*

—ED. RENDELL,
Personal Letter, January 9, 2001

Late in 1999, I went to see Peter Paul for the first time in years.

Brilliant and imaginative, he had reinvented himself once again. He had a beautiful new wife, Andrea, new offices on Ventura Boulevard over in the Valley in Encino, and an entirely new line of work. Fabio was history, along with most of the other people from the old days. Peter had cast his lot with Stan Lee.

Stan Lee was a legend, a genius who had created a long list of comic-book superheroes, such as Spider-Man, The Incredible Hulk, X-Men, Daredevil, The Fantastic Four, The Silver Surfer, and many, many more. When the two men met, Stan was doing okay, but was no longer in his heyday.

It was Peter's own genius to see unlimited opportunity where others might see only a guy past his prime. Peter had a vision that was bold and adapted to a world that was changing drastically right before our eyes. We put our difficult past behind us and talked about the future. Though much of it was beyond me—I barely knew what the Internet was, for example—I smelled money, and lots of it.

And money was important. More than usual.

DESPITE THE FACT I'D PRODUCED two major events in 1999—Entertaining Liza! and A Family Celebration—as well as several smaller ones, I was piling up debt faster than I could manage it. To keep my head above water, I did whatever I could, mainly borrowing and shifting money around from account to account.

I'd gotten used to the money-shuffling gambit hanging around Cynthia and watching Gershman Foundation assets do amazing things. Initially, I used my own nonprofit, AFPA, to handle the money for her. Later, I ran cash through a series of at least a half-dozen DBAs opened at banks around town by Blake Lindquist and one of my attorneys Eddie Jamison. That Blake was charging me a hefty fee didn't help. But I had no credit of my own, and this was one of the only ways I could stay a step ahead of people coming after me for money.

I would take receipts from one event, pass them through a bogus account, and then use the money to meet obligations from a previous event. That was not only illegal, it was crazy. I kept thinking that in the end I'd be able to make it all gel. I'd pay all my creditors and make good on all my loans, the charities would make tons of money, and those who bad-mouthed me today would thank me tomorrow. Even though I didn't use drugs, from my thinking you'd have never known it.

Something else that doesn't make sense: through it all, I continued to live in near-poverty. I only kept enough to eat and live in my run-down, one-bedroom apartment. Money itself never mattered that much to me. But now I needed lots of it.

I did have many financial angels. Whenever I was in deepest need, incredibly good and generous people would appear to lend or give me money. Steve Fox lent me millions. Brad O'Leary more than a million. Joni and Jody Berry supported my events continually in a very big way. Others did as well, some of whom I'll discuss later.

For now the important thing was Peter Paul was sailing high again, and he needed me.

IN 1998, PETER PAUL AND STAN LEE founded Stan Lee Media (SLM), a publicly owned corporation that they financed by selling stock (NASDAQ: SLEE). The goal was to create a branded, global entertainment franchise that would merge film, radio, TV, and music, using the Internet to tie the whole package together.

Peter described a big place for me in this enterprise, because of the extensive access to famous personalities I already had and my skill at continually meeting and befriending new ones. That could really help them get the thing off the ground, he told me. The price of admission was twenty-five thousand bucks, which he said I actually still owed him from years earlier. He was prepared to sue me to get it. BS, of course, but here was my choice: walk away and face a lawsuit with all its attendant bad publicity (more of which I certainly didn't need), or pay him and snag a piece of what might be the biggest cash cow of my life. This was a no-brainer. I borrowed the money, paid him, and moved into a vacant office at SLM as a consultant.

Right off, Peter wanted a gala public launching for the new company—a big, glittering party with entertainment and Hollywood stars. He had already lined up Jerry Lee Lewis to come and sing, but he wanted as many more celebrities as he could get. That was my job.

First thing, I brought in Lynne Cohen from Malibu. Lynne was a very competent publicist and budding film producer who had helped me with A Family Celebration. Peter hired her on the spot to be our event planner.

We settled details fast. Time: February 29, 2000. Place: Raleigh Studios, right across the street from Paramount. Publicity: Jeffrey Lane. Production: Dick Clark Communications, with Clark announcing.

Then I went to work packing the house with guest celebs. I reached into my own bag but also enlisted the aid of new friend Alana Stewart. Alana had been married to both Rod Stewart and George Hamilton and was doing a great job raising the children she'd had with each of them. She was one of the most decent, honorable people I met in Hollywood, loyal and beautiful, with a great sense of humor. What's more she was resourceful and hard working. Together we got her ex, George, along with James Caan, Nicolette Sheridan, Chaka Khan (who sang), Joey and Matthew Lawrence, Anthony Michael Hall, Dean Cain (my own personal money pit), Lou Ferrigno (the original Hulk), Harry Hamlin, Red Buttons, and others.

Peter and Stan were using the event to showcase SLM's product: weekly, episodic, superhero Webcomics. The first, *The Seventh Portal*, was shown, and a second blockbuster, due in June, was announced: *The Backstreet Project*, which would cast pop mega-stars, the Backstreet Boys, in an online game in which they were granted super powers. If all went as planned, cash would flow in torrents from the merchandising offshoots of these and other animation efforts.

The big bash came off without a hitch. It was an historic happening. The whole affair was Webcast in real time. Dick Clark Communications was ecstatic to be part of it. The company turned the Raleigh Studios sound stage into "an immersive, global, cyber-techno experience," in the words of executive vice-president Jeff Salmon. "[This is] the first convergence of film, radio, television, music and publishing with the Internet." Roving reporters treated the broadcast audience to interviews with executives and guests, who enjoyed food and a martini bar set up under huge renderings of the new, online comic book characters.

We had ourselves the best send-off we could have imagined. We were on our way, and really pumped up.

Suddenly, Peter Paul and I were fast friends again. So, naturally, the next thing we did was illegal.

I BROUGHT PETER UP TO DATE on Cynthia Gershman, and he immediately started scheming ways to get his hands on her money. He came up with the idea of persuading her to invest in the new venture. He still had his own 501(c)(3) nonprofit, the

American Spirit Foundation (ASF), and it was perfect for shuffling Cynthia's foundation money around without unwanted scrutiny.

The way it worked was that Cynthia would write a check from the Gershman Foundation to the ASF. One charity to another, no problem there. In return, however, Peter would gift her with an equivalent value in SLM stock to put into her personal account. That's not so kosher. Peter would write Cynthia the same kind of tax letters that I used when we were doing this with my American Foundation for the Performing Arts. Additionally, he assured her that she would make a fortune as the stock increased in value, and he sweetened the pot still further by promising her roles in the movies SLM would produce, as well as other unspecified contributions to her career.

That was all Cynthia needed to hear. She was off, madly writing checks in no time. She had her quid pro quo, and Peter had a nice infusion of cash. I have no idea where most of the money went, but a little of it came to me to pay off debts and give back to Cynthia and Peter.

An example of one of Peter's "helpful" moves in furtherance of Cynthia's career: In November 2000, SLM sponsored the 69th Annual Hollywood Christmas Parade. A joke of an event, Peter nonetheless saw some useful publicity value and media exposure in it. To pay for his involvement, he went to Cynthia and offered her a chance to ride in the parade as a famous movie star, to be seen in that role on national TV. Knowing Cynthia, he calmly asked for a cool quarter of a million dollars. For her, this was a dream come true, so she willingly paid up (with foundation money, of course).

The thing was a fiasco. Cynthia was put in a car carrying

Hal Linden of *Barney Miller* and his grandkids, and they had the place of honor, sitting up on the back deck of the convertible. Cynthia was shoved down onto the seat, while I rode up front, waving and pretending there was some reason for me to be there. To make matters worse, the TV announcer characterized Cynthia as a "philanthropist" and made no mention of her acting career.

On top of all that, Alana Stewart and George Hamilton had been hired as co-hosts, and Peter never paid them. Peter thought the entire affair was hilarious, but it was an embarrassing experience for me, and it made Cynthia more furious than I had ever seen her before.

I don't think Stan Lee ever knew what was actually going on. He would stop by my office sometimes, shake his head, and say, "I don't know how you do it." He didn't want to know.

In any case, on we went, Peter and I. We were moving very fast, into all kinds of areas. Weeks before the SLM bash, in fact, we were already wheedling our way into the world of big-money politics.

EARLY IN 2000, I MET a political operative named Terry New. Employed by a Sacramento-based lobbying group, she was a strong Clinton supporter from Arkansas and had close ties to the Democratic National Committee (DNC). After talking about what I did, she wanted to know if I'd be interested in participating in a Democratic fundraiser.

"Can I meet the president?"

Terry said yes.

"How much to sit with him and have my picture taken?"

"Thirty thousand," she said.

I got a few more details, then took her business card and said I'd call if I could swing it.

Immediately, I went to Peter Paul and told him about my encounter. Without really being sure I could deliver, I said I could get him and Andrea and Stan Lee into a private dinner with President Clinton, and that they could sit at his table. How great would that be for SLM, and for only thirty grand!

I quickly overcame Peter's initial reluctance to part with that much money by just talking it up, and eventually he wrote the check. I delivered it to Terry New, and, just like that, I popped onto the radar of the DNC. This was a whole different group from those I met through Denise Rich, so there was no fallout from what had happened in New York. I don't think they would have cared anyway. This check cleared, and thenceforth I was treated like gold . . . or maybe fresh meat.

The event at which we were to meet Bill Clinton was scheduled at the Café des Artistes in Hollywood, on February 13, 2000, for the benefit of the DNC. We made arrangements for Peter and Andrea to sit at the president's table, and for Joan and Stan Lee to come to the pre-dinner cocktail reception. Peter wanted to sit right next to Clinton, but the organizers wanted an extra twenty-five grand for that. Nix.

As all this was happening, my own wheels were turning. During my conversations with the Democrats, I saw how they absolutely loved Hollywood celebrities, and I thought, *What if I brought some of my friends?* If I could set up some entertainment, and invite a few stars to attend, might that not increase my access to power? I knew it'd be an easy thing to accomplish, and besides, I loved doing it.

Needless to say, my new buddies went nuts for the idea. This was great for them as fundraisers, and it'd really jazz up the event for the president.

So I called country singer Mac Davis out of the blue, off of some old mailing list I had. I invited him, and he accepted. Then I approached Alana Stewart, asking her if she thought she could get her good friend Olivia Newton-John to perform. *Sure,* she said, and she did it. Olivia agreed to sing for free, if I would do her the favor of meeting with the heads of a charity she was involved in to see if I could help them. No problem.

I had our performers. But I also wanted a few stars to sprinkle among the crowd. I went to Neely Swanson and asked her to invite Calista Flockhart for me. I'd already met Calista a couple of times, and she was very nice. You'd think I wouldn't have to pay to arrange the thrill of a lifetime for Calista (or anyone else), an evening with the president of the United States, and probably if it had just been the two of us, I wouldn't have. But I had to work through Neely Swanson, and with Neely, nothing came free. I paid, and Calista showed up. So did Gregory Peck and music producer Kenneth "Babyface" Edmunds.

The only other person I had to pay for was Jim Brickman, a famous musician in his own right, who was going to accompany Olivia. I almost died of embarrassment when one of the Clinton staffers came up to him while he was standing by his instrument before the show and asked if he'd play some background music for the cocktail guests.

The event was perfect. It was a magical evening, very intimate, with only sixty guests. The president was gracious, as he always was, and quite friendly to me. He thanked me for what I'd done for the fundraiser and said he remembered me from Denise Rich's. Maybe it was even true. He does have an extraordinary memory.

Clinton especially seemed to like chatting with Alana Stewart, who had a seat next to California Governor Gray Davis. She *was* a gorgeous woman, after all. Like everyone else, he enjoyed Mac Davis, but he positively loved Olivia Newton-John. He even mentioned her in his speech.

A final incident should be mentioned here because of its far-reaching significance.

I had spent several thousand dollars to purchase CDs and cassette recordings of music by my headliners, Mac Davis and Olivia Newton-John. I saved the receipts and afterward tried to give them to one of the members of the DNC. I wasn't expecting reimbursement; I just wanted to further ingratiate myself by showing how much I'd spent on behalf of the organization.

To my surprise, the woman didn't take the receipts. Instead, she took two steps back, recoiling like I had the plague.

"Please," she said, holding up her hands. "I don't want them. Forget it. Just throw them away." And when I asked why, she said, "Because they would be applied to the political contributions."

"Oh," I said, though I had no idea what she was talking about. Soon I would learn what it all meant. Boy, would I ever.

Now, as I traveled the American political landscape, I would come to learn that financial funny business is not confined to one party. However, since I was primarily involved with the Democrats, it was their practices I most closely observed.

At the time of the Café des Artistes event, though, the incident barely registered. I was on a roll now.

PETER KNEW I WAS BUSTING my *tuchas* for SLM and wanted to show his appreciation. He also knew I constantly needed money.

Peter and Stephen Gordon helped me open an account at Merrill Lynch, so that Peter could deposit stock into it for me. I didn't know the first thing about stocks, or how an account worked. But in no time, I had a hundred thousand dollars of unrestricted SLM stock, which was selling for about six bucks a share.

Peter wouldn't let me sell it. Instead, I learned about my margin account, through which I could now borrow cash against my holdings, up to 50 percent of their value. Cool. All of a sudden, I was worth something, at least on paper. Better yet, I could use my holdings to put real dollars into my hand—like having a big personal ATM machine.

I immediately margined the whole thing. I took out fifty grand and paid off some of my debts. For the next several months, I didn't have any big events, and that's what I lived on. Peter would give me more stock, and I'd turn it into cash on margin.

No one filled me in on what would happen if the stock price went down. It wasn't the sort of thing I would have wanted to hear anyway: that if the value of my account sank to a certain level, I would get a "margin call" and have to figure out a way to pay back the money I'd withdrawn.

I also had no inkling of the manipulations of SLM stock that Peter Paul was involved in—or was about to be. In the months to come, this would play a major role in my life.

PETER WAS DESPERATE to build a close relationship with Bill Clinton, for three main reasons.

First, anything he did with the president would be great immediate publicity for Stan Lee Media. It would raise the profile of the company, attract investors, and boost the stock price.

Second, he had this idea that he could persuade Clinton to join the board of directors when he left office and become the corporation's global goodwill ambassador. Whatever that cost—and Peter would eventually be prepared to offer him millions—the company would reap much more in benefits around the world from the prestige of being associated with a former and very popular U.S. president.

Third, there was always the possibility that, if enough money were paid to Democratic causes, Clinton could be persuaded to pardon Peter from his previous criminal convictions. Time was growing short on this one, with the president due to leave office the following January. Peter moved quickly to ingratiate himself.

I was definitely with Peter in wanting SLM to succeed. The price of the stock was steadily rising, from six dollars into the teens and beyond. I thought we were all going to get big-time rich. At the same time, I wasn't really a member of the team; I was only an outside consultant, by choice. I had my own dreams and wanted to remain my own person this time around. So my primary hope for my involvement with SLM was that it would get me out of debt. I was in very deep, and getting deeper. If I was to have a chance to branch into TV production, always a long-term ambition, I had to pull myself from that hole first.

Forging a relationship with the Clintons became an integral part of Peter's plan, and thus of mine. Not that I minded. I enjoyed them, loved being around them and meeting those who traveled in their circles. But how to get closer to the president, that was the question. We thought about it and decided that what we obviously needed to do was to meet with him in some more intimate setting.

With this in mind, I brought in Cynthia Gershman. She was very pleased to become "politically active." Of course, politics didn't have the slightest bit to do with it. There was nothing in the world she would value more than to count a president and first lady among her acquaintances. She was tired of the *schmos* and *schleppers* she'd been hanging out with, she told me. Moving in the highest political arena, she thought, would elevate her standing in the community, and attract a higher caliber person to her social affairs. True to form, she also believed that it would somehow give a boost to her non-existent acting career.

Originally, I thought fifty grand would do it, and that's what I told Cynthia. *Donate that much to the party and you'll get an audience with the president.* Turned out I was a few bucks shy. I conferred with Stephanie Berger, the DNC's Southern

California finance chairwoman, and she told me the going rate: five hundred thousand dollars bought a fundraiser luncheon with either Clinton or Gore; dinner would cost a cool million.

That sat me down in a hurry. But I thought it over. Maybe between SLM and Cynthia we could raise the money, especially if Peter were allowed to make corporate stock a part of the deal.

I went back to the DNC. They said they would accept a combination of stock and cash, but that neither Clinton nor Gore would go to dinner with just me, Cynthia, Stan and Peter, and their wives. It wouldn't look proper, they said. It would look like we were trying to buy influence. Hello!

However, they told us what we *could* do: donate the required amount of money and then invite a number of people to the luncheon or dinner, so that it at least looked as if more than just a few had contributed. Then it wouldn't matter if all the money had actually come from the four of us.

I told Peter the deal, and I could see his mind working. This was a golden opportunity for us to use a political contribution (a big one) to befriend an outgoing president who could bring great international publicity and prestige to a hot young company. Heck, Stan Lee could even make Bill Clinton one of his Internet superheroes.

We tossed the idea back and forth, and in the end decided there was only one real question: how much could Cynthia Gershman give?

We went back to the DNC with a deal: a guarantee of five hundred thousand for the Gore campaign, to be raised at a dinner at the Beverly Hills Hotel on June 8. Stephanie told us she'd have to check it out with her boss, the DNC chair. That she did, and he gave us the go-ahead. At the same time, we confirmed two events for Hillary—a small luncheon at Spago and a tea at Cynthia's, both scheduled for the following day, June 9.

For the initial event, Peter Paul pledged a hundred fifty thousand dollars to Gore, in restricted SLM stock that would become negotiable in September. And Cynthia pitched in with a hefty sum as well.

SINCE PETER WAS SUPPOSEDLY guaranteeing the take, I began to look at the Gore dinner as more of a private party than anything else, to use however I wanted. Some people were paying twenty-five or fifty thousand dollars for a table, while I invited a lot of friends and comped them. So did Peter and Cynthia, and I think Stan Lee as well. Not many of our friends or business associates had that kind of money to blow on a meal. It was quite a special gift to drop in someone's lap. The schnorrers swarmed.

I brought a whole slew of stars: Jamie Foxx, Jon Lovitz, Donna Mills, Frances Fisher, Red Buttons, Suzanne Somers (and husband Alan Hamel—Lord, wasn't I a glutton for punishment?), Olivia Newton-John, Alana Stewart, and so on. I paid for a luxury weekend for Michelle Rella and her husband Frank, comping them tickets to the Gore dinner and the Gershman tea for Hillary. Michelle stayed true to form, shaking Al Gore's hand and saying, "Hi, I'm Denise Rich's best friend, Michelle Rella."

In addition, I was doing some romancing of people I thought might be useful to me in the future. One was Arnold

Stiefel, manager of Rod Stewart, with whom I wanted to do a big event. I was already connected to Rod through Alana, but I needed Arnold as well. A second guy was the Rodeo Drive designer Bijan, who owned an "appointment only" boutique, sometimes called the most expensive store in the world. He drove a yellow convertible Bentley and was in the midst of an ad campaign with Michael Jordan. I wanted to know him, so I invited him to the next day's luncheon with Hillary Clinton as well.

Then there was Gary Smith. My ultimate goal was television production, and Gary was highly respected in that arena. He was doing the Democratic Convention that year, so I invited him to the Gore bash so that he could see what I could do. Maybe I'd hire him for something. I did, shortly thereafter, but that project wouldn't be a TV show. It would be the Hollywood Salute to Bill Clinton in August.

Finally, there was Edward G. Rendell. Since the party at Denise Rich's, Steve Grossman had resigned as general chairman of the DNC. The new guy was Ed Rendell, who was between jobs. He'd been mayor of Philadelphia for eight years, through 1999, and was preparing to run (successfully, as it turned out) for governor of Pennsylvania in 2002. In the meantime, Ed was spending a lot of time in California.

My early contact with Ed had been by phone, through Stephanie Berger, as we planned the three June events. I wouldn't actually come face to face with him until the night of the Gore dinner, and at first I didn't quite know who he was. He knew me, though, and knew that I was connected to serious money, so he immediately hit me up for help with his Pennsylvania campaign. I said *sure*, not really meaning it.

Pretty quickly, though, I caught on to the fact that the new DNC chairman had a lot of juice, including access to the first family. He worked tirelessly. After I got to know him better, I used to joke that every time I turned around, there was Ed, raising money. I wondered when he found time to spend in his home state. He pushed me very hard to go out and raise money for his gubernatorial effort whenever I saw him. I did eventually help out.

Because of Peter and Cynthia's big financial involvement, we got a private audience with Al Gore prior to the dinner.

I didn't find him particularly engaging. He wasn't as personable as either of the Clintons. But he was nice enough not to embarrass Cynthia by trying to carry on a conversation with her after he quickly discovered how inarticulate she was. He talked mostly with Peter and Stan, which was what they wanted anyway.

For me the big payoff was the incredible access—and not just political access. I immediately found that I could call the biggest, most inaccessible stars and get a hearing. If I invited them to one of these functions for the president, vice-president, or first lady, they would get back to me right away. The answer was almost always, *Yes!* and I was able to chalk up another connection made that could later be turned to the good of my charities.

It was the bridge I had been looking for. It felt almost like a secret weapon that granted me entrée into the entire Hollywood community. My life was on a new and exciting path.

When the night was over, the press reported that the dinner netted $1.4 million for the Gore campaign. Pure bunk. Taking into account the expenses for putting it on, and the fact that the room was filled with non-paying guests, I'd be surprised if they cleared anything at all. At the head table, which is where the high rollers are supposed to sit, there wasn't anyone who had paid a dime. On top of that, although Peter claims to have honored his financial commitment, I believe he stiffed them. I think Cynthia failed to honor her pledge, as well, although I know she funneled a bit of cash through Peter's American Spirit Foundation that went toward covering some of the evening's expenses.

I don't know what the gaudy reports of monies raised were about. Maybe the candidate's handlers were trying to make it look like their man was out there pulling down crazy cash.

After it was all over, the same thing happened as had happened with the Café des Artistes event. I tried to give the DNC people an accounting of expenses I'd paid, for Olivia Newton-John and her band, for party favors at the tables, for the event planner's fees, and so on. Despite the fact that the affair was lavish and expensive—or more to the point, perhaps because it was—they once again wanted no record of them. I didn't understand why, but I was quickly discovering that it was in a campaign's best interest to avoid expense reporting. I'd find out soon enough. But at the beginning, I just took it for granted that this was some minor offense that everyone did and kept quiet about.

I was a babe in the woods when it came to politics.

AFTER THE GORE DINNER, I could barely sleep, thinking about the day to come. I was going to escort the first lady of the United States, and a Senate candidate to boot, to not one, but two functions. And the icing on the cake was that I really liked her. I'd felt a warm, solid connection with her from the beginning. Much more than with her husband.

A year earlier, this new world had been completely unattainable to me, and now it was wide open. All that it had taken was money. I'm not sure what I had thought about the relationship between politics and money before I got involved. I probably didn't think about it at all. But I was getting a first-hand education in a hurry.

The two events of June 9 were very different from each other. First, there was going to be lunch with the first lady at Spago, with only twelve invited guests. Nice and intimate, a chance to really get to know her. Then we would all go to Cynthia Gershman's home for an afternoon tea for about one hundred. Another great opportunity to build the relationship.

How much all this had cost, I have no idea, but it was loads. I knew that Cynthia had given money, of course, since I handled a lot of her donations. Peter says that he kicked a hundred fifty thousand into the Senate campaign fund, although whether he actually paid it, I don't know for sure. Most of what he did with SLM stock was out of my sight. Terry New had also worked hard to bring in money, as had I. Ditto for David Rosen.

One of the things I had noticed about Hillary Clinton was how young so many of her staffers were. I already knew Stephanie and Terry, and would this day meet two more who were part of the innermost circle: longtime aid Kelly

Craighead and Rosen, who was director of finance for Hillary's Senate campaign. All young, all dedicated, energetic people. I suppose that's why she liked them. But another characteristic of youth is the willingness to take risks, and in that way some of them did not serve her nearly as well.

Take Rosen. Though I hadn't met him in the flesh yet, I'd worked closely with him by phone. He was my consultant on money matters, since I had only a passing acquaintance with campaign finance law. If there was any question in my mind, I'd call David. The problem was, whenever I asked for advice he would invariably laugh off my concerns and say, "Don't worry. Just raise as much as possible. Just keep at it."

Here's an example: I came up with what I thought was a great idea to make it look as though support were coming from a lot of little donors, instead of one big one. I proposed that Cynthia would write a check for forty grand, which she was willing to do, and I would run it through one of my accounts and emerge with cash and started giving it out in one-thousand- or two-thousand-dollar chunks to twenty or thirty people. They would then turn around and write personal checks of their own for the same amount, and that would be "their" contribution. Sounded good to me, but when I presented it to David he laughed for about three minutes straight. When we got down to it, though, he told me to go ahead. I should have been suspicious when he added, "Just don't tell anyone." Later, he would pull me aside at Spago and reemphasize the point: I was to keep that little trick of mine quiet, "very quiet."

He was equally adamant concerning expenses. Here, as with all the previous political fundraisers, I was pointedly told they didn't want the receipts I had, and that I was, under no circumstances, to report expenses for which I didn't have a receipt, such as the twenty thousand in cash that I paid Dionne Warwick to sing at the Spago luncheon. "Throw them out," David told me. "Don't write them off on your taxes, just get rid of them. I don't want to know about them. What we want is the appearance that expenses were minimal."

I went along. I didn't know any better. Eventually, I would become a lot more familiar with Federal Election Commission requirements, and see exactly how much misreporting had been done on the things I was involved with. *Tons.*

At the time, though, all I had to go on was that this was the head money guy for a U.S. Senate campaign speaking, and he was greenlighting whatever I did. Even if some of it seemed dodgy, I had no choice but to trust him and assume that he knew what he was talking about, didn't I? Well, not completely. Concerned that some day this stuff might come back to haunt me, I saved all the receipts.

None of that, however, was going to spoil June 9 for me. The Spago luncheon was for just twelve people and was held in a private room rather than in the restaurant's general seating area. This was very understandable, both for security reasons, and because the first lady would have caused too much commotion if she were out in the open. That really bummed Cynthia. She was going to be there with her new "best pal" Hillary Clinton, and she wanted all the regulars in the place to see.

Before lunch began, I met Kelly Craighead and David Rosen. David and I visited for a little bit. He knew that I was a Republican, but didn't hold it against me because I said I would work hard for the Democrats if it meant helping the

Clintons. I really wanted Hillary to win. *I'll do anything*, I told him. *Use me as much as you can.* He did. Very shortly I would find myself deeply immersed in another campaign fundraiser, this one back in Chicago, and then . . . the biggest of them all.

My connection with Rosen meant that I was mostly finished with Terry New. I'd now moved up in the organization. We'd do one more thing together, for Governor Gray Davis, but that was it. It was too bad. Terry was great. She had done a lot for me, had introduced me to a lot of important people. Much later I would try to show my appreciation for her by sending her a check for twenty-five hundred dollars. She returned it uncashed, saying she had just been doing her job, and that to take the money would be unethical. How rare and refreshing that was!

Back to Spago for the luncheon. I went into the private party area, where there was a room for a reception and another for the lunch. Security was tight. Secret Service men, looking tough and stern. We were all tagged. No one could get in or out. My event planner had done her usual fabulous job creating the right atmosphere. There were beautiful flowers and place settings. Everything. Over in the corner was a little electric piano and a mike. Dionne Warwick was going to sing "That's What Friends Are For."

Yeah, I thought. *I'd be a friend too, for twenty grand.* She was still mad at me for things she hadn't gotten last time around, so I'd had to go through my "buddy" Barry Krost to get her. Pay him, pay her. Her normal fee was around thirty thousand for a complete show with orchestra. Here, twenty for one song. Cash. As usual, it was a "business expense" that came out of my pocket. No way the campaign was going to reimburse me.

But so what? The guests all arrived, and they were excited. There was Joan and Stan Lee; Andrea and Peter Paul; Shawn King (Larry's wife); Alana Stewart; Olivia Newton-John; Bijan; Angela and Gerry Harrington, manager of Sylvester Stallone and Nicholas Cage, among others; Susie Tompkins Buell, founder of the Esprit clothing company, a friend and supporter of Hillary Clinton's; Cynthia Gershman; and me. There was also a last-minute addition: Barbara Lazaroff, Wolfgang Puck's wife.

When Hillary arrived, I was the first to greet her. We stepped into a small, private room adjacent to the luncheon area, embraced, and kissed on the cheek. With her staffers and Secret Service agents guarding the door, I said something so bold that I almost can't believe it.

"I am so happy you are here," I said. "I'm going to do everything I possibly can to raise money for you to win this Senate seat. I hope I am not overstepping my boundaries here," I added, "but you have been through so much embarrassment, you deserve this."

Not only did she not take offense, but I felt that we definitely connected at that moment. My Republican friends were always telling me how evil Hillary was, but that was not my experience. I was quite enamored with her. She was obviously maternal in nature, very engaging, warm, and genuine.

Just as we were getting ready to eat, someone told Hillary that Marvin Davis was outside in the restaurant. You always knew when Marvin was on the way, because all of his favorite restaurants kept a special chair for him and put it out when he was expected. He needed an enormous, oversized chair because he was too obese to fit into a regular one. His excessive eating was peculiar because I never thought he could manage a fork and knife too well. Hillary wanted to go out and see him and, because I was her official escort for the afternoon, she asked me to go with her.

It was something. Spago was full of people, the regular Friday lunch crowd, all *kvetching* and *kvelling.* Until Hillary Clinton walked into the room, that is. At that point, it went dead silent. Jaws dropped, forks stopped in mid-air. I stood by her as she said her hellos to Marvin. He didn't get up, because it was too much of a physical strain for him. She made it quick, and we hightailed it out of there before they swarmed all over her.

The luncheon went well. It was nice to be in such an intimate setting, where people could have a real conversation with Mrs. Clinton, and get to know her a little bit. There were only a couple of problems—the biggest was, predictably, Cynthia.

Her beloved dog, T.J., had died, so I bought her a new one. He was a black poodle, really ugly and long like a dachshund, and had cost me a lot of money because he supposedly came from some kind of championship breeding stock. Cynthia had unimaginatively named him Pepper. The dog went everywhere with her. He was completely disruptive, barking and jumping in and out of his dog-carrying bag. He even barked twice while Dionne Warwick was singing. As if that weren't bad enough, Cynthia fed him some leftovers, which he noisily scarffed— against all health code regulations, and annoying to boot.

Cynthia didn't care. She thought he was cute. And this was our host for the tea to follow.

THE CHANGE OF VENUES was going to be a big adjustment, moving from an intimate gathering to a mob scene with over a hundred people, all wanting a piece of Hillary. I asked David Rosen if I could ride with the first lady.

"You're not supposed to do that," he said.

I didn't understand. "Why?" I asked.

"Because you are now a big donor and this is a fundraiser." He paused. "But let me see what I can work out."

Here was a new sensation and always a surprise to me: people thinking of *me* as a big donor, a guy who barely had two nickels to rub together. But they didn't know that, of course. All they saw was the money coming in. Mine, someone else's, it didn't matter, what mattered is that *I* brought it.

This was also reflected in the way some of the people around Mrs. Clinton (and President Clinton, too) deferred to me. I didn't get it at first, but I slowly put it together. These people were thinking about their careers after politics, what might be available to them outside of their associations with the Clintons. The president was leaving office soon; Hillary might or might not get elected to the Senate. They never knew when they would be looking for a new job. So when I came along, they had no idea of my real financial situation. I had money in hand, I might be a guy they wanted to know in the future, and so they wanted to stay on my good side. It was kind of fun.

Soon David came back. He had gotten me not only into the motorcade, but right into the van that was transporting him, Kelly, Susie, and the first lady, along with two very serious-looking guys in suits. It was a great ride. Six or seven police cars, front and back, with their lights going. Motorcycle cops.

Unmarked vehicles. We were surrounded on all sides. It was probably the most secure I'd ever felt.

We all talked and laughed as we drove down Sunset Boulevard. Hillary made several calls on her cell phone, mostly to thank donors to her campaign. I had a chance to scope out the relationships among these people. Kelly had been with the first lady for seven or eight years now, and although she was firmly in place, she was always careful and respectful around her boss. David was the new kid on the block, very professional but still a little insecure. He definitely deferred to Kelly.

When we got to Cynthia's Beverly Hills estate, I felt I had to say something.

"Mrs. Clinton," I said as we were pulling in, "I know you've been all over the world and have seen a lot, but I have to prepare you for something. The inside of this house is like the *Beverly Hillbillies,* only worse. It is a seven-million-dollar shell around a nightmare. I just wanted to warn you."

She didn't bat an eye. With a straight face, she said, "That's all right. I used to live in Arkansas."

MY POLITICAL CONNECTIONS were mounting faster than I could keep up with them, and with that came much easier access to Hollywood personalities. It was like being the head of a studio. There was no better way to establish instant credibility with some hard-to-reach movie star than to have the first lady on your arm, giving you her personal endorsement.

That was what Hillary did for me. After I introduced her at Cynthia's tea, she got up on stage and during her little speech thanked me, saying, "Aaron is a new friend of mine. Those of you who have known him longer are very fortunate."

When she said that, Stan Lee pointed to Peter Paul's video recorder and said, "Take that to the bank and play it for your loan officer!" We laughed. My credit rating was a bad joke. Being a friend of the Clintons certainly couldn't hurt.

But there were problems—all the schnorrers, for instance. I'd done my part by getting a couple dozen of them to write small checks with Cynthia's money, but as I looked around I could see that the take wasn't going to be very good, especially considering expenses. The whole thing had just gotten too extravagant. How it all worked out, I don't know, but I think Peter and Cynthia must have written checks or moved some stock around.

For my part, I knew what was coming, and sure enough, David later came to me and said, "Just forget about the expenses. No one will know the difference." It was becoming a common refrain, like a radio jingle you never forget.

AFTER JUNE 8 AND 9 I was no longer a mere organizer of celebrity charity events. I was also a full-fledged producer of political fundraisers. I only had a few under my belt, true, but what a choice few they were: the vice-president and the first lady.

Trouble was, I was barely sustaining myself financially. I was margining stock and taking a commission for handling Cynthia's foundation money, and the income from those activities was going to pay off stars and old debts and the loan sharks I'd been forced to turn to when all else failed. There was nothing left for myself, but I was hoping that my new political connections were going to lead to paying jobs. Unfortunately, it didn't work out quite that way.

The first thing that happened, during the Hillary tea, was that David Rosen took me aside, reminded me of my earlier pledge to help whenever possible, and asked if I could do something for him. *Of course,* I said, *what?* It seemed that Mrs. Clinton was supposed to make a speech in New York City the next week, but now she had to be somewhere else. They needed someone to take her place. *Like maybe Dionne Warwick?* he said. I guess he was thinking of how nicely she'd done at Spago.

I'll ask, I said. I wasn't sure Dionne would do anything just for me, but I went and found her and gave it a try. I offered to fly her to New York. Since she had a home there, that would save some money. I hoped that might be it.

Of course it wasn't. She made like she was really reluctant to commit until I offered to throw in five grand—cash.

I went back to David and told him I'd gotten Dionne. I said I'd fly her back East immediately, and then he could coordinate things from there. *Great,* he said, *thank you.* Then I explained what the terms of the deal were, the airfare and the money.

Oops. "Thanks, but I don't want to hear about that," he said. Once again, I was going to be stuck with the bill. In any case, Dionne did her part, and afterward David called to tell me that it went really well. Over the next month, Hillary called several times, leaving messages on my answering machine or thanking me personally, telling me how much she enjoyed getting to know me and what a great job I'd done on her fundraisers.

Then, right on the heels of the early June events, I got a call from David, asking me if I could co-host a dinner in Chicago in a private home. I asked him what that meant. Give fifty grand, he said, and bring some talent that will help sell more seats for Hillary.

I agreed on the spot. I was the ultimate *yes man* when it came to Mrs. Clinton. I used no discretion at all and jumped right in, ignoring the advice of long-time supporters of mine like Brad O'Leary. *Be careful,* Brad was warning me. *You're going to get yourself in a lot of trouble with the Clintons.*

Oh, little did either of us know.

fourteen

THE PRESIDENTIAL SALUTE

Thank you for that incredibly wonderful trip to Washington—I don't think we will ever forget it.
—CHRISTIAN SLATER,
Personal Note, January 1, 2001

Chicago—the gig David Rosen had asked me to do following the June 9 Hillary luncheon—was coming along fine if you didn't count the expense. I had to fork over some serious bucks to snag my performer on such short notice, and the expense snowballed. Getting Olivia Newton-John turned into transporting a party of seven and putting them all up at the Four Seasons Hotel. When I added up Olivia's fee, food, lodging, transportation, shopping sprees, and I don't know what all else, the bill was around eighty thousand. Another "political contribution" that I told David Rosen about the night of the event, and another one he didn't want to hear about.

I FLEW OUT TO CHICAGO a day early because this was an opportunity for me to catch up with my old friend Stuart

Goldberg and his mother Rhea. Stuart had mostly given up his screenwriting career and returned to his law practice. I hadn't seen them in a while.

It was a great reunion. On the day of the event, we all met at the Four Seasons, and I had limos come and pick up everyone. Rhea and Stuart rode in a limo with friends of Olivia, and by coincidence they arrived at the home at the same time as the first lady. So as Rhea got out of the limo, she found herself going inside right behind Mrs. Clinton, which meant the news cameras were running and she was on TV all over Chicago. She got a kick out of that.

The place didn't look like much from the outside, but inside it was beautiful and spacious, furnished with a lot of impressive Asian art. There was a cocktail reception for about one hundred and fifty people downstairs, followed by dinner upstairs in the loft for the seventy-five top donors. Hillary took the time for pictures with my friends, Stuart and Rhea, and to talk with them. She seemed very happy. Olivia looked darling in a dress with a diamond-studded belt. Everyone enjoyed her performance. The food was great and graciously served. All around, a wonderful evening.

At one point, Mrs. Clinton went into a private room to freshen up with Kelly Craighead, so I decided to follow. I just wanted to talk to her for a minute; I'm not certain why, but Kelly looked nervous. I told Hillary again how thrilled I was to be able to do all of these things for her, and anything she wanted from me, she should simply ask.

Thus it came as no surprise when David Rosen approached me after the dinner and said that there was someone he wanted me to meet, a good friend of the president and a big fundraiser for both Clintons. A few minutes later, Kelly brought over a tall, good-looking guy around fifty, in excellent shape, with a dark tan. His name was Jim Levin. Was I up for drinks? I said yes—I had an idea to pitch.

We went outside and the valet brought around a top-of-the-line, two-door Mercedes. As he was getting in the driver's side, I said to Jim something like *this is a beautiful car*. At that, Kelly turned to me and said with a smile, "It won't be around for long. He gets his cars repossessed every few months." We laughed and got in. I liked Kelly, and not just for her access to Mrs. Clinton. She was cool, very loyal to the first lady, and wasn't judgmental of others.

Jim drove us to a bar. Even with my bizarre career, this seemed an odd choice for a business meeting. Turned out to be typical of Jim, as I learned. We talked for a couple of hours.

"Tell me exactly what you want to do," said Jim.

I told him I wanted to put on something spectacular, something that would honor the president and first lady out in Hollywood, something that would be an appropriate send-off for Bill Clinton after eight years in the White House, something that people would talk about for years to come.

I didn't really put a political fundraising twist on it at first. That was Jim's idea. He was more a friend of Bill's than Hillary's, but he said the president would want it to benefit his wife's Senate campaign. Kelly liked that. Jim said he was going to see Clinton July 4 weekend at Camp David, and he could bring it up then, if I was serious.

Oh yes, I was serious, I said. I got more and more excited the more I talked about it. It would be first class all the way, I assured him, a star-studded evening with only A-list people there. I could do it. I had the experience and the contacts. All I needed was some time to put it together.

No dice. I would have to pull it off relatively quickly because it would probably have to be around the time of the Democratic Convention, in mid-August. I almost died. That was only six weeks away. No one that I knew of had ever organized and produced something as big as I envisioned in that short a period of time.

But I said *sure* anyway. What the heck. This was too big an opportunity to worry about a silly thing like time. Best of all, I added, I knew some people—Peter Paul, Stan Lee, and Cynthia Gershman—who would underwrite the event.

"Are you sure?" he asked.

"Yes," I said, although of course I wasn't. Cynthia would go for it, of that I was certain, but the others, I didn't know. But I thought Peter would because of how badly he wanted to befriend the president. And Stan would probably follow. It was a risk worth taking and a promise worth making.

So they came on board to my grandiose idea. Kelly would go back to Hillary Clinton and present the plan. At that time, Hillary was struggling to raise money and would see this as a godsend, although I didn't know it. Jim would meet the president at Camp David and see what he could do there. And that was the way we left it.

For some reason, it didn't enter my mind that the Clintons would turn me down. On the plane ride back to L.A., I went over and over in my head how I was going to approach Peter to persuade him to pay for the celebration. I knew he had the money. Seemingly overnight, SLM had taken off. It was growing, the stock was appreciating, and everyone connected with the company was living high, except for me. Peter had a new multimillion-dollar home in the Valley. He was buying twenty-thousand-dollar rugs to hang on the walls and driving a new Benz. Everybody had one. In fact I used to joke that Mercedes was the company car.

Being confident that I would land this event didn't stop me from being careful, though. Hollywood is, after all, a land where there's very little happiness for other people's success. Everyone competes with everyone else, and standard operating procedure involves crushing your competitor's dream if you can. Screw unto others is the golden rule. I had to consider the possibility that someone would say something negative about me to the Clintons, and so I talked about my new relationships with Peter and Cynthia, and almost nobody else. There would be plenty of time to savor my accomplishments later.

If I could pull this off, and no one interfered with my plans, then maybe I could begin to find my way out of the ongoing financial disaster I was living in. I was broke, deep in debt, breaking laws, when all I wanted to do was establish a solid legitimate base for my business and build an honest reputation. I was ends-justifies-the-meansing my way through professional and personal hard times, and it seemed like everything I did worsened my predicament.

I went to Peter Paul and pitched him on the idea of a tribute to President Clinton. Initially, he didn't want to do it. It would be too much money.

"Five hundred thousand," I said. "I can do it for that."

"No," he said, "it'll be more expensive."

"I organize and produce these kinds of events," I said. "It's what I do. Half a million should be the cost."

I pitched him all the pluses: the great publicity, the access to Democrat movers, the ingratiation to Clinton. If Peter really wanted the president to join the company after he left office, this could go a long way toward making that a reality.

Still, he was hesitant. I couldn't figure it out. He was living high. The company must have been growing like crazy, because he was taking over other floors in the office building and adding more and more employees. The only thing I could think was, *There must be more to his financials than I know about.*

After much haranguing, Peter finally gave a conditional okay, dependent on my getting Cynthia to commit half of what I thought we needed, a quarter of a million dollars. That was a piece of cake. As soon as Cynthia found out the details, she jumped on board as a co-host.

I put Peter in contact with Jim Levin, and they started discussing details. Then Jim went to Camp David to meet with the president. Afterward, he called us. President and Mrs. Clinton had agreed, provided only that the tribute be first class all the way. No problem.

WE SET THE DATE FOR AUGUST 12, which gave me barely a month to produce a mega-event, from beginning to end, a process that usually demanded half a year. I can't believe I took it on under those conditions, but I did. If anyone could do it, I could. The Hollywood Gala Salute to President William Jefferson Clinton—our official title—was going to be a monster success if it killed me. Failure was not an option.

I hit the ground running and never stopped. The first details fell into place quickly: I lined up my event planner and the venue and put Alana Stewart to work recruiting celebrities and making introductions for me, as a supplement to my own efforts.

I wanted top performers and plenty of A-list stars in attendance. Damn the cost. Very, very bad judgment. Expenses were bound to spiral out of control, and my talent should have been thrilled with the mere invitation to appear. Sing for the president and the first lady, are you kidding? The publicity alone was worth a fortune. Instead, once again, they had their hands out, palms up. Big time. I found myself in my usual position of handing out expensive gifts, airline tickets, and checks to celebrities and their representatives. And cash. Lots and lots of cash.

We also had to have a stage show producer, and I tapped Gary Smith. Gary was a professional with a great reputation. I also had a secondary motive in wanting him; I still hoped to get into a TV project with him. Beyond producing the show, we needed someone to produce an edited videotape record of it, with the idea that the tape could be used for promotional purposes for SLM, or even released commercially. Gary got both jobs, a decision that had its ups and downs.

Shortly after Jim Levin had called to say the Clintons were in, we were told that David Rosen was coming out to California for the duration, to watch over things "in house." He moved in immediately. I gave up my office at SLM to him, and started working either out of Peter's office or the boardroom next door. This was a very important development: as the official on-site representative of the various committees sponsoring the event, as well as Hillary's finance director, Rosen was in on everything we did.

David got more than my office. I put him up at the Beverly Hills Hotel and lent him my car. I was driving a leased Porsche Carerra at that time. My one-bedroom dump of an apartment no one saw. My car they did, and so I needed to look successful in public. I even bought airline tickets for David one time. For his part, he made it crystal clear that I was not to tell anyone that I was doing these things for him.

THE CLOSER THE CLINTON SALUTE GOT, the more often Peter Paul would call David and me into his office and scream at us about the cost overruns. Expenses quickly soared over the originally-budgeted half-million. Stan Lee put up a couple of hundred thousand personally, backed by a note from Cynthia Gershman, but even that left us way short.

"I hope Mrs. Clinton appreciates this, and understands everything I am doing!" Peter would say, and David would have to reassure him that, *yes, she does.*

But as much as Hillary may have been pleased, there was one person who definitely wasn't, and that was Al Gore.

Here's some in-fighting between the two camps that I got to sit in on: The problem was that the night after our Salute to Clinton, Al Gore was having his own concert fundraiser, with Barbra Streisand performing. His people were having trouble lining up other entertainers, and they felt like we were responsible, because of all the headliners who had committed to our event. Terry McAuliffe, who would become the new chair of the DNC early in 2001, forbade us from even going near Streisand. I went to the Clinton staffers, and told them about the pressure I was getting, being told to stop asking so many stars to perform because it was hurting Gore. I guess my comment worked its way to the top, because Jim Levin called and gave us a message from the president: *go ahead and invite anyone you want.* David Rosen told me that pissed off the Gore camp, big time.

Anyway, with regard to money going out, I was paying, so was SLM, and so was Peter Paul personally. On and on it went. Peter claims that he eventually put up around two million dollars for the Salute, and he has filed suit in California Superior Court to get a big chunk of it back. His contention is that, since most of the money was never properly reported, it technically wasn't spent and should therefore by law be returned to him. I can't speak to what Peter paid, or how he paid it, or what he may now be owed. I can only report my own spending. It was considerable, and, in part, it looks something like this:

First off, there was Alana Stewart, who got fifteen thousand dollars to help out with a lot of the arrangements, plus a slew of first-class travel which included tickets to Europe. But that wasn't so bad, considering the problem came when I went after Cher. I really wanted Cher; she was such a legend, so perfect for a glitzy night. The best way, according to Alana, was through her friend Loree Rodkin, a famous Beverly Hills jewelry designer. Rodkin is the ultimate example of the "best friend"—she even dresses, collagens her lips, and wears her hair like Cher! She also costs. It set me back $18,750 to get hooked up with her idol.

Now, Cher herself. She would cost me and/or SLM a total

of close to a hundred grand before it was all over, in her personal expenses, expense money for her makeup artist, and tens of thousands in free travel that I gave her afterward. In return, I got myself a big pain in the butt.

Next, Alana introduced me to Paul Bloch, co-chairman of the Rogers & Cowan public relations firm. They handled Diana Ross, and I wanted her.

Bloch warned me she was trouble, that working with her would be nothing less than a nightmare, and that her diva behavior was as bad as diva behavior could get. At least he did that. But I chose not to believe it, so I took her, and paid her hotel and airfare expenses.

Rogers & Cowan also handled John Travolta, whom I was after. His career was enjoying a big comeback, and he was very popular. Bloch delivered him, for whatever that may have been worth. The guy had a list of special requirements that might have made you think the Pope was coming. He had to have a seat right up front at the concert. Not only did he want to be first to toast the president at dinner, but he wanted to be the *only* one to do so. He demanded to be seated at the presidential table, which meant we had to move Brad Pitt and Jennifer Aniston to Hillary's. Luckily, the newlyweds were gracious and uncomplaining throughout.

We hired Bloch's company to do our PR for us, but Peter didn't trust them and wasn't paying to their satisfaction, so they quit. For his efforts, though, Bloch demanded and got a free twenty-five-thousand-dollar dinner ticket and eight thousand dollars worth of gifts from me to keep him appeased so that he didn't pull out his clients, Ross and Travolta. I kept the thank-you note he sent me (at least he took the trouble to send one). "One thing this has taught me," he wrote, "is that I have nothing but respect and admiration for Aaron Tonken."

Blossette Kitson, who I met through Denise Rich's "best friend," Michelle Rella, was someone I thought could open doors for me, and she did knock a few ajar. After promising much more, she got me Patti LaBelle, for whom I paid through the nose. Tens of thousands in cash, free concert tickets for her and a friend, her Four Seasons Hotel bill, and about fifteen thousand bucks for her and her band.

Muhammad Ali I didn't have to pay, but I did have to charter a private jet to fly him and his entourage out to the gala. Another twenty-five thousand.

I hired an old-time, veteran publicist who for five thousand (cheap, compared to some of the others) promised to get four huge stars—Jack Lemmon, Goldie Hawn, Michael Douglas, and Shirley MacLaine—to come and be featured speakers. All of them were accordingly listed on the invitation, but only MacLaine actually showed up and spoke. At least the publicist had the decency (very rare) to send me a letter of apology, saying, "I am embarrassed by what happened with the stars who agreed early to participate and then, for highly unusual circumstances, canceled at the last minute."

Garry Thompson was another person I hired to deliver talent. Thompson was a tall, fat, unattractive guy with no connections that I met one day in the SLM offices. He was meeting with Peter Paul about something or other, and when I talked with him afterward, I decided that he could get some people for me. Well, he could, but that was only half the story. What I didn't know at the time was that he was a scumbag and not to be trusted. After I got embroiled with him, I remember

Peter saying, "Why didn't you ask me about this guy first? Just because you see someone in my office doesn't mean that I would recommend them." I wished I'd known.

Thompson told me he could bring Stevie Nicks, Michael Bolton, and Toni Braxton, and he was paid tens of thousands and free concert tickets to do it. Bolton and Braxton did perform, but that was about the only thing he delivered. Nicks, who he promised would show, never did so; he told my event planner I'd comped him ten tickets when I'd only comped him two; he got me supposedly free CDs, then billed me for thousands of dollars; and much more. He did attend the Salute, though, coming in a Cat-in-the-Hat type of hat, about three feet tall, and looking like a complete fool.

Afterward, when I tried to not pay him the full amount for his stars, since Nicks hadn't come, it got really ugly. He tried to scare me by cc'ing me on faxes to his lowlife lawyer, filled with all kinds of legal threats. He also threatened to trash my car and kick my tail. Cute stuff like that. Peter advised me to get him out of our lives and pay him. I eventually did, including legal fees.

For my final entertainer, I turned again to Alana Stewart, who had me hire her son, Ashley Hamilton. Ashley knew Mark McGrath of Sugar Ray, and he got them to agree to perform. McGrath and company got transported on a private Gulfstream—they wouldn't fly first-class commercial—and, for the dubious privilege of securing their services, I paid Ashley thousands of dollars plus a trip to Hawaii that cost eighteen thousand five hundred.

Bonus: band members totally trashed their makeshift dressing room—the beautiful office of one of our co-hosts, Ken Roberts.

The money spout was wide open. Even Norby Walters, the premier schnorrer that I thought I'd rid myself of, got in on the act. He hounded me for tickets for him and his family. I ignored him until he sent me an eight-page, handwritten fax, saying how important it was that I use him on this event, more important than any before. "The President and Mrs. Clinton are both huge starf—ers!" he wrote, and I had better be sure there were plenty of stars there for them. Once again, I succumbed to self-doubt and gave in to Norby, who took forty thousand to bring his usual clump of B-list personalities. I also gave him his tickets, which meant I had to watch him chase Brad Pitt around like a slobbering dog. It was disgusting. ABC's *20/20* did a report a few weeks after the event in which you can actually see Norby in hot pursuit of Pitt.

Then there were the gifts for the first family. I had a solid gold watch for the president, engraved on the back with a commemoration of the Salute, and also a custom humidor for his cigars, from Alfred Dunhill. These ran me well into the five figures. Hillary got an eight-thousand-dollar necklace, which she later returned because she didn't like it. President Clinton claims he never got his gifts, but I personally put them into the presidential limo as they were leaving, telling them to open the packages later. I suppose it's possible that someone ripped off the president of the United States.

I also incurred a couple of major expenses in favors for the guests. There was my usual CD gift bag, featuring music by the scheduled performers. Cost: about twenty-two thousand. And there were the director's chairs I bought that people were allowed to take home with them as souvenirs. Cost: thirty thousand.

Okay, there you have a partial list. Ten grand here, ten

grand there—pretty soon we're talking real money. I'll never know exactly how much I spent, but it was a huge amount. Peter Paul's lawsuit states that he provided me with six hundred thousand in cash from margined SLM stock to help pay for everything, but the final total was surely higher.

Remember that this list for the most part is exclusive of the "fair market value" of the stars' performances (estimated by Peter in his suit at one million dollars), and of the escalating expenses that Peter says he was personally footing the bill for (which, as I said, came in at around two million dollars by his accounting). Those included things like the cost overrun with Gary Smith, for example.

NOW, GARY WAS GREAT. He was a pro who did a wonderful job with the stage show. In addition, it was a positive experience to work with him. He didn't get emotional, was respectful and decent to everyone around him, and was a team player who listened to other people's ideas and took them into consideration. But he was big bucks.

His initial estimate was so high (eight hundred fifty thousand) that Peter had to go to David Rosen and ask him to get Hillary to intervene. Hillary had some clout with Gary because they were friends. He was also producing the upcoming Democratic Convention, and sure enough she was able to get him to lower his price by fifty grand. (I sweetened the pot by giving him an eighteen-thousand-dollar gold Rolex Daytona, which he apparently never reported. I heard through the Hollywood grapevine that *after* he discovered I was involved in a criminal IRS investigation, he quickly filed an amended tax return.)

But then, with the day of the Salute drawing near, he demanded an additional seventy-five grand, to be paid through Smith-Hemion Productions, as a "personal production fee" for the concert portion of the event. He threatened to quit if he was not paid the additional fee. Once again, Peter balked and went to Rosen for help. But this time, Hillary refused to enter the fray. David told Peter that we couldn't afford to lose Gary at this late date and to pay, which Peter did.

We were taking a financial bath. Personally, I thought it was worth it.

THE NIGHT ITSELF WAS MAGICAL. I hit the highlights in Chapter One, so I won't rehash any of that, except to reiterate that the guests were uniform in their praise, the vendors got paid (for the most part), and I was basking in the glow of a major success that would also cement my relationship with the first family. I also came away with the priceless memory of a hug and kiss from Hillary and Chelsea, and a big hug of thanks from Bill Clinton at the very end—all on stage, in front of a crowd of over two thousand people.

Everyone was happy.

Well, except for Peter Paul. I don't know the details of whatever else he was doing besides this event, but his high-flying lifestyle suddenly collapsed. Within a few months, I was under federal scrutiny, and while I was answering my first questions from the FBI, he would flee to Brazil.

Which brings me to the Clinton Salute shenanigans. These are what wound up tainting the crowning achievement of my life.

To know what was really happening, you have to understand a little about campaign finance law, which is something I never bothered with as I was getting into these fundraisers. First of all, at that time personal donations to a specific political campaign were limited to a maximum of two thousand dollars (one thousand for a primary, another thousand for the general election). This was what was known as "hard money," that is, it could go directly toward paying campaign expenses.

However, campaigns could also benefit from so-called "soft money," which could be contributed into more general funds not subject to these restrictions on amount. For example, you could give generously to the Democratic or Republican National Committees, because the money was not targeted to a specific candidate.

Let's look at the Clinton Salute to see how this worked out in practice. The event was sponsored by an umbrella organization called New York Senate 2000, and defined as a joint fundraising committee authorized by Hillary Rodham Clinton for U.S. Senate Committee, Inc.; the Democratic Senatorial Campaign Committee, Inc.; and the New York State Democratic Committee, Inc.

The hard money raised (all those one- and two-thousand-dollar tickets to the reception and stage show) could go right into Hillary Rodham Clinton for U.S. Senate Committee, Inc. But the rest of it (the twenty-five-thousand-dollar dinner tickets, for example) had to go into one of the more general funds.

It is, however, just a little more complicated yet. There is also a category called "in-kind" contributions. This covers, among other things, expenses incurred in the putting on of such events as the Salute. These are supposed to be meticulously recorded and accounted for when a political fundraising entity makes its annual report of income and expenditures.

Thus, if Cher agrees to perform for a fundraiser, she can elect to do it for free, in which case the campaign is not obligated to place a value on her performance and report it. On the other hand, if she is paid by the campaign, that is a reportable expense. If she is paid indirectly, by someone like me, then I become the donor of record and her performance becomes an in-kind contribution. It must be reported. Also included, and therefore subject to reporting, would be such things as air travel expenses, hotel bills, ground transportation, and so on.

It is these in-kind contributions that, in my experience, are seldom properly reported. Certainly, that was the impression from my dealings with Hillary Clinton's staffers. All told, I spent millions on expenses for fundraisers that I organized for her. How much was ultimately reported I don't know, but it couldn't have been much, since no one ever asked me for a detailed accounting. And, as I have noted, when I tried to offer campaign officials receipts, they were refused.

Considering these irregularities, the naturally-occurring questions are: who knew what, and when did they know it? Those are the questions that have started many a political figure's downfall.

All I can say is that David Rosen, Hillary Clinton's director of finance, worked out of our offices and knew about every dime that was being spent. More than that, he *participated* in the spending.

To take one small example, at the end of the Salute, he directed that I purchase very expensive gifts for some of the people involved. I paid for them personally. He told me he wanted to develop ongoing relationships with some of the stars, for the benefit of his boss, and that if I would do this for him, he would see that I was taken care of in other ways. I took that to mean I would be granted the kind of access to the president that I wanted. These gifts added up. Here's the price list:

Lindsay Scott, Cher's manager:	$1,000
Jay Kenoff, Gary Smith's lawyer:	$300
Jim Levin:	$750
Michael Bolton:	$1,000
Jonathan Krane, John Travolta's manager:	$350
Paul Anka:	$1,000
Mark McGrath:	$1,000
Melissa Etheridge:	$800

You can see how stuff like this adds up.

Apart from David, I worked closely with three women from the White House: Kelly Craighead, of course; Patti Solis Doyle, Hillary Clinton's scheduler, who became the executive director of her Political Action Committee, HILLPAC, in early 2001; and Capricia Penavic Marshall, a dynamic young lawyer from Cleveland who was White House social secretary.

My impression was that Kelly knew virtually everything that went on with Hillary's campaign and, in addition, received from me a gold watch (which she hastily returned when I started talking to law enforcement officials) and an all-expense-paid trip to Hawaii (which she took).

The other two women served as liaisons inside the White House, and both came out to personally inspect the site of the Salute, the night before it happened. They could not have been unaware of the costliness of the event, considering how lavish what they saw was, and in any case I bragged about how much I was spending. I often did that with people, in order to win favor with them and show how first-class my productions were.

What did these four people report back to headquarters? Well, that's what the FBI wanted to know too, when they questioned me. (They were especially interested in Kelly's Hawaii trip, perhaps because I saved the receipt with her name on it.) I can't say for sure; the reader will have to draw his or her own conclusions. But we do know this: I paid the money, they were political contributions, and, to the best of my knowledge, they were not properly filed.

As to Hillary Clinton's personal knowledge, I will address that question shortly.

fifteen

WHITE HOUSE REGULAR

Money, money, money. I always made so much for other people, never for myself. And I spent and spent. Borrowed and borrowed. My finances were messier than a plane wreck.

As I became enmeshed in the organization and production of my next charity gala, A Family Celebration 2001, I didn't know how I was going to make it. But somehow, I continued to get by. For example, after the salute to Bill Clinton, Ken Roberts—the man at whose magisterial estate we held the Salute—took pity on me and, seeing how much I was struggling, gave me a loan.

Ken was very active in charitable and community endeavors, things he was able to do because he had made a whopping fortune in the Los Angeles radio market. He once owned KROQ-FM and two other stations. I doubt that I ever would have met him, except that we shared an acquaintance who offered to provide an introduction. I had to pony up seventy-five hundred bucks for it. Turned out to be some of the best money I'd ever spent. Ken has been nothing but good to me.

Then there was Michael Moskovitz. Michael was a sweet guy from back East who was dying of some degenerative disease. All he wanted to do during the time he had left was to meet movie stars, have himself photographed with them, and add their autographs to his enormous collection. For this he was willing to pay, and pay well. Over a couple of years he gave me more than half a million dollars, and I got him personal meetings with many stars, as well as invitations to parties, galas, and every other thing I was involved with. He considered it money well spent.

In summer 2000, I had also made another new "friend." One day while preparations for the Clinton Salute were underway, I went into Peter Paul's office and there was a stranger in there, a very big guy wearing dark glasses. Peter introduced him as Stanley Myatt, a businessman from Florida who was there to help out with the development of Stan Lee Media.

Stanley always dressed casually and was quite friendly. He carried a large black pocketbook with him. I don't know for sure why he was there—I believe he was there to help Peter with the company. Stanley was a money guy. I found that out one day when Peter wasn't around and, needing cash as usual, I asked if Stanley could float me a loan. *Sure,* he said, *how much? Oh, twenty-five grand,* I said. He said he would do it and then pulled the money out of his bag.

Of course, when the loan came due, I couldn't pay him back. Stanley was pissed. He told Peter, and Peter blew up at me. I should never have borrowed money from Stanley, Peter told me. He was the one guy I did not want to screw over, whether intentionally or not.

Eventually, I did pay Stanley back. Moving money from here to there. I got very adept at using current proceeds from something to pay past debts from something else. After we settled that initial situation, we got pretty friendly, and he loaned me money on numerous occasions.

Over time, I heard a lot of speculation about Stanley Myatt. That he was a former CIA agent who had been present when Salvador Allende was murdered. That he was a Mafia fella. That he was an informant for the FBI. That he had friends at high levels in the government. Who could say? He was kind of a mystery man. Peter seemed to know him from back in his Florida days, and all he ever said was that Stanley was "connected."

For me, Myatt was a lifesaver. Without his financial help, I never would have been able to stay above water long enough to put on A Family Celebration 2001.

My other main source of funding during this period was Robert (Bobby) Freedman—less a financial angel than a financial fallen angel.

Bobby was a guy with some kind of checkered past; I was never quite sure what. But in Los Angeles, he was what I would call a loan shark. He characterized himself as a "private lender," which technically is what he was. In California, believe it or not, anyone can lend money, at any rate of interest they choose. All they need to do is get a license from the state. I've never understood why anyone bothers to do illegal loan sharking, when for fifty bucks they can do it under protection of the law.

I met Bobby at the Café Roma in Beverly Hills, where he

hung out and made a lot of his deals. It turned out that Ken Roberts knew Bobby from long before, which was invaluable to me. When I tried to borrow money from Freedman, he would many times call Ken, and ask, *Will you guarantee the loan for this guy?* And Ken would say yes. I don't know what I did to deserve such a good friend.

Bobby would take ruthless advantage of that friendship. He already charged interest of 50 percent, and if I was a little late he'd be all over me. For example, my first loan with him was for around a hundred and twenty-five grand, due on a Friday. I'd paid off the interest, but didn't have the principal, although I told him I could get it on Monday. Knowing I was scared of losing Ken's friendship, he threatened to call Ken on me and only let me off the hook when I agreed to pay him another twenty-five thousand in interest. That's what a "private lender" can do.

But what was I to do? I was barely keeping my head above water then.

THE ENORMOUS SUCCESS of the Clinton Salute had me riding high, at least in reputation. Personally, emotionally, I was a wreck, besieged by worry and doubt, as my mountain of debt grew ever higher. There was only one thing to do, and that was to continue to fall upward. Despite my financial struggles, I piled on the events, buoyed up by my ongoing relationship with the first family. I also attended a couple of functions that I didn't organize or produce.

The first one came the day after the Salute. It was a

fundraiser for the Clinton Library, held at the oceanfront home of Barbra Streisand, down past Malibu. Price of admission was a hundred thousand, which Cynthia Gershman committed (but later reneged on). With Cynthia and me also came Andrea and Peter Paul, Jim Levin, and Michael Moskovitz. Despite the fact that he was desperately ill by this time and had been recently hospitalized, Michael dressed nicely in a suit and carried a little Instamatic-type camera.

Security was very tight at the Streisand estate because Bill Clinton was there, along with Chelsea. It was a lovely home, a little more modest than you might expect, but built on a ledge right over the ocean. Everyone inside was wandering around, seemingly more interested in how Barbra lived than in who was there. I saw very few celebrities and VIPs, like Robert Johnson of BET and Casey Wasserman, Lew's grandson. Conspicuously absent were any female stars or beautiful young women at all.

Several people came up to me, including presidential staffers and Bill and Chelsea Clinton, to thank me for the night before and congratulate me on the success of the event.

Finally, out came the hostess, with her husband James Brolin, a nice guy, very cordial. I shook his hand while Barbra fawned over President Clinton. She paid no attention to anyone else for a long time, but eventually came down the line to meet her guests. I waited there with Michael.

When she got to us, she walked right by my offered hand. She ignored Michael as well, but her manager didn't. He was right behind her, and when he reached Michael, he started yelling at him, grabbed the little camera out of Michael's hand, and smashed it to pieces on the floor. I was horrified and had to restrain myself from punching this jerk out right there. Hollywood is hardly the Make-a-Wish Foundation.

Barbra never did greet us, or Peter or Cynthia. Cynthia, who pledged big bucks to get in, was understandably pissed. But it was Michael I was concerned about. After we left, I apologized. He thanked me for bringing him in spite of it all, and told me that he enjoyed the Salute much more, anyway.

"Besides," he added with a smile, "I didn't really want the picture. She looks so terrible without her makeup."

WITHIN DAYS OF THE SALUTE, I went back to work. I made a little excursion into California state politics, by accepting an invitation to organize a hundred-thousand-dollar fundraiser for California Governor Gray Davis's reelection campaign. It was a dinner for twenty people at the Beverly Hills Hotel, and it was one of my most lavish. There was one long table, laid out so beautifully the room looked like the interior of Versailles. I spent eighteen thousand on the flowers alone, which caused Governor Davis to joke that the room looked like a funeral home. But by the time the night was over, he was very impressed.

The guest list was also impressive: Diahann Carroll, publicist Dale Olson and client Shirley MacLaine, Joan and Stan Lee, Andrea and Peter Paul, famous sculptor Robert Graham and wife Anjelica Huston, Jim Levin, Alana Stewart (who got paid for getting Anjelica), a couple of TV stars, and last but not least, Dean Cain. Why I continued to associate with this creep, I really don't know. Probably because he'd come to the opening of a flower. He demanded five grand in cash to show up, and the first thing he said to me when he walked into the cocktail reception was, "Where's my money?"

Rosemary Clooney came and sang two songs. For twenty-five grand. All told, I spent sixty-five thousand on the dinner, not a penny of which was reported, as far as I know. I did, however, get a handwritten note from the governor, thanking me. I had bought myself access to the CEO of the great state of California.

I used it immediately.

To get Olivia Newton-John to sing at the February 13, 2000, DNC event with Bill Clinton at Café des Artistes in Hollywood, I'd agreed to meet with the heads of a charity with which she was involved: Nancy and James Chuda of the Children's Health and Environmental Coalition. Nancy heard I was now pals with the guv, and she got in touch, begging me to set up a meeting with him for her, her husband Jim, and Olivia. There was a bill pending in the legislature that they were desperate to have passed. I knew Davis was very busy with the campaign and the Democratic Convention, but I'd earned some points with him because of the fundraiser, so I called.

Davis resisted at first, due to his hectic schedule, but I pushed. *I would consider this a personal favor,* I told him. *It's important.* Finally he said, *Yes, I'll do it.*

They met, and, later on, the bill was passed. Nancy told me it was because of me. I was really learning how the political game was played now. If you could raise money, you got access, and through access, you got results. That was the way things were done in America. It made me wonder what else I might accomplish through the contacts I was making.

In the end, even though I'd lost money on the dinner, I had

the personal satisfaction of knowing that my efforts hadn't been for nothing. I'd helped make the environment safer and healthier for children. I was proud of that.

THINGS WERE STILL GOING STRONG in the Clinton department. I had phone calls and cards from Hillary, and she left messages on my answering machine saying things like, "You really outdid yourself, my friend," and, "Hope to see you soon, thanks for *everything!*"

A personal, handwritten note from the president arrived, thanking me for what I'd done, and the boost I'd given to his wife's campaign. I'd gotten signed letters from presidents before, Ford and Reagan, as well as Clinton. But that one, all in Bill's own hand, was a special treasure.

I also made certain to keep on the good side of Kelly Craighead, my number one contact with the first lady. I gave her a beautiful gold watch with diamond bezel, from the Beverly Hills Watch Co. More than a year later, when the FBI came knocking to ask about the Salute, one of their first questions concerned personal gifts. I told Kelly that over the phone, and the next day, without a word, she FedEx'd back my watch. It still looked new, so I gave it to some other celeb.

One day, I received in the mail an envelope from the White House. I opened it and, to my shock, found an invitation. The president was hosting his last formal affair of the year (and, as it turned out, of his time in office) in late September, the black-tie India State Dinner, and he would be honored to have me as a guest. I was beside myself.

One of the things you have to go through if you're invited to the White House is a background check. You have to supply a lot of personal information, and then submit to being investigated. Somehow I passed. It must have been a little sticky, since I'd had several lawsuits filed against me, but Jim Levin handled it. At the dinner, Jim joked with me, saying it hadn't been easy. President Clinton said I should really pay my bills.

Peter Paul, who wanted an invite like this more than anything, didn't get one. I'd warned him during the preparations for the Salute to just put out that Stan and Stan Lee Media were sponsoring this, and to personally keep a low profile. He didn't listen. He arrogantly stuck his own name out there every chance he got and, sure enough, it all came back to bite him on the *tuchas*, as I knew it would.

Some newspaper printed the story that the guy who was doing this stuff for the Clintons was a convicted felon. The end. Despite all of Peter's efforts on his behalf, the president never invited him to anything. Never mind the notion of getting into business together. It was a shame. Surprisingly, however, there was no fallout from this on me. I continued to be treated like royalty.

As I prepared for my trip to the White House, I decided to ask Kelly for a favor, not having any idea that these state dinners tended to be small affairs, and that I was actually asking for quite a lot. I wondered if it would be all right for me to bring another guest, along with Cynthia and me. She got permission.

The guy I wanted to take was Robert H. Lorsch. Bob was a wealthy, ardent conservative Republican who had made a killing in the pre-paid calling card business. He was about 5 feet 8 inches and looked like a redheaded version of the

Pillsbury Doughboy—or maybe a fat Howdy Doody. He lived in a twenty-million dollar estate up on Mulholland Drive that looked like a French estate; he bought it from the brother of the Sultan of Brunei in a kind of distress sale.

I was hooked up with Bob for two reasons. One, he had a large charitable foundation, and I was courting him to try to develop an event for it. And two, he'd recently been diagnosed with a rare form of cancer, and I wanted to do something nice for him.

When I invited Bob, he was thrilled and immediately accepted.

Then, I somehow talked Kelly into letting me bring one more guest: Joseph Lake, co-chairman of the Larry King Cardiac Foundation and retired co-founder of the Children's Miracle Network. Joe was another staunch Republican, a Mormon from Salt Lake City—a decent, honorable man of his word who became my friend and stuck by me to the end. I really wanted to produce a series of events for his foundation, and had been trying to get in with Larry King for years, lavishing gifts upon him and his wife Shawn. To no avail, supposedly because Mrs. King didn't like me. So I thought maybe I could work through Joe instead.

Equally as impressed as Lorsch, Lake also accepted the invitation. It is a measure of how far the Clintons were willing to go to accommodate me that they approved my attending a small, prestigious state dinner with two big, well-known Republicans by my side—and Bob, also a heavy GOP contributor.

Off we went to D.C., me with my new tuxedo that I had to have tailor-made for this black-tie affair, because my weight had shot up to over three hundred pounds due to the stresses of my life, and Cynthia with a boxful of new jewelry she'd purchased by funneling charity money through one of the DBA accounts I controlled. We stayed at the Watergate Hotel, again courtesy of Gershman Foundation money.

THE BIG NIGHT FINALLY ARRIVED, and the four of us went over to the White House in our limo. It was a long line to get in, and we had to wait for quite a while, as bomb-sniffing dogs checked our car.

Then we had to run the press gauntlet. News cameras everywhere, a ton of media. I immediately turned to Cynthia and said, "This is not a charity event with *paparazzi* looking for stars. These are sophisticated journalists who are going to ask you serious questions. *Stay away from them!!*"

"I am an actress," she mumbled, "and that is what I will tell them."

No, I told her again.

Yet when we got out of the car, she spotted ABC set up nearby, and immediately dashed over to the cameras as if she were running to save a little child playing in the street.

They, of course, asked her why she was at the dinner, and Cynthia said, "Well, I have nothing to do with India, but I am a big donor to the Democratic Party and a friend of Bill and Hillary's."

I never heard any of this, but that was when I pulled her away, telling her to keep her mouth shut. She promptly lied about what she'd said, and I didn't find out until I saw her on TV. It made the *Nightly News* that evening and *20/20* a few months later. A real embarrassment. There was a lot of talk in the media at that time about the ethics of big donors buying access to the White House. The Clintons must have been really ticked off at Cynthia, but luckily it never came back on me.

At the final checkpoint, we were to present identification before being permitted into the building. I'd forgotten mine. Everyone looked at me like, *Oh my God, we came all this way and now we're going to have to go back.* So I immediately began carrying on the way I was so good at, with my voice rising and everything. But the police and Secret Service were unmoved. *This is a high security area,* they said. *We don't care who you are; if you have no ID, you don't get in.*

Fortunately, one of them radioed inside, and someone in there cleared the way for me. In less than five minutes, I was admitted without my identification. We walked through the gates and into the White House!

If you've never been to something of this kind, you can't imagine what it's like. Everyone was dressed to the nines. Tuxedos on the men, beautiful evening gowns on the women, and tons of expensive jewelry. Indian women in saris. VIPs left and right. It felt like being among the richest of the rich, or in a palace with royalty all around.

There was a long receiving line, but the wait was pleasurable because my neighbors were interesting. I met two ambassadors, where I'd never known even one before. At the end, we were *announced,* something else that had never happened to me. These days, I figured that was only done in the scripts of period movies.

Then we entered the cocktail reception area and spent about forty-five minutes there. I recognized many, many faces from both the political and entertainment worlds. Madeleine Albright was one of the first people I saw. From my coast, there was Chevy Chase and Goldie Hawn.

At one point, I heard the name Tendo Oto, as he was introduced. It sounded familiar, and I turned and looked. There was the Japanese guy that Peter Paul, Jim Levin, and David Rosen had smuggled into the Clinton Salute. Now, Jim Levin was all over him, acting very nervous.

When I asked Jim what was up, he said he was waiting for Capricia Marshall to get there, so she could escort Oto to the Oval Office for a photo. He was doing it for Peter Paul, he said. Later, he came up to me and told me he got it done. Oto had a picture of himself sitting in the president's chair. Jim now seemed relaxed and proud. I had no idea what was going on, but I suspected some kind of scheme.

This was confirmed a little later in the year. Peter told me that his mother, who is a world traveler, was in Japan, and Peter had told her to stop in and say hello to Tendo Oto while she was there. She did, and who should she find in Oto's office when she arrived but Jim Levin. Peter was livid. He never knew Jim was going there, and might never have found out. It convinced him that Levin was trying to cut some sort of side deal of his own with Oto.

At the time, though, I also thought, *That must have set Peter back a bit, to get his prospective foreign business partner into the Oval Office.* Little did I suspect just how much, but I would find out. A couple of months later, I got one of my own clients in. It cost me a two-hundred-thousand-dollar donation to the Clinton Library (which I later stopped payment on).

After cocktails, we went into a huge tent for the dinner.

Usually state dinners are held in the White House, dignified and intimate affairs. This was something entirely different, hardly intimate and a few degrees shy of dignified. People laughed about it. The Clintons were using the dinner to reward their supporters, they said, and the horde to whom they owed favors was so big they had to put us all in a tent outside. I overheard people joking about how half the attendees were people who'd given big bucks to the first lady's Senate campaign.

Despite the "prestige inflation" because of the over-packed guest list, our table was great. We were right in front of the long head table where the president, first lady, and dignitaries from India were going to be seated. People like Goldie and Chevy were well behind us. More proof that money talks.

Seated at our table was Rodney Slater, then the secretary of transportation—a major honor. When we all sat down, before anyone got a chance to introduce themselves, Bob blurted out something like, "Guess we're not going to be telling any Firestone tire jokes at this table tonight." Firestone had issued a major recall of its tires because they were unsafe, having at that time already been linked to hundreds of injuries and dozens of deaths. With all the problems in the press, Secretary Slater was surely feeling the pressure. Jay Leno and David Letterman could be forgiven making light of it on their shows, but in front of the secretary at an official government function? We were all stunned by the comment—and silent. Then, just when I was sure Bob had botched it for us, Slater laughed out loud. *Whew!* Close call. You've got to admit, it was pretty funny.

I spotted Denise Rich across the room. She had on an incredible gown and probably a couple million in jewelry. She was, I would later find out, always there. I don't know what it meant, but on each of my several official visits to the White House, every single time, I saw Denise.

The first family came in, along with the prime minister of India and his wife. Hillary was wearing a sari. The Clintons walked right by our table, smiled, and waved to Cynthia and me. It was a great dinner, with an extensive menu of interesting food, and a long list of new and interesting people to meet. I kept going to the bathroom by myself, in case I might run into someone there that I could strike up a conversation with.

Afterward, we waited in a long line with everyone else to have our pictures taken with the president and Mrs. Clinton. I ran into Denise there. She hadn't seen me before and, after getting over her initial shock, said she wasn't surprised I was there. She laughed, but in a nice, not a jealous way.

When we reached the Clintons, it was almost embarrassing, the warm, open-armed greeting we got from them. It seemed genuine, though. Cynthia, of course, put her foot in he mouth by saying, "I just wish everyone in Los Angeles could see this; they would just die!"

Back at the Watergate, Joe thanked me profusely, and Bob enthused about how I'd done wonders for his spirits. I could only wonder at this amazing turn my life had taken. Everything had changed so quickly. The president and the first lady addressed me by name and considered me a friend. My family could never have dreamed I'd be in a situation like this.

Yet in spite of my newfound fame, my new friends couldn't have guessed how screwed up my personal life was. Though this evening would have been one of the highlights of just about anyone's life, the truth was that I couldn't relax or enjoy myself. My financial woes were weighing too heavily on me.

AFTER THE INDIA STATE DINNER, I was getting all kinds of invitations to the White House. It still seemed almost like a dream. But I was scrambling so hard for money, I couldn't afford to keep flying to Washington all the time. Plus, I was trying to gear up for my next big charity event, A Family Celebration (AFC) 2001, to be held the following April at the Regent Beverly Wilshire Hotel. I was determined to make it spectacular.

David Rosen called me and asked if I could attend a small dinner for twenty at the Georgetown home of Elizabeth Bagley, former ambassador to Portugal, and benefiting Mrs. Clinton. Hillary wasn't going to be there, but the president was. Could I give ten thousand? I hesitated. It would be great to be part of such an intimate gathering with the president. On the other hand, I couldn't really afford it. I told him I'd think about it.

Then I got a call from Ed Rendell, who was stepping down as DNC general chairman after the November election. Ed and I had gotten to be pretty good friends. He wasn't going to be at the dinner, but he strongly urged me to go, saying that he was arranging a little surprise for me.

So I margined some more stock and made plans to go. I decided to ask Chaka Khan to accompany me. She was a new friend, and we were going to do a fundraiser together for her charitable foundation. That was still in the planning stages, and I figured we could talk some business on the trip if she went with me. When I invited her, she said *okay,* but only if her sister and manager Tammy could come too.

More expense. But I bit the bullet and said *sure.* It turned out to be a lot of fun. Both Chaka and Tammy were nice and down-to-earth.

We arrived in D.C. with only a short time to change before the limo picked us up to take us to Georgetown. The two ladies were dressed beautifully, each with a jewel on her forehead between the eyebrows. In the limo, Ed Rendell called me once again on my cell phone to say that the surprise was in place. He still wouldn't tell me what it was. It was pouring down rain.

At Ambassador Bagley's home, there were valets waiting with umbrellas to walk us inside. There were more Secret Service than guests, who all seemed to be big money donors. A computer guy from Malibu, someone from Ohio who owned a steel mill.

Even here, among the country's business elite, star power ruled. Everyone wanted to meet Chaka Khan. She handled all the attention with grace.

President Clinton arrived, and he greeted me by name. We chatted for a few minutes, during which he thanked me for coming. Then we had dinner. The president sat there, asking questions and answering them, in a spirited session. It was very intimate, something rare and special to share with the country's leader. Halfway through, he switched tables and did the same thing with the other ten guests.

Afterward, we retired to the living room where Marvin Hamlisch played piano and sang for us. I sat on the couch between my two ladies. Both seemed very pleased.

After a few minutes, a gentleman approached me. It was

Orson Porter, introduced as the Midwest political director at the White House.

"The president would like you to join him in his limousine, just you and him, for the ride back to the White House," he leaned in to say.

Ed Rendell's surprise! I was stunned and speechless (a weird experience for someone *never* at a loss for words). The only thing I wanted to say was: *For what?* But I couldn't. It took me about thirty seconds to find my voice again. Then I just said *okay.*

Orson said he would let me know when to get ready.

As the shock wore off, I wondered what I was going to do with my two guests. Orson told me they couldn't ride in the limo, but they could ride in the motorcade. For some reason, I persisted. I guess I wanted someone else there to share the experience. *What about just Chaka?* I asked. He checked that out with the president and said yes, that would be all right.

"Nice dinner, wasn't it?" Clinton said when we were all in the limo.

"Yes," I said.

"Too bad Hillary couldn't be there."

We small-talked about various Hollywood personalities we all knew—meaningless conversation that somehow made it easier to be in the near exclusive presence of the most powerful man in the world. As I became more comfortable, I emphasized how much I was trying to do for Hillary and what she meant to me. I offered to do anything I could to help her raise money for her campaign. I also told him I was going to bring him some new donors for his library. He was very appreciative and thanked me again for everything.

In no time, we were at the White House. The ride had seemed very short, but it was unquestionably the greatest one I had ever taken in my life.

President Clinton excused himself, saying he had to retire, but invited us to take a tour of his office with Orson if we weren't too tired. *Too tired?* I was blown away. We thanked him, and he said he'd see me soon, and Chaka next week in L.A. at the home of Tracy and Kenny "Babyface" Edmunds. She would be performing there with Lionel Richie.

Orson took Tammy, Chaka, and me up to the Oval Office, where we all had our pictures taken. I wasn't as bold as Tendo Oto, and didn't sit in the president's chair, but got photographed standing behind it. After those photographs, we sat and talked on the couches in the sitting area in front of the desk.

This was my first intimate visit to the White House—as opposed to the more formal functions like state dinners—but it would not be the last. I would be back several more times before Bill Clinton left office. Each time I would learn and see something different.

IN NOVEMBER, I MADE ANOTHER fateful political contact who would play a big part in my story down the road.

I met Noah Mamet at one of my earlier political soirées. He was the regional director of finance for the Democratic Congressional Campaign Committee and was in charge of fundraising for Congressman Dick Gephardt. Mamet took an interest in me as the new kid on the block. He began romancing me, hoping I could help him channel money to his client. He kept telling me that Gephardt would be running for president one day, and that when he won, we'd be smoking cigars on the White House balcony whenever we wanted to.

Noah invited me to a Democratic fundraiser at the Brentwood home of Michael King, the president and CEO of King World Productions, one of the most powerful companies in the TV business. *Come as Dick's and my guest,* he said. He told me the president would be there.

It was a great night, very lavish, for 225 people or so. I recognized many of the heavyweights from the industry. The biggest of the big. Canadian composer and producer David Foster was in charge of the music. Nita Whitaker sang, and actor Christian Slater performed a song as well. Bette Midler was there, but when they tried to get her up on stage, she refused.

There was a long cocktail hour, but even though I didn't drink, I didn't mind at all. I just wandered around, to see who I could meet. Events like this always resulted in adding names to my Rolodex.

Bill Clinton arrived, spotted me, came over, and gave me a big, warm hug while the cameras flashed.

When we finally went to dinner, and I was shown to my seat, I was shocked. I was seated right in the center of the action, at the head table, the president's table. I couldn't believe it. Seating placement is everything in Hollywood. It absolutely defines where you are in the pecking order. I hadn't contributed a penny, yet I was in one of the most prominent chairs in the house. Hundreds of eyes were watching.

I looked around, to see who *didn't* get seated up front. There at one table were Sylvester Stallone and his wife Jennifer Flavin. At another, Bernadette and Sugar Ray Leonard. At another, Bette Midler. At another, Barbara and Marvin Davis. At yet another, Christian Slater and his wife Ryan Haddon.

At my table were the hosts, Jenna and Michael King; Bill Clinton; Motown founder Berry Gordy; writer/producer Suzanne de Passe, one of the most powerful women in town; Christine Peters, film producer and wife of the infamous Jon Peters; Sumner Redstone, CEO of Viacom; some computer exec from Silicon Valley; and me, there amongst all the moguls.

When the president leaned across the table to ask me what I was up to these days, I immediately captured everyone's attention. Those who didn't know me were wondering who I was, and making plans to introduce themselves. I could feel it, and I *loved* the feeling.

I wound up taking a couple of new contacts away with me from the dinner table. Christine Peters and I became fast friends. She was a decent soul in a rough town. I also became friendly with Michael King's wife Jenna, and they ended up supporting some of my events in a big way.

Later that night, I approached Slater. He'd seen my close interaction with the president, and I figured it couldn't hurt. After some small talk, out of my mouth popped an invitation for him to join me on an all-expense paid trip to Washington that would include dinner at the White House. I wasn't 100 percent positive I could deliver on this, but I was pretty confident. I had a couple of promised invites from Kelly Craighead, and she'd always let me bring other people along before. And this was a movie star. There should be no problem.

In a way, it seemed odd to me that here I was, asking a perfect stranger to accompany me on a trip to see the president. Yet that was my new life. My association with the

Clintons made a lot of things possible in terms of growing my business that just hadn't been there for me before. I was going to take full advantage.

Of course, there was the question of how I was going to pay for first-class tickets to Washington, accommodations at the Four Seasons, and limo service. But I just had my normal response. That would all work itself out.

I MADE SEVEN TRIPS TO THE WHITE HOUSE between late September and the end of Clinton's term in January. Someone joked that I went back and forth to Washington like I was taking bathroom breaks.

Once, President Clinton asked me if I had a tape of the concert from his Salute in August. He wanted to make some copies for Christmas gifts. I immediately called Peter and found out that Gary Smith, who was supposed to do this as part of his contract, hadn't even edited the material down yet. He was demanding more money, on top of the huge salary he'd already received and the gold Rolex I'd given him. Peter was really ticked. But for all his jumping on Gary's back, Clinton never got his tape.

Around Christmas, I made a couple of visits to the White House. One was with Diahann Carroll, who'd become a good friend and one of my favorite people in Hollywood. She's extremely beautiful, refined, and thoughtful. I enjoyed traveling with her as my "date," and invited her to accompany me to a fancy, black-tie dinner honoring Barbra Streisand, Maya Angelou, and many other famous artists.

During the day, I did some business in D.C., including helping Ed Rendell with his gubernatorial campaign. I was now the bright and shining new star among Democratic fundraisers because I was bringing in new donors, new arteries to tap.

That night, as we were checking our coats at the White House, who should walk up behind us but Barbra Streisand and James Brolin. For about fifteen minutes, I stood there, making small talk with Brolin, while Barbra and Diahann chatted. Streisand snubbed me again, of course. Later that night, so did Martha Stewart. The dynamic witch duo.

But who cared? There were plenty of other people to meet. I can't even recall them all. Madeleine Albright again, Mikhail Baryshnikov, Spike Lee and his family. I talked shop with Ed Rendell and Terry McAuliffe, his replacement-to-be. The real highlight, though, was meeting Elie Wiesel, the Holocaust survivor and winner of the Nobel Peace Prize. That was truly a memorable and special meeting.

A shuttle then took us to a big tent that was set up outside on the lawn. It was beautiful. There was even a symphony orchestra playing. We were seated at a table with some foreign ambassador and TV personality Star Jones.

We'd barely settled in when I hear a loud voice behind me calling my name. When I turned around, there was Shirley MacLaine, with whom I'd become a little friendly since the Salute. I liked Shirley. She had great spunk and tremendous wit and always made me laugh. I'd introduced her to Peter Paul, which was apparently a mistake.

"Aaron," she said in that loud voice, "that Peter Paul is a crook! You know, the guy you introduced me to!"

I was so embarrassed, I just wanted to slide down under the table. I didn't know if she was kidding, or what Peter might have done to her. But that was it. She talked with Diahann for a few minutes, introduced us to her date, some general whose name I've forgotten, and then she moved on.

The other thing I remember from that dinner was who was seated at the head table. On one side of President Clinton was Denise Rich, on the other, Barbra Streisand and James Brolin. Rich looked stunning in a gorgeous gown and multimillion-dollar necklace. I also knew her to be an outgoing, fun-loving, free-spirited woman, exactly the kind of person Streisand wouldn't want to be compared to. I could see the looks Barbra gave her.

Like I said, whenever I was there, Denise was there. Later, when we ran into one another, she gave me a hug and a kiss and said, "I can't believe you're here again."

"What about you?" I said. "Do you have a room here?" And we both laughed.

The fact was, I wasn't the only one to have noticed her continued presence. Four other people came up to me that night and asked the same question: "Is Denise f—ing the president?" As if, because she was an acquaintance of mine, I'd be an authority on the subject.

I could only shrug and say, "You'll have to ask her."

MY NEXT TRIP TO WASHINGTON, also during the Christmas holidays, involved my last visit to the White House—or, more accurately, series of visits.

The first was the Christian Slater fiasco. I didn't know him ahead of time, which was okay, because he turned out to be a sweet guy. But his wife . . . *oy!* She kept me, and a couple of other guests who were going to the dinner with us, waiting for an hour, then lit into me in front of everyone as if it were *my* fault. The story is pretty funny. I called Christian at the Four Seasons to tell him when I'd be there to pick them up. Well, he apparently fell asleep and never told his wife. When we arrived as scheduled, they were not downstairs. They weren't ready at all. Finally, after patiently waiting for the tardy couple, I called upstairs. When they got down, Ryan ripped me a fresh one, cussing me up and down about how I hadn't given her adequate time to get ready. Christian just stood meekly by while his wife went off on me. *Whipped.* Finally, he told her that the miscommunication was his fault and did his best to calm her down, though it was clear who wore the pants in that family. (Her terrible temper would get her arrested for domestic violence in Las Vegas a couple of years later, when she allegedly broke a glass on her husband's face.)

After the rocky start, the evening went pretty well. I saw a lot of familiar people at the cocktail reception and dinner: Deepak Chopra, Al Franken, and of course Denise Rich, once again seated next to the president. Later, Ryan and Christian got to see the Oval Office and have their pictures taken with the president in there. Ryan had to boss her husband around, telling him where to stand and what he could touch, like a little child. I don't know how he stood it.

THE FOLLOWING DAY, THE HAPPY COUPLE was gone and I could get down to my more serious business. I had two new clients that I had brought to town for a meeting with President Clinton: Loreen Arbus and her husband Norman Chandler Fox.

Loreen was part of one of the first families of the entertainment industry. She was the daughter of Leonard Goldenson, founder of the ABC television network, and a so-called producer in her own right. She had access to lots of money. She was also, well, a bit eccentric, a plump woman with jet black hair extensions, ghost white makeup like Morticia from *The Munsters,* and Mary Jane shoes. For some reason, she didn't want anyone to know she was married to Norm Fox, and she was absolutely paranoid about concealing her age. When the White House staffer asked for her birthdate, as they do with everyone who visits, she at first wanted to cancel the trip, her office told me, rather than give it, but settled for swearing them to secrecy. As if their purpose in life was to dig up this piece of vital information and release it to the world.

Back in November, I had met her through her publicist, in conjunction with the planning for AFC 2001. I pegged her for a *starf—er* from the beginning. I told her about all the celebrities and politicians who were committed to the event, which was to benefit eighteen different charities, and that President Clinton would be there as one of the honorees. I emphasized the political, because it was evident that she was hungry to expand her circle of acquaintances from Hollywood to Washington. Then I asked her to donate a hundred and fifty grand.

She thought it over and said she would do it if I would honor her with the Heart of Giving Award. Now I really had her pegged. She was one of those people who will contribute large sums to charity, as long as she's the center of attention. Once she gave a hundred grand to Project Angel Food, and in return insisted not only on being honored, but on being allowed to dance the tango on stage for fifteen minutes. Which, embarrassingly, she did while the audience watched and laughed.

So I agreed. Give her some dumb award, who cared? What was important was that she was hooked. I said that for another two hundred thousand dollars, to be donated to the Clinton Library, she could host the president and twelve of her friends at an intimate, private luncheon before the celebration, and that Bill Clinton would personally present her with the award later that night. Without hesitation, she said yes to that as well.

To solidify the deal, and to demonstrate to her that I had real credibility with the Clintons, I had arranged for a meeting with the president at one in the afternoon on the day the Slaters left.

I actually wound up going to the White House early, as I sometimes did, to hang out with Kelly and Orson Porter and other friends I'd made among the staff. I would wander different places, see all these people coming and going, having meetings, getting yelled at a lot about security violations. It was exciting. I'd also meet lots of new people like Sandy Berger, not realizing who they were, only that they were important.

One of the reasons I was tolerated was that I was always cultivating members of the president's staff, sending them flowers and cards, as well as presenting them with expensive gifts. So many people there had my gold watches that the place was like an advertisement for the Beverly Hills Watch Co. This was not at all ethical. I shouldn't have been offering these things, and they shouldn't have been taking them. But it happened with few exceptions. For example, Orson Porter never accepted a thing. And when I left a set of fine luggage for Doug Band, an aide who always traveled with the president, he immediately sent it back with a thank-you note inside.

Late in the morning, I left the White House and met at a nearby hotel restaurant with Terry McAuliffe, the incoming general chair of the DNC. I was on Terry's radar screen now, but I don't think he knew what to make of me yet, and he wanted to kind of feel me out. For my part, I wanted to make certain I had a firm commitment from the president to appear at AFC 2001.

The restaurant was crowded and obviously a hangout for Washington political types. All of them knew Terry. We couldn't go five minutes, literally, without being interrupted by somebody who wanted to say hello to him. I found him to be quite different from Ed Rendell. Terry had a stronger personality. He struck me as more of a hustler, where Ed had been gentler, less ego-driven, more humble. I liked Ed a lot.

I reiterated to Terry what AFC 2001 was all about. It was to benefit eighteen different charities, and Bill Clinton would attend and receive its first annual Award of Merit. I'd already worked this out with the president's staff; I was just looking for confirmation. Terry said fine, but that I would have to pay.

Sure, I said, feeling secure because I had the two hundred grand coming from Loreen Arbus. And what about everything I had done for Clinton in the past, and was continuing to do for his wife? Did that get me a discount?

We both laughed.

I figured I was on pretty solid ground with Terry McAuliffe for another reason. He was going to have a big

340

dinner party in D.C. soon, to celebrate becoming party chair. I had been asked to get a performer and then volunteered to bring Olivia Newton-John to town to sing at that affair and was paying the expenses for her and her crew.

"Of course," he said. "We will take good care of you."

Then he got down to business. *I can get you Bill Clinton right out of the box,* he told me. Meaning that this would be the first thing Clinton did after leaving the presidency. He made out what a big deal this was, both for me and for them offering it to me. I didn't think through that, in reality, it would mean less to have an ex-president than a sitting one. And as things turned out, it was a disaster. Because of the controversy over his last-minute pardons, sponsors were pulling out right and left (I wound up losing seven hundred fifty thousand in corporate sponsorships). But at the time, I accepted what Terry told me, that he was about to do me a huge favor.

"Okay," he said, "I can get him there for sure for a donation of five hundred thousand to the library."

That knocked me for a loop, but I immediately responded, "How about three hundred thousand?"

He told me this was a great gift he was giving me, and he couldn't *guarantee* anything for three. What could I do? I grudgingly agreed to this tenuous arrangement, although I knew it'd be a stretch to come up with the extra three hundred thousand dollars.

When I told him I was introducing the president that day to Loreen Arbus, who would put up two hundred thousand, he said, "Did she bring the money?"

"No," I said, "her foundation is going to send it." I explained that the foundation was tapped out for the current year, but that they would come through right after January 1. Loreen was a very trustworthy person, I added. I'd already taken her word on the hundred and fifty grand for AFC 2001.

Not good enough. "Well, you better bring your checkbook, then," he said, and he chuckled.

He wasn't kidding, either, but that wasn't the worst of it. I later found out that instead of dealing with him, I should have just worked through Clinton's new schedulers, who were booking his post-presidency appearances. If I had, I'd have found that his full fee was going to be a hundred twenty-five thousand dollars. So much for Terry McAuliffe's "generosity." Instead of handing me this great gift, what he'd actually done was take advantage of me as a supporter and new friend of the first family.

Our meeting with Clinton was delayed and delayed. I sat in the White House and waited. In the interim, I must have made or received twenty-five calls. I talked with the guy from the Clinton Library foundation and tried to renegotiate with him. Then McAuliffe called and asked me why I'd done that, and I said I thought Loreen's offer of two hundred thousand was very generous. Then the library guy called again and instructed me to leave three checks for one hundred thousand each with the president's secretary. He said I could post-date them. I wrote the checks, figuring I could get Cynthia Gershman to cover them. She loved doing stuff for Bill Clinton.

Finally, at about 5:30 P.M., we were shown into the Oval Office. It was filled with camera lights and studio equipment and a big camera. Dan Rather had interviewed the president and was just leaving, and man, was Bill Clinton pissed. He was complaining to one of his in-house counsels about how Dan

Rather kept harping on Monica Lewinsky, how that was all he wanted to talk about.

After I introduced him to Loreen and Norm, he calmed down, though, and warmed up to the situation. I explained why we were there and that she was a two-hundred-thousand-dollar donor to his presidential library, and we talked about A Family Celebration 2001 a little bit. Then pictures were taken all around. I even have one of the three of us standing next to the president, me with my checkbook in hand.

Loreen and Norman were thrilled, despite the delay. I had my honoree for the charity event. And then President Clinton was immediately off for New York by helicopter. On the way out, I forgot to leave the checks with his secretary.

sixteen

SHAKIN' IT DOWN

Lord knows why, but even after all of my troubles with Cher at the Clinton Salute, I continued trying to build a relationship with her.

In the early fall of 2000, I took Cher and "best friend" Loree Rodkin—whom I'd come to think of as *Cher: The Homely Jewish Sequel*—to dinner at Mr. Chow, another trendy Beverly Hills restaurant. There I laid out the plan I'd devised for her. Since she was already involved with the craniofacial disease cause, I suggested that she establish her own foundation, in her name. That foundation could then, in turn, donate money to the primary charity in this field, the Dallas-based Children's Craniofacial Association (CCA). I explained why this would be a good move, both for her and for them.

"It'll give a higher profile to your good works, of course," I said. "But I also think that people would be more willing to give, those that know you personally and those that just know your name. Most importantly, I believe we can get big sponsors to support an annual fundraiser, the way Elton John and Sting do with their foundations. You could really give this charity a huge boost."

At that point, I was already involved with preparations for a mega-mega-event, A Family Celebration 2001, to be held (appropriately, as it turned out) on April Fool's Day of the following year. And I was doing my political fundraisers. So I probably shouldn't have taken on still another major project like this one. Nevertheless, I told Cher I would work my butt off to make it happen. In addition, I said, I had already talked it over with Cynthia Gershman, and she was willing to put some money behind it to get it going.

Cher loved it.

We batted the idea around for a while, and there was enough enthusiasm that eventually I felt comfortable bringing up another subject that was on my mind. It wasn't a quid pro quo exactly, but . . .

For weeks, Ed Rendell had been calling, begging me to try to get Cher to headline a New Jersey fundraiser for Al Gore's presidential campaign, and to perform for free. Because of the Salute, Ed probably thought I was tighter with the singer than I actually was. What I did know about her was that she never did anything for free. It would be huge to ask this of someone I wasn't yet close to.

I *really* didn't want to do it. Ed persisted, though, saying it would be a great personal favor to him. I had to give that some consideration. I liked Ed personally, that was one thing. Beyond that, he was powerful. As chair of the DNC, he was in a position to further my career by introducing me to useful people. There was a good chance he'd be the next governor of Pennsylvania, a great contact for me to have. And, of course, he had done *me* a great favor, by arranging the limo ride with President Clinton. That tipped the scales.

I waited while Dennis Miller came over, and Cher had a few words with him. Then I popped the question. Would she fly to Jersey to sing a couple of songs in support of the candidacy of Al Gore? They couldn't pay her, I added.

Okay, she said. Just like that. I couldn't believe it, but, boy, was I relieved. I called Ed Rendell immediately, and he was very happy, I could tell. Now, I figured, the DNC owed me.

I THREW MYSELF INTO WORKING toward setting up Cher's new foundation. One of the pleasures of the job was meeting the ladies from Dallas who headed up the CCA. They were great, dedicated people who made me proud to be working for them.

What with all the balls I had in the air, I didn't have time to take direct control of providing the stage show for the Al Gore fundraiser. So I got my old reliable, Sandra Furton Gabriel, to produce it for me. I knew she would do a bang-up job, and she did. In addition to Cher, she got Sister Sledge, Michael Bolton, Hootie and the Blowfish, and others to perform.

When Cher heard she would be sharing the stage with Bolton, she had a fit, saying that he was so tacky.

"What do you mean?" I asked. Michael was a big star.

"Well, just look at him." That was all she said.

But Sandra could handle Cher. She could handle anyone. The fundraiser, on September 12, was a big success, with a showstopping finale that Sandra arranged: Sister Sledge leading all the performers in singing "We Are Family." Al and Tipper got up and danced too.

I GUESS CHER WAS REALLY GETTING into this political stuff now, because next she agreed to co-host with me a tea for the benefit of Hillary Clinton's senatorial campaign on September 29. It was originally supposed to be at her Malibu home, but she got cold feet about that and we moved it to the Casa del Mar Hotel in Santa Monica.

As always, I paid for everything. I asked David Rosen over and over where to send the receipts, but again he said *forget about them. Okay,* I said, but I wanted to be certain that Mrs. Clinton knew everything I was doing for her. I'd just spent thousands on this fundraiser for her, and could he please tell her that? He said he would.

The tea was a success. Sean Hayes, from *Will & Grace,* was there. Christian Slater and Ryan Haddon. Robert Shapiro, the famous defense attorney from the O.J. Simpson trial, and from the other side of the courtroom, Los Angeles D.A. Gil Garcetti. Cynthia Gershman. And my favorite sweetie, Melanie Griffith (who took Cher aside, right there at my own event, and told her I was a crook—outrageous behavior even by Melanie's standards).

At least Melanie paid for her ticket. *All* my schnorrers had wanted in on this one, and I had generously comped them:

Carol Connors, Nikki Haskell, Loree Rodkin, Blake Lindquist, and Arnold Stiefel.

The guest of honor, Mrs. Clinton, was gracious as ever. I introduced Cher, who introduced the first lady. All very nice and civilized as you please—except that most of my friends who had never seen her up close couldn't stop making derogatory remarks about Cher's face. It was so smooth and wrinkle-free that it didn't look real. This was plastic surgery gone very, very wrong, everybody said.

But the highlight (or lowlight, depending on your sense of humor) of the afternoon was probably a guest appearance by Janice Combs.

One of the people in my life who was really getting on my nerves was Blossette Kitson. I'd gifted her with close to a hundred grand in free travel at this point, in the expectation that she was going to help me meet music business personalities. So far, all she'd delivered was Patti LaBelle.

Now I wanted some contacts in the area of rap and hip hop, where I had none. I knew that producer/artist Sean Combs (a.k.a. Puffy, Puff Daddy, P. Diddy) was a very big name in hip hop, even though he was embroiled in controversy because of his upcoming trial on weapons possession and bribery charges. I thought that some day maybe I could work with him. So I went to Blossette and asked her to hook me up.

I realized, of course, that the last person Hillary wanted to see at her little soirée was an accused felon. But I was thinking of the future, and believed that the way to get to him later if he was acquitted (which he was) might be through his mother Janice. Blossette agreed to put me in touch (for a ten-thousand-dollar fee), but counseled me that Janice Combs, a former model, might not be what I was expecting.

What did that mean? I asked. Well, Blossette explained, Mama Puffy is kind of like P. Diddy in a wig, with breasts. She wasn't real good with the social graces and might not, um, present herself appropriately for a meeting with the first lady. Thus was I warned. But naturally I went ahead anyway.

On the afternoon of the tea, I drove to Janice's hotel to pick her up—the Four Seasons where I had paid for her suite, still never having met her. I almost couldn't believe my eyes. She was everything Blossette had said, and then some: huge platinum blonde wig, skintight, lime green pants, overflowing blouse, the whole nine yards. To top it all off, when she climbed into the passenger's seat of my car, her painted-on pants split right up the rear.

I asked her if she wanted to go back inside and change.

"No," she said. "We don't have time. I don't want to be late."

And that's the way we went. I have great pictures of Mama Puffy with Hillary Clinton and Cher, all of them looking like they're wondering what they're supposed to do next. Luckily for Janice, they don't show the split pants.

One thing about Hillary, she was very attentive to the little details. I believe she is genuinely considerate in that way. The very next day, she sent me a thank-you note, partially handwritten, in which she said: "Your ongoing support of my Senate candidacy is especially important to me, and I am grateful for your continued friendship."

Take a good, long look at the first half of that last sentence. I did, and it made me wonder: Did she really know what was going on? I think David Rosen knew; I think Kelly Craighead knew; I think Jim Levin knew. But Hillary? It was very possible that they hid it from her. In a way, that was their job. Protect the candidate.

That was all about to change.

THAT TEA, UNFORTUNATELY, was not the end of Cher's involvement with the politics of year 2000.

The Democrats really loved her apparently, because at 11:30 on the Sunday night before Election Day I got a call from Jennifer Ruiz, Cher's assistant. She told me that Cher had been asked to fly all around the country the following day, to help campaign for Al Gore. She was willing to do it, but only on a private plane.

"I don't have anything to do with this," I said, and I didn't. "I don't know why you're calling me."

Because Cher needed someone to foot the bill for the private jet, of course.

"She's going to be doing this big charity event with you," she said. "She'd take it as a personal favor."

Pressure, more pressure. That was the last thing I needed.

"I can't afford to do it," I told her. "I don't have the money. I would have to borrow from what I've already raised for CCA."

I thought that might get to her. Surely she wouldn't want me to do that. Guess again.

"Do whatever you have to do to make Cher happy," she said.

Twenty minutes later, at midnight, Alana Stewart called. She said she had Cher holding on the other line. Cher asked her to intercede with me to get her what she wanted. She needed the plane, and would in return do anything for me and my charities that I asked of her. That was her promise.

And I believed her. A fatal and stupid mistake on my part. I told Alana that I would do it. I ordered up a Gulfstream G-4 for the day for Cher. It cost me more than fifty thousand dollars. I didn't have the cash on hand, so I had to get one of my crooked "business partners" to charge the bill on his credit card (at 20 percent interest), and then pay it back with money that was supposed to be used to fund the charitable event Cher and I were doing together.

I felt guilty as hell. I was really fond of this charity, and of the ladies I'd met who were so dedicated to it. And here we were, basically stealing from needy kids so Cher wouldn't have to lower herself by flying first class. To ease my conscience, over the next few months I collected a hundred thousand dollars from people in my donor base and paid it directly to CCA. The contribution gave them a much-needed shot in the arm. That helped a little.

I sent the receipts to the Gore campaign. Predictably, they sent them back. Even though the campaign had benefited from Cher's help, they apparently didn't want the cost of her junket to count against the campaign's take.

DABBLING IN POLITICS wasn't the only thing I was up to. I also was actively pursuing new sources of money. One of the reasons I was doing this with such determination was that the situation with Cynthia Gershman was undergoing some changes.

Biggest of all, she had a new boyfriend, Hector, whose arrival left me looking distinctly like the proverbial third wheel. She met him at a dress shop he owned in L.A. He was in his thirties, she in her seventies.

It was kind of comical, really. After Cynthia got paired up with Hector, his whole family adopted her. Mama and a bunch of sisters—they traveled in a pack. We called them Hector and the Tijuana Brass. They ate together, went to the bathroom together, danced together, everything together. When they would go out to dinner, the family would surround Cynthia, like circling the wagons, and not let her mix with anyone. Not that she was ever much of a mixer.

By the same token, Cynthia adopted them. Threw parties for them, gave them all expensive presents. I would bet that she didn't have a Judith Lieber handbag left in her closet. In addition, she would buy her own clothes only from his store, spending a fortune there every month. Hector would turn around and buy her small gifts in return, essentially with her own money.

She gave Hector control over her checkbook and bill paying. He would do her budget for her, and whatever was left over from her monthly allowance would go to him for these services and for escorting her around town. On one hand, that was a relief for me, because I didn't have to do it any more, but on the other, I hated the thought that Hector was using her.

Naturally, I didn't want to forfeit my pipeline to Gershman Foundation money, since it was the source of so much funding for my own projects. I desperately needed her financial backing for my AFC 2001 event, for example. But there was more than that involved. I was getting scared. Cynthia's mishandling of foundation money was ever-increasing. And I was helping her, mostly because it would have been catastrophic for me to lose her. Yet one of these days, I feared, we were going to get caught. It was a vicious circle. I was afraid of losing her, which made me do things that made me more afraid of getting caught, which made me do more things to avoid losing her.

I had long since overburdened my own American Foundation for the Performing Arts with our shenanigans, so, after I'd gotten back with Peter Paul, I went to him for help. The master con man. He'd obliged by giving me permission to use his own nonprofit, the American Spirit Foundation. It was in good standing, he said, so I converted it to one of my own DBAs and was supposed to give Peter a cut of every transaction I ran through it.

This allowed me to hide money from my creditors, and also to accommodate Cynthia. She would write a check from the Gershman Foundation to the ASF for, say, half a million, and I would provide her with the usual tax letter. Then I would take maybe 40 percent of that money and use it to finance a charity event, at which she would get free tables for whomever she wanted, plus an award honoring her for her philanthropy, the chance to make a "speech," and so on.

The other three hundred thousand, however, would go right back to her, in cash, and she would spend it on Hector or whatever else pleased her. There were incredible trips to Europe that I set up for her, lots of them, with accommodations in the finest hotels money could buy. We're talking seventy-five grand a trip, and up, because Hector insisted on flying his family and friends also. There was jewelry and gold watches. A new Mercedes, a super-stretch limo, and a Bentley. And more.

One night Cynthia called me, crying hysterically. Hector was going to leave her if she didn't give him a hundred thousand to buy him some land in Mexico that he wanted to turn into a mall. He got the money. Another time, she paid him forty thousand in cash just to accompany her on a weekend trip to Palm Springs that he didn't want to make.

On yet another occasion, I watched her use her foundation credit card at a charity function, so that Hector and his sisters could buy whatever they wanted from the silent auction. Did they ever: jewelry, clothes, luggage, trips, on and on.

"You *know* this is wrong, Cynthia," I said to her. "You can't let them make purchases on your foundation card!" She knew that, she told me. But she thought it was worth taking the chance to keep Hector happy.

Cynthia was going broke, and no one could understand it. She got eighty thousand a month for crying out loud, and a free mansion. But I knew why.

Bad as this was, the bad news had only begun. She was wrecking the Gershman Foundation. The foundation, like most of its kind, was set up so that it contained interest-bearing investments, like bonds. The interest money generated by these was what the foundation used for its yearly disbursements; the principal was not supposed to be touched. This ensured that the foundation would be able to function as a charitable organization in perpetuity.

Cynthia had begun selling bonds. I don't know how she got away with it, but she did. Whenever the cash balance in the foundation account would get too low, Cynthia would call up the bank and have them break a bond, as she called it. And she continued to do it right up to the moment the California Attorney General's Office got involved.

THE MONSTER ITEM ON MY PLATE was still the following April's Family Celebration 2001. I'd started on it in September, giving myself seven months to organize it—an eternity by my standards—but certainly not an excessive amount of time for something of this magnitude.

One of the things I envisioned was a kickoff for the event itself, to be held sometime in December at one of the local upscale restaurants, and I had begun searching for the right one. This kickoff would serve my publicity purposes, of course, but it would also give me a much needed financial boost. Not only was I trying to get AFC 2001 up and running, but I had also stupidly taken on an event called Celebrating Diana, with Diana Ross as the honoree. I was overextended, and I was broke.

I did have money coming, the two hundred thousand dollars committed by Loreen Arbus that was scheduled to arrive after the first of the year, and I had Bob Lorsch's promise of one hundred fifty thousand. (Even so, I was still short just on the basic half-million for the presidential library, the figure I'd foolishly agreed on with Terry McAuliffe.) But I had no immediate, start-up cash, and I was frantic to get some. Peter was fading from my life; Cynthia was tied up with Hector.

So I turned to Bob Lorsch, thinking that with his hundred and fifty in pocket, I could really get moving. Bob had a reputation around town as a big philanthropist. Like Hal Gershman, he had set up his own nonprofit, the Robert H. Lorsch Foundation Trust, to act as a vehicle for his charitable disbursements.

I met with Adam Krajchir, trustee of the Lorsch Foundation, who handed me a multi-page, handwritten contract. I often did major things just on a handshake, now here was a full contract.

Bob was offering me a hundred fifty thousand dollars, split into two equal halves. Seventy-five was to go toward my AFC 2001, and the other seventy-five to Celebrating Diana. In return, Lorsch only wanted the world.

First, he insisted on having the kickoff event at his Beverly Hills home, probably just so he could laugh with his Republican friends about how he had entertained Hillary Clinton (who was scheduled to attend) at his house. That was a budget buster right there. I'd been negotiating with restaurants to hold the function on premises, which is a great deal cheaper. The restaurant will comp you some things, plus a catering job is always expensive compared to an in-house dinner. Everything is simpler.

Next, he required two prime-location, free tables at each event and multiple free ads in the tribute journals. He was to be honored at AFC 2001, prominently seated near two ex-presidents (I was nearly finished working out the details to bring Gerald Ford, as well as Clinton), and allowed to make a speech to the whole gathering.

In addition, President and Mrs. Ford were to come to his house the night before the kickoff for a more intimate cocktail and dinner reception. I'd had a preliminary look at how much the Fords were going to gouge me for the main event; this little add-on would negate the value of Lorsch's "contribution" all by itself—and then some.

But it was the final condition that really took the cake.

For underwriting two *charity* events, Lorsch demanded not only to be recognized as an underwriter but also a beneficiary. As the contract puts it, "The Robert H. Lorsch Foundation Trust will be recognized as a benefiting charity of the event [Celebrating Diana] and will receive funds equal to the greater of $150,000 or 50% of the funds raised by the event." So much for charity. He wanted it all back, and then some, if he could get it. "The greater of" meant there was no ceiling. If my event took in a million bucks, then I would have to rebate half a million to his foundation. And this would come directly out of the net proceeds. Bobby Freedman, my own personal loan shark, never charged me that much. I said I couldn't sign something like that. But inside, I knew he had me. I was in desperation mode. Bob knew it, and he was prepared to take full advantage of the situation.

No signature, no money, he said.

I signed, setting me up for the incredible financial bath that I would take between then and April.

I WAS CLOSING IN ON my other honorees for AFC 2001. At that time, *Ally McBeal* was a big hit TV show, and I decided to go for the entire cast. That was becoming one of my specialties. *Friends. The Practice.* Now *Ally McBeal.*

To get them, I had to go back to my old "friend" Neely Swanson, director of business affairs for the hottest production company in town, David E. Kelley Productions. I had to, because they were the creators of *Ally McBeal.* But I also wanted to get Kelley himself, and his wife Michelle Pfeiffer, to act as co-hosts of the event. I was ambitious, but believed I should never aim low. I wanted every gala of mine to be more spectacular than the last.

Neely was her usual grabby self. For the *Ally McBeal* cast, she wanted an expense-paid summer trip to Europe for her and her family. I agreed. A short time later, she made a second demand. For Michelle and David to come and be dinner chairs, I would have to pay for a first-class European vacation for Pamela Wisne, the president of the company. I had never even met Wisne. This was getting very expensive, but I couldn't afford to risk losing hosts and headline honorees, so again I agreed. *Done.* Michelle and David committed, and I was hooked up with Marsue MacNicol (cast member Peter MacNicol's wife), who would coordinate everything with regard to the cast. Marsue was a good person, and did a good job.

I have detailed in this book any number of instances in which employees of talent or publicity agencies hustled me for expensive foreign travel or other expensive gifts, in return for providing access to their clients, or doing other special favors. This may or may not seem like a reprehensible practice to the reader—though I hope that it does—but is it a crime? I believe so, and, as I see it, should be called *commercial bribery.* This is the relevant California statute:

Any employee who solicits, accepts, or agrees to accept money or any thing of value from a person other than his or her employer, other than in trust for the employer, corruptly and without the knowledge or consent of the employer, in return for using or agreeing to use his or her position for the benefit of that other person, and any person who offers or gives an employee money or anything of value under those circumstances, is guilty of commercial bribery.

That is clearly what happened to me, over and over again. I would provide these people with lavish gifts; they would use their influence within their companies to get me stars that I wanted. The only gray area lies in that word *corruptly.*

The statute goes on to define it like this:

"Corruptly" means that the person specifically intends to injure or defraud (A) his or her employer. . . .

So, was what they did corrupt, and therefore criminal? Again, I think the answer is yes, but the appropriate authorities will have to decide. To help that decision along, I have provided a mountain of material to the authorities that I believe documents numerous instances of commercial bribery, boxes and boxes of letters, receipts, and invoices.

To return to my story, with Election Day just around the corner, I got a final call from Neely Swanson that turned out to be one of the most fateful of my life. She knew of my friendship with Hillary Clinton, so what she wanted was for me to arrange for the first lady to visit the set of *Ally McBeal* and meet the cast. Could I do this favor for her? It'd be a real feather in her cap, and she would not forget it, she told me.

Now that was about the last thing I wanted to do. In the first place, it was the run-up to the election, and Hillary's schedule was already jammed. And in the second place, it would be incredibly crass of me to presume on my relationship with her to that degree. Neely, however, was holding the good cards, and she knew it. It was so hard, she said, keeping the whole cast in line to be honored at my event.

Then there were the cast members' lists of friends and wealthy associates. I needed those to help solicit contributions, especially considering how rapidly event costs were escalating, and considering that I didn't have enough even to pay myself a starvation wage for my efforts. The clear implication was that those lists might not be forthcoming if I didn't do this for her.

I told her I couldn't do it. But Neely does not like taking *no* for an answer. She continued to call me, pestering me, pressuring me, until I finally said that I would give it a try.

No way, Hillary's staff said.

Not only was the first lady too busy, but there was another problem, they explained to me. She was already coming to California a lot to raise money, and was being attacked as a friend of the Hollywood liberals. They didn't want that label stuck on her any more than it already was. A visit to the set of some TV show would not help.

Now I was the one who wouldn't give up. I kept calling her office, and finally she told me she would do it. She was coming out to the coast, would go from the airport to the studio, and make a quick stop before going on to her other obligations.

THE DAY OF HER VISIT I went over to David E. Kelley Productions an hour early to make sure everything was in place. The Secret Service was there in force. When I got there, Neely informed me about a change of plan. Mrs. Clinton now would be taken to the set of each of their hit shows, *Ally McBeal, The Practice,* and *Boston Public,* then meet David in his office.

Then she told me that company president Pam Wisne would be Hillary's escort, not me. "What about David?" I asked. She's taking the trouble to come here, and he isn't even going to come out of his office long enough to take her around? I couldn't believe it.

I didn't like these developments, but went along. However, I made certain we still had our understanding about pictures. There were to be none. No press, nothing the company could use to exploit this. It was a private visit. *Of course,* she said. (Somehow, naturally, the whole thing ended up on *Entertainment Tonight,* and I got chewed out by the White House, as if I were somehow part of it.)

When the motorcade arrived, Neely tried to shove past me, saying, "Okay, now Pam is taking over."

I shoved right back. "No, she isn't," I said. "I am not going to let a bunch of strangers greet the first lady when I am the one who invited her to this f—ing thing. *Unfortunately.*" I pushed my way through the gawkers. The door of her van slid back, and out stepped Hillary Clinton. She looked great, with a smile on her face, ready for a day of campaign fundraisers in Beverly Hills.

She greeted me with a big warm hug, and I said, "Thank you so much for coming."

I introduced Neely and Pam to Hillary and Kelly Craighead, who also gave me a hug.

Once again, Neely tried to take over, saying, "Pam can take it from here." But I shook my head. What chutzpah.

We walked briskly into the building, and Hillary toured the three sets as quickly as she could without being rude. She must have met two hundred people in thirty minutes, shaking hands and greeting each one personally. It was nice and all, but not what she was looking for, trust me, which was solid donations to her Senate campaign, and she wasn't going to get that here.

Still, it was fun to watch the scene unfold. We walked through a number of sets—lawyers' offices and fake courtrooms—and finally got to the one where Dylan McDermott and Camryn Manheim were shooting for *The Practice*. We walked through the door and there were the stars, the judge, all the extras in the jury box and courtroom observer seats. We took everyone by surprise. Imagine it: the first lady walks through the door of a fake courtroom with me by her side. The jury's mouths dropped. I could actually see it happen in slow motion. Just as sudden, they all broke into huge smiles. Camryn, a major left-wing, bleeding heart and butt-kisser, ran to Mrs. Clinton enraptured. Dylan McDermott, much more dignified, approached her and said what an honor it was to meet her.

I stood back and watched it all, thinking, *I got the wife of the president of the United States of America to come to this.* I would have rather had her meet my family, but with my father having passed away and the rest basically abandoning me, they might not care or appreciate it anyway. After all, I was involved in it. I snapped back to consciousness and watched the first lady work the room. When she was done, everyone gave her a standing ovation and wished her well.

At the last set, for *Boston Public*, Kelly Craighead grabbed my arm and whispered to me, "This is going to cost you. I cannot believe you got her to do this." Quite tense. I just ignored her.

After the sets, we met with David E. Kelley in his office. They talked for quite a while, and I could see her staffers getting nervous. I got up and left the office three times, trying to get Neely to pull the plug on this, but she was afraid to. Finally, I had to do it myself, or Kelly would have killed me.

What a waste, except . . . when we got back to the van, Mrs. Clinton asked me if I would like to ride along for the day. She was going all over the area, to hotels and private homes, raising funds, and winding up at Barbara and Marvin Davis's estate.

I was literally struck dumb. This was an unbelievable offer. I couldn't get a word out, and finally Kelly said yes for me and we all got into the van—two Secret Service agents up front, Kelly and Hillary in the middle, David Rosen and me in the back.

What a day that was. I saw the interiors of many beautiful homes and met many interesting people. We would stop, Hillary would do a quick pitch, and then we'd move on. In between each of them, Hillary would make twenty or thirty phone calls. As the day wore on, we all got more relaxed, but tired. It was exhausting, even Mrs. Clinton said so. How she did it, day in and day out, I don't know. Nevertheless, I wouldn't have missed it for the world. It was a joy for me, and a real bonding experience for both of us.

Late in the day, both Kelly and David had other things to do, and suddenly (except for the Secret Service) I was alone in the van with the first lady. She asked me what new projects I had planned. She knew about the AFC 2001 honoring her husband, of course, but I told her about some of the others.

Then I did something I hadn't been planning to do. It just came out.

I'd spent odd moments alone with her before, primarily in the evening at the White House. But this was my real shot to talk to her with no one else around, and what I wanted was to let her know how much I admired her, how much I was behind her, and most important, what I had already done for her. It was, quite by accident, the moment of truth.

I didn't know how you earned someone's trust and friendship, except by giving them money and gifts and doing extravagant favors for them. I liked Hillary Clinton so much and wanted so badly for her to be my friend. So I did the only thing I understood: I told her about virtually every penny I'd spent on her behalf. I let her know what I was doing and had done for each event of hers. I spoke about the money and what a pleasure and honor it was to spend it on her candidacy for the U.S. Senate.

Once and for all, I wanted it clear in her mind who was the person really doing things for her. There was so much jockeying for position among those around her: Kelly, David, Jim Levin, and so on. People taking credit for stuff. I thought I might have been short-changed, and I wanted to correct that. I believed that once she knew the facts, she would see how valuable I was to her and welcome me into her inner circle.

The whole thing was intended to be solely for my benefit. I never wanted to hurt her. I could tell she wasn't entirely comfortable with this conversation, and yet I couldn't stop.

It wasn't until much later that I fully realized what I had

done. Whatever protection her staff had built around her, however much in the dark they had kept her, that was over.

Now she knew.

BEGINNING IN SEPTEMBER, after the Clinton Salute, I had begun to extricate myself from Stan Lee Media. I left their offices and worked out of my one-bedroom apartment. The only connection I maintained was through Stanley Myatt.

I never knew the details of what was going on there, only that something was. Peter Paul had taken a financial bath at the Salute, and it hadn't paid off in terms of access to the president. His plan to bring Bill Clinton into the business was in shambles. And the value of SLM stock was plummeting. Peter must have been doing something behind the scenes to shore up his finances—later he would be charged with all kinds of illegal stock manipulations—but I remained in the dark.

There were only a couple of things I knew for sure. One was that if Peter was going down, anyone around him would be in the line of fire. When he got into trouble, it was always someone else's fault. I didn't want to be that someone if I could help it.

The other was that I had begun to get margin calls from Merrill Lynch. I didn't have the foggiest notion what a margin call was, but I learned that the money I had borrowed on margin against my SLM stock now had to be paid back in some way.

One way to do it would have been to sell some stock, but I wasn't supposed to do that, because it would hurt the company. In fact, Peter and my broker had told me that a lot of the stock he'd given me was restricted, and I couldn't sell it. *False.* All of it was unrestricted, and I could have sold out at any time, including when the stock was selling in the mid-twenty-dollar range and my holdings were worth millions.

Peter covered my margin calls for a while, but then one day he called me up and said he wasn't going to do it any more. "Do what you have to do," he said. Trouble was, I didn't have a clue what I was supposed to do, so I didn't do anything. To this day, I don't know what Merrill Lynch did. Maybe they took it upon themselves to sell some of my stock on its way down and recoup some of their losses. In any event, the last I heard, my brokerage account was now worth in excess of negative four hundred thousand.

This is the strange part. That was the last thing I heard. Merrill Lynch never called me in, not even after SLM disintegrated and trading in the stock was halted. I can't figure it out, but the fallout from a margin call of close to half a million simply disappeared. Today, my statement shows that the account is worth plus two dollars. Go figure.

AS PETER'S TROUBLES WERE BREWING, I was totally consumed with all my various charity and political projects, so I didn't think much about it. Then one day, late in 2000, I got a call.

One of Peter Paul's companies was called Mondo English. This was the vehicle for a grandiose scheme of his, a worldwide Internet hookup that would teach people in out-of-the-way places how to speak English. I don't know if it was eventually intended to merge with Stan Lee Media or what, but he definitely had high hopes for this idea.

Now, he told me, he had to go to Brazil, to oversee the branch of Mondo English that he had set up there. He needed me to buy some airline tickets for him and, later, for his family to join him there.

Then he warned me that I could find myself in big trouble. I had never really considered the possibility that I could be implicated in any of Peter's shenanigans. He mentioned the Clintons and my Merrill Lynch account and a lot of other stuff I didn't understand. His usual scare tactics, I think, so he could manipulate me for his benefit.

So maybe I shouldn't have done the favor for him, but I did, and on December 22, 2000, Peter Paul flew to Brazil on an eighty-eight-hundred-dollar ticket I bought him. A month later his wife and kid followed, to the tune of another fourteen thousand. I have the receipts to this day.

Shortly thereafter, Peter was arrested and thrown into a Brazilian prison, where he was stuck for two years. I didn't lay eyes on him again until late in 2003, after he'd finally been extradited back to the U.S. to stand trial for stock fraud.

seventeen

ONE BIG HAPPY FAMILY

Hillary joins me in extending best wishes to all for a memorable celebration.

> —PRESIDENT BILL CLINTON,
> *Letter, March 20, 2001*

Mrs. Ford and I thoroughly enjoyed the delightful dinner at Bob Lorsch's gorgeous residence on Saturday and it was an equally delightful evening on Sunday at the Regent Beverly Wilshire Hotel. . . . I look forward to your coming to Rancho Mirage . . .

> —PRESIDENT GERALD FORD,
> *Personal Letter, April 6, 2001*

Bill Clinton was the first ex-president I got to be an honoree at A Family Celebration 2001. But was one chief executive really enough? I decided that it wasn't and went after Gerald Ford.

His Palm Springs office staff referred me to Betsy Berg, his booking agent at the William Morris Agency in New York City. I called and explained about the event that I was producing, that we were benefiting eighteen different charities, and that I wanted to honor President Ford with the Special

Giving Award. I said that we would pay him a fee, plus expenses—which wouldn't be much, because he lived so nearby. I offered fifty grand, which was his usual asking fee, and which I figured I could get someone to underwrite.

Betsy said she'd get back to me, which she did pretty quickly. No deal. I raised the offer to a hundred thousand and got turned down again. Then I sucked it up, knowing full well the risk I was taking, and went to a hundred-fifty. Back came Betsy with Ford's counter-offer. A two-hundred-thousand-dollar personal speaking fee for himself, and a further commitment of another two hundred thousand dollars for the Betty Ford Center.

Gulp.

Further, William Morris made me sign an agreement that I wouldn't take the money for Ford out of the proceeds from the event. So I didn't. I borrowed the money, mostly from Stanley Myatt, and got Cynthia Gershman to guarantee the contract, promising her that I would funnel more money through my DBAs for her to spend on Hector. I put the money into the event bank account and began paying it out on a fixed schedule to the former president.

It was a stupid deal. Yes, it increased the prestige of AFC 2001, but not by a whole lot. One of the things I was thinking, though, was that I would make it back through ads and tickets I would sell to wealthy friends of the Fords who wanted to honor them. Didn't happen. Not one person came out or bought ads to support Betty and Gerald Ford.

As if this weren't bad enough, as the event approached Betsy got back in touch with me. She told me that her boss, William Morris Chairman Norman Brokaw, had received a call from a distraught Gerald Ford. Ford told Brokaw that he'd been contacted by Marvin Davis who said I was a bad guy and to make sure to get all the money up front. I'd never even met Marvin Davis, unless you counted the time in Spago when Hillary Clinton went to his table to say hello and I was following her. All of my contact had been with his wife and daughter. I couldn't believe it.

Here's how I think the scenario played: The charity fundraiser business in Hollywood is cutthroat. So when on March 25 the *Los Angeles Business Journal* ran a page-one story about me, it was a huge red flag waved in the faces of my competitors.

I always tried keeping a low profile. Mainly because I wanted the events to get the attention, not me. Plus, as my business affairs got more tangled, I simply didn't want any extra scrutiny on myself.

Andrea Mitchell of NBC had bugged me constantly at the time of the Clinton Salute for a story, which she never got. I even told Julie Nathanson, a great lady from Rogers & Cowan I'd hired to help me, to keep my name out of the media.

When the *Business Journal* came calling for an interview, I said my standard, *No thanks.* They were welcome to do a story—in fact, that would help me—but I wasn't going to cooperate. Curiously, even though I'd given no interview to any of their reporters, the *Journal* ran an article full of quotes from me.

But here's where the real damage was done—in the lead of the story:

With an A-list guest roll that includes Elizabeth Taylor, Whoopi Goldberg and Sylvester Stallone, an annual charity fund-raiser that quietly began only last year has already emerged as one of L.A.'s hot-ticket philanthropic galas. The second annual "A Family Celebration," to be held April 1 at the Beverly Wilshire Hotel, is already being compared to Marvin and Barbara Davis' Carousel Ball, Ronald O. Perelman and Lilly Tartikoff's Fire & Ice Ball, and other prestigious events.

They quoted Julie Nathanson—who had loyally tried to protect me by talking only about the gala—as saying, "It absolutely could grow to be as prestigious as any other major (charitable) event in Hollywood."

Barbara Davis must have hit the roof when she read this stuff. How dare they compare my event to hers? Feeling threatened, I believe she decided to try to do what she could to sabotage my event. With President Ford and, as we shall see, also with Sly Stallone.

I was so enraged that I called up Nancy Davis for the first time in a long while and chewed her out, up one side and down the other, for allowing her mother to stab me in the back after everything I'd done for their charities over the years. She denied it. I called her a two-faced liar and slammed the phone down; it was the last time Nancy Davis and I ever spoke. With all the stress in my life, constantly broke and scrounging for more money than most people make in a year—or two, or three, or four even—I was more stressed than ever before in my life. Not sleeping. Sometimes I thought of getting out. Even ending it. And then this kind of stuff happens. It was the very last thing I needed—one more weighty straw on the camel's back.

Whatever the actual story, President Ford chose to believe Marvin and stuck to his demand. Payment up front, or he was canceling his appearance at the event. And what about the Betty Ford Center money? If I shifted money to him, it could end up shorting them, and would at the least delay their getting paid.

Luckily, I had a good relationship with the Betty Ford people, so I was able to restructure their payments in order to get the president his money. I had to borrow more money, stick it in the event account, and hand-carry a cashier's check over to William Morris at the last minute. Literally the last minute. Ford was waiting, not getting into his car to come to the event before he knew the money had been delivered.

And that was my interaction with Gerald Ford, recipient of the Special Giving Award. It should have been called the *Special Taking Award*.

ABOUT THREE MONTHS AFTER the Clinton Salute, with everything else that was going on, I got a call from Stanley Myatt. Peter was preparing to flee the country (although I didn't know that), and all was not well with Stan Lee Media. Myatt warned me that I could get caught up in things. "You never know what the government can do," he told me, "even if you're innocent. I want to protect you and try to help you."

Of course, I owed Stanley a growing amount of money at that time, so he did have a certain degree of self-interest. But I'd also heard that he was, or had been, part of the FBI's Organized Crime Task Force, and maybe the CIA too—that whole man of mystery shtick—so he was a guy who should probably be taken seriously.

"Here's what you should do," Stanley advised me. "Make copies of all your documents relating to the Clinton Salute, and take them to a private meeting with a guy that I'll set up for you, Ron Moretti." Moretti, it turned out, was a special agent for the FBI, based in New Jersey.

I didn't see why I needed to do this, and I resisted at first. But Stanley persisted. "Show him what you have, that's all." I had never been involved with law enforcement before, at least not at this level, and had no idea what this all meant. I was a little scared, but didn't think that anything could happen to me. I hadn't done anything.

Still, I brought my friend and lawyer Phil Levy in on it.

Though he was a civil lawyer without much experience in criminal matters, he said, "This is highly unusual. I know there should be two FBI agents present at all times, and the meeting should be recorded and they should take notes. Plus you should have a lawyer with you."

But Stanley had reassured me that this was a very informal meeting, just a look at what I had and some conversation. I wanted to do as he said. More than the government, I was scared of Stanley Myatt. I was so far in debt to him and didn't want him any angrier at me than he already was. So I didn't listen to Phil.

I went to Atlantic City and met with Moretti in my casino hotel room. He had on golfing clothes. He showed me his badge, which could have been bought at a toy store, for all I knew.

We spent a couple of hours together. He was friendly, asked a lot of questions, didn't record the conversation or take notes.

I gave him the copies of my documents, and he kept them. Then he gave me several phone numbers and told me if I had any further concerns about this meeting, to call him, but that he probably wouldn't need to meet with me again. I flew home thinking it was all over. But no.

Next thing I knew, I got a call from FBI agent David C. Smith, who was investigating New York Senate 2000, one of the organizations benefiting Hillary Clinton's campaign. I thought it was a joke. I told him I'd already met with the FBI. But he'd never heard of Agent Moretti and wanted to come over and meet with me. I said okay.

This time there were two agents, as he was joined by Kevin Horn. Both were young guys, special agents with the Los Angeles office of the Bureau. They seemed very honorable and just interested in the truth about the Clinton Salute. Once again, I didn't feel intimidated, or that I needed to have a lawyer present with me.

I was completely cooperative. I thought that the best way to handle this was to give them what they wanted, answer everything truthfully, show them the mountain of stuff I had. I'd saved my receipts, money orders, cashier's checks, invoices, and correspondence. The whole story was there for anyone to see.

Since they interviewed me in my one-bedroom apartment/office, they could also see how crappy my living situation was. Nobody could possibly think I was making money off of all this. That probably gave me a feeling of immunity. They couldn't be after me. I was a witness, not a target.

My viewpoint was strengthened by what they were asking me. They were very focused on David Rosen, Kelly

Craighead, and Hillary Clinton herself. I went through the whole scenario for them, demonstrating how there was no way for them not to know about the expenses—even Mrs. Clinton. Looking back, it seems odd now that I never thought, *What is this about? Who is in trouble and for what?*

I still thought of myself as a minor player. Peter had donated the big bucks. I was glad it was Peter, and not me. Mostly I just went along, letting the FBI lead me wherever they wanted to. I guess what I was actually doing was steering them toward other crimes, the different fundraisers I'd been a part of, whatever.

Month after month this investigation went on. My life began to seem surreal. Here I was, doing charity events where there was fraud involved; continuing to expand my political contacts, fielding telephone calls from President Clinton, the first lady, and Gerald Ford; and at the same time being enmeshed in an FBI probe.

NO MATTER HOW WEIRD MY LIFE GOT, though, I still had to keep working. I had a mega-event to put on. AFC 2001 was coming along in some ways, however costs were soaring and the money flow was ebbing. Some time before, I'd hired away a first-rate event planner from Nancy Davis: I'll call her Ellie Spock. In this situation as in all others, she was doing a great job and helped get things under control. But with everything else going on, I was still losing steam, both physically and emotionally. We needed another body.

Sometime after the first of the year, 2001, I hired David

Rosen to assist with the money end. He was young and energetic and wired into some very prominent circles. I thought he'd be perfect as a fundraiser. He didn't have a commercial fundraising license, but hey, I didn't know that he needed one. I didn't care that his asking price was high. I only cared whether he could get us a much-needed infusion of cash, and with his résumé, how could he not? I remember our first strategy meeting, at the Regent Beverly Wilshire, where he and Ellie and several others had gathered with me to discuss AFC 2001, how it was going and what we needed to do.

For one, we needed someone to headline the stage show of AFC 2001—and it came about in an odd way.

There was a man named John Cassell, whom I had met at Stan Lee Media. He was a tall, really skinny guy, and he was doing something with Peter Paul, I don't remember what. He carried himself with a big air of self-importance, but seemed more like a loser to me. One day, he overheard me talking to Peter about my big event and said he would like to get involved with me.

So I said, "Okay, bring me a big name act to be honored, and I'll hire you to work on the event if you're capable." Thinking there was no way he'd come up with anything I'd be interested in.

But he answered immediately, "I can get *NSYNC to come and sing, and be honored."

He had my ear. *NSYNC was one of the hottest musical groups in the world. They were just another boy band to me, like a lot of others, and I didn't care for their music. But they were a top act, and I wanted them. Plus, my wheels were turning here. There was always the possibility that along with them I might also get Britney Spears, another mega-hot performer, because she was dating Justin Timberlake, one of the members of the band.

"What'll it cost?" I asked.

Answer: twenty-five thousand for him and another five grand for his roommate Sarah, who was the actual friend of Lance Bass and Justin Timberlake. Wasn't that typical. It cost me five times as much for the introduction to the person with the connection as it did for the connection herself. It was steep, but I figured with the band's drawing power, I could make it up in journal ad sales, as well as increased ticket and table proceeds.

The only other stipulation was that we would have to make a generous contribution to *NSYNC's favorite charity, Challenge for the Children. That was no problem. I knew that Cynthia would come through on that one.

I met Sarah at the Polo Lounge in Beverly Hills Hotel and laid out the deal. *NSYNC would be honored at AFC 2001 with the Harmony and Spirit Award. They would sing a couple of songs. Afterward, the Gershman Foundation would match the events net proceeds on a one-for-two basis and donate that money to Challenge for the Children. In other words, if AFC 2001 raised a million dollars, she would contribute half a million to their charity. Sarah took the offer to *NSYNC, they accepted it, and that was that. No contract, which was the way I usually did things. I had my share of no-shows, as we've seen, but truthfully, most of the time my handshake deals were honored.

So John Cassell got me my headliner, and I kept my word by hiring him to help out with the event. This was a windfall for him since, as he kept crying to me, he was broke and out of a job. He had no office. I set him up in my one-bedroom apartment with his own "office." What I would do is get up in the morning, put my mattress in the closet, and set up a folding table for him. I also installed phone lines and other equipment for him, and that was his office. Mine was the living room. That was all I could afford.

A week later he "had to have" an assistant, which I had no money for. So, of course, he threatened to pull *NSYNC on me, and I had to give in. That sure was a familiar story. Since I had no money, I had to borrow it from Stanley Myatt to keep paying now two guys.

The demands kept coming. Next, Lance Bass wanted to have a coming-out party for his new film production company, A Happy Place, at the Sundance Film Festival. John asked me to sponsor it. I looked at him like he was crazy.

"Look at how I live!" I screamed at him. "Don't you hear the bill collectors calling me every day?"

Didn't matter. The following day I found out Lance was going to pull out if he didn't get what he wanted. Same old story. It was too late for me to lose my headliners. So I borrowed twenty grand from Bobby Freedman at 100 percent interest and gave it to Lance, who called me up to thank me and to say that he was going to make sure that this charity event was the greatest ever.

I didn't take credit for the Sundance party. I let John Cassell pretend to have sponsored it. I didn't even go; I was way too busy with AFC 2001.

In return for all this money I put out I got . . . nothing. All of Lance's promises weren't worth ten cents. He had promised me a list of people to whom I could send fundraising letters.

Didn't get a single name. I was depending on *NSYNC's popularity to bring in a lot of money in tickets, tables, and ad sales. Now I had to do it myself. I researched who they were, who their supporters and vendors were, anyone connected to them who might give money. Then I reached out to these people on my own, and I did sell some tables—only a very few for reasons that later became apparent.

One day I got a call from someone I was soliciting, to tell me that he had contacted *NSYNC's office and their rep had said, "Oh no, that's not our event, don't do that."

That was it for me with these guys. This was about raising money for charity, and you make someone an honoree at one of these affairs for only two reasons: One, they deserve it— clearly a joke with some stupid boy band. Two, because you can get a lot of charitable contributions based on their name.

So much for that delusion. Instead, I had to pay for them to work against me.

THE KICKOFF FOR AFC 2001 was held on December 3, 2000. Ellie set it all up at Bob Lorsch's estate up on Mulholland.

Ellie did her usual fabulous job, especially considering how much Bob grew the guest list. He was making this thing into his own private Christmas party. We had to rent a huge tent to accommodate everyone, and our expenses ran to seventy-five thousand dollars—an insane amount for a kickoff.

The event was attended by everyone, including all the members of *NSYNC, except for Justin Timberlake (who would, however, show for the formal event in April). Jean

Karlson came with new sponsors because I was very involved again with *Vanity Fair* and its sister Condé Nast publication, *Traveler* magazine. Olivia Newton-John came with her daughter; ditto for Rod Stewart, his daughter Kimberly, and manager Arnold Stiefel; most of the cast of *Ally McBeal;* and Camryn Manheim and Dylan McDermott from *The Practice.* Eric McCormack of *Will and Grace* co-hosted (for approximately twenty thou), along with my friend Alana Stewart, and Terry Bradshaw, a good guy who asked for nothing in return.

*NSYNC's representative was a girl named Melinda Bell who, unfortunately, treated everyone around them like crap. I had given out several invites because the band was going to be there, just to do kindnesses to people. Jenna King, Michael's wife, brought her kids and stepdaughter specifically to meet them and thanked me later. Stanley Myatt brought his daughter for the same reason. And there was a group of girls from over in the Valley, whom I'd heard about on the radio. They'd been stiffed by some crooked ticket agent, gypped out of seeing an *NSYNC concert that they'd paid for. I'd also invited them. I'm sure all the girls loved being around the band, but it would've been nice if their rep wasn't so rude to the group's fans.

The reason Eric McCormack was there was because I wanted some hot new blood to work with, and I'd gotten Camryn Manheim to get us together. I'd given Camryn two center-court tickets to the Lakers, which set me back five grand—we're talking playoff action. In the process of developing my own relationship with her, I also gifted her with a custom Harley-Davidson motorcycle for twenty-five thousand dollars.

But my favors for Camryn Manheim didn't stop there. While she was at my "office" picking up her bike, the phone rang and it was President Clinton, calling from the Kennedy compound in Hyannisport, Massachusetts. Clinton wanted me to get a star for him, for something or other that he was doing. That really blew Camryn away, seeing me dealing so casually with the president from my folding-table desk in a one-bedroom apartment. She flipped—immediately bugging me about getting her an invitation to the White House.

In actuality, I'd already put out feelers about that, but had been rejected because White House staffers were bothered by a *People* magazine article that said Camryn Manheim and Monica Lewinsky were becoming fast friends. She swore it wasn't true, and I told her I could fix the situation, which I did. Within a short time, I took her to meet the president.

AFC 2001 WAS REALLY SHAPING UP. This was now what it looked like:

> Honorary Chairpersons: President and Mrs. Clinton
> Dinner Chairpersons: David E. Kelley and Michelle Pfeiffer
> President Bill Clinton: Award of Merit presented by Elizabeth Taylor
> President Gerald Ford: Special Giving Award presented by Larry King
> *NSYNC (Lance Bass, JC Chasez, Joey Fatone, Chris Kirkpatrick, and Justin Timberlake): Harmony and Spirit Award presented by Britney Spears

Sylvester Stallone: Outstanding Creative Achievement Award presented by Congressman Richard Gephardt

Bob Newhart: Lifetime Achievement Award presented by Suzanne Pleshette and Tom Poston

The Cast of Fox's *Ally McBeal* (Gil Bellows, Lisa Nicole Carson, Portia de Rossi, Calista Flockhart, Greg Germann, Jane Krakowski, Lucy Liu, Peter MacNicol, Vonda Shepard, and Courtney Thorne-Smith): Outstanding Television Drama Award

Jeffrey Bonforte: Internet Entrepreneur of the Year Award

Loreen Arbus: Heart of Giving Award presented by President Clinton

Robert H. Lorsch: Humanitarian Award "Celebration of Life"

Hosted by Carson Daly of MTV

Special Guests: Whoopi Goldberg, Britney Spears, and Elizabeth Taylor

Featured Performers: Marc Anthony, Ray Charles, Josh Groban, B.B. King, *NSYNC, Rod Stewart, Tiffany, Luther Vandross, and Dwight Yoakam

Musical Producer: David Foster

Associate Producer: Sandra Furton Gabriel

Announcer: Ed Hall (from *The Tonight Show*)

Executive Producer: Aaron Tonken

Event to benefit: Alzheimer's Lakeway Program, Broadway Cares/Equity Fights AIDS, Challenge for the Children, Locks of Love, Starlight Children's Foundation, Wildlife Waystation, and others

This, of course, is not to say that the planning came off without the usual glitches. There were plenty of those. In fact, financially it was the worst it had ever been for me.

Foolishly, I had re-hired Garry Thompson, the sleazebag lowlife who had gotten me a couple of performers at the Clinton Salute. For seventy-five thousand, he promised to get me Clint Black, Dwight Yoakam, and Marc Anthony. About the only positive thing I can say is, well, Dwight and Marc did show.

I doubt Thompson ever had any intention of delivering Clint Black, but that was the least of my problems with him. In addition to the money I paid Garry, I also had to agree to pay expenses for Marc Anthony's entourage, about forty musicians and friends, before he would play for "free."

Even worse was that one day Garry brought by someone who could supposedly deliver radio stations across the country that would buy twenty-five-thousand-dollar tables (fifteen or twenty of them) and do listener giveaways in conjunction with the event. All for only ten grand. Great. I gave the guy his ten grand and—surprise, surprise—that was the last I ever heard from him.

It got worse yet. One day, Garry came to me and asked for two hundred letters on event stationery, over David E. Kelley's signature, and said he was going to send them out to friends and vendors who would donate items to the auctions. Out they went. I even paid the postage. When nothing came back, he told me that, well, it hadn't worked out, tough luck. Later, though, I received phone calls after the event from different companies, asking for tax write-off receipts for stuff that I'd never received.

When I confronted him, he gave me reason to believe he was going to beat the crap out of me if I didn't back off.

I did.

Besides Clint Black, I lost several other entertainers. Tiffany was supposed to be delivered by John Cassell, who kept promising that yes, yes, she would be there. Nope—not that John didn't take a chunk out of me anyway. Luther Vandross simply didn't show up, without any explanation.

Rod Stewart had also committed to being there. But then Arnold Stiefel, his manager, demanded an all-expense-paid European trip in payment and, for once, I put my foot down. I felt as if, this time, I had enough top-drawer performers that I could afford the loss. When Stiefel threatened to pull Stewart out, I called his bluff and said *go ahead.*

Neely Swanson told me to go ahead and give Rod's manager whatever he wanted, saying Rod Stewart was a listed performer and it would be terrible if he withdrew. Sandra Furton Gabriel was against my paying him anything; she kept saying, *No, this is for charity.* She was right, and I was not going to relent. Stiefel was not going to get his vacation on my dime. Neither would I get Rod.

Neely was very upset. "[I]t is . . . disturbing that an artist of Rod's stature would choose to cancel at the last minute." It is, but that's how some of these guys play the game.

It would have been much worse for me to lose my dinner chairs, which I almost did.

Turned out that Michelle Pfeiffer and David E. Kelley were vacationing in Hawaii and were having such a good time they didn't want to come home. I had to call Neely Swanson and scream at her about the lavish gifts I'd given her and how she was obligated to produce her boss and his wife. Not to mention the incredibly crass behavior of Pfeiffer and Kelley. What kind of people sign on to be *chairpersons* of a huge, wonderful event raising money for charity and then think they don't have to show up if they're having more fun doing something else? *You better get them there,* I told Neely. And she did.

Then there was the change of venue, which happened as a result of fallout from the Marc Rich pardon. I had originally arranged to have AFC 2001 at UCLA's Royce Hall, which can accommodate fifteen hundred. That would make it my biggest event yet, but I felt it wasn't overly ambitious, considering the glittery list of honorees and scheduled performers. Then, on his way out of the White House, Clinton pardoned Rich, and the country was hit with a storm of protest that eventually found its way to the likes of me.

Suddenly, Bill Clinton, who left office on a wave of popularity, was poison. Corporate backers began pulling out of AFC 2001 by the boatload. And it really wasn't just the pardon. Neely Swanson wrote me in March from David E. Kelley Productions:

I very much regret that numerous underwriters withdrew their support because of President Clinton's participation . . . although I am still a fan of President Clinton, he by no means represents the best that family values has to offer. As you recall, you suggested Nicolas Cage back out of the event when he got his girlfriend pregnant while still married to Patricia Arquette; and yet now the event is giving its "highest honor" to a man whose sexual proclivities were a best seller on the internet.

In all, I lost seven hundred fifty thousand dollars in sponsorship money. That scared me. I began to worry that I wouldn't be able to fill Royce Hall, and I didn't want the place to be half-empty. If nothing else, it wouldn't look good for me. So I transferred the event to the Regent Beverly Wilshire ballroom, which held only half as many people. I was probably wrong, because we packed the place, but the deed was done.

OF ALL MY MISHAPS, though, the Sylvester Stallone fiasco was the pits.

I had met with manager Gerry Harrington and had been greasing the skids with freebies for both he and his wife. I was trying to land Nicholas Cage for the event, but Gerry warned me that Cage didn't really fit the family celebration theme too well, since he had a reputation as a philanderer. So Gerry pitched me Stallone.

This was my choice? I knew that Stallone had a reputation as an abusive person, but I settled for him and arranged to offer him the Creative Achievement Award. "Next year," Gerry said, "we'll try to get you someone better."

The problem arose when I told Neely Swanson. *He's a joke in the industry and a scumbag,* she basically told me. *Nobody here wants to be involved with him.* No joke. One by one almost every member of the cast of *Ally McBeal* said the same thing to me, directly or indirectly. I stuck to my guns out of loyalty to Gerry, but then a little while later John Cassell came to me and said that *NSYNC also preferred not to be associated with the Italian Stallion. Two very different groups of people saying the same thing. I still backed Sly, though.

Then, about a month before the event, Stallone was accused by some woman of sexual assault. *Oy.* And Nick Cage was supposed to be the bad bet?

It got worse. With two weeks to go, the Davises struck again! Stallone had gotten a call from them, just like Gerald Ford, and been told that he should get some money up front from me. I didn't even owe the guy any money! Gerry was the one I'd paid off; Sly was just supposed to come and be honored.

"For *what?*" I said.

"For his maid's daughter, who is ill," said Gerry. "She needs a hundred thousand dollars."

What in the hell did that have to do with me? This mega-zillionaire couldn't afford to help out his maid's daughter and was expecting me to do it instead? I exploded. "Are you f—ing *kidding?* How can you do this to me after all I've done for you? *NO F—ING WAY!!*" I hung up.

A couple of hours later, I got a call from Paul Bloch, who was Stallone's publicist at Rogers & Cowan. This was another guy I'd spent thousands on. He said the same thing Gerry had said. I can't do it, I told him. I didn't have the money. Then, he said he would pull Diana Ross, whom he also represented, from her upcoming event.

"This is so unethical," I said. "I will have to borrow money at a huge interest rate to get it."

"Do whatever you have to do," he said. (Amazingly, Paul Bloch had the chutzpah to ask me to give money to his favorite charity, last minute.)

After we hung up, I decided not to do it. It was totally unfair. Besides, I didn't need Sylvester Stallone. I had a great list of stars already, and nobody wanted him there in the first place. But I made the mistake of discussing my problem with Neely Swanson, and suddenly she switched sides! I couldn't take him off the list at this late date, she informed me, because that would embarrass David E. Kelley and that would reflect badly on her.

Shoot me.

I couldn't win, no matter what I did. So Stallone's maid's daughter got thirty thousand, courtesy of my personal loan shark, and me, I got nothing except snubbed backstage by Sylvester Stallone.

CRAP LIKE THIS IS COMMON when you work with prima donnas and greedy SOBs. How, some people wonder, does a huge gala ever come off?

With great difficulty. Every time.

If you don't make at least a few really good decisions, you're screwed. With that fact in mind, I brought in David Foster to put together my musical production. David is a major producer, one of the most prestigious and well respected people in the music business. I needed him, badly. I'd had to move the venue, the sheer number of acts was intimidating, expenses were spiraling out of control as the artists began making their outrageous demands. I just wasn't capable of producing the show on top of everything else I was doing. Could he take over? I asked.

Without any hesitation, he said he would do it. "I know

you're trying to do good work here, and that is what counts," he said. "I will help and not charge you." All he wanted in return was for part of the proceeds to go to his charity and for me to allow two of his singers, Josh Groban and Nita Whitaker, to perform. After all I'd been hustled and pressured for, that was nothing. A pleasure.

Foster did a superb job. He brought in a six-piece house band to play behind the performers, which because it was David made it good enough for everyone but Ray Charles and Marc Anthony, who demanded their own huge bands and all the expenses that went along with that.

David also worked tirelessly on rehearsals and production. He helped bring down the cost substantially. And not least, he was extremely supportive of me. When the Stallone thing blew up in my face and stuff was hitting the fan, he was there, counseling me to turn the other cheek and trust in God. That meant a lot.

IF LAST-MINUTE SCREW-UPS were a dime a dozen, then last-second ones probably went for a nickel.

The night of the event, Ray Charles was up in his suite, with his ridiculous eighteen-piece orchestra waiting in the wings, when they sent word down that Ray wasn't going on until he got an extra twenty thousand in cash (ten grand for each of the two songs he was supposed to sing). No shame. I had to go out on the street to get it right away, then carried the wad of bills up to him and counted it out to his road manager. With the twenty grand already on the barrelhead, I asked his manager if Ray would sing a patriotic song instead of one of the two that were planned, and thus make his performance really special. Without batting an eye, the guy told me that that would cost double, because there were two presidents there.

IT REALLY WAS A BEAUTIFUL, incredibly gala night. Many who attended said it was the greatest thing they ever saw. The stage setting was perfect, the food was superb, and the entertainment was top-notch. Everyone seemed honored to be there. Even if Sly Stallone never cracked a smile, Bill Clinton more than made up for him, pleasantly engaging people, letting them have pictures taken with him. And Red Buttons, the last of the great Borscht Belt comedians, was terrific, with a wit that's quicker than almost anyone out there today.

If I'd wished for anything, it would have been that my dinner chairs not be so sour. They looked like they wished they were still back in Hawaii. Michelle Pfeiffer and David E. Kelley were to give our welcoming speech, but right when that was supposed to happen, Neely Swanson came up to me and said they don't get up on stage and give speeches. This was news to me. But that was it; they weren't budging. Nor were they smiling. I asked Neely if they would just grin and wave from their dinner table; for goodness sake, they were our dinner chairs. She told me they didn't want to do even that. There was nothing for me to do but go out there and welcome everyone myself. Without their permission, I had Carson Daly introduce Michelle and David, so that everyone would be sure to know they were there, at least. (And, boy, did Neely chew me out for that.)

I also would have liked to have my award plaques there. But I was now so broke that I didn't have enough money to get them from the store where they had been made. The store wouldn't let them go without payment. So I had no hardware to present to the honorees. Improvising on the fly, I picked up a large glass vase that I found at the hotel. It weighed about twenty pounds and looked impressive. That was my award for the night. We presented the same vase, over and over, and later, after I'd gotten the real ones out of hock, I mailed them to the proper recipients. Only a few people were in on the vase joke.

Still and all, the show went on. Gerald Ford, eighty-seven years old, was the hit speaker of the night. He got up and gave a very moving speech about his childhood, his abusive father, and the stepfather who had come in and given his family the strength to sustain them through hard times. In life, in the long run, "it's family that matters," he concluded. The crowd was touched and gave him a two-minute standing ovation; they obviously didn't know how he'd put himself ahead of Betty's clinic that night.

He even outdid Bill Clinton, who gave a nice speech of his own, which included cautioning the audience that they must never stop supporting charity events such as this. The big ironic line was, "Government alone cannot do this, and we must thank the hundreds of entertainers who give their time and spirit to these gatherings." If he only knew.

Britney Spears was a bust. She was supposedly committed to presenting the *NSYNC boys (including her boyfriend Justin Timberlake) with their award. This had really been hyped up beforehand, but when the time came, she refused. She was literally standing a few feet away backstage while they were waiting, and she wouldn't make the trip out there for five seconds. No reason, just didn't feel like honoring her obligation. Someone else had to do it.

When she and Justin went back to their table, they were immediately surrounded by their security detail, which consisted of half a dozen or so goons, all of them seeming to be about seven feet tall. They stood there through the whole show. This meant that many who had paid big money couldn't see because the goons wouldn't either sit down or move out of the way. There were a lot of people furious about that. (Britney and her friends in the band had been comped, of course.)

Bill Clinton presented Loreen Arbus the Heart of Giving Award. As it turned out she probably earned it, having personally given the Clinton Library two hundred thousand dollars. I knew she was so star struck that if I got him to present to her, she would be an unending source of money in the future. I caught Clinton offstage and tossed him the vase. It surprised him, but he caught it, went onstage, and presented it to Loreen.

Whoopi Goldberg was great; she got out on stage and toasted President Clinton. She said Bill Clinton was one of only a few men who could get her out of the house on a third Sunday of the month. And the cast of *Ally McBeal* was wonderful. They all showed up; some even thanked me from stage for the evening.

Elizabeth Taylor, however, was pretty sad. Once one of the most beautiful women in the world, now ravaged by age, alcohol, and medications. She'd gone downhill so much since I first met her a few years earlier that I almost didn't recognize her. She looked like my Jewish grandmother. Still, she was trying to hang on to her glamour by wearing a green velour dress a couple of sizes too small for her. When she sat at her table, she took off her diamond ring to pass around for the other women to look at and try on.

For the climax of the evening, David Foster persuaded Bill Clinton to climb up on stage and wail away on his saxophone, jamming with legendary guitar player B.B. King, on an improvised version of "Blues in F." The crowd went absolutely nuts. Whatever else he may have been, Clinton was surely the first rock star president.

AS SOON AS IT WAS ALL OVER, I began getting congratulatory messages. There were twenty-eight of them waiting for me on my answering machine that same night, when I got home at two in the morning. A couple in particular stood out.

"Aaron, it's Hillary Clinton. I just wanted to call and wish you well for this evening. I'm so sorry I can't be there, and I'm delighted that Bill will be there with you. But I just wanted to tell you how much I appreciate everything you do for everybody. Have a great, great evening. Say hello to everyone for me. Breathe deeply. It's going to be wonderful. Take care, my friend. Bye." I saved this very special message from Hillary on tape.

Another, from Jean Karlson of *Vanity Fair*: "Aaron, this was the best that you ever put on. My clients sitting at our table said it blows away the *Vanity Fair* Morton's Oscar party. You did an amazing job and let's talk about our next project together." This from a magazine that would later say they hadn't had anything to do with me since 1997.

The next morning Bill Clinton, always thoughtful, phoned on his way to the airport. "You did a superb job, Aaron" he said. "You should really be proud of yourself. Is there anyone else I should send a note to, to thank?"

"Well," I said, "how about a couple of three-way calls right now, to some of the main sponsors?" My office staff were amazed—couldn't believe what they were witnessing.

"Sure," he said, and so I hooked him up with Bob Lorsch, Loreen Arbus, and a couple of the top donors, each time saying, "Hi, it's Aaron, and I've got President Clinton on the phone, who'd like to say a few words to you personally." Then I'd three-way it and bring the president onto the line. They were blown away, all of them.

AFC 2001 raised a lot of money, at least for the various charities. We came out with six hundred fifty thousand to distribute. Not bad at all. Plus Cynthia was supposed to match half of that as part of her agreement with *NSYNC. She'd been billed as the event underwriter, spoke from the stage, was honored, and even given special recognition by Gerald Ford. Unfortunately, she'd blown so much by that time that she was forced to renege, despite all she'd gotten out of the event. *Blown it away on what?* A Bentley she had me buy for her, jewelry, and lavish trips for boyfriend Hector and his family. Cynthia might have been trying to redefine charitable giving there, I don't know. One way or the other, it took a long time to straighten out the money mess.

For me, it was another financial bloodbath. When were they not? This one I would never really recover from. I had to borrow over a million dollars from a wealthy Beverly Hills businessman by signing over Cynthia's five-million-dollar life insurance policy as collateral to cover all the outlandish demands before the event.

Of all those there that night, I probably enjoyed myself the least. I simply couldn't, knowing all the angry creditors I would be facing the next day, and the day after that, on into the future, and knowing that eventually there would be no one left who would lend me any more money. My long, wild ride was coming to an end.

eighteen

DROPPING THE DIME

Thank you for your graciousness for the lovely gift. The next box should be full of cash.

—PAUL ANKA,
Personal Note, August 28, 2002

The two years following AFC 2001, I was doing whatever I could to hustle up money, scrambling for capital from every conceivable source, dealing with loan sharks, borrowing from financial angels, shifting cash from point A to point B, essentially constructing a personal Ponzi scheme, by which money intended for present obligations actually went to settle past ones. All the while trying to put together more extravagant events, none of which would come off—in some cases, because of others, but ultimately because the government would shut me down. I never defaulted on events and always planned on following through in the end.

Celebrating Diana, a benefit to honor Diana Ross and raise money for the Joan English Fund for Women's Cancer Research, was hampered by the demands of Ronnie Caan, brother of actor James Caan, who helped raise seventy-five grand in seed money to get the event up and running but asked for ten grand for himself, making me swear I wouldn't tell anyone on the charity's board. "But," I protested, "your *brother's* on the board."

"Yeah," he said, "I'm splitting it with him." *Imagine that,* I thought, *I've just been shaken down by Sonny Corleone.* Basically, the Caan job was a commission for putting me in contact with the charity.

Worse than Ronnie Caan, however, was Diana's agent, Paul Bloch from Rogers & Cowan.

Paul had me meet with Diana Ross one morning at her Malibu Colony home. There was just a handful of us, and I made my pitch, discussing the details of the plan. She was cold as ice and disengaged. Bad sign right there—and, remember, this was after she'd already sung for me at the Clinton tribute. Diana had a longtime associate there who Paul insisted I fly out, covering her accommodations, *before* he even guaranteed any deal with me. Finally I received a letter on Rogers & Cowan stationary from Paul:

> This letter will confirm that we are looking forward to honoring Diana Ross in September 2001 and to meeting with you, Ms. Ross, and her attorney . . . to finalize the details in January.

Based on the commitment, I started raising cash for the event. Lots of it. But there was Paul like a vulture picking what he could from the corpse of my dying career. I had to pay Diana's longtime associate thousands even though we were months from the event. I also had to pay Bloch's company for publicity work that wasn't even being done because the event was still so far out. For all the money I raised, it wasn't enough. The event was killing the event.

Then there was Diana herself. The event would eventually fall apart when, after spending the fund's money, and some of what others had donated, and after having pre-sale solicitations printed up, as well as paying tens of thousands to Rogers & Cowan for publicity—Diana decided she didn't want to do it, after all. Just didn't feel like it. None of the PR was actually done because there was no event, but that didn't mean they were going to return the charity's money.

In an attempt to salvage things, and under pressure from Loreen Arbus to come up with a replacement for Diana, I tried to rebuild the event around Bill Cosby. I asked William Morris Agency what it would cost to get him to come and accept a humanitarian award from a women's cancer charity, and they said a hundred thousand. I negotiated it down to seventy-five plus ten grand in expenses (fuel for his private jet, transport to the event, etc.).

When this substitute event also fell through, the media got wind of Cosby's proposed compensation. His team went on the defensive immediately. "A Cosby spokesman said the comic instructed his agent to tell the charity he would donate his fee to the group if the event had gone forward," reported Michael Cieply and James Bates in the *Los Angeles Times*. "The spokesman said he didn't know why Cosby didn't just forgo the fee." Eric Shawn of Fox News also questioned Cosby's representatives about it. They responded that the entertainer routinely donates such fees he receives to charity. Okay, Shawn persisted, could they give him an example of at least one charity that had benefited in this way? Well no, they replied, they didn't disclose information like that. Cosby finally wrote a letter to the editor at the *L.A. Times* and basically said a charity would be thrilled by having a check coming from him personally. Maybe. But it's probably hard to feel grateful when you realize it's just your money coming back. It'd be like paying seventy-five thousand dollars for Cosby's autograph. Some deal.

There was also the Great Men in Music fundraiser that would honor four or five great musical artists who had influence in different fields, as well as a Nelson Mandela birthday tour. Neither would ever happen.

In the first case, Arnold Stiefel, manager of Rod Stewart (who was slated to be one of the honorees, not to perform), made a lot of promises and never delivered to my satisfaction. He took twenty-five grand as a deposit (toward a much larger sum from charity proceeds) for his services and just sat on it.

In the Mandela tour, the one I was really pumped about, we had the grand plan to have him come to the United States in 2003, in celebration of his eighty-fifth birthday, and go on a three-city tour that would honor him and raise money for charity, especially his own Children's Fund. But my contact with Mandela turned out to be a rip-off artist. While my expenses mounted, shuttling him back and forth to Africa, it appeared he was working his own deal with Mandela on the side. About a year and a half after our deal collapsed, I encountered this guy again. I had begun cooperating with federal law enforcement officials, and, after one of my court appearances, I was assaulted in a parking lot outside Kinko's. It was my Mandela contact. He stole my briefcase, which had money in it, and threatened to have me killed if I did anything to hurt him or the Mandelas.

As all this nonsense was going on, I was trying to maintain my political involvements, which didn't end when Hillary became Senator Clinton. I still did a lot of work for Ed Rendell, the former chair of the Democratic National Committee, culminating with his election as governor of Pennsylvania in 2002, hoping against all hope that if he won the seat he just might give me a respectable, legitimate position.

I was also simultaneously assisting with fundraisers for both Governor Gray Davis and his opponent Bill Simon, during the 2002 California gubernatorial contest. I even got Dean Cain— the money pit, again!—to be a celebrity attendee at a sixty-five-thousand-dollar dinner for Gray Davis in L.A., then turned around and paid him to fly to San Francisco, where he participated in a sit-down dinner for Simon. Absolutely absurd.

Of course, the politicians didn't care, so long as the stars showed up to lend a little glamour to their fundraisers. And they were equally bad with their finance reporting. I sent copies of my bills to both camps, and both sent them back. I not only had to pay for Cain's travel expenses for these fundraisers—expenses which are supposed to be recorded and declared by a candidate's campaign committee—but I also had to provide Cain with quid pro quos— a paid vacation trip for his entire family to Ibiza, for example. Once, when I tried to bring these matters up with the Davis campaign, his staffer just laughed at me. "What the government doesn't know," he said, "and what the public doesn't know, won't hurt them." It was the same on the other side of the fence; my fundraising contact in Simon's campaign didn't want to know what I had spent to bring Rick Schroeder, Roseanne Barr, and others to one of his events.

Even though he was generally hated in Hollywood, I also wanted to try to develop a relationship with President George W. Bush, similar to what I'd had with Clinton. To that end, I co-hosted a breakfast for him (and fundraiser for Simon) and brought Roseanne, Kelsey Grammer, Paul Anka, and others. All told, I spent directly or indirectly ninety thousand dollars on Bill Simon's campaign.

IN EARLY 2002, I WAS IN DIRE STRAITS, despondent and hopeless, starved for cash, and feeling that the only way out might be to get a foothold in a new field, the one that had always been my goal: television production. Such was my misery and desperation that I did something completely insane.

I became Roseanne Barr's manager.

Roseanne's career was pretty much in the toilet after she'd disgraced herself by grabbing her crotch during a performance of the national anthem. That incident, as you probably remember, got intense TV coverage and made newspaper headlines all over the country. It resulted in Roseanne becoming *persona non grata* just about everywhere.

Yet foolishly, I set out to resurrect her.

What I had in mind was to start a charitable foundation for her, to better her image, while managing her as a performer. I'd had some preliminary discussions with other artists' agents about managing them, and I thought that if I succeeded with Roseanne, I'd be in demand. I'd be the miracle worker. That could mean, potentially, another career for me. What I got instead was an unending nightmare of expense and a payoff that never came.

Roseanne . . . what can I say? A pig with rabies, that's the best way I can think of to describe her. She is rude, crude, totally without class. For seven months, she used and abused me, and worst of all, cost me a lot of money. I paid for everything, from vacations for her right down to her shoes. In all, over two hundred and fifty thousand dollars.

Why? Because I believed I could make her a star again, and then, she promised me, I would get rich from my 10 percent manager's fee, which she would start paying me. Any day now.

It was a sucker's bet. I worked hard. I tried to assemble a good new team for her. I got her a new agent, United Talent Agency, after ICM fired her. I got her a new publicist and, when he resigned after two weeks, got her another, paying for both. UTA, with whom she'd landed due to my efforts, lined up a new TV show for her. I took her calls at three in the morning and let her cry on my shoulder, drunk, complaining bitterly about how much she hated her life. I even set up a dinner date with the president—formal intros and photo op included.

That's right. This woman, who was unwelcome just about anyplace else, who had disgraced America's anthem for all the world to see, went to dine with President George W. Bush. All I had to do was donate one hundred thousand dollars to the Republican Party. You think money doesn't talk in politics? And I got her in with the Democrats too. Here, believe it or not, is an actual letter from my pal Noah Mamet, who headed up Dick Gephardt's Political Action Committee:

Dear Ms. Barr

Leader Gephardt would like to invite you to Washington, and honor you as an outstanding citizen and humanitarian and also recognize you for your many accomplishments. During this ceremony, high-ranking members of the House and Senate will be joining us in the Capitol building, which is home to the United States Congress. We would like to recognize your tremendous contributions in comedy, television, and the arts, which has influenced millions of Americans. We are working with Aaron Tonken on scheduling this sometime during the week of August 19, 2002.

We thank you for the example you have set which has encouraged young people to reach for the best in themselves and work for the common good of society. We appreciate the time and talent you have dedicated to helping young people through your philanthropic and charity work. It has undoubtedly made a lasting difference in the lives of numerous kids.

Leader Gephardt cherishes his friendship with you and looks forward to organizing an event in Washington in your honor. We look forward to continuing to work with you in the months and years ahead to create a better, more just and more livable world.

How's that for a rehab job? Even at the time, I knew it was a joke. Here's how this "outstanding citizen" behaved—just a few examples, of course, but very much in line with the kind of stunts she would always pull.

I had told Roseanne about this fantastic joint for rib

barbecue that I remembered from my days in Windsor, Ontario. So late one afternoon she called me and said she wanted to go there and eat some ribs. I said okay, I'd make hotel and plane reservations for some time in the next couple of weeks.

"No!" she yelled. "I want to go NOW! I have a craving for barbecue!" She said she would only go private, not even first class. We're talking G4 here.

I asked her who was going to pay for all this, and she said, "You, if you want to keep managing me."

So I flew her to Detroit and then took a limo forty-five minutes to Canada. She was already drunk when we got on board, dragging a big red plastic cooler filled with beer. *What kind of person travels with her personal cooler?* I wondered. I suppose the beers were to go with the $125 an ounce Beluga caviar that she wanted, to be served on the plane with mother-of-pearl spoons.

When we got to Windsor, we went to Tunnel Bar-B-Q. Roseanne got her ribs, which she complained about, of course, then went on a shopping spree that cost me thousands more. Altogether, a very pricey dinner date.

Then there was my birthday. For weeks beforehand, she told me that she wanted to take me out to dinner in recognition of all I had done for her. *Don't make any other plans,* she said. She was going to treat me to a really special evening.

She finally decided on Nobu, a Japanese restaurant in Malibu she wanted to try, and presented me there with my birthday gift: a copy of her book and a card. A used birthday card, no less, that had originally been addressed to somebody else. Roseanne had scratched through the name and written mine in.

You can probably guess what happened when the check came. Roseanne reached for her wallet, then gasped in "surprise." Oops, forgot it. "You don't mind paying, do you?" she asked.

When the night was over, and she dropped me off, she hit me up for twenty bucks, for gas.

I fired her a couple of weeks later. Still, she kept after me, demanding money and gifts that she said I "owed" her. My lawyer had to send her lawyer a letter, forcefully requesting that she cease and desist. He was troubled by the increasingly vile tone that her e-mails were taking.

At first, she wrote to me: "I am sorry that things have not worked out and I have decided not to hold any hard feelings toward you, as many of the things you did were encouraging and sweet. I wish you good luck in the future."

Two days later, she was writing: "You must live with a lot of pain inside to be able to be unconcious [sic] of the damage you inflict on other people. I suggest you ask your version (however corrupt it is) of Jesus Christ to forgive you and heal you of the need to be so greedy [!], so sick and so deceptive."

And then, the same day, this capper: "Satan will soon be twisting your entrails onto his pitchfork and roasting them over a never ending fire hotter than a million suns. Love, Roseanne."

Smarting from another quarter of a million of debt, I was quite happy to be rid of her.

MY EVENTUAL DOWNFALL was, predictably, tied to yet another spoiled Hollywood princess.

Cher had agreed to fly commercial to Georgia for the

annual opening of a camp for kids with craniofacial disease. I was still hoping to help her establish a charitable foundation of her own, and had already sunk a fortune in borrowed money into a proposed event with the Children's Craniofacial Association (CCA). Now I was paying for Cher's travel to kick off the summer camp. I had the tickets and everything.

Then, late one night in June of 2001, Jennifer Ruiz, Cher's assistant, called to say that her boss wasn't feeling well and needed to travel by private jet.

Now, this camp was a fine thing—a chance for all these kids whose faces were seriously deformed to be with one another in a fun setting where they wouldn't be teased—but I really had nothing to do with it. Cher was supposed to go no matter what. It was not my responsibility to make sure she got there in maximum comfort. So I told Jennifer that a private aircraft was too expensive, I couldn't afford it.

Next thing I knew, Cher herself was on the phone saying, "Aaron, you know I love you and will do anything for you and our event. Just do this thing for me, please. I really need you to. I'm not feeling good."

Well, I was thinking to myself, *how will it make you feel better by going on a private plane versus first class non-stop?* But I didn't say that to her. After four separate calls from her and her friends and associates, I gave in. Since I didn't have the money, I borrowed it from one of my attorneys, Eddie Jamison, and charged it on his American Express card, which he was happy to do since he not only charged me commission but could then browbeat me until I let him come along with us. He'd never been on a private plane before, and he wanted to meet Cher. Cost: over fifty thousand.

Cher kept us waiting at the plane for over an hour. When she finally arrived, she didn't say hello, just went to the lounge area at the back of the aircraft and locked herself in. No *thank you*, nothing. Not from her or Jennifer.

After we landed in Georgia, as Cher was getting into her own limo, I told her I had paid for a non-refundable, round-trip charter and we had the plane for two days. It would be on standby for her when we were finished, to fly her back to L.A. Or up to New York, if she would prefer. What did she want to do?

"Oh, I don't need it," she said, "I'm going to Europe after this."

"Are you sure?" I said.

"Yes."

So I told the plane to leave. That night I met with the sweet ladies from CCA; we had dinner and mapped out our plan for the future fundraiser. It all went well. The day after that Eddie and I flew home commercial.

It was evening in L.A. when I arrived, and I went immediately to the Four Seasons, where I was due to meet someone for a drink. I was just sitting down when my cell phone buzzed. It was Jennifer Ruiz.

"Cher has changed her mind," Jennifer said. "She doesn't want to go to Europe after all. She wants to go back to Los Angeles."

"What!? Are you *kidding* me?"

"No," she said. "Come on, you know Cher loves you, we all do, and we're going to do that big event with you for the kids. Just get her a plane, okay?"

I wanted to throw up. But by now I was already in so very deep financially with her that I had no choice but to do it. I called my travel agent, Alan Krausen, and begged him to find me something for the next morning, knowing it was going to be awfully difficult on such short notice in the middle of the night. I told him he could charge it to Eddie's card once again, at 100 percent interest.

My travel agent came through. He managed to persuade a charter company to reroute one of its Gulfstream G3's from Colorado to Georgia, which meant they had to fly all night in order to be able to pick her up in the morning.

As the plane was landing in Atlanta, Cher decided that she wasn't going to take it after all. Cancel the flight. Cher, it turns out, didn't fly G3's, only G4's! I, of course, was still held financially responsible, for the full price. I received a bill for twenty-eight thousand for a plane that Cher didn't go on. What I never did receive was an apology. Three weeks later, after all the work I had done and the money I had raised and spent to develop the CCA event with Cher, I was notified through a third party that she was not going to do anything further with me. No explanation.

But that wasn't the worst of it.

I paid for the plane. But the important thing is *how* I paid. When you have cascading debts, like I did, you never know for sure where you will find future money to settle past accounts. It was because of that phantom plane ride that my frantic money shuffling finally caught up with me.

IN SEPTEMBER OF 2001, I got mixed-up with a photographer who worked with a charity for children. We started working on an event that would benefit his charity, along with Children's Craniofacial Association (trying to make up for the money they lost when Cher stiffed me), and the Mark Wahlberg Youth Foundation (which I hoped would get me closer to the famous actor).

This guy was very upfront about his motivations. "I need to make money personally," he told me. "You can take whatever you want, just get me some money quick."

I was willing to do just about anything to start the ball rolling—I would get closer to Wahlberg and I'd make sure the charities made money—so I told him I could make that happen for him. All we needed to do was create the event, and I could immediately begin raising funds against it. For maximum marketability, he needed to get Mark Wahlberg's commitment, in writing, to participate and be honored. No problem, I was told.

I did my part. I got a couple of sources to donate startup money, a hundred thousand worth. I also began negotiations designed to bring Britney Spears and former president George Bush on board as additional honorees.

October came, but no Wahlberg. That didn't stop this guy from demanding the "personal use" money I'd promised him.

I finally took him with me to the City National Bank and deposited all the money I'd raised into his charity's event account, which he controlled. Private lender Bobby Freedman, whom I talked about earlier, was with us too. Since I'd become his most valued client, he was virtually camped out at my apartment, hitting on one of my assistants and waiting to make the next loan to me at his exorbitant rates of interest.

Ken Roberts was still guaranteeing some of those loans for

me. When the FBI later asked him why he'd done it, Ken told them that he's always been on the side of the underdog, and that when he saw me struggling, he wanted to help out the same way he'd been helped when he was young and just getting started. I was very fortunate to have had him on my side.

As soon as the hundred thousand was banked, I asked this photographer to write a check to Bobby Freedman for sixty thousand dollars, telling him that it was going to cover expenses already incurred on our upcoming event. He did. In truth, though, I was covering the balance due on Cher's private charter flights. I simply trusted that I would find another source of income to make the account whole again.

He then asked if he could have five grand for himself personally, and I agreed. In return, he gave me multiple blank checks from the charity, already signed.

I laughed and said, "You know, you have a fiduciary responsibility to your charity not to do stuff like this."

And he said, "I know, but just keep the money coming to me and I won't care."

As time went by, he made an unauthorized payment of ten thousand dollars to a vendor who had performed no services for us and should not have received any money until we were certain there was going to be an event. He also moved more thousands out of the charity account, for legal fees and other purposes of his own—money that was only intended for foundation business. A lot of it is still unaccounted for.

He then, as I understand it, grew worried. His solution was to create trouble for me. He hired an attorney, and they demanded receipts that would give a full accounting of how I had spent money on behalf of our event.

They knew that I couldn't produce any such receipts. In fact, I was so busy working on this event, along with all my other projects, that I couldn't be bothered with these two guys and their questions. I treated them as an annoyance and blew them off.

Big mistake. I had no idea who I was dealing with, but the hired attorney had formerly been an assistant United States attorney, and he had a lot of old pals in the legal system. So when he smelled a rat, he dropped the dime on me, phoning one of his buddies at the California Attorney General's Office. Before I knew it, I was under investigation, and representatives of Attorney General Bill Lockyer were knocking on my door.

I will never forget the first time they came calling. It was one of the most horrible moments of my life, but believe it or not, I was so naïve that initially I didn't know what I'd been served with. I just held onto the papers. When I finally called my attorney, Vicki Roberts, she told me to send those papers to her right away, and then to get my records in order.

Sure. No problem.

Still, I would be able to pull off one final extravaganza, a last hurrah so to speak, even as my world was crashing down around me.

I'D FINALLY MANAGED TO PREVAIL upon Rod Stewart to open his home to a fundraising event, and the result was Unified in Great Cause for an Evening to Remember, September 19, 2002. It was to be one of my most magnificent accomplishments, with Jack Nicholson as honorary chairman, Kelsey Grammer receiving the Outstanding Achievement in a Television Comedy Award, and Arnold Schwarzenegger receiving the Heart of Giving Award. Beneficiaries were charities selected by Stewart (City of Hope), Schwarzenegger (Inner City Games Foundation), and Grammer (Toys for Tots), as well as the Performing Arts Foundation. Musical performance by Lionel Richie. Catering by Wolfgang Puck.

As our press release and invitations put it:

Guests will enjoy an exclusive evening at Rod Stewart's estate, dine by candlelight surrounded by orchids and cascading white flowers. A live auction will include a basketball lesson with Shaquille O'Neill, a tennis lesson with André Agassi, a walk-on role in the new Jim Carrey comedy *Bruce Almighty,* and a walk-on in an episode of *Will & Grace.*

There was also nine holes of golf with former President Clinton and much, much more.

Spectacular, beautiful, exclusive, and, needless to say, disastrous. My most hellish experience ever. I raised a fortune that evening, hundreds and hundreds of thousands, and if expenses had come in as projected, everyone would have been very happy. As it was, though, the charities got none of the immediate proceeds. Every penny went into the outstretched hands of the undeserving, and I had to do my best to make up the difference out of pocket.

Jack Nicholson, my honorary chair, whose name was at the top of the invitation, dropped out. I shouldn't have been surprised, since he is a very private person who rarely does things like this. He hadn't asked for anything for himself, but wanted a hundred thousand committed out of the take to his choice of charity. Which was fine with me. But then he stipulated that he was only lending his name to the event, not his presence. That was not fine with me, so he was gone.

Lionel Richie cancelled at the last minute, after I had paid his representative five thousand dollars to get him there (predictably, he never returned the money). So I had to run around like a maniac, searching for a replacement who could come on extremely short notice. The best I could do was Charlotte Church, who sang two songs, accompanied only with an acoustic guitar, and pocketed twenty-five thousand for the effort. (Lionel's daughter, Nicole, had the nerve to come to the event after her dad reneged on his commitment. All I could think of to do was gesture toward Charlotte Church and say to Nicole, "You know, your father cost me an extra twenty-five grand." Toss in the agent's commission and makeup, and it was an even thirty thou.)

My nemesis Arnold Stiefel hit me up for tens of thousands in cash, plus airline tickets, expensive gift certificates, and luxury cruises for himself and his assistant, Annie Challis. Whenever I would balk at his demands, he would threaten to pull Rod Stewart's support from the event, so I paid.

Kimberly Stewart, Rod's daughter, got ten thousand and an airline ticket worth two grand, for helping get her father to agree to do it.

Camryn Manheim, in return for playing hostess, got a trip to Hawaii for her and some friends that she didn't take because she didn't like the four-star hotel I'd booked her into.

The friends were less picky, though, and went. She also asked for an around-the-world trip for her brother, a successful lawyer who wanted to take a sabbatical, and his companion. That, they never got.

Kelsey Grammer was a decent man who came for free, but I had to give his agent two first-class tickets to Europe to close the deal.

Our genial host even got in on the act. Rod Stewart demanded a private plane to fly him back from New York to the event. If he didn't get it, he said, he would cancel the whole thing.

Then there was Schwarzenegger. As one of our two featured honorees, Arnold was guaranteed fifty thousand for his Inner City Games Foundation. But that, apparently, wasn't enough. (*Never enough* was the key phrase when I dealt with Hollywood stars, always.) At that time, Schwarzenegger was making his first foray into state politics, by raising money and campaigning for the passage of Proposition 49, an initiative on the November ballot that would boost spending for after-school programs. I'm sure it was a worthy cause, but it was politics, not charity, and he should never have mixed the two.

In addition to the money promised to his charity, Arnold demanded that an additional hundred twenty-five thousand be donated to his political fund. (Note that the political require-ment was more than twice as much as the charitable one.) Obviously, I couldn't take money that the donors intended for charity and divert it to this political effort. So I had to come up with a creative way to meet Schwarzenegger's demands. Naturally I turned to Cynthia Gershman and got her to pledge the full amount. Of course, Cynthia's money was tainted too, since it came out of her charitable foundation and was funneled through one of my DBAs. But they didn't know that.

In any case, the event happened. I'm sure everyone had a grand time. And then came the final accounting.

We had raised a lot of money. The live auction alone—basketball with Shaq, tennis with André, golf with Bill Clinton—brought in over two hundred grand. But because of all the outrageous, last-minute expenses, there was nothing left. Thus, despite my dire personal financial straits, I had to borrow some more. Fifty thousand from Bill Austin, to meet my obligation to Inner City Games Foundation. Sixty-two thousand five hundred from Bobby Freedman, at his usual exorbitant interest, to the Performing Arts Foundation. Its director, Charisse Browner, was one of the few selfless individuals involved with this fiasco, and I wanted her to get her money.

Then I had to deal with Arnold. Cynthia was tapped out with her Hector expenditures, among other things, and she defaulted on her commitment. That left me having to get the Prop 49 money from somewhere. I borrowed another sixty-two five from Bobby and gave that to them. I don't know if this was even legal—to borrow money from a third party to make a political contribution—but no one cared where I got it, as long as I did.

In order to try to force the money from me, Arnold's attorney sent a letter to my lawyer, threatening to turn me over to the attorney general if I didn't pay up. I didn't have either the means or the will to take action against them. I just wanted to be done with it, and eventually they settled for the sixty-two five and got out of my life.

The Rod Stewart disaster was the culmination of a very bad

year for me. I was drowning in debt; I had endured the incredibly abusive relationship with Roseanne; Blake Lindquist was threatening to turn me in if I didn't keep him on the payroll; my primary money faucet, Cynthia Gershman, had finally been turned off; and so on. Throughout the year, I had also been called in to testify to the attorney general's investigation and, upon the advice of my attorney Vicki Roberts, I took the Fifth Amendment. I had no idea what they were up to, but suspected the worst.

I was, understandably, an emotional wreck. In the months following Rod Stewart, mostly what I did was call my lawyers and cry. I was having night sweats and couldn't sleep. I was raving, hysterical, calling anyone who would take the time to listen. I even persuaded a supposed friend to loan me his gun, and I took a cab to the store and bought bullets for it. My plan was to check into a hotel and shoot myself, just like the disgraced studio head David Begelman. I went so far as to prepare a note, apologizing to all those who had lost money because of me.

In the end, though, I couldn't do it. I became so ashamed of myself. Maybe deep down I was afraid too. My lawyer Phil Levy talked me into giving him the gun; he returned it for me unused.

In November 2002, I closed down my business and sold everything I had of any value. I put a mere five hundred dollars in my pocket. All of the glitz and the glamour and the high society and the Spago dinners and the limos and the private jets, and five hundred bucks is all I had to show for it. Well, that and a law enforcement investigation.

I relocated to Florida for a short time. It was my intention to rehabilitate myself and start over. Stanley Myatt was offering me help to do that. But I didn't know what to do with myself. I did some work for the Larry King Cardiac Foundation with Joseph Lake and *Ocean Drive* magazine. It never panned out. When Stanley got tired of lending me money, I moved back to L.A. and, utterly destitute, became dependent on the kindness of others. I slept on a couch in Phil Levy's office for six months.

My Hollywood soirees were over—my long legal night-mare had begun.

nineteen

Miscarriage of Justice

In *January 2003, my civil attorney* Phil Levy and I met at the Friar's Club with a private investigator who said he had some information for me. He did. He told me the California Attorney General's Office was about to come down with a criminal indictment of me and others. That turned out to be false, but it spurred me to action.

I left my longtime attorney Vicki Roberts, who'd helped me a lot, and went instead with a criminal lawyer named George Bird, whom Phil introduced me to. Together, George and I decided that, in order to help myself with whatever Attorney General Lockyer planned to do, I should meet with the feds.

It was a fateful decision that put me on a collision course with Joseph H. Zwicker.

On March 13, the AG's Office filed suit against me, Cynthia Gershman, Kevin Clarke, Bobby Freedman, and Does 1 through 100 (other defendants to be named later).

The same day, George Bird and I set up my meeting with federal officials, and on March 19, we met with Assistant U.S. Attorney (AUSA) Zwicker and two FBI agents, Isaac DeLong and Kevin Horn. The FBI had questioned me a couple of times before, as I've noted, but I'd never been charged with anything. What I *had* done was provide assistance with ongoing investigations into Hillary Clinton's fundraising.

That didn't have anything to do with Zwicker, though. As a result of our March meeting, I signed a plea agreement a couple of months later, in which I pled guilty to one count of mail fraud and one of wire fraud. This was done even though I was charged with crimes I never committed, and the AUSA had not yet bothered to learn all of the facts (and never did).

In order to understand why I did it, you have to understand what it's like to be in my situation. It's completely intimidating. They have all the power, you have none. On the one hand, they offer you the carrot: *cooperate and we will seek a downward departure when you're sentenced.* Then they bludgeon you with the stick: *if you don't sign this, we'll throw the book at you, and you'll be looking at more prison time than you can imagine.* Put just about anyone in that position, and he'll be scared, I guarantee it. He'll even confess to things he didn't do, just to get it over with.

I offered them my total honesty in whatever ongoing investigations I could help them with and also gave them a mountain of documents—more than two dozen boxes full, something like ten thousand sheets of paper—that led to the initiation of new cases, by either their office or one in a different geographic region. I told both state and federal officials on several occasions that I wanted to make early restitution (all ignored me).

Still, in recognition of my efforts, the prosecutor was bound by a plea agreement to recommend a downward departure from federal sentencing guidelines when I finally went before a judge. That is common practice where plea agreements are concerned. However, all such "promises" are conditional upon the government agreeing that I had given "substantial assistance." They get decide if enough is enough. Thus their agreement to recommend a reduced sentence is entirely at the prosecution's discretion and is subject to abuse. Defendants should never operate under the belief that they are automatically going to benefit, despite the wealth of assurances they get. They should also be aware that the information they secure may be used to bury them, should it prove inconvenient to authorities. I know.

From the beginning, it was clear that mine was going to be a high-profile case. I naïvely assumed at first that this would work in my favor, that the idea of going after famous defendants would be enough to gladden the heart of any prosecuting attorney. How wrong I was.

For the next year, I was enmeshed with the law enforcement establishment, dealing with first one of its arms, then with another. I spent literally hundreds of hours with these people. Along the way, I got an in-depth education as to just how twisted and perverse our "justice" system really can be.

Here are the highlights.

Outside of Los Angeles, I participated with investigators from an organized crime and racketeering investigation pending in Washington; a special agent for the Office of the Inspector General, Investigations Division; a special agent with the IRS, Criminal Investigations Division; and investigators and U.S.

attorneys regarding the New York Senate 2000 Hillary Rodham Clinton and Marc Rich presidential pardon investigations, including the chief of the Major Crimes Unit in the U.S. Attorney's Office. FBI Special Agent David C. Smith must have liked what I gave him because, after five letters and six calls from George Bird, he refused to return the documents I gave him on Hillary Clinton. On my own turf, Attorney General Lockyer's investigations in support of his lawsuit expanded, resulting in additional claims against Cynthia Gershman and the addition of several people to the list of defendants, including Eddie Jamison, Blake Lindquist, and others.

I also did my best to assist Joe Zwicker. But despite the twenty-five boxes of documents and financial records I provided, with regard to complex trails of criminal behavior, the FBI and AUSA often seemed unable to follow them, resistant to pursuing them and inept at follow-through.

All this time, I felt under nearly constant threat of physical violence. The AUSA never did anything to protect me. First, the threats came from unknown persons. While working with the New York Senate 2000 investigation, someone e-mailed me a copy of the so-called "Clinton death list," a compilation of about thirty-five people who have died mysteriously after crossing the Clintons. The implication was chilling. Next, I received vicious e-mails from someone I believe was Blake Lindquist. Then, from Bobby Freedman, who made numerous threats, including a message left on my answering machine, after I turned down the offer of a hundred-thousand-dollar bribe to keep my mouth shut about him. I believe that Lindquist was also behind the bloody animal parts that I received in the mail, the lawnmower delivered to my residence

COD, and pornographic and harassing letters sent to me and my lawyers, Phil Levy and George Bird. Finally, there were threatening AOL Instant Messages that began appearing on my computer screen, such as *you're a f—in' dead man,* and references to *fat jew, kike,* and *Jewbie Wan Kanobie.* I believe both Eddie Jamison and Lindquist were responsible for these. Both Phil Levy and his paralegal Heather Medina witnessed the messages. Eddie also called Phil and said, "Tell Aaron to leave it alone or I'll f— him up."

The FBI's response to all this? Indifference, or worse. When I tried to give an agent one of the threatening letters, he laughed and told me he didn't want it; no fingerprinting was ever done. When I got the bloody animal heart in the mail, with the manager of Mail Boxes Etc. as a witness, I called the agent, who once again laughed and told me to just throw it away. When I was assaulted, again in front of a witness, he wasn't even interviewed; there was no investigation, much less protection offered to me. When I received a telephoned death threat, which I recorded in the company of my attorney, no one from the FBI ever came to pick up the tape.

Does this sound like normal behavior on the part of law enforcement officials involved in a major investigation? I didn't think so, either. I could only conclude that they weren't truly interested in protecting their primary source—perhaps because they had made up their minds about me before hearing the whole truth. Maybe they even wanted me to come to physical harm, I don't know. What I do know is that I was in continual fear for my life—to the point where I had to flee to the East Coast—and was not taken seriously.

With all this, you probably wouldn't think that it would be

me who'd be blamed. Think again. Those Instant Messages, unbelievably, would wind up getting me into serious trouble. Not the sender. Me.

When I started getting them, I reported them to Joe Zwicker with my lawyers on the same phone call. He asked me to document them. I knew that that was virtually impossible to do, and I'm sure the sender did, too; that was why he was using them. But one way is to have a "sniffer" installed on your computer. This is a device that can definitively search out the source of AOL IMs, and Zwicker told me the specific FBI agent to call to have that done. I phoned him repeatedly. At first I was told that it would be several weeks before they could get to me. Then he stopped returning my calls.

In the meantime, I block-copied some of them and pasted them into the e-mails that were arriving at the same time and appeared to come from the same source. These I forwarded to Zwicker's office, per his specific instructions. Apparently, Zwicker didn't understand that these were patched-together documents and not actual e-mails, even though he'd clearly been told that's what they were. Based on this evidence, Zwicker obtained search warrants for the computers of the two people who were probably involved and conducted a raid. Naturally, the incriminating e-mails weren't there, since that wasn't the way I'd received the messages, and IMs don't leave their own footprint on the source computer.

Zwicker was incensed. Despite the fact that all offending e-mails and IMs ceased after his raids, and even though he knew I had two witnesses who'd seen the Instant Messages (he interviewed neither of them), he accused me of having fabricated the whole thing. Stating that his office had been embarrassed and involved in the harassment of "innocent" people, he threatened to charge me separately with obstruction of justice and violation of my plea agreement and made it clear that he would not be seeking any downward departure for me. It was an astonishing development. Because of his own screw-up—searching for something he'd clearly been told wouldn't be there—he was going to screw me.

And that is exactly what he has done.

Thinking about what happened to me over the course of the past year and a half, I have been forced to the inescapable conclusion that I am the lamb to be sacrificed in order that others of greater position and power might go free. And it was not a great feat of deductive logic to get to this point.

Consider Attorney General Bill Lockyer first. He has a boatload of evidence implicating very prominent people in all sorts of illegal activities, but he has yet to file criminal charges against anybody, and even in his civil suit has named only me and other lesser-known figures. He showed no interest in numerous persons who, like me, were ignoring the law and doing fundraising without a license. Additionally, his attachments to the suit contain supporting statements contributed by some of the very people who demanded money and gifts from me.

I tried to settle with the AG's office. I made four separate offers through four different law offices—Joel Spivak, George Bird, Phil Levy, and Phil Dapeer's—all of which said I'd give in to the AG's demands. Not only did Lockyer not give in, he didn't even get back to us with a no. Instead of settling, he wasted California taxpayer dollars by pursuing a costly action against minor players.

The fact is that Lockyer is a Democrat with gubernatorial aspirations. Hollywood is top-heavy with wealthy Democrats and will undoubtedly serve as his fundraising base. Can he then be expected to be impartial in a case like this, to go after those upon whom he will later depend for financing? You decide.

Next, think about all those investigators from different agencies who interviewed me and to whom I provided evidence of malfeasances that pointed to the very highest levels of government. Is it possible they would be just a little bit reluctant to open that particular can of worms, regardless of their political affiliation, considering where it might eventually lead?

Finally, let's take a close look at the federal prosecutor, AUSA Joseph Zwicker.

First off, he has shown very little inclination to follow the trail of evidence wherever it might lead. He received his initial information about this case from the California Attorney General's suit and seems to have relied upon it, despite its inaccuracies and the fact that there is so much more to the story. The more complex and far-reaching that story became, the less inclined he became to stay with it. (This is equally true of the FBI.) Perhaps it was too much work for him.

Second, he made a very serious error in his investigation, and falsely shifting the blame will help him look a lot better.

Third, like Bill Lockyer, he is a Democrat being confronted with allegations—directed against fellow Democrats for the most part—that could seriously undermine the national standing of his party among voters.

After encouraging my assistance for over a year, in the summer of 2004, Zwicker suddenly and completely turned on me. Not only did he negate my plea agreement and refuse to petition for a downward departure because of my cooperation, but at the end, he even opposed a request for a simple continuance by my two criminal lawyers, George Bird and Alan Rubin.

I was scheduled to be sentenced on August 23 by Judge Dale Fischer. She was known as the strictest law-and-order judge in the California system, unsympathetic to defendants of any kind, much less those who had been stripped of prosecutorial assistance. Many prominent and well-respected defense attorneys refer to her as vindictive and vicious.

My pre-sentencing report had been prepared under federal guidelines that had been thrown into question by the U.S. Supreme Court's August 2 decision to hear arguments as to their constitutionality. It was a major development, affecting a huge number of pending cases. All over the country, attorneys were filing requests for continuances in order to see how the Supreme Court ruled, and judges were routinely granting these requests. Not mine. At Zwicker's urging, Judge Fischer turned me down on August 11.

Even worse were the grounds argued by Zwicker and accepted by the judge. They demonstrate clearly the AUSA's rush to get me out of the public eye and in to prison as quickly as possible, at the expense of justice. My attorneys filed an emergency motion for continuance on August 16 in response to Zwicker's claims.

Zwicker, for instance, had claimed my "fabrication of evidence . . . breached defendant's plea agreement." Replied my attorneys: "Ever since the government made a mistake in their interpretation of information that Tonken gave them concerning a death threat . . . they have tried to shift the responsibility for their own error to Tonken . . . [and] gone on a campaign of vindictiveness and punishment that is truly remarkable."

Then he had this to say: "Defendant's motion [for continuance], if granted, risked additional delays far beyond his proposed sentencing date. . . . Defendant's plea agreement [which, remember, they claimed I had already breached] obligates the government to bring to this Court's attention any cooperation defendant provides in other investigations." Under those circumstances, "defendant may not be sentenced until the government has fully evaluated his cooperation, and calculated the proper sentence reduction." This is a bewildering assertion that turns common sense on its ear. Basically it shows that the AUSA was so anxious to imprison me that he was willing to deny other agencies the benefit of talking to me. That seemed to suit Zwicker just fine. In fact, only a month before, Zwicker had even received a letter from one such agency regarding my desired cooperation in a high-level federal investigation.

My attorneys' outraged response: "[The prosecution asserts] that it is improper for the defendant to try and provide additional cooperation to other Government investigators in the next few months *as if that were a bad thing* [emphasis theirs]. . . . With all due respect, *their job is to investigate crime and bring prosecutions. Information that helps that cause is a good thing* [emphasis theirs]. It is frankly amazing that the Government would argue that a court has to sentence a defendant immediately because if it does not, he may give us information that we can use to prosecute criminals that we do not have now."

Finally, Zwicker contended, "The district court was also presented with evidence that defendant's motive for filing the motion was improper. Defendant informed the government that he required a continuance to publicize his impending book about Hollywood and certain politicians."

I had told them no such thing. However, the fact that they chose to cite this at all creates some implications that are frightening, as my attorneys recognized: ". . . with this argument it appears that the Government was extremely unhappy about defendant's decision to write a book. Whether or not that had a role in their decision not to make the motion for a downward departure raises the issue of whether the decision was based upon the exercise of defendant's First Amendment rights."

Maybe they thought they could get me inside before I finished. And that after spending years in prison, no one would be interested in my story any more. Well, if that was their intention, they have failed. This is still America. I still have a constitutional right to be heard, and the reader has the right to make up his or her own mind. I have not allowed them to silence me. I have told my story, just the way it happened.

IT STILL GOES ON. Shortly after I was incarcerated, Zwicker retired. Maybe he rushed my case through so he could hurry up and go into private practice—shoving me into a cell being one last thing on a to-do list before he could jump ship. This, despite the fact that I was still helping in ongoing federal and state investigations.

Some of these investigations might still bear fruit. In early

October 2004, the Associated Press and Fox News reported David Rosen, Hillary Clinton's finance director, with whom I'd worked so long and hard, was the subject of a grand jury criminal investigation looking into the financial shenanigans of the Clinton Hollywood Salute.

Specifically, said the reports, the grand jury examination focused on underreported expenses to inflate the take for the first lady's Senate bid.

AP quoted part of a twenty-two-page FBI affidavit, signed by Special Agent Smith on May 30, 2002—just a snippet. It's worth noting here that *Insight* magazine scooped the mainstream media two months before and quoted the same affidavit in more detail:

> The event's costs exceeded $1 million, but the required forms filed by New York Senate 2000 with the Federal Election Commission ("FEC") months after the event incorrectly disclosed that the cost of the event was only $523,000. It appears that the true cost of the event was deliberately understated in order to increase the amount of funds available to New York Senate 2000 for federal campaign activities.

I could have told them that. I was there—and it was worse. *Insight's* August 13, 2004, report didn't stop there, either. Writes editor Paul M. Rodriguez: "Agent Smith's sworn declaration also mentions interviews he and FBI Special Agent Kevin J. Horn conducted with several people with firsthand knowledge of behind-the-scenes activities associated with the fundraising events, including an apparently false FEC report that SLM, Inc. donated $366,000 to the Clinton campaign—a report that was filed by her campaign committee and, to date, has never been corrected."

Rosen's attorney maintains his client's innocence: "From my review of all the facts, I am convinced that Mr. Rosen has done nothing improper."

He should have talked to me.

EPILOGUE

Aaron, I so regret the troubles you have had. As I
am sure you have thought long about it and now
realize, you became a victim of the lure of
celebrity . . . and a pawn of some of the people you
surrounded yourself with. . . . I do hope you can
come out of this with a better understanding and
can utilize your talents in a productive way.

—DALE C. OLSON,
Personal Letter

Among the many stars I met in Hollywood, one I remember with great fondness and regret is Brian Keith—the father in *The Parent Trap* and TV's *A Family Affair,* and President Teddy Roosevelt in *The Wind and the Lion.* After Tippi Hedren's ROAR Foundation fundraiser, I became very close with Brian and his family, his lovely wife Victoria, and his daughter Daisy. Brian was an enormously kind man, very patient with me, providing counsel. He truly cared about me and was concerned for my welfare.

Unlike the long line of stars I met who always had their hands out, palms up, Brian never asked for anything—except to be a friend to his daughter, who was only a little younger than me. Daisy was a sweet, dark-haired girl who laughed a lot. She seemed to have not a care in the world. But, of course, if there's anything I learned in Hollywood, it's that appearances are deceiving.

Her parents were concerned. They tried to tell me in subtle ways that they felt she was troubled and in need of some good friends. They even encouraged me to co-rent a house with Daisy, so that I could befriend her and stay close by. But I was never able to properly read between the lines. I did look at places in Malibu with Daisy and Victoria, near where she and Brian lived, but it never happened.

I was becoming so selfish, so wrapped up in my own world then, and so used to dealing with superficial people that I was losing the nerve—even the sense—to do the right thing. I now have nothing but sorrow that I couldn't give Brian the one thing he ever needed from me.

One afternoon, as Brian and I were strolling along the beach in Malibu near his home, I saw Rob Reiner knee-deep in the surf, playing with his kids. I was still impressed, being among the stars.

At the same time, Brian was trying to tell me something very important. "Slow down," he said. "Make sure you're doing the right things, because otherwise Hollywood will eat you up. Just try to get as many good people around you as possible." That was the best advice I ever got. Never really took it. I surrounded myself with many who brought out the worst in me.

We shuffled through the sand in our bare feet for a while, as I tried to take in his words. Then, after lunch, as I was leaving, Brian took me aside and gave me a gift: a small crucifix on a chain.

"I feel like there are demons around you," he said. "You

have a lot of turmoil ahead. Pray to Jesus and wear this cross to remind you of the way."

I will never forget that moment. I stayed close to the family until spring 1997, when Daisy tragically committed suicide.

Although I spoke with Victoria after that, Brian wasn't able to come to the phone. I never spoke with him again. Two months after Daisy died, distraught over her loss and suffering from a serious illness himself, Brian took his own life. I went to the funeral, and that was the last time I saw Victoria before she moved back to Hawaii. I lost other friends in Hollywood that I loved, but this relationship was more of a treasure than any. And because I didn't listen and follow Brian's counsel, I was headed for my own suicide of sorts. I was killing myself, professionally, spiritually, morally, even legally.

I AM ASHAMED OF WHAT I HAVE DONE. I have embarrassed my family and friends, and ruined my good name.

I thank God my father isn't alive to see what has become of me. He tried everything he could to be a moral leader to me, and I let him down. From his many attempts at inspiring responsibility and a strong work ethic in me, to his attempts at staying in contact with me after I had left home in disgrace, he loved me and tried to be there for me at every opportunity.

Still, despite everything, I feel that God has watched over me in all of this. Believe it or not, He never gave me more than I could handle and always put people in my life to help me and have mercy upon me when I deserved neither. Many of these people have vouched for me even now, writing to the federal judge in my case. I've excerpted some of these letters below:

Aaron Tonken was, and I am sure still is, the most talented organizer and producer of charitable events this town has ever seen. Early on he realized that the key to putting on "Big Hollywood Events" was to have close personal relationships with talent. Aaron's problem was that he was also a "fan" and never wanted to say no to anybody. . . . Many took advantage. . . . I know Aaron has suffered tremendously over the past year, but also has learned from his mistakes.

—JONATHAN SILVERMAN,
actor/producer, July 23, 2004

[Aaron and I] only worked together once and it was a pleasurable, fulfilling and honorable experience. He delivered on all his promises, and many good things came out of the "Celebration" night that I helped put together musically. Not only did my new artist, Josh Groban, get to share the stage with many notable and successful artists, but his career really was kick-started that night. Aaron was professional, detailed, and as a result of our hard work together, the David Foster Foundation (helping kids that need organ transplants) received a very generous donation from Aaron. He also was very caring towards my children. For those of you that are parents, I'm sure you'll understand how important that is.

—DAVID FOSTER,
fourteen-time Grammy-winning musician,
composer, and record producer, June 14, 2004

I have attended and contributed generously to many events that Aaron Tonken has produced during the past six years. The charitable events that he has organized have been professionally arranged and have benefited many worthy endeavors. . . . Aaron had done much good for charities in the past, and I believe that he has the ability and willingness to act honestly and with integrity in dealing with charitable organizations and others in the future.

—Jo Ann Berry,
Joseph K. and Inez Eichenbaum Foundation,
August 6, 2004

As an old character actor in Hollywood *(Quiz Show, Serpico, Disclosure, Amistad* and sixty other features, miniseries, and MOWs), Aaron invited me to partake in one of this charity evenings called "A Family Celebration" in 1999. . . . Aaron promised my charity $75,000 which it subsequently received. . . . [M]any of the people he dealt with took advantage of his naivety and vulnerability.

—Allan Rich,
president, We Care about Kids, June 9, 2004

Aaron is facing some very serious charges. I also know that he did not benefit in any way that would provide him with a life of luxury then or now. I look at Aaron as a victim of a Hollywood that none knew existed. Shame on those celebrated people of motion picture, television, and music. . . . I truly believe that Aaron was overwhelmed by the greed of the celebrities. There were no books of reference regarding how to deal with these stars when they demanded a Rolex watch or an all-expense paid trip to Europe. . . . This was a new discovery, and it was unfolding as the event itself unfolded. . . . Incarceration of Aaron Tonken will deprive the public . . . of an opportunity to learn how to understand the truth behind fundraising.

—CHRIS HARRIS,
Harris & Delorean Public Relations, June 7, 2004

My office staff and I worked with Mr. Tonken and his staff . . . arranging all sorts of travel for Mr. Tonken's clients, including airline tickets, airplane charters, limousine, hotels, and cruises. Between the spring of 1999 and the end of 2002, Aaron spent well over 1.3 million dollars with The Travel Authority. Many of the clients that Mr. Tonken was working with were stars, their managers, or high profile people that were very demanding in their travel needs. Mr. Tonken's clients were very insistent on what they wanted. They would often demand certain airlines, flights, and hotels, irrespective of what it may have cost Mr. Tonken or the charities.

—ALAN KRAUSEN,
president/owner, The Travel Authority, June 25, 2004

Aaron combined excellent taste, morals, fantastic connections, and a wonderful gift of salesmanship with unfortunate, extremely very poor business judgments. The Gala that Aaron produced raised millions of dollars ostensibly for the benefit of charities and political campaigns . . . however, much of the monies never went to those areas where the money was intended. The reason for this was not that any of the monies went into Aaron's pocket, actually to the contrary. . . . Consequently, with each event Aaron fell further and further into debt. And many of the celebrities, renowned for their generosity, profited. Unfortunately they did so at the expense of Aaron Tonken.

—RAYMOND CALDIERO,
chairman, The Sequoia Group Inc., June 28, 2004

There came a time in mid 2000 when Aaron . . . asked me if I would be amenable to hosting an event at my estate honoring President and Mrs. Bill Clinton. . . . The evening was a tremendous success and I would venture to say that it was one of the most acclaimed events ever held in Los Angeles. I firmly believe that the ultimate success of this and many other events was due to the diligence and professionalism of Aaron Tonken. . . . Unfortunately when I heard about some of his problems it didn't surprise me inasmuch as I felt that Aaron always tried to accommodate everyone especially the celebrities . . . and I knew that their demands would get the best of him. . . . To this day I don't believe that Aaron ever intentionally tried to deceive anyone but rather got caught up in the domino effect of trying to please everyone. . . . It is also my opinion from what I've seen that Aaron never personally benefited financially from the disaster. . . . To me this is obvious by the fact that he . . . wound up sleeping on a couch in his attorney's office, destitute. . . . I believe that Aaron Tonken has learned the hardest lessons the hardest way . . . and if allowed the opportunity he could have a very productive and respected future.

—KEN ROBERTS

There can be no doubt that Aaron has transgressed as he has quite obviously entered a guilty plea to the charges leveled against him. . . . It is apparent to me by both Aaron's word and, more importantly, his deeds, that he has genuine deep remorse for his actions and realizes that he must answer for them.

—BRAD LEE AXELROD,
attorney, July 23, 2004

I do answer for them and will continue to do so. Even though I will now be spending several years in jail, my imprisonment is better than the life I was living while free. Almost from the beginning, I suffered at my own hand, for my selfish and self-indulgent decisions. This was not what God put me on earth to do.

For the first time in my life, I believe I will be able to search for God's plan for me, rather than working against it. I am grateful for a chance to put my terrible decisions behind me, decisions for which I must now pay the price. While I look forward to getting out of jail and starting a new life, I also look forward to making changes in myself while I am imprisoned, even if they are small ones, so that I can begin to grow into the man my father always wanted me to be, and tried so hard to teach me to be.

Through the years, there have been some very special people who tried with great moral force to set me on a better path (even if I never heeded their advice) and forgave me my transgressions. I will always be grateful that they were there—Philip Levy, George Bird, Bradley O'Leary, Ken Roberts, Joni and Jody Berry, Steven Fox, Rhea and Stuart Goldberg, "Ellie Spock," and all the others who stood by me to the end. Many thanks to Esther and Norman Acker, Geri Jones, Chad Mouton, John Murphy, and Danny Welkes. *Very special thanks and gratitude to Philip Dapeer and Mike Walker.* Thank you all. I now have the opportunity to start over fresh, and I intend to put it to good use.

Acknowledgments

I *thank each of you* for all that you have done to make this book a reality for me—for your endless patience, love, and encouragement:

Bradley O'Leary, my friend. Thank you for introducing me to David Dunham at Thomas Nelson Publishers. May you be continually blessed for all the loving strength and compassionate support you have given me.

David Dunham, my publisher and friend. What a fine example you have been to me. Thank you for your patience and for sharing with me the love of Christ.

Joel Miller, my editor. Thank you for being so kind and for the excellent work you have contributed to making my book a success. Thanks for your constant diligence.

Jennifer Willingham, my publicist. Thank you for all the work and effort you have put into this project. Thank you for your patience with me and for your wisdom and guidance.

I WOULD LIKE TO THANK ALL who helped me along the way, unafraid, enriching my life with your friendship and offering endless moral support. You stood beside me and never judged.

I want to thank *Alan I. Rubin, Esq.*, for bringing his dedication to my legal team, showing his support and guidance 'till the end.

To my lawyer and defender, *Philip Dapeer, Esq.*, thank you for your outstanding hard work getting me out of a heck of a lot of problems.

Thank you . . .

Brad Lee Axelrod, for all your never ending love, support, encouragement, and skilled negotiation on my behalf; you are one of the most ethical and honest men I have known.

Selma and Army Archerd, for your kindness and support. Army, thank you for believing in me and always writing the good things about me and my events through the years at *Daily Variety*.

Adam Bellow, for all your good ideas and encouragement.

Red Buttons, for staying my friend through the whole mess.

Ray Caldiero, thank you for believing in me and for always offering forgiveness and help. For all the good times we had together and all the time you gave me in New York (that helped keep me sane).

Michael Cieply, former *L.A. Times* reporter, thank you for telling the truth, for being an example to me and the world that you can be well respected, ethical, and successful.

David Foster, who is a super success in Hollywood and in the music business, yet has always remained grounded, humble, and filled with love. You are an honest and decent man.

Acknowledgments

Ron Greene, the very best CPA in Los Angeles, thank you for guiding and counseling me. Thank you for your generosity and patience.

Rhea Goldberg, for your loving kindness and friendship, and for your never ending loyalty.

Chris Harris, for making me laugh out loud and often during the time that I needed it most. For all of your good ideas and suggestions.

Geri Jones, you are like a second mother to me. I love you for being so loving and generous to me and my family.

Tricia Jones, my friend and supporter, thank you for all of your advice and love.

Alan Krausen, for your patience, trust, and support.

Heather Medina, for putting up with all my craziness and for making me laugh in very tough times.

Chad Mouton, for being a superb assistant and putting up with more than any person should ever have to. For never leaving me alone, without help.

John Murphy, for always being my friend and never judging me. For caring about me and supporting me during my darkest days.

David Niven Jr., for your support and kindness as well as never being afraid to stand up and tell the truth!

Suzanne Pleshette, for being my friend and displaying backbone and courage.

Alan Rich, a prince of a man, for being one of my biggest defenders and supporters, for loving me with all of his being, and for encouraging me to see a good psychiatrist!

Eric Shawn of Fox News Channel, for always reporting my problems from a fair and balanced perspective and for taking the time to understand not only me but also my life's journey before reporting it.

Bradley D. Simon, a fine attorney who encouraged me to fight and demand my rights, for your guidance and expert council.

Joel Spivak, Esq., for all your council, support, and compassion.

Susan Tellem and *Marshall Thompson,* two true friends who never judged me, for your guidance and suggestions, being wonderful friends.

Mike Walker, my new friend, another great example of someone who is fair, honest, and not afraid to write the truth!

Grant Woods, former attorney general of Arizona, for not being afraid to stand by me, guide me, and for giving me your encouragement, support, and the benefit of your knowledge, I thank you and will be grateful to you always.

Dr. Michael Zola, the best dentist in California, for giving me great treatment and care, even when I couldn't afford it, with a smile on his face!

Thank you to those I love and have hurt:

S.H.

B.N.

J.S.

Y.P.

D.C.

J.L.

Acknowledgments

I HAVE BEEN GIVEN SO MANY GIFTS and talents from God and have been so fortunate. His blessings continue to flow. Jail will be tough for me, but I hurt people who didn't deserve it. I look forward to starting a new chapter in my life, allowing me to do good every day, helping others. I hope that, in the end, as I have forgiven others, I will also be forgiven.

APPENDIX

I provided the federal government thousands of documents that span my career as a political and charitable fundraiser. Here is just a small sample. —AT

BILL CLINTON

8/19/00

Dear Aaron —

The event was wonderful. I can't thank you enough. And I'm very grateful for the book & gave Hillary's campaign —

Sincerely,

Bill Clinton

HILLARY RODHAM CLINTON

June 26, 2000

Mr. Aaron Tonken
269 South Beverly Drive, #372
Beverly Hills, California 90212

Dear Aaron:

Thank you for your warm welcome while I was in Chicago and for hosting yet another wonderful event! It was great to see you again.

I cannot thank you enough for all of your efforts on my behalf. I appreciate everything that you are doing in support of my Senate candidacy, and I am grateful for your continued friendship.

With warm personal regards, I am

Sincerely yours,

Hillary

Hillary Rodham Clinton

Thanks for everything

WWW.HILLARY2000.ORG

Paid for by the Hillary Rodham Clinton for U.S. Senate Committee, Inc.
Contributions are not Tax Deductible for Federal Income Tax Purposes

Recycled Paper

HILLARY RODHAM CLINTON

August 18, 2000

Mr. Aaron Tonken
269 South Beverly Drive
#372
Beverly Hills, California 90212

Dear Aaron:

Thank you so very much for hosting Saturday night's tribute to the President and for everything you did to make it the great occasion that it was. We will remember it always.

With gratitude for your friendship and warm regards, I remain

Sincerely yours,

Hillary

Hillary Rodham Clinton

You were the real star!
Thanks for everything!

Paid for by the Hillary Rodham Clinton for U.S. Senate Committee, Inc.
Contributions are not Tax Deductible for Federal Income Tax Purposes

Recycled Paper

March 20, 2001

Warm greetings to all those gathered in Beverly Hills for the
second annual *A Family Celebration*. It is my privilege to be an
honorary chairperson for this extraordinary event, and I am
honored to receive the *A Family Celebration* Annual Award of
Merit. It is truly a pleasure to be with our distinguished
dinner chairs, David E. Kelley and Michelle Pfeiffer, and all of
the generous sponsors and supporters who helped make tonight's
festivities possible.

I join you in congratulating my fellow honorees who so willingly
share their time and talents to make a difference in their
communities and our world: President and Mrs. Gerald R. Ford,
for their lifelong commitment to public service; N'Sync, whose
smooth harmonies have captured America's heart; the creative cast
of *Ally McBeal*, one of television's most innovative series; the
incomparable Sylvester Stallone, who has created some of the most
memorable characters in film; Bob Newhart, legendary actor and
comedic genius; Loreen Arbus, a strong and compassionate voice
for women, children, and working families; Jeffrey Bonforte, a
trailblazer in information technology; and Robert Lorsch, a
gifted businessman and renowned philanthropist.

This annual celebration reminds us if we are to make our world a
better place, each of us must take responsibility for solving the
problems around us. Families are the vital foundation on which
our nation stands, so we must reach out to help families who are
in need and ensure the well-being of all our nation's children.

I commend the honorees and the charitable organizations they have
selected for special recognition this year for setting an example
of leadership in this endeavor. By providing children and
families with the services, assistance, and opportunities needed
to enjoy a better quality of life, you reflect America at its
best, getting things done and reinforcing our nation's deepest
values of community, compassion, and responsibility.

Hillary joins me in extending best wishes to all for a memorable
celebration.

Bill Clinton

Some people were not happy with President Clinton's inclusion at Family Celebration 2001. This was one of the rejections I received. —AT

BECAUSE OF THIS COUNT US OUT!

Warm greetings to all those gathered in Beverly Hills for the second annual *A Family Celebration*. I am pleased to join you in congratulating this year's outstanding honorees who so willingly share their time and talents to make a difference in their communities and our world.

This annual celebration is a powerful reminder that we are all part of a larger family, composed not only of our immediate relatives, but also of our neighbors, colleagues, communities, and fellow citizens. As members of this extended family, we must reach out to help those families who are still in need, and we must share responsibility for the well-being of all our nation's children.

I commend your honorees and the charitable organizations they have selected for special recognition this year for setting an example of leadership in this endeavor. By providing children and families with the services, assistance, and opportunity they need to enjoy a better quality of life, you reflect America at its best, getting things done and reinforcing our nation's deepest values of community, compassion, and responsibility.

Hillary joins me in extending best wishes to all for a memorable celebration.

Bill Clinton

453

April 1, 2001

A Family CELEBRATION

As Mayor of the City of Los Angeles, on behalf of its residents, I am honored to greet the members, friends and guests who have gathered for "A Family CELEBRATION", honoring outstanding individuals who have dedicated their time and efforts toward the betterment of their communities.

Congratulations to this years' honorees: The Cast of Ally McBeal, NSYNC, Sylvester Stallone, Loreen Arbus, Jeffrey Bonforte and Robert H. Lorsch. You are being recognized for the wonderful contributions you have given to society through your professional and personal endeavors.

I join with other members of the community in commending A Family CELEBRATION for your hard work and outstanding contributions which have not gone unnoticed. Your generosity in giving of your time, energy, experience and expertise has truly touched the lives of many and is worthy of praise and recognition.

Again, congratulations to all and best wishes for a most enjoyable and memorable celebration.

Sincerely,

Richard J. Riordan
Mayor

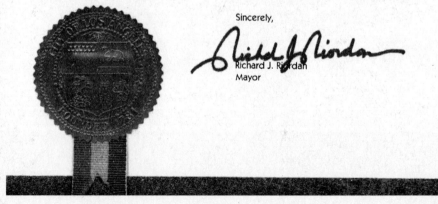

454

Welcome

A Family Celebration 2001

April 1, 2001

It is a great pleasure to extend a warm welcome to all who have gathered for *A Family CELEBRATION 2001*. This celebration is a wonderful opportunity to bring people together for an exciting and enjoyable event while also helping their community.

From fostering new voices in film to providing valuable services for those affected by breast cancer, the supporters of these outstanding charitable organizations are making a positive and lasting impact. I salute their remarkable efforts to make a difference by sharing their time, energy and resources.

I am also pleased to recognize this year's honorees for their extraordinary compassion and generous service. Their hard work and unselfish dedication serves as a model for all Californians.

On behalf of the people of the State of California, I extend best wishes for continued success.

Gray Davis

Governor Gray Davis

DIANNE FEINSTEIN
CALIFORNIA

United States Senate
WASHINGTON, DC 20510–0504

April 1, 2001

Dear Friends,

I would like to welcome all of you to the second annual *A Family Celebration*. This event provides a wonderful opportunity to recognize those who have made a positive impact in the lives of others, and to raise awareness about a number of worthwhile causes. The charitable organizations that will benefit from *A Family Celebration* are excellent examples of how committed individuals can make a difference to their community and the nation.

I would also like to congratulate tonight's honorees: the cast of *Ally McBeal*, the members of *NSYNC, Sylvester Stallone, Loreen Arbus, Jeffrey Bonforte, and Robert H. Lorsch. As actors, entertainers, writers, artists, and businesspeople, all of you have touched the lives of countless people in a unique manner. In addition, the charities that you have selected to benefit from tonight's event are truly worthy ones, helping those in need and allowing people to achieve their dreams.

I hope that this will be a memorable evening for all those involved. On behalf of the people of California, I commend each of you for your efforts, and wish you all the best in your future endeavors.

Sincerely yours,

Dianne Feinstein
United States Senator

United States Senate

HART SENATE OFFICE BUILDING
SUITE 112
WASHINGTON, DC 20510-0505
(202) 224-3553
senator@boxer.senate.gov
http://boxer.senate.gov

April 1, 2001

"A Family Celebration"
Los Angeles, CA

Dear Friends:

I send my warmest greetings as you gather for the 2nd annual "A Family Celebration" benefit. The success of last year's event was remarkable, and I extend my best wishes for an even more successful one this year.

This event provides a special opportunity to recognize those who have made substantial contributions to the community. I commend all those in attendance for their tremendous efforts to benefit charitable causes. Through your work, you continue to enhance your community and provide valuable assistance to all involved.

I understand that the proceeds raised from this benefit will be directed to specially selected charities and organizations. The leadership and concern you show for the community has enriched the quality of life for many Americans.

You have my best wishes for your continued success and a spectacular event.

Sincerely,

Barbara Boxer
United States Senator

1700 MONTGOMERY STREET
SUITE 240
SAN FRANCISCO, CA 94111
(415) 403-0100

312 N. SPRING STREET
SUITE 1748
LOS ANGELES, CA 90012
(213) 894-5000

501 I STREET
SUITE 7-600
SACRAMENTO, CA 95814
(916) 448-2787

1130 O STREET
SUITE 2450
FRESNO, CA 93721
(559) 497-5109

600 'B' STREET
SUITE 2240
SAN DIEGO, CA 92101
(619) 239-3884

201 NORTH E STREET
SUITE 210
SAN BERNARDINO, CA 92401
(909) 888-3525

PRINTED ON RECYCLED PAPER

William S. Clinton

POSTAGE AND FEES PAID

WILLIAM JEFFERSON CLINTON

September 5, 2001

Aaron Tonken
Number 372
269 South Beverly Drive
Beverly Hills, California   90212

Dear Aaron:

Thank you so much for the videotape of the
Family Celebration event. It's a great
reminder of the evening.

Thanks, too, for sending the award -- I was
honored to receive it.

All the best to you.

Sincerely,

A *Family* CELEBRATION 2001

HONORARY CHAIRPERSONS
President & Mrs. Clinton

DINNER CHAIRPERSONS
David E. Kelley & Michelle Pfeiffer

March 20, 2001

Mr. Garry Thompson
Global Access Advisors
Via Fax: ▮▮▮▮▮▮▮

Dear Garry,

This letter will serve to supersede my earlier letter to you of this date as follows:

As you know, we have attempted to secure, through your offices, Marc Anthony's assistance and presence at A Family Celebration 2001 charitable event scheduled for April 1, 2001. As per our most recent conversation, after utilizing our best efforts to secure the necessary funds/underwriting, I regret to inform you that the charity will unfortunately be unable to assume the additional cost of the private air transportation for Marc Anthony and his entourage. As I previously mentioned to you, Delta Airlines is an underwriter of this charitable event and has graciously offered to provide the necessary first class accommodations for Marc Anthony and his entourage on the April 1, 2001 flight departing LAX at 10:10 pm, so he may be able to return to New York for his scheduled function.

In the event that the generous offer made by Delta is not agreeable to Mr. Anthony and/or his representatives, we unfortunately will have to forego Marc Anthony for our function.

Please advise us in writing, in the manner set out hereinabove, as to whether Marc Anthony will accept this proposal.

I apologize for the confusion, and thank you for your cooperation in this matter.

Sincerely,

Aaron Tonken

201 North Robertson Blvd., Suite G, Beverly Hills, CA 90211
Phone: 310-247-1000   Fax: 310-247-1449

The Honorable Dale Fischer
U.S. District Court Judge
Edward R. Roybal Center and Federal Building
255 East Temple Street
Los Angles, CA 90012

Your Honor

I am Alan Krausen and have been the president and owner of The Travel
Authority since 1992. The Travel Authority is a full service travel agency serving
both corporate and leisure clients.

We were introduced to Mr. Aaron Tonken in the spring of 1999 by one of
our long time corporate clients, Mr Brad O'Leary of the PM Consulting
Group. At that time Mr O'Leary asked if we could help Mr Tonken with
travel arrangements for his "Family Celebration" event, and we did. After
that event, Mr Tonken called and thanked me for all the help that our
agency provided for his event. At that time he asked if he could use our
agency to help with future travel arrangements for events that he had
planned, and I said we would be glad to.

My office staff and I worked with Mr Tonken and his staff for the next
few years, arranging all sorts of travel for Mr Tonken's clients, including airline,
tickets airplane charters, limousine, hotels and cruises. Between
the spring of 1999 and the end of 2002, Aaron spent well over 1.3 million
dollars with The Travel Authority. Many of the clients that Mr Tonken was
working with were stars, their managers, or high profile people that were
very demanding in their travel needs. Mr Tonken's clients were very
insistent on what they wanted. They would often demand certain airlines,
flights and hotels, irrespective of what it may have cost Mr Tonken or the
charities.

For example, I remember one specific time when Rod Stewart's manager
called me after Aaron had generously given him a cruise for him and his partner.
The cruise was worth over $50,000.00 and at the last minute the manager
called me out of the blue and said he wanted to be upgraded for no apparent
reason to the owner's suite. I told him Aaron Tonken would have
to pay for this and right now he was complaining he was short on funds. The
manager said he didn't care, and that he would pull his client at the last minute
from a charity event at his client's own home if I didn't make the upgrade,
and he didn't care if it had to come out of the charity's pocket.

Many other times I personally told Aaron's clients that it was going
to cost Aaron and the charities more money because of what they wanted.
Not one person ever said "OK, I will change my plans" or "I would be happy
to take a different airline or flight." It was not uncommon that we had to call our
supplier's VIP desk, or our sales representatives, to get what we would need
for his clients.

I always felt that Aaron was under a lot of pressure to give the stars and high
profile people what they wanted. Whenever we would book anything for Mr.
Tonken's clients, Aaron always was very insistent that we treat his clients
with the utmost professionalism, and he always checked to see if we were in
contact with them. It was not uncommon for Aaron to call the clients and
see if The Travel Authority was taking care of everything for them. In my dealings
with Aaron, he always wanted everything to run very smoothly .

In all the years that we where working with Mr Tonken he always came through
for his clients. Not until late in 2002, after his indictment, did he have a problem,
and to my knowledge that was just one client. Mr Tonken was slow paying
for some of the travel sometimes, but always made good on what he owed
The Travel Authority.
I cannot say first hand whether Aaron ever benefitted from any of the
events he did while working with The Travel Authority. It always seemed
that he was short of funds. The only way he may have benefitted would
have been if he traveled with one of his clients somewhere, but this
was very rare.

It is my feeling that Aaron always wanted to do the right thing, but
because of all the demands made on him by the stars he was not able to.
As I understand it Aaron produced some great events during the years that
The Travel Authority was doing business with him. Aaron has an
ability to put together some of the greatest events, and if the travel
demands had not gotten out of hand I think the events would have been
even more successful. I hope that I have been able to give you some
insight into my relationship with Aaron.

Respectfully ,

Alan Krausen

GERALD R. FORD

April 6, 2001

Dear Aaron:

Mrs. Ford and I thoroughly enjoyed the delightful dinner at Bob Lorsch's gorgeous residence on Saturday and it was an equally delightful evening on Sunday at the Regent Beverly Wilshire Hotel. I was honored to speak at the Sunday event. I have received many very favorable comments on my speech.

I compliment you on arranging this superb program under the generous support of Cynthia Gershman. She is most impressive and a delightful dinner partner.

I thank you for the opportunity to meet so many attractive individuals.

During the weekend you suggested you had clients who would be willing to support the Betty Ford Center for alcoholism and chemical dependency. Mrs. Gershman has already made a commitment. Mrs. Ford looks forward to giving her a personal tour of the Center when she comes to Rancho Mirage. Hopefully you know others who will donate to the Betty Ford Center. Enclosed information on the Center.

We also discussed possible donors for the Gerald R. Ford School of Public Policy at the University of Michigan. I am extremely proud of the Ford School. Enclosed some excellent materials describing the school. Donors have numerous options – professor's endowments, funding of a new building, student fellowships and other specific academic programs.

I look forward to your coming to Rancho Mirage so you can join me for lunch.
I strongly hope you can be helpful with your friends and clients. Mrs. Ford and I will be most grateful.

Warmest regards,

Gerald R. Ford

Mr. Aaron Tonken
269 S. Beverly Drive, Suite 372
Beverly Hills, California 90212

GERALD R. FORD

August 1, 2002

Dear Aaron:

I profusely thank you for sending the beautiful MONTBLANC
Charles Dickens limited edition set. You are most thoughtful for
remembering me on my 89th birthday, which incidentally we
celebrated very quietly.

With appreciation and my warmest regards,

Mr. Aaron Tonken
Aaron Tonken & Associates
269 South Beverly Drive, 372
Beverly Hills, California 90212

State of California
DEPARTMENT OF JUSTICE

1300 I STREET, SUITE 1130
P.O. BOX 903447
SACRAMENTO, CA 94203-4470
Telephone: (916) 323-5076
Facsimile: (916) 444-3651
E-Mail: diane.erbeznik@doj.ca.gov

October 12, 2001

AARON TONKEN
269 S. BEVERLY DRIVE, PMB 372
BEVERLY HILLS, CA 90212

RE: **NOTICE TO REGISTER AS A COMMERCIAL FUNDRAISER OR
FUNDRAISING COUNSEL FOR CHARITABLE PURPOSES**

Based on information reported to the Attorney General's Registry of Charitable Trusts,
your organization has provided services as either a Commercial Fundraiser or Fundraising
Counsel for Charitable Purposes and, therefore, must register with the Attorney General and file
annual financial reports accounting for all funds collected (Commercial Fundraiser only).

Enclosed is a copy of Government Code, Section 12599. Once you have determined
whether you are a Commercial Fundraiser or Fundraising Counsel, please go to our website at:
http://caag.state.ca.us/charities/forms.htm scroll down to the "CF Forms" to download the
appropriate form. If you do not have access to a computer, please feel free to contact me and the
appropriate form will be mailed to you.

**IT IS UNLAWFUL FOR YOU TO SOLICIT FUNDS IN THIS STATE FOR
CHARITABLE PURPOSES UNLESS YOU HAVE COMPLIED WITH THE
REGISTRATION AND FINANCIAL REPORTING REQUIREMENTS.** Unless and until
you are in full compliance with the law (filing your annual financial report, annual renewal
registration, renewal fee, and bond), you may not solicit funds for charitable purposes. **If you do
solicit, it is grounds for civil action, including injunction and penalties of up to $2,500 per
solicitation.**

Sincerely,

DIANE L. ERBEZNIK
Staff Services Analyst

For   BILL LOCKYER
Attorney General

Enclosures

And how about all the others that were not registered? —AT

March 15, 2002

Personal & Confidential

TO: Cynthia Gershman
FROM: Aaron Tonken

Dear Cynthia,

Let this letter confirm that when I sell your Corniche Rolls Royce I will have ten business days to purchase/replace with the car with a car of your choice. In this case you have chosen Roger Dauer's Bentley. I will advance the $14,000.00 in sales tax and take it out of your foundation at a later date. In addition, I will be using the $70,000.00 from the sale of your Rolls Royce to make a payment for the Roseanne investment. It is $85,000.00 so I will be advancing $15,000.00 towards the payment. This also can be taken out of your foundation at a later date. Once the Bentley is paid for then I owe you no more money personally and you will return all the checks you have in your possession.

Sincerely

Aaron Tonken

Please furnish me by fax your insurance information tonight.

465

AARON TONKEN & ASSOCIATES
Marketing • Management • Production

August 20, 2002

Ms. Renee Croce
Renee Croce and Associates
Via Fax: ████████████

Re: Event on 8/23/02

Dear Renee,

Regarding the dinner with President George W. Bush and Bill Simon on August 23, 2002, please find the enclosed payment in the amount of $10,000.00 to reserve two seats and photo opportunity with President Bush for Aaron Tonken and Ken Roberts. I have enclosed personal information for both below:

Kenneth J. Roberts
ss#: ████████
dob: ██████

Aaron Tonken
ss#: ████████
dob: ██████

If you should have any questions or need any additional information, please contact me at (310) 659-79680.

Sincerely,

Aaron Tonken
President

AT/cm

June 14, 2002

Mr. Aaron Tonken
269 S. Beverly Drive PMB 372
Beverly Hills, CA 90212

Dear Aaron:

Thank you for participating in the President Bush and Bill Simon dinner on April 29, 2002. Because of your efforts, it was a huge success. We raised over $3 million. The photos with the President and Bill Simon have finally arrived. Thank you for your patience during the processing.

Enclosed is your complimentary 8x10 photo. If you would like to order reprints or enlargements, you may place your order directly with *Balfour Photography* at (626) 403-4200. Please have the number located on the back of your picture with you when you call to place your order.

Please call me if you have any questions (818) 905-5420. I hope we can count on you for further support before the November election. Thank you again for all that you have done. Bill will be our next Governor!

Sincerely,

Alice

Alice Borden
Bill Simon for Governor

Both photos are great!! Especially Rosanne's —

P.S. I'm enclosing a copy of a NEWSWEEK article that came out this week. Thought you would enjoy it.

*All the best
Alice*

c/o Alice Borden Company • ████████████████████

www.SimonforGovernor.com

Paid for by Bill Simon for Governor Committee - FPPC ID# 1233478

David H. Murdock
cordially invites you to join in welcoming
The President of the United States
George W. Bush
At a breakfast Honoring
Bill Simon
The Next Governor of California
Saturday, August 24, 2002
8:00 a.m.
at
The Regency Club
10900 Wilshire Boulevard
Los Angeles

Reply Information Below   Business Attire
Doors will open at 7:00 a.m. and will be closed at 8:00 a.m.
For security purposes, all guests must arrive prior to 8:00 a.m.
Space is very limited. Please phone or fax your reservation immediately.
For more information, please call ▮▮▮▮▮ *or fax* ▮▮▮▮▮

☐ Yes, I would like to be listed as a Breakfast Chair and contribute $25,000.
  Includes: 1 table of 10
               2 photos (two people per photo) with President Bush ✗

☒ Yes, I would like to be listed as a Co-chair and contribute $10,000.
  Includes: 2 tickets
               1 photo (two people per photo) with President Bush. ✗

☐ Yes, I would like to attend and serve on the Host Committee and contribute $2,500 (per person).
  Includes: 1 ticket to breakfast

☐ I cannot attend, but would like to support Bill Simon for Governor. Enclosed is a contribution of $_____ .

Contributions cannot be accepted without the following information:

Name (as you would like it to appear on the invitation): AARON TONKEN
Company   AARON TONKEN AND ASSOCIATES
Address (no P.O. Box) 269 S. BEVERLY DR #372
City/State/Zip: Beverly Hills, CA 90212
Phone 310·659·9680   Fax 310·659·9865   Email
Occupation   producer   Employer
                        (If self employed, name of company)

Credit Card Contributions:

☐ MasterCard   ☐ Visa   ☒ AMEX   Amount of contribution $ 10,000.00
Credit Card # ▮▮▮▮▮▮ 3002   Expiration Date   1/04
Name as it appears on the card   EDDIE JAMISON
Authorized signature (must be same as name on card)   Eddie Jamison

Please make checks payable to Bill Simon for Governor Committee and mail to:
                        Bill Simon for Governor
                        ▮▮▮▮▮▮▮▮▮▮▮
                Or fax to: ▮▮▮▮▮▮
For further information, please call the Alice Borden Company at ▮▮▮▮▮

Contributions to the Bill Simon for Governor Committee are not deductible as charitable contributions for federal income tax purposes. U.S. citizens, permanent residents and U.S. corporations may contribute. There is no limit to the amount of your personal, corporate or PAC contribution.
Paid for by the Bill Simon for Governor Committee – FPPC ID# 1233478

A Breakfast with President George W. Bush

Saturday, August 24, 2002

The Regency Club

☑ Yes, I would like to be listed as a Breakfast Chair and contribute $25,000.
Includes: 1 Table of 10 for breakfast
2 Photos (two people per photo) with President Bush

☐ Yes, I would like to be listed as a Co-chair and contribute $10,000.
Includes: 2 Tickets to breakfast
1 Photo (two people per photo) with President Bush

☐ Yes, I would like to attend and serve on the Host Committee and contribute $2,500 per person.
Includes: 1 Ticket to breakfast

☐ I (we) cannot attend, but would like to support Bill Simon For Governor. Enclosed is a contribution of $ _____.

Contributions cannot be accepted without the following information

Name AARON Tonken Spouse _____
Company AARON TONKEN AND ASSOCIATES
Address (no P.O. Box) 269 S· BEVERLY DR· #372
City/State/Zip Beverly HILLS CA 90212
Phone 310 659·7680 Fax 310 659-9865 E-Mail _____
Occupation producer Employer _____
(if self-employed, name of business)
Credit Card Contributions
☐MC ☐Visa ☑AMEX amount of contribution $ 25,000.00
Credit Card # ▓▓▓▓▓▓▓ 3002 Expiration Date 1/04
Name as it appears on the card EDDIE JAMISON
Signature (must be same as name on card) Eddie Jamison

Please make checks payable to **Bill Simon for Governor Committee** and mail to:

Bill Simon for Governor

▓▓▓▓▓▓▓▓▓▓▓▓▓▓

You may FAX credit card contributions to ▓▓▓▓▓
For further information, please call Alice Borden Company at ▓▓▓▓

Contributions to the Bill Simon for Governor Committee are not deductible contributions for federal income tax purposes. U.S. citizens, permanent residents and U.S. corporations may contribute. There is no limit to the amount of your personal, corporate or PAC contribution.
Paid for by the Bill Simon for Governor Committee – FPPC ID#1233470

469

Orange County welcomes

The President of The United States

George W. Bush

at a reception for

Bill Simon
The Next Governor of California

Friday, August 23, 2002 at 5:30 p.m. - doors open at 4:00 pm
St. Regis Monarch Beach Resort & Spa

☐ **Yes, I/we would like to be a Co-Chair and give $25,000.** Checks made payable to Team California.
Includes dinner hosted by Gerry Parsky with Karl Rove, a Team California membership, a photo with President Bush for 2 people, reserved, VIP admittance to the President's reception for 2 people and 10 tickets to the general reception.

☒ **Yes, I/we would like to be on the Host Committee and give $10,000.** Checks made payable to Team California.
Includes a photo with President Bush for 2 people, reserved, VIP admittance to the President's reception for 2 people and 10 tickets to the general reception.

☐ **Yes, I /we would like to attend the President's reception.** Please reserve _____ tickets at $1,000 per person.
Checks are made payable to <u>Bill Simon for Governor.</u>

☐ **No, I (we) cannot attend the reception,** but would like to support Bill Simon. Enclosed is a contribution of $_____.
Checks are made payable to <u>Bill Simon for Governor.</u>

Contributions cannot be accepted without the following information:

Name AARON TONKEN   Spouse _____

Address (no P.O. box) 269 S. BEVERLY DR, #372 City/State/Zip BEVERLY HILLS, CA 90212

Phone 310·659·7680 _____ Fax 310·659·9865 ____ E-Mail _____

Occupation PRODUCER _____ Employer _____

Company (if self employed) Aaron Tonken and Associates

If your check is written on a joint account, please check whether it is attributed to: Husband_____ Wife_____ Both_____

Credit Card Contributions (You may fax credit card contributions to (949) 756-8033):

☐ MC ☐ Visa ☒ AMEX Amount $ 10,000. Credit Card # ▮▮▮▮▮▮▮ 3002 Expiration Date 1/04

Name as it appears on the card ____ EDDIE JAMISON

Signature (must be same as name on card) ____ Eddie Jamison

For further information, please call Renee Croce at ▮▮▮▮▮ or
send your contribution to Renee Croce, ▮▮▮▮▮▮▮▮▮

Hosting a HILLPAC Fundraiser

- Receive final sign-off for date, time and location

- Work with the Finance Director to determine a financial goal and budget

- Create a Host Committee when applicable

- Submit Host Committee names for vetting, when applicable

- Determine method of invitation

- Create invitation and receive sign-off from Finance Director (allow one week for vetting)

- Develop a guest list. HILLPAC-NY will mail the invitations from Washington.

- Make personal follow-up phone calls (invitations should be sent 4 weeks prior to the event)

- Relay any commitments to Finance Director

- Event costs (food, beverage, photography, etc) will be paid for by HILLPAC-NY and should not exceed 10% of the lowest estimated intake (including any related travel expenses). Keep hospitality and refreshments to a minimum.

- Determine RSVP process with Finance Director. Guest information must include name, occupation, business, mailing address, e-mail address, phone number, fax number and a brief biography, method and amount of donation.

- When applicable, event photographer must be screened by the Finance Director prior to contracting services.

- Name tags provided for all guests

- No press or unauthorized release of information including amount raised, guests in attendance, etc.

- United States Secret Service personnel will contact you directly in the preceding days of the event. Be sure the logisitical information you provide has been cleared by the Finance Director.

- All donations should be collected PRIOR to the start of the event.

- Contributions can be made by check or credit card.

- Corporate contributions are prohibited, but partnerships and limited liability companies are not.

- Event program (including any speaking or photo arrangements) will be determined by the size and nature of the event.

- A full briefing including guests lists, and guest bios must be submitted to the Senator's Office by close of business the day before the event.

###

471

MEMORANDUM

TO: Aaron Tonken
FROM: Edward G. Rendell
RE: Philadelphia Event 9/12
DATE: August 23, 2000

Aaron,

I'm sorry to ask you for assistance again, but we need your help for our Philadelphia event on September 12th, with the Vice President. The following artists are performing in Philadelphia or Atlantic City around that time:

Boys II Men and Luther Vandross, (they are performing in Philadelphia on 9/9). As you may know, Boys II Men performed at the Shrine Auditorium with Barbara Streisand, and they know me pretty well. (Again, thanks for all your help in making the Shrine Gala such a success).

Bruce Hornsby (he will be performing in Philadelphia 9/16). I know he is a Democrat and has performed in DC for us in the past.

Richard Lewis (he will be in Atlantic City 9/16). I actually spoke to him at the Convention in Los Angeles and he said that he would like to be helpful.

The Gypsy Kings (they will be in Atlantic City 9/8). I do not know if they are Democrats or if they support the Vice President.

Cybil Shepard (she will be in Atlantic City 9/9- 9/14). I am not sure if she is a Democrat, but I have a feeling she is. I was hoping we could bring her to Philadelphia to do our event and then have her do her show later that evening. (Philadelphia is 55 minutes away from Atlantic City).

I know how much you have done for us, Aaron, but this is for me personally and it will mean so much– and you will be helping me make Philadelphia great!

Thanks.

Suzanne H. Itzko
Executive Director

MEMORANDUM

TO: Aaron Tonken

FROM: Edward G. Rendell

DATE: 12/19/00

RE: Our Conversation

Thanks for speaking with me today. It's always great to talk to you.

As always, I appreciate your willingness to help me as I turn my attention in part to 2002.
My goal for the end of this year is substantial but I believe we can achieve it. Towards
that end, it would be great if you could send me as substantial a check as possible dated
before December 31st.

Thanks, again.   *Aaron - Thanks! You're the best!*
                    If you could do as much
                    as possible - it would be terrific!
                                                    Ed

P.S. As you probably know, there are no limits under Pennsylvania's law; however, no corporate checks
are allowed.

Paid for by Rendell '02 Committee; David L. Cohen, Treasurer ████████

473

███████

Suzanne H. Itzko
Executive Director

<u>VIA FACSIMILE</u> ███████

MEMORANDUM

TO: Aaron Tonken
FROM: Edward G. Rendell
DATE: 12/26/00
RE: The Grinch

I hate to be a Grinch at this time of year and I know you have been swamped with holiday parties, gift purchases and the spirit of this wonderful holiday season. The Grinch that I am, however, I want to give you a gentle reminder that in order to accomplish our goals, we need checks dated by December 31st and received by this Friday, December 29th.

You know how much I appreciate your willingness to help me and I hope you understand my time constraints.

Thanks, again, for all you've done for me.

P.S. Checks should be made payable to "Rendell '95".

P.P.S. Please feel free to bill overnight shipping charges to our UPS account--#A7050V.

Paid for by Rendell '95 Committee; David L. Cohen, Treasurer ███

Check 1021 (register stub)

1021

Date *Nov. 1, 2001*

To *William J Clinton Pres. Fd.*

Previous Balance	
Deposit	
New Balance	
This Check	*100 000* 00
Balance Forward	

Check 1021

ENCINO   ENCINO, CA 91436   1021

DATE November 1, 2001   11-4288/1210

PAY TO THE ORDER OF William J. Clinton Presidential Fd. $ 100,000.00

One-Hundred-Thousand dollars and xx/100------   DOLLARS

AARON TONKEN
DBA AMERICAN SPIRIT FOUNDATIO
269 S BEVERLY DR STE 372
BEVERLY HILLS CA 90212-3807

Aaron Tonken

1021

Check 1004 (register stub)

1004

Date *July 1, 2001*

To

For *William Clinton Pres. Fd*

Previous Balance	
Deposit	
New Balance	
This Check	*100,000* 00
Balance Forward	

Check 1004

ENCINO   ENCINO, CA 91436   1004

DATE July 1, 2001   11-4288/1210

PAY TO THE ORDER OF William J. Clinton Presidential Fd $ 100,000.00

One-Hundred-Thousand Dollars and xx/100-------   DOLLARS

AARON TONKEN
DBA AMERICAN SPIRIT FOUNDATIO
269 S BEVERLY DR STE 372
BEVERLY HILLS CA 90212-3807

Aaron Tonken

1004

Check 1005 (register stub)

1005

Date *September 1, 2001*

To *William J. Clinton Pres. Fd.*

For

Previous Balance	
Deposit	
New Balance	
This Check	*100,000* 00
Balance Forward	

Check 1005

ENCINO   ENCINO, CA 91436   1005

DATE September 1, 2001   11-4288/1210

PAY TO THE ORDER OF William J. Clinton Presidential Fd. $ 100,000.00

One-Hundred-Thousand Dollars and xx/100-----   DOLLARS

AARON TONKEN
DBA AMERICAN SPIRIT FOUNDATIO
269 S BEVERLY DR STE 372
BEVERLY HILLS CA 90212-3807

Aaron Tonken

1005

RICHARD A. GEPHARDT
HOUSE DEMOCRATIC LEADER

July 23, 2002

Ms. Roseanne Barr
5 Crest Road West
Rollling Hill, CA 90274

Dear Ms. Barr,

Leader Gephardt would like to invite you to Washington and honor you as an outstanding citizen and humanitarian and also recognize you for your many accomplishments. During this ceremony, high-ranking members of the House and Senate will be joining us in the Capitol building, which is home to the United States Congress. We would like to recognize your tremendous contributions in comedy, television, and the arts, which has influenced millions of Americans. We are working with Aaron Tonken on scheduling this sometime during the week of August 19, 2002.

We thank you for the example you have set which has encouraged young people to reach for the best in themselves and work for the common good of society. We appreciate the time and talent you have dedicated to helping young people through your philanthropic and charity work. It has undoubtedly made a lasting difference in the lives of numerous kids.

Leader Gephardt cherishes his friendship with you and looks forward to organizing an event in Washington in your honor. We look forward to continuing to work with you in the months and years ahead to create a better, more just and more livable world.

Sincerely,

Noah Mamet

430 South Capitol Street, SE · Washington, DC 20003
Contributions to this committee are not tax deductible.
Paid for and authorized by the DCCC

476

ATTORNEYS AT LAW

A LAW CORPORATION

GEORGE F. BIRD, JR.°¹
KAREN HUNTER BIRD¹
KRISTIN J. HANSEN¹¹

°CERTIFIED SPECIALIST - CRIMINAL LAW
THE STATE BAR OF CALIFORNIA
BOARD OF LEGAL SPECIALIZATION

¹ALSO ADMITTED IN NEW MEXICO

¹¹ALSO ADMITTED IN
NEW YORK & NEW JERSEY

3424 CARSON STREET, SUITE 460
TORRANCE, CALIFORNIA 90503

TELEPHONE ███████

FACSIMILE ███████

E-MAIL ███████

July 3, 2003

Agent David Smith
Federal Bureau of Investigation
11000 Wilshire Boulevard
Los Angeles, California 90024

VIA FACSIMILE
(310) ███████

Re: Mr. Aaron Tonken

Dear Agent Smith:

Enclosed herewith please find a copy of the Beverly Hills Hotel bill for Mr. David Rosen. Mr. Tonken recalls that he reimbursed Mr. Rosen with cash that he obtained from Stanley Media for Mr. Rosen's hotel stay. Additionally, Mr. Rosen used Mr. Tonken's porsche to drive around the entire time he was in Los Angeles working solely on the Hollywood Tribute to President Clinton for Mrs. Clinton's United States Senate Campaign. Lastly, Mr. Rosen told Mr. Tonken to never discuss or tell anyone about the reimbursement or the fact that he was utilizing Mr. Tonken's automobile.

In the meantime, if you have any questions, please do not hesitate to contact us.

Very truly yours,

BIRD & BIRD

George F. Bird, Jr.

GFB/srv.
Enclosures as referenced.
cc: Mr. Aaron Tonken

477

ROSEN, MR DAVID   7/30/00
450 7TH AVE #804   Arrival   8/19/00
NEW YORK, NY   Departure   1
10123   No. in Party   360.00
                                           Rate

                                    245
Account No.   Room No.

No	Date	Description			Amount
A-STANDARD FOLIO					
1	7/30/00	LOCAL CALL	245	7300082003	$1.00
		20:29 3109430177			
2	7/30/00	LOCAL CALL	245	7300111067	$1.00
		20:33 3109430177			
3	7/30/00	ROOM SERVICE	245	210693	$28.82
		20:33			
4	7/30/00	ROOM	245	207	$360.00
5	7/30/00	ROOM TAX	245	208	$51.00
6	7/30/00	ROOMS SURCHARGE	245	209	$4.32
7	7/31/00	OVERNIGHT PARKING	245	8	$21.00
8	7/31/00	OVERNIGHT PARKING	245	16	$21.00
9	7/31/00	ROOM	245	243	$360.00
10	7/31/00	ROOM TAX	245	244	$51.00
11	7/31/00	ROOMS SURCHARGE	245	245	$4.32
12	7/31/00	LOCAL CALL	245	7310549153	$1.00
		22:42 3109430177			
13	8/01/00	LOCAL CALL	245	8010649006	$1.00
		07:54 3109430177			

Continued..

*The first page of David Rosen's Beverly Hills Hotel bill
for his work during the Clinton Salute. —AT*

ROSEN, MR DAVID
450 7TH AVE #804
NEW YORK, NY
10123

		7/30/00
Arrival		8/19/00
Departure		1
No. in Party		360.00
Rate		

Account No.   7   245   Room No.

No	Date	Description			Amount
	A-STANDARD FOLIO				
183	8/18/00	ROOM TAX	245	247	$51.00
184	8/18/00	ROOMS SURCHARGE	245	248	$4.32
		• BALANCE DUE	•		$9,280.58

Several pages later, here's the final total. —AT

Philip A. Levy
Law Offices of Philip A. Levy
A Professional Corporation

███████████████

Tel: ███████████   Fax: ███████████

July 6, 2004

The Honorable Dale Fischer
U.S. District Court Judge
Edward R. Roybal Center and Federal Building
255 East Temple Street
Los Angeles, California 90012

Re: Mr. Aaron Tonken

Dear Judge Fischer:

I am writing to you on behalf of Aaron Tonken in the hope that you will have mercy on him in connection with the sentence to be rendered by the Court.

I am an attorney and have known Aaron Tonken since approximately 2000. I represented Paula Abdul in a dispute she had against Mr. Tonken. Mr. Tonken then engaged my services to negotiate with his other creditors. In the course of my representation of Aaron I met him, on several occasion, at his home - a rented, modest one-bedroom apartment on Veteran Street, in Los Angeles. It would be hard to imagine a more austere residence - his living room was furnished with 2 picnic tables, and some chairs, on several occasions he left the door to his bedroom open and I saw it was furnished only with a mattress on the floor.

At no time during the 4 years that I have known Aaron did he ever live in anything that could be considered luxury. At no time that I have known Aaron did he ever live in conditions any better than in his Veteran Street apartment. One thing is clear to me from knowing Aaron, Aaron did not take money so he could live in luxury. From what I understand now, Aaron was continually behind in his obligations, took from one event and used what he took for other events or to pay those who pursued him for money lent for previous events. I think Aaron was always "upside down," as to the expenses of his events, took from one to pay off another, and this irregular "wheel," lurched downhill toward disaster for Aaron.

Aaron aspired to put on the most wonderful parties which, in his mind, were always for the benefit of charities. Aaron was a poor fiduciary, and a worse businessman, but I think it is important to recognize something about Aaron's misappropriation and

-1-

480

commingling - he did not take for himself, to the contrary, he incurred vast personal obligations, some from unsavory characters, to put money *into* events. The "why of it" is puzzling, but the answer, I believe, is to be found in his character.

I do not believe that Aaron is a malicious person. He is, without a doubt, the most disorganized, hyperactive, distracted, hysterical yet creative people I have ever met. He always seemed on the verge of a nervous breakdown, was driven by panic and obviously made some terrible choices.

Had Aaron personally benefitted from his misconduct, I would not be writing this letter.

I have had an opportunity to observe Aaron after the commencement of the civil lawsuit brought against him and others by the Attorney General of the State of California. Aaron did not know how to stop the "wheel," but the commencement of the Attorney General's civil action put an end to Aaron's 'business.' The dominant emotion I observed in Aaron at that time was relief. Aaron voluntarily met with the United States Attorneys Office and attempted to inform the investigators of all the wrongdoing he was involved in, wrongdoing regarding which other people, including some very prominent people, did benefit and benefit greatly.

From what I have observed, I would say that Aaron engaged in this process not only to seek the benefits of cooperation, but to cleanse himself and therefore his cooperation was enthusiastic and complete.

Aaron is still scared, and for perhaps the first time in his life, reflective. He now understands that his conduct was wrong and hurtful. At the bottom of it all, I believe that Aaron is a gentle person, though subject to fits and storms which obliterated his judgment. Except for his ability to put on a great party, he was totally unequipped to engage in the business of fundraising - unequipped by lack of education, lack of good judgment and a lack of common sense.

I believe that Aaron, in his own confused way, had always hoped to do good. I believe Aaron can do good. I also believe that a long sentence will crush Aaron.

I therefore hope this court will have mercy on Aaron. I truly believe he deserves your mercy.

Sincerely,

Philip A. Levy

-2-

481

STEVEN FOX

July 7, 2004

The Honorable Dale Fischer
U.S. District Court Judge
Edward R. Roybal Center and Federal Building
255 East Temple Street
Los Angeles, California 90012

Dear Judge Fischer:

Approximately ten years ago, I was introduced to Aaron Tonken for the purpose of discussing a charitable event I wanted to put on in order to raise money for the Tommy Lasorda Jr. Memorial Foundation of which I was a Founder and Director. At the time, Aaron was one of the most popular and powerful people in Hollywood and I felt his association would guarantee success. After the initial meeting, Aaron agreed to orchestrate the event that would eventually raise hundreds of thousands of dollars and enable the Foundation to build a sports center in Yorba Linda in honor of Tommy Lasorda Jr. This was Aaron's first major event, and the one that would launch his "fund raising" career which, as you know is now under investigation and the reason for my letter.

What should be very clear by not only the success of the world class event Aaron put on for TLJ Memorial Foundation, but also the beginning of what would eventually become his downfall, his inability to say "no." This is not an excuse for his actions but a perspective of reason as to why I am writing this letter. You see, I have first hand knowledge of the actions of some of Hollywood's most popular stars who use their star power to extort gratuities from charitable fund raisers such as Aaron, with no conscious thought whatsoever. This would eventually lead to Aaron's downfall and the resulting circumstances under which he has now found himself in.

I, personally can attest to the fact that Aaron is a very sincere and caring individual whose extraordinary ability to raise charitable funds has been overshadowed by the very people he counted on to perpetuate the fund raising. I truly believe you must look at the fact that he gained nothing monetarily from any of the events in question but rather became the "pawn" by being manipulated by the very people who knew his fear of failure was greater than his ability to say "no."

I know Aaron has suffered immeasurably physically and mentally over the last several months but continued to assist in both the State and Federal investigations. I also am aware from statements made to me by Federal Agents that his assistance in these investigations is without question, the key to what will eventually lead to convictions of the people who profited from Aaron's efforts and who are the real criminals.

I would hope that upon review of the facts, you will find that Aaron has been completely forthright in assisting to uncover the misuse of funds and contributions regarding charitable and political fund raising, and is given absolute consideration for his cooperation, his sincerity and his complete remorse over the circumstances which have brought him before you.

Sincerely,

482

July 19, 2004

The Honorable Dale Fischer
U.S. District Court Judge
Edward R. Roybal Center and Federal Building
255 East Temple Street
Los Angeles, CA 90012

Your Honor,

I first met Aaron Tonken in late 1998 as an honoree at a major Hollywood fundraising event. The honor came at a time when I was receiving notoriety in my profession as a political consultant and for the fact that I raised over $1 billion for causes and candidates that I supported, such as Senators John McCain, George Allen and Orrin Hatch and forty-seven other past and present members of the U.S. Senate. The honor also came at a time when I had just purchased a partial ownership in Chasen's restaurant in Los Angeles.

The event was very successful and I was particularly impressed by the amount of money being raised from new donor sources for these charitable organizations.

Aaron Tonken did not ask me for any funds to aid or assist with this particular event but he asked me at a later point in time if my restaurant would sponsor a Liza Minelli fundraiser to which I agreed. At no time did Mr. Tonken ask me for any funds for his personal use and I was impressed by the fact that his lifestyle seemed frugal enough to convince me that fees being paid Mr. Tonken were not being spent on things I considered frivolous or extravagant.

Around this time I was also dealing with my daughter who was having a great deal of difficulty dealing with her latest bout with multiple sclerosis and the poor medical advice she received from doctors pushed her to the brink. She'd all but given up on life.

When Mr. Tonken learned of my daughter's plight he arranged for me to meet with a number of people that helped my daughter receive superior medical care. Today she is not only progressing well with the disease but has married and now has twin boys that she is healthy enough to raise.

483

I was so grateful for Mr. Tonken's assistance that I offered to pay a personal fee or retainer for his services but he refused to accept anything from me. He did, however, ask me to make some direct contributions to charities and organizations he was supporting or helping.

Although I was impressed with Mr. Tonken's fundraising skills, I felt he was a bit unorganized and prone to allow celebrities to take advantage of him. He subsequently asked for my help in trying to straighten out his business and I arranged for him to meet with a certified public accountant to try to structure his business so that all of his profits did not end up paying for expenses for unreasonable requests he would sometime receive from celebrities.

Mr. Tonken subsequently involved himself with Mr. Stan Lee and Mr. Peter Paul in a business project I thought was sound enough that I actually invested my money in some stock in the project. I can readily understand why so many sophisticated investors and Mr. Tonken were seduced by the project as it was presented. Unfortunately he found himself working with partners who were way in over their head in putting a major business together and I believe Mr. Tonken was led down a very destructive path.

At the same time he became involved with fundraising for politicians who, for an unsophisticated person such as Mr. Tonken, were able to lure him into doing things he otherwise would not normally have done.

Certainly, staying at the White House and forging a personal relationship with the President and the First Lady for someone with Mr. Tonken's background was not only seductive but of great help to him in dealing with the celebrities, the great majority of whom, shared the political philosophy of the President and Mrs. Clinton.

I know Mr. Tonken has documented an incredible amount of activity during that time – no doubt the result of his meeting with a certified public accountant and from a personal sense of responsibility Mr. Tonken felt towards the donors to the charities with which he was involved.

I understand that much of that documentation has been helpful to four or five grand juries and may indeed be helpful to the ████████████████████ and possibly to one Congressional investigation in redressing some of the failures or weaknesses of the political and charitable systems of fundraising that have resulted in at least new laws being written in California to prevent such future abuses in the system.

I did a rather extensive background check on Mr. Tonken before I got to know him and found that the only legal problem he'd ever had was an incident involving his driver's license. Many of the charities I spoke to who might have been unhappy with Mr. Tonken's results nevertheless admitted that he had raised funds that sources they never would have otherwise considered and admitted they'd been seduced by the names of celebrities that made themselves available to help but failed to understand that many of the celebrities had no personal attachment to the charities they were helping.

Mr. O'Leary letter, page three

During the time I have known Mr. Tonken he hasn't asked me for money for his personal use and I feel he is sincere in his desire to help people – particularly with respect to my own situation with my ailing daughter.

I also believe that he is very talented but exceptionally naïve in believing each step of the way he would be able to secure contracts to raise money that would help him fulfill any obligations to which he committed.

The only special favor Mr. Tonken ever asked me to fulfill for him was an opportunity to meet a religious leader that he admired so that he could spend some time discussing some of the conflicts he had between his religion and his personal life in order to achieve some inner peace.

There is no question in my mind that a number of people took great advantage of him in part because he allowed it to happen only because he truly wanted to help the charities with which he became involved.

I believe that Mr. Tonken can and should be rehabilitated and can serve a meaningful role in society. Hopefully he has already learned great lessons from his mistakes.

Sincerely,

Bradley S. O'Leary

Bradley S. O'Leary
President
PM Consulting Corporation